Utopian Lights

Utopian Lights

THE EVOLUTION OF THE IDEA OF SOCIAL PROGRESS

Bronislaw Baczko

Translated by Judith L. Greenberg

PARAGON HOUSE
New York

First American edition, 1989

Published in the United States by

Paragon House
90 Fifth Avenue
New York, NY 10011

Library of Congress Cataloging-in-Publication Data

Baczko, Bronisław.
    [Lumières de l'utopie. English]
    Utopian lights / Bronislaw Baczko; translated by Judith L.
Greenberg. — 1st American ed.
      p. cm.
    Translation of: Lumières de l'utopie.
    ISBN 1-55778-026-9
    1. Utopias—History. I. Title.
HX806.B2313   1989
335′.02—dc19   88-30123
                                    CIP

Manufactured in the United States of America

For Rela

Contents

Preface

What do the glittering fires of utopias light up and what do they hide beyond the dazzling transparency of the imagined and desired New City?

Utopia and history: complex relationships that this book proposes to bring out through the study of the social imagination at work in the eighteenth century, and in particular during the course of the revolutionary period.

Utopian lights: When utopian dreams light up the horizon, a horizon of expectations and collective or individual hopes, they shed new light on the social landscape. Men and objects appear caught up in the glare of these lights. Although of variable intensity, their effect remains the same. Utopian representations arrange and lay out black and white, opaque and transparent, visible and invisible differently. Modifying the lighting also changes the way people see, causing the possible and the impossible, the past and the future, the real and the desired to be seen differently. Caught in the light of utopia, glances are turned toward visions of an *alternative society*, contrasting with the existing society because it is reconciled with reason, history, happiness. Imagining the New City doesn't necessarily mean abandoning oneself to a sleep filled with dreams. The production of social dreams can become a specific intellectual practice such that it imposes imprescriptible demands. Once they are produced and diffused, the utopian idea-images penetrate into the circulation of symbolic representations. It is thus that they are presented with historically variable opportunities to intervene in conflicts and strategies in which the symbolic power of the social imagination is at stake. The plan of this book is to show how the fires of utopia during the eighteenth century are lit and extinguished. The history of utopias, and particularly of those of the Age of Enlightenment, is not, certainly, a new subject; nevertheless, it seemed possible to us to approach it in a new way. We have not followed the systematic procedure that would venture to confine utopian representations in a particular formula of discourse, only then to attempt to bring out their continuity, if not to impose it. The discontinuity of this book does not arise solely from our determination not to be exhaustive; it is deliberate, chosen for reasons of methodology. We have proceeded by thematic sections and investigations, trying in this way to show how the history of social dreams is made up of discontinuities and ruptures only beyond which are found certain revealing aspects of the mentalities of the era. Sociologically, the population of utopians is particularly heterogeneous, and the most diverse figures pass one another on the paths of utopia. The frontiers of utopia are mobile and it is to their displacement that we paid most attention. Utopian discourse is never closed in on itself. It draws from the collective imagination by exploiting old myths; it establishes itself in the realms of knowledge and ideology by opening up an imaginary time-space for itself. Utopian discourse easily adapts the languages of philosophy and politics, as well as those of history, science, and architecture. It can neither be limited to a matter of language, nor confined within it. The practice of utopian discourse also has a certain practical application: specifically that in which the representations of the New City are set up. But in seeking the bursts of utopian light where they succeed in shining, the historian inevitably finds utopia burst, shattered, the dreams broken. Does the utopian imagination not reproduce, in its own distinctive mode, the historical evolution, whence it emerges and where it founders?

Light of utopia, utopias of light . . . the brilliance of dreams and the fragmented dreams that we have sought belong to one era that, to define itself, borrowed the symbolism of light. A secular symbolism, certainly, but one that utopias charged with new meanings. In defining their era as "our enlightened century," contemporaries contrasted it with the shadows in which the past had too long been immersed. But the symbol of lights contrasted, too, if not primarily, with any opaque society that hid its workings and its mechanisms. The multiple utopian dreams of this "enlightened century" intersect in the representation of the City that would form, at least virtually, a transparent whole such that it would be entirely perceptible in each of its parts. But, by the same token, nothing in the imagined social life could escape the synthesizing scrutiny. Paradoxically, this dazzling transparency casts a shadow; it hides as much as it reveals. This shadow cast by the transparency blurs the differences among social dreams, even among the most diverse fantasies, just as it makes it difficult to perceive the multiple functions these dreams assumed for the mentalities of the time. The transparent City that, in utopias, represents the final stage of a road to be followed is only a crossroads to which the most sinuous paths lead and from which leave several paths leading in socially and ideologically opposite directions. This is particularly striking during the revolutionary period, the height of which is marked by conquering utopia. Utopias are at that time more or less durably engraved in mentalities and ideologies. They become essential as guiding images and key ideas that orient hopes and mobilize collective energies. The revolutionary period both inherits numerous utopias and produces them in abundance. Once begun, the revolutionary impetus gives a particular thrust to the utopian imagination, modifying above all the modes of producing and diffusing social dreams, if not of imposing them. Is the power of the dream not harnessed to the service of the machinery of power and is the energy of the dream not converted into the weighty inertia of a discourse of oppression, in the shadow cast by the representations of the transparent City?

Is utopia a true light or is it rather a will-o'-the-wisp? Perhaps the problem has never so fiercely discussed as it is in our time that is unable either to live with utopias or to do without them, an era that seeks new ones, although distrustful in advance of the dangers and risks they entail. The historian of utopias cannot cherish the illusion that he can completely escape the pitfalls of this debate, even if he doesn't accept its terms. He would, however, like to elude its constraints, as far as possible. True lights or will-o'-the wisps, the lights of utopia, like searchlights for the historian's scrutiny, spotlight the men of an era producing and grappling with their dreams. To compose the history of the utopias of this "enlightened century" is, in the last analysis, to note that it could not have done without them. Its place in history has reference, too, to the creations of its imagination. Social dreams were as much the products as the conditions of the several important choices of this decisive era and thus entered into the realization, through these choices, of *one of the possible histories*. Whether the best or the worst, the century passed it down to us and it has become *ours*.

Writing a preface is always an enterprise fraught with ambiguity; this one is no exception to the rule. Is it not drafted when the book is already finished, yet with the intention of placing it at its beginning? Does it not propose a path to follow, whereas the author has already done it time and time again, getting lost who knows how many times? Does it not overemphasize the effort accomplished and understate the enormous work that remains to be done in order to attribute to social dreams the true richness of their history? Thus it is with relief that the author leaves the shifting sands to set foot on this terra firma from which he can express himself with greater confidence. From this place, my warmest thanks to my friends Jean Ehrard, Krzysztof Pomian and Paul Viallaneix, for their stimulating, faithful, and efficient help throughout this long work. This book is dedicated to my steadfast and generous lifelong friend, to my wife.

I
The Social Imagination and Utopian Representations

1
The Concepts and Meanings of "Utopia"

"Utopias are often only premature truths." These words of Lamartine have become almost a dictum. They summarize a certain perspective, a certain way of envisioning utopias: the basic issue would seem to be their relationship to the future. The value and importance of a utopia in the *present* would depend on its "truth"—that is, its ability to *predict the future*. Lamartine's words attest to a certain rehabilitation of utopia, and show both the anxieties and the hopes of his time. They attest to the perplexity of an era teeming with semi-utopians and semi-prophets; Saint-Simonians, Fouriérists, and "Icarians"; and semi-social and semi-religious sects. What exactly are these utopias? Do they, despite their oddities, foreshadow the future? Do they fill the place formerly occupied by the prophets? In order to judge, one must first question to what extent utopian dreams, in anticipating the realities of tomorrow, espouse the "march of history" and predict the answers that the future eventually brings to the dilemmas and anxieties of the present.

The lapse of historical and sociological time that separates this mid-nineteenth century from our era can be measured by comparing Lamartine's dictum with the text by Berdiaieff quoted by Aldous Huxley as the epigraph to *Brave New World*: "Les utopies sont beaucoup plus réalisables qu'on ne le croyait. Aujourd'hui nous sommes confrontés à une question nouvelle qui est devenue urgente: comment peut-on éviter la réalisation définitive des utopies? Les utopies sont réalisables. La vie marche vers les utopies." But, if the haunting fears and hopes (and also the disillusionments) have changed, the two texts cited show a similar approach. Major questions recur: to what extent is such and such a utopia realizable? What is the relationship between the future predicted and foreshadowed in and by the utopia and the present? What varies is the assessment of the future forecast by "utopian truths."

3

Lamartine worried particularly about the lack of maturity in his contemporaries, who were incapable of grasping the hopes announced by utopians. In Huxley, distrust and the feeling of danger predominate: utopias demand vigilance, and the present is already too mature to make them realizable.

The approach shown in the question, "Can utopias be realized?" is imposed, in a way, by the utopian texts themselves. The proposals, the detailed accounts of ideal societies, have an obvious or scarcely hidden intention clearly aimed at a certain attitude in the reader. This provocative intention is an element of the utopian process and of the structure of the text. The utopian is often a visionary in the etymological sense of the word—he *sees* his new City. Thus the utopian asks that the reader seek correspondences and oppositions between the dreamed City and the present, that he see them as two plans of society and that he compare them. If the particular reader who is the historian responds to this challenge, he is compelled to wonder immediately about the chances of achieving such a utopia, if not in its entirety, at least in its elements. History seems to offer him the unique opportunity of verifying, of studying the validity of premature truths, of assessing to what extent a utopia really foreshadows the future. The temptation is all the greater as the historian is often struck by the prescience and the premonitory values of a particular text, by the prophetic force of a particular utopian reality. One would almost wonder whether Le Corbusier didn't hit the nail on the head when he said that "utopia is never anything but tomorrow's reality and today's reality is yesterday's utopia."

This approach suggested by the utopian texts, especially prevalent in nineteenth-century studies on utopias, but still occasionally found in contemporary studies, doesn't seem promising to us. Indeed, it distorts historical perspective by making at least two presuppositions. First, that the utopian finds himself, so to speak, facing a ready-made and finished future; it is, then, only a matter of whether or not he has succeeded in deciphering it. The era when the utopian creates his work and the place from which he sees and tells his social dream are seen then as comprising only one possibility of evolution, precisely the one that the future will realize. But each era always offers a set of possibilities and the course of events results from the choice of certain possibilities and hence, from the rejection, the elimination of the others. As Max Scheler said, the past is always indebted to us, since it contains possibilities not realized in the real. Present reality tells us only indirectly and partially what were the *other* possibilities of history, the *other possible futures that forever remained at the level of pure possibility*. But there is yet another essential reservation. Focusing attention on the verification of utopias often reduces the function and action of utopias to the value of their prediction, and may even lead to the supposition that a utopia's influence and effectiveness are the province of its realism, of the extent to which it proved to be realizable. Even supposing the utopia to be perspicacious to the highest degree, it is obvious that its prophetic force could only be noticed and appreciated after the fact. Utopias do not influence the course of events by the realism of their predictions. Of course, certain utopias have been more interdependent with the real course of events; others have—from this point of view—succeeded less well. But it is equally obvious that *no* utopia has been totally and completely realized in history; it is obvious, too, that the overwhelming majority of utopias have not been realized in any of their predictions. However, that is in no way prejudicial to their *real* influence and historical function. It would be only too easy to show that the most stirring social dreams were by no means those that were distinguished by their realism. Moreover, one of the greatest historical successes of utopia consists of the fact that, beginning with a certain era, utopian discourse becomes essential as a way of speaking of and visualizing the future, by substituting itself to the former means of doing so, those of a secular tradition, such as prophecy or astrology.[1]

Utopias are involved in historical realities and intervene in ways other than by foreshadowing the possible future. As Renan said, the utopian is the "friend of the impossible." For the historian, the paramount interest of the study of utopias is the fact that the utopian places himself in the dimension of the impossible, that the utopian process doesn't resign itself to looking at the present social reality and its projection on the future as the only ones possible; the utopian shifts the very limits of what is accepted as possible or even as imaginable. "If instead of spending twenty-one years figuring out the 'theory of association,' " Fourier asserted, "I had said that *it would be too much to hope for, therefore it is impossible*, the theory of association would not yet have been discovered. The *sect of impossibilities* did the human race much wrong and I do not think that there exists any that is more harmful."[2] The historian of utopias is not the verifier of such calculations; the focus of his concern is not the relationship between the utopia as prediction and the future to be predicted. Rather, he wonders how, in what specific manner, the realities of a certain present, its modes of thought, belief, and imagination are translated in or by utopias, how utopias participate in the present while endeavoring to go beyond it. A sole utopia, however farseeing it might be, presents less interest to the historian as a social phenomenon than does the presence, at such and such an era, of a series of utopias, even if their projective force into the imaginary is only mediocre and limited. Utopias are specific demonstrations and expressions of a particular era, showing its obsessions, haunting fears, and revolts; the scope of its expectations as well as the paths taken by the social imagination; its way of envisaging the possible and the impossible. Going beyond social reality, even if only in dream and as an escape, is part of that reality and offers revealing testimony about it.

"*Utopia*," (by Thomas More), said Lucien Febvre, "like all subsequent works that take as a generic name the proper name of the *libellus aureus* of Erasmus's friend . . . translate the need both to escape from present realities and to plan and work out future realities, thereby furnishing the historian with one of the most deliberately unfaithful but also one of the most unconsciously faithful interpretations of the reality of an era and a milieu—a mixture of anticipations and observations, the lineaments of the seen world; the characteristics divined, foretold, and prophesied of the world of tomorrow or the day after. It is at times of trouble and transition that soothsayers and prophets are given free rein. . . . They speak when humanity, in its anxiety, seeks to specify the broad outlines of the social and moral upheaval everyone feels to be inevitable and menacing. For that reason, their works are, to the historian, always interesting —often pathetic testimony, not only of the fantasy and imagination of some of their predecessors, but of the innermost condition of a society."[3]

Certainly, the concept of utopia is only one of the many possible demonstrations of the anxieties, hopes, and pursuits of an era and of a social milieu. The questioning of the legitimacy and rationality of the existing order, the diagnosis and criticism of moral and social defects, the search for remedies, the dreams of a new order, etc.—all these favorite themes of utopias are found in political systems and popular myths, in religious doctrines and in poetry. If the critique of social reality and the expectation of a new City turn toward utopia, that means that a choice has been made among available forms of discourse. What is said in utopia and as utopia cannot be said otherwise. There are "hot" eras when utopias flourish, when the utopian imagination penetrates the most diverse forms of intellectual, political, and literary activity; eras when opposing points of view and divergent main themes seem to rediscover their point of convergence in the very invention of descriptions of utopias. But there are other "cold" eras, when utopian creativity is weakened and cut off from social, intellectual, and ideological activities. Manifestations of a social situation and of an orientation of mentalities, utopias influence them in turn. It might well be that utopias "foreseeing the future" sustain models of ideal societies that come to the fore as guiding images of a collective action. But it most frequently happens that the overall attitude toward the present reality changes as soon as visions of an alternative society, at odds with the dominant social order, arise and are disseminated. Existing social evils are seen and judged in another way once social systems that can eliminate them are imagined. The present order is no longer presented, then, as the ultimate, definitive reality, but as the counterpart of other imaginable orders. Even if the imaging activity is only practiced as a game, consequences result that affect both the way of living in the present and that of awaiting what is to come.

Up to now, we have used the concept of utopia without having defined it exactly, only referring to more or less vague intuitions or else to classic examples, such as Thomas More's *libellus aureus*. The existence of the utopian phenomenon is a fact on which historians and philosophers, sociologists and the "literati" can readily agree. As soon as one goes from isolated examples to a definition of the utopia and its specific domain, in an attempt to define the concept, it complicates and spoils things. It is useless to insist on the fact that methodological choices, and hence, the way of approaching and conceptualizing an entire field of research, are involved in the definition of notions of that type. Moreover, utopia is not in the least a neutral concept but, on the contrary, strongly valorized and valorizing. How rare it is to find an author who defines his work as *utopia* and, therefore, calls himself a *utopian*. Most often, it is others who, in calling him utopian, designate him thus as a fanciful dreamer, a chimera-maker.

Utopia was charged with this valorizing role very soon after the neologism was invented by Sir Thomas More in 1516 (what a rare opportunity it is for a historian to be able to date with such precision the birth of the key concept of his discourse . . .) and never lost it. Moreover, diverse and even conflicting values are thus successively taken on. It is not only utopias that have a history, but also discourse on utopias. In becoming a generic name, the word "utopia" extended and diversified its semantic content, but lost precision.[4]

The first and fundamental ambiguity of the term stems from the neologism and was certainly intended by More himself. "Utopia": is it "*eu*-topos," the region of happiness and perfection, or "*ou*-topos," the region that nowhere exists? Or, rather, does *utopia* not designate both things together—justice and happiness united in a social order that nowhere exists?[5] During the seventeenth and eighteenth centuries, other ambiguities that stem, on the one hand, from the extension of the meaning and, on the other, from the valorizing function taken on by the term, were added to this original ambiguity. Thus any text that follows More's narrative model was called "utopian": the account of an imaginary voyage at the end of which the narrator discovers an unknown country where the ideal social order, recounted in detail, reigns. But the designation "utopian" is also given to texts that do not fall into this literary genre and that had been conceived of several centuries before "the very excellent man," Raphael Hythloday gave Thomas More an account of his trip. Plato's *Republic* is most often cited as the typical example of this other model of utopian discourse, namely a *proposal for ideal legislation*. "Utopia: region that exists nowhere; an imaginary country. The word utopia is sometimes used figuratively of the plan of an imaginary government, following Plato's *Republic*."[6] To this is added the valuing function. *Utopia* is synonymous with *impossible*, with *chimera*, particularly in the political and social domain, and it is only political dreamers who fabricate utopias. *Utopia* is the generally used designation for an imaginary plan of a government where all is ruled for the common happiness, e.g., "Every dreamer imagines a utopia."[7]

In the nineteenth and twentieth centuries, due to several factors, the word became enriched with new meanings and new ambiguities. First of all, utopian discourse changed paradigms. Fourier, Saint-Simon, Enfantin, and Cabet, described as well-known utopians and social dreamers, do not write imaginary voyages, nor do they propose dream governments. The visions of ideal societies that they put forward are presented as so many consequences of social theories, as scientifically grounded truths. It is no longer a question of imagining faraway islands inhabited by ideal peoples. The New City must be established *hic et nunc*, in the very near future. Its advent is inevitable because the march of historical evolution and its universal laws that have been discovered guarantee it. If Cabet has recourse to the paradigm of the imaginary voyage, he only uses it as a literary expedient to insure the best diffusion to ideas he had formulated elsewhere in a theoretical and scientistic, if not scientific, discourse. Moreover, those chimeras that find partisans are greeted by some as guiding images of their actions, and by others as a real social danger. This evolution, which has repercussions on vocabulary as well as on attitudes toward utopias, is in fact recorded around the middle of the nineteenth century in a book that attempted to combat utopias by writing a critical history of them. "Doubtless, at first glance, these excursions into the domain of the imagination can be seen either as an innocent diversion or as a useful exercise for thought. . . . However, when the chimeras become too ambitious, writers have another duty, that is to lead minds back to an awareness of realities and to assign limits to fantasy."[8]

However, interest in utopias doesn't cease growing and they have become the object of systematic research which retraces their history and questions their scope and functions. These questions extended the frontier line of the "kingdom of utopia" well beyond mere literary genre, and conquered distant provinces. Scientific research, philosophical reflection, and sociological analysis discovered the complexity of the utopian phenomenon. The presence of the ideas—utopian images in the most diverse works and activities—is noticeable in the major social movements, even if they claim to be distinct from and opposed to any utopian process. It is not for us to discuss either the diverse methodological procedures that presided over the study of the utopian phenomenon, or the new ambiguities that accrued. It is, however, important to note that a common tendency can be seen in all these widely differing approaches. First of all, the traditional meaning of the word is no longer satisfactory. The awareness of the complexity of the utopian phenomenon is translated by the setting up of a meta-discourse on utopias, characterized by attempts at redefinition of the very concept of utopia. On the one hand, the opposition utopia/non-utopia tends to characterize not works but collective attitudes, social movements, currents, and trends in ideas. Finally, there is an attempt to bring out historical and social conditions that favor the creation and diffusion of utopian representations. Let us cite only three examples of these diverse approaches that have in common their positing utopia as the term of an opposition: utopia/science, utopia/myth, and utopia/ideology.

The most complex and most remarkable case is certainly that of Marxism. The opposition *utopia/science* or, more exactly *scientific socialism/utopian socialism* is found in Marx and Engels, and then in almost the whole Marxist tradition. This opposition implies several different perspectives that reveal the history of Marxism as well as of the representations it forms of itself and its history. On the one hand, utopias are considered premonitions or prefigurations of a knowledge, of ideas that, with Marxism itself, acquired the status of a science. "Scientific socialism," said Engels, "raised itself on the shoulders of Saint-Simon, Fourier and Owen, three men who, despite all the fantasy of the utopianism of their doctrines, are among the greatest minds of all times and have brilliantly anticipated numerous ideas whose scientific accuracy we demonstrate today." Marx's theory is, then, in relation to the "fantasies" of utopians, what chemistry is to alchemy. The utopias provided with socialist idea-images, and notably the utopias of Babeuf, Saint-Simon, Fourier, and Owen, corresponded to a specific social stage, namely that of the birth of capitalism and translated the "immaturity" of the proletariat at that time. With Marx's discoveries, every utopia becomes an anachronism. On the other hand, however, Marxism recognizes the manifestation of the profound feelings of the oppressed masses in "socialist" ideas of utopias dating from the sixteenth and seventeenth centuries. The persistence and continuity of the utopian phenomenon bear witness to the constant and faithful aspiration of these classes to immemorial values: equality, liberty, social justice, the community of goods, and so forth. From the first perspective the stress is primarily on the "scholarly" aspect of utopias; their "maturity" is valued, that is, the fact of having formulated or foreseen such and such a thesis that entered into Marxism as "scientific." This view supposes (or even imposes) a certain teleology in the development of utopian ideas that, throughout history, "mature" in the direction of Marxism. The other perspective emphasizes the imaginary and the emotional; utopias become primarily repetitive manifestations of feelings of social revolt and of the hopes of a communist or rather communal future. In relation to utopias, "scientific" socialism is thus defined as both continuity and rupture—continuity, because it takes on the ideas, images, and values it recognizes, in light of its theory, as scientifically valuable; but rupture, as well, since it contrasts with utopias as the solitary does to the multiple. There were several utopian socialisms, but there can be only one "scientific socialism." Continuity, for socialism, having become a science, is the only legitimate heir to all the hopes that nourished the revolts of the oppressed in the past. But rupture is also involved, because it is not only the proletariat, armed with a scientific theory, who can and must necessarily transform dreams into reality. Rupture and continuity operate again in relation to the representations of society to come—rupture, because scientific socialism, contrary to utopias, refuses to elaborate in detail the image of the society whose advent is nevertheless considered the ineluctable result of the historical evolution and the ultimate objective of the class struggle—but continuity, too, for, despite this automatic refusal, the overall vision of the community of the future is permanently in play in the theoretical and political discourse of Marx and Engels. Thus, the opposition utopia/science at once masks and reveals this vision of the social otherness, showing at once its presence and its absence. In fact, it is remarkable that a "scientific" Marxist reading of the works of the utopians particularly stresses the distinction between their "fantasies" and their "anticipations." Moreover, such a reading, at once selective and valorizing, has, as a condition of possibility, a vision of the community to come, whether the latter is explicit, or suppressed in what is unsaid in "science." In fact, how can what is and what is not anticipation be judged, if not according to the ideas one forms of the social state on which it is anticipated? This vision of communist society can be read, veiled, just below the surface in Marx. He occasionally speaks of it, but only in a secondary discourse. It seems in that case that he almost distrusts giving his imagination free rein, being afraid to fall into illusion and reverie. And yet his entire work conveys this vision, making it a potent, stirring dream that renewed the collective imagination.

We have emphasized only the outline that is found as a commonplace in a certain Marxist or, if you will, Marxist-Leninist orthodoxy. On the other hand, the formation and evolution of the concept of utopia in Marx and Engels have yet to be studied. Such a study could contribute to a better clarification of certain trends in their work as well as the variable structural relationships of its constituent elements. The very notion of "scientific socialism" has been defined in relation—and in opposition—to what the authors of the Communist Manifesto consider "utopian." But there is also interaction: the notion of utopia is crystallized from a certain idea of science whose formation and evolution have yet to be explored, although it remains considerably dependent on the representations of a future society that would be imbued with a scientific rationality. Let us remember, too, that the opposition science/utopia enters the conceptual network of Marx and Engels fairly late. Their attitude is marked by feelings of continuity and rupture in relation to the utopians, but the weight of each varies under the influence of diverse factors (for example, their interest in the Russian *obstchina*, the rustic village community). It is, finally, useless to insist on the fact that Marx's theoretical thinking, like his critique of capitalist society, postulates the vision of a different society—one promised, if not assured, by the course of history and the laws commanding it.

There is still another study to be made of the importance accorded utopian representations in the course of the evolution of Marxism. It is obvious that it changes from one ideology to another, even during what is known as the "classical" period (more important, e.g., in a Lafargue than in a Kautsky). But the most fascinating chapter of the changing attitudes of Marxism toward utopias would be, perhaps, on Russia during the first years after the October Revolution. On the one hand, the newly dominant ideology seeks to acquire its own cultural tradition, whence the growing interest in utopian texts. This interest corresponds, on the other hand, to a proliferation of plans and proposals for communal life, but also to more or less ephemeral experiences. There is a wish to change life, to immediately put into practice, in several types of communes, the overall representation of communist society. In search of models, there is a turn toward certain texts of Marx and Engels, but also to "classic" utopians, from More to Tschernyschevski and Kropotkin. How do utopian idea-images, combined with revolutionary myths and symbols, mark the mentalities of militant minorities during this period? How do they perform their function of mobilization and concealment? These questions would require another study, one that would be extremely promising, and not only for the history of utopias.[9]

Let us go on to the two other oppositions that we will take up much more briefly.

In Sorel, the precise meaning and pejorative valorizing of utopia are expressed by the opposition utopia/myth and Marxism is specifically reproached for having fixed a myth in a utopia. By utopia, Sorel means the artificial model of an ideal society presented to the masses as the ultimate objective and final realization of their aspirations and struggles. Utopias are the product of an intellectual and speculative work. Their producers are intellectuals outside the spontaneous movement of the masses, the manipulation of whom utopias can only facilitate. The political myth, on the contrary, in Sorel's sense of the term, is a particular form of the collective conscience; it is summarized in a key idea that is the watchword of both the struggle and its line of action. The myth is produced by the spontaneity of the revolt of the masses; it is never finished or fixed. Utopias are structures composed of imaginary institutions, models to which existing societies can be compared in order to gauge any good and bad that would result. Utopias, like any social institution, can be discussed, and lead minds toward pertinent reforms. On the other hand, the political myth cannot be broken down into parts that one might try to apply here or there. The myth is not debatable; it takes possession of men and inspires their combat. The Marxist idea of socialism on the one hand and the idea of a general strike on the other are, for Sorel, contemporary forms of utopias and of the political myth respectively.[10]

A final example: the opposition utopia/ideology proposed by Karl Mannheim. What is striking, at first, in this redefinition of utopia is the extension of the concept. The "topos," the "place," of which utopia is the negation, is always historically determined: it is the set of social relationships to which a rising social class is opposed. The aspirations, ideals, and value systems of important social movements manifest themselves in utopias; they are, therefore, coherent and structured overall visions of the world, and represent the profound needs of an era. Ideologies, too, are overall systems of ideas and values; they translate, however, the deformations and limitations of the social conscience of classes opposed to social progress, supporters of the status quo, of a conscience that is always marked by the tendency to mystify reality and history. The concept of utopia is not, then, attached to any precise form of literary expression; it is a global vision of the world, a manifestation of an essential dimension of the historical conscience. The concept of utopia marks the totality of the culture of an era; it constitutes an essential factor in every mass movement and every radical historical and social change.[11]

Additional examples seem unnecessary; the aim of this brief review, limited to approaches that have already become standard, was only to bring out the difficulties research on utopia entails. On the one hand, historical research must take into account the broadening of the field of studies as well as the complexity of the phenomenon brought to the fore in methodological discussions. But, on the other hand, any philosophical, sociological, and anthropological reflection on utopian phenomena must be based on thorough, detailed, historical studies; otherwise it risks foundering in vague generalities. The fact that these postulates are commonplaces does not by any means make their realization easier.

One final observation on the uncommon interest that utopias arouse today. The number of works published during these last thirty years is as impressive as it is significant.[12] Paradoxically, scholarly discourse *on* utopias, meta-discourse, now prevails over utopian creativity itself. (The work of Ernst Bloch is, perhaps, the only case where, in a thought in search of Hope as the founding principle of Being, this meta-discourse is in harmony with a powerful utopian impulse.) Certain specific tendencies of the recent evolution of the interests of the human sciences have surely contributed to this renewal of research on utopia. Such is the case with the prominence given the importance of prophetic and utopian visions in social movements; with the growing awareness of the roles played in social life by so-called marginal groups and phenomena, and with the questioning of the structures and evolution of collective mentalities. The attention paid to utopias indicates, above all, a more general tendency to restore the value of the imaginary and the imagination, to recognize them as a specific and indispensable social mode of the collective life. As every field of social experience is surrounded by a horizon of refusals and expectations, of fears and hopes, it is impossible to study the mentalities of an era without taking into account precisely those horizons on which utopias are situated. And refusing to reduce the imaginary to the illusory, one then tries to show how reality contains and conceals the dreams of the social actors and what are the social functions of these dreams.[13] All these are questions to which we will return.

Last but not least, the growing interest taken in utopias is not merely a matter of scholarly preoccupations. It responds to more than one of the questions about our century. It could be said that the term ''utopia'' has become the focal point, if not the symbol, of our own haunting fears and hopes. Never, perhaps, have utopias been so violently denounced and so ardently praised. Thus, profound anxiety is evinced about the danger to our times of the absence of utopias suitable to them, at the horizon of our expectations and in the use of our imagination. ''Our era,'' said Bernard Russel, ''can no longer believe in the dreams of utopians. Even the societies dreamed of by our imagination only reproduce the evils we are accustomed to in daily life." *Utopia or death*, proclaims the title of a recent work pondering possible responses to the degradation of our ecological condition. Quite recently, graffiti calling for *power to the imagination* were erased from the walls of Paris. But at at the same time, interest in utopias reveals conflicting feelings and attitudes. It is not only a disillusionment that is coming to light, but a profound distrust of utopias, because of the social dangers that their influence on mentalities might entail. We are more conscious than ever that utopias are apt to become not only powerful instruments of action and social mobilization but also the instruments of tragically effective manipulations. Did the totalitarian experience in Russia as well as in Germany not show how utopias, joined to myths and amplified by omnipresent and oppressive propaganda, enslave and degrade minds and imaginations?

We scarcely harbor any illusions about the possibility of the historian studying utopias without consciously or unconsciously taking on the fundamental preoccupations of his time. Moreover, we do not by any means seek to escape from this. That having been established, the object and intention of this work nevertheless remains historical. It does not concern utopia in general, but rather considers utopian phenomena during a specific period, the eighteenth century, which at least for the sake of convenience, will continue to be called the "Age of Enlightenment."

2
The Utopian Sphere and Its Frontiers

During certain eras utopias represent only a marginal, isolated phenomenon; during others, utopian creativity is intensified. While the number of utopian texts grows, a singular affinity links utopias to the mental structures and principal ideas of the times. Utopias then maintain multiple and complex relationships with philosophical ideas, literature, social movements, ideological currents, collective symbolism, and the collective imagination. It is thus that the Age of Enlightenment is a "hot" period in the history of utopias, as does the Renaissance, or the first half of the nineteenth century. So the study of the utopias of this period offers the historian a double opportunity: while contributing to a better knowledge of the mental structures and latent tendencies of the movement of contemporary ideas, it can lead to a better understanding of the complexity of the utopian phenomenon, as well as the lines of its evolution, and the historical characteristics of its social functions.

The utopian sphere in the eighteenth century is both fascinatingly rich and disturbingly ambiguous. That is why before beginning to explore it we must first pave the way, planting guideposts and proposing a conceptual grid, if only to reduce the risks of misunderstanding, to delimit the field of our work, and to specify the orientation of our research. That sometimes calls for reservations: we are afraid of putting the cart before the horse. In such a preliminary presentation, necessarily succinct and schematic, there is great risk of putting forward definitions and propositions that would give the impression of being a priori, if not arbitrary. In fact we propose only an elaborate set of tools, adapting them to the progress of the research itself. By this procedure we will no doubt anticpate the results of the research. If certain preliminary developments concerning, in particular, the structural relationships that are brought out in utopias prove to be too abstract or schematic, we ask the reader to wait patiently until they are given concrete form in the explanation of the historical development that inspired them. If he is still somewhat disappointed afterward, let him not accord excessive importance to formulas that prove to be too general when put to the test. Their only value is in the extent to which they open on realities and, by conceptualizing them, bring out their richness. On the other hand, they are condemned in advance once they close in on themselves and compose a discourse whose sole justification is found in the hollow cavity of its own practice, in the contemplation of its own navel. This kind of discourse is too widespread and contagious for us to feel completely safe from its dangers; thus our insistent warnings.[14]

a. There is no utopia without an overall representation, the idea-image of an alternative society, opposed to the existing social reality, and its institutions, rites, dominant symbols, systems of values, norms of interdictions, hierarchies, relationships of dominance and property, its domain reserved to the sacred, and so forth. In other words, *there is no utopia without a synthetic and disruptive representation of social otherness*. The degree of this otherness could, in some way, serve as a scale for a classification of utopias. The ideal type of utopia would be the overall representation of a New City, which would be radically at odds with the existing society, and would refuse any continuity and would imagine history beginning again from square one—a synthetic and disruptive idea-image of an alternative society and a better social life. It is up to the utopian City to take hold of the idea of collective happiness and to give an image to public felicity.

Utopian representations, then, go hand in hand with critical attitudes toward social realities. The starting point of the utopian enterprise is the feeling, if not the clear consciousness, of a rupture among what ought to be, the ideal and social reality. Utopias aim at a new life in the name of values that transcend existing reality and that alone are judged capable of regenerating individual and collective life. Utopias, then, tend toward radical criticism of existing society. Singularly sensitized to the evils of established society, they very often perceive it through anguish, they see it at the height of crisis, dominated by evil and injustice. There is then no utopia without an ideal opposed to reality—although not every ideal engenders a utopia. In this sense, and only in this sense, it could be said that every utopia is more or less unrealistic, that it accommodates and expresses sometimes latent tendencies to escape from history and society. But, on the other hand, imagining an alternative and better society is also a specific way of approaching and living the realities of one's time. The opposition utopia/reality is both derivative of and a part of history, not only in the sense that every utopia is produced, imagined, and dreamed in a given moment of history, but also and above all because the imagined social otherness refers, at least implicitly, to historical realities, if only by refusing and going beyond them.[15]

b. The representations of a different and happy City are the products of a particular way of imagining the social; utopias are one of the places, occasionally the privileged place, where the social imagination is put into practice, where individual and collective social dreams are welcomed, gathered, worked on, and produced.[16] Moreover if utopian imaging activity is focused on overall and synthetic idea-images, it nevertheless is developed through day-to-day reality. The dreams of the happy City are, then, articulated with images of a renewed daily life, and utopias often offer a great luxury of detail in their descriptions of individual and collective daily life.[17] The structural relationships between the representation of the overall society and the detailed images of the ordinary aspects of life are as complex as they are revealing. On the one hand, in utopias accumulated descriptions of the everyday only become functional insofar as they put into more concrete form the imagined overall society, particularly the principles that command it. At most, each detail is only a symbol, while all the details are only signs that signify a sole idea, the representation of the New City. Thus, society is imagined as "readable" on all levels. Utopias represent transparent societies: the whole is entirely perceptible in each of its parts (hence, every part is always visible and nothing in the social life ought to escape the synthesizing gaze). Such a transparency, the result of the play of images, is also put into a deliberate image, affirmed as a fundamental principle of the society. The *alternative* society is precisely the one that dissimulates nothing of its machinery, cogs, and wheels. But, on the other hand, the images of the everyday and of the individual gain autonomy and acquire their own specific density, if only by virtue of their accumulation and their symbolic surcharge. The participation of each individual and each instant in the common synthesis must be imagined through institutions and activities that would unite the whole and its parts. Thus, new modes of socialization are imagined in detail, with particular emphasis on the family, the educational system, the living conditions, celebrations, and the like. These institutions and activities are consequently presented as just so many collective rites perfectly internalized by each individual and rigorously respected by society as a whole.[18] All these levels of the imaginary sometimes make explicit what remains unacknowledged in the overall representation, an opacity that is the shadow projected by the dreamed transparency.

    c. In utopias, the exercise of the imagination is already limited by the relationships established among the representation of the overall society and the images of the everyday and the individual. The social imagination is again (and differently) limited by the interference of knowledge. The alternative society is not only imagined, it is also thought to be consonant with reason, and prides itself on the rationality it brings into play. Utopias want to install reason in the realm of the imagination; in utopias, constant exchanges among social dreams and critical, theoretical, and normative reflection are carefully worked out. The term idea-image to which we often have recourse has the sole aim of bringing these distinctive characteristics of utopian representation to the fore. In imaginative, scholarly, and theorizing utopias, the social dream is always organized and premeditated, but knowledge is fed, if not guided, by the dream. Utopias are relay stations where encounters and amalgams, if not impossible fusions of both, are made and unmade. The global representation of the different City is certainly imagined, but it strives to visualize frequently abstract principles and values on which to base the just and virtuous happy City. The everyday and its ritual are certainly imagined; but, at the same time, they are deduced from the idea-image of the overall society as well as from its directing principles. This complex interplay reveals not only the diversity of the utopian realm of imagination, but the contradictions that shape it as well. In the ideal model of utopia, it could be said to be almost a question of thinking the unimaginable while imagining the unthinkable.

d. Utopia is not only imagined and thought; it is made intelligible and communicable in a discourse by which the merging of the idea-images and their integration into a language is accomplished. As already stated, two classic paradigms were imposed in utopian discourse from the sixteenth through nineteenth centuries. The first is the *utopia of the imaginary voyage*. The text is presented in the form of a quasi-novelistic discourse. The narrator, who most often speaks in the first person, tells of his discovery of the ideal City situated in a distant, previously unknown land; it is generally a region isolated from the rest of humanity, preferably an island. After his return from this country "nowhere," the traveler tells of his adventures. He describes the City itself, with its inhabitants, institutions, morals, religion, history, and so forth. The genius and the success of the work of Thomas More lie in the invention of a paradigm that responds to the curiosity of his time about distant lands, that lends itself wonderfully well to the exercise of the social imagination by a play of mirrors between the image of the overall society and the images of the everyday, which blend the serious aspect of moral and social criticism with free intellectual, humanistic, and scholarly play. The other paradigm is that of the *utopia-proposal for ideal legislation*. The ideal City is imagined by means of detailed legislation, a code of reason or nature, whose beneficial effects are shown by images of renewed individual and social life.

There are many variants of these two classic paradigms, and exchanges between them are particularly frequent in the eighteenth century. We run across numerous examples of imaginary utopia-voyages when the description of the ideal society, the essential argument of the book, is only an ideal proposal for government badly linked to the pseudo-novelistic story. Often a secondary narrator expounds the proposal that is the basis of the City visited by the traveler and gives a detailed commentary on it; sometimes the imaginary legislator himself does this. But too, by an inverse movement, the political literature of the time seizes upon ideas advanced in fables as well. The paradigm of the imaginary voyage spreads easily and holds sway over an entire literary genre, the political novel, which, moreover, suffers increasingly from its rigidity, its paradigmatic fixity. It is, in fact, an easy genre, perhaps too easy. It lends itself all too readily to imitation and repetition, and there is a marked mediocrity of imagination in the majority of these imaginary voyages. Certainly, even when utopian discourse only reproduces the classic paradigms, it is never closed on itself. It draws from the depths of the collective imagination, exploiting, for example, the myths of the land of milk and honey or of paradise lost. On the other hand, it adapts diffuse social dreams, as well as the moral, political, and philosophical ideas of its times. But, most important, utopian creativity does not confine itself to classical and more and more worn-out, hackneyed, paradigmatic forms. "The utopian field is not reduced to the creation of some few lampoons, however illustrious they may be. . . . It covers a vast cultural field."[19] First of all, there are numerous cases when the utopian enterprise goes beyond the scope of the discourse, extending into practical application; furthermore, utopia can be expressed in modes other than the novel or the code of perfect legislation; it can use other languages.

e. Every utopia is not necessarily proposed as a program of action or even as a model that would demand intellectual or emotional support. The novelistic utopias are offered most frequently as intellectual games. They only seek to stimulate both the imagination and the critical and moralizing reflection of the readers (if they're not offered as a simple diversion, in which case, the novelistic elements predominate in the text). However, sometimes even the utopias presented in the form of an imaginary voyage inspire a will to act and to give some of their ideas a practical application. Bacon s *New Atlantis* is a classic example. The dream of the "House of Solomon," of a community of scholars that, by maintaining unprecedented progress in the sciences and the arts, directs the life of the ideal City, served as catalyst to the founding of the "invisible college," the forerunner of the Royal Society.[20]

But there are utopias that proclaim themselves as both a prophetic and a founding word, and that find their extensions in the establishment of exemplary communities professing to put them into practice. The communities attempt to materialize the idea-image of social otherness by the word "utopian" in their institutions, their way of life, their social and human relationships, and so forth. They are characterized, on the one hand, by the wish to isolate themselves and to form a sort of island within the society but, on the other hand, they seek to open themselves to the world, if only by offering it the masterful example of new community life. During the era that interests us utopias are put into practice primarily in Protestant countries, particularly England and America. There, on new land and in a break with the old world, there is an increase in the community experiments intended to regenerate social life. It is significant that nearly all of these utopias put into practice are marked by a strong religious tone, by a messianic if not millenarian faith.[21]

Certainly, the dichotomy utopian discourse/utopia put into practice is only relative. Is a minimum of discourse on the New City not a necessary preliminary requisite to utopian practice? However, in utopian communities the play of principles and of the everyday does not take place on the level of discourse, but in a lived collective experience. The coherence of a discourse-proposal is not sufficient to assure the effective coherence and life of a community. Thus, practiced utopias engender their particular mechanisms and contradictions that, most often, lead to their breakup.

f. The frontiers of the utopia are still shifting in other ways. That is the case particularly when utopian discourse is expressed in languages and modes other than those used in the classic paradigms. In fact, utopian idea-images have the distinctive characteristic of being easily articulated in political, philosophical, architectural, and pedagogic language. It is not the language borrowed but its specific use that characterizes utopian discourse, although the language borrowed is not immaterial either to the mutations of the discourse or to the formation of new paradigms. Certainly, it is neither only nor primarily a question of language. If utopian idea-images are more or less durably associated with a certain language, that attests to the fact that those who practice it think, imagine, and act in function of the utopia. Let us take one example. During the Age of Enlightenment, the practice of the sciences and the arts as well as reflection about their rapid development took place in conjunction with predictions of their beneficial social effects; these are the desires and wishes, dreams and hopes lived by the intelligentsia of the time and are part of its ideology. Presumably, then, the future progress of reason in general or even in a particular science must necessarily lead to the regeneration of the overall society or to the formation of the new man. This expectation is sometimes strongly charged with utopian content or, it might be said, it is utopian idea-images that are formed on the horizon of expectations. Approached in this way, the social imagination forms fringes of the utopia, representations of the more or less elaborate social otherness that, by a retroactive effect, stimulate and consolidate diffuse expectations. These displacements of utopias, their localizations and anchorages, their rises and falls, are thus precious indications both of the field of the experiences and of the expectations and hopes of a social group, of a milieu, of a sphere of activity. In these forms, utopias take on the most complex functions—they serve as relay stations between the practical application and the dream; they stimulate ideological commitments, like flights from realities, they clarify certain aspects of those realities, not without masking others. Certainly, in these multiple and complex relationships the contours of the utopian idea-images occasionally become indistinct, but the richness of the utopian phenomenon stands out all the more clearly. It is true that the field of research is being dangerously broadened so that its limits are less clear than in the case of the classic utopia. But is it not a worthwhile risk if it shows promise of better bringing out both the utopian structure and its manifold functions and facets?

Let us here stop our preliminary observations on the domain of utopia and its frontiers. At once too long and too succinct, they leave us with the feeling of having said both too much and not enough. Nevertheless, they lead us directly to the object of our research and its orientations. In fact, the domain of utopias during the Age of Enlightenment is characterized, on the one hand, by the rapid development of the utopia in its classic paradigmatic forms, and on the other by the renewal of utopian creativity, the mutation of paradigms, and the increase of the fringes of utopia.

The eighteenth century, we have said, is a "hot" period in the history of utopias, as much because of the number of utopian texts as by virtue of the richness of the themes and forms of discourse. We find communal and egalitarian utopias, but also utopias aspiring to an equitable bourgeois property; spontaneist utopias and those with anarchistic leanings, but also statist utopias where the power rules all the details of life; agrarian and urban utopias; retrospective and primitivistic utopias closely associated with the themes of Arcadia, the Golden Age, and the Noble Savage, but also prospective utopias turned toward the progress of science and technology or simply toward Progress itself; utopias contenting themselves with dreaming of the elimination of abuses and others imagining a radical transformation of human relationships. Imaginary voyages are made to "austral lands," to the Barbary Coast, to the moon, under the sea, and to the interior of the globe, and proposals for legislation include the establishment of perpetual peace, happiness, virtue, abundance, and perfect rationality. The eighteenth century is also the era when the weakening and wearing out of classic paradigms becomes more and more obvious. But under other forms, the encounters of utopia with the great hopes and key values of the Enlightenment, the utopian sphere is broadened and its frontiers are extended. Thus, metaphysical reflection is seen to combine with the most audacious social dreams, the arts and sciences give themselves visionary extensions, and proposals for partial and limited reforms merge with representations of a regenerated nation, populated by "new men." Utopias are responses given to the anxieties, to the unsatisfied hopes and dreams of the century; they thus appear as limits toward which reflection and imagination tend, as hidden dimensions of ideas, as distant horizons of searches. Utopian representations served as stones and mortar in the construction of the imaginary society spoken of by Tocqueville. "Above the real society whose constitution was still traditional, confused, and irregular; where laws remained different and contradictory, classes and ranks clearly defined, conditions fixed and responsibilities unequal, little by little an imaginary society was built, in which everything seemed simple and coordinated, uniform, fair and in conformity with reason."[22] And it is during this century that history seems to open itself to the dream as a vast work site, and the utopia, focusing on a distant horizon of expectations, establishes itself at the very heart of a lived collective experience.

We do not propose to cover this entire wide field and our inquiry does not profess to be exhaustive. It will proceed by sections and investigatory probes, seeking thus to bring out structural relationships between utopian representations and discourse, the registers and orientations of the utopian imagination. We shall examine the pressure exerted on ideas and mentalities by the utopian imagination but we shall seek, too, to analyze the historic and social limits of the social imagination, the weight of its inertia. We are interested, certainly, in classic utopias, but even more so in the moving frontiers of the utopia and in the movement of these frontiers. Thus, as specific examples, we will see utopian imagination at work in discourse on politics, metaphysics, and history. But, on the other hand, our inquiry will be extended to the conquering utopia, namely, to the utopian representations that are imposed as guiding images and directive schemata in attempts to renew collective time and space, in particular during the revolutionary period (new calendar, festivals, imaginary architecture, and urbanism). Thus, we will turn our regard as much toward history in utopia as toward utopia in history.

3
Utopias, Utopians, Reformers

B*efore* turning to these inquiries, let us give a brief survey, as global as it is rapid, of the scale of magnitude of the utopian phenomenon in the eighteenth century. Semantic data bring us the first indications. The extensive meaning given the word "utopia" as well as its polysemy reveal the diffuse presence of the phenomenon as well as the differing attitudes it gives rise to. As we have already observed, the majority of dictionaries of the time record the generalization of the generic use of the word. *Utopia* denotes an imaginary country that exists nowhere but it is also used for any plan of ideal government; in the broadest sense, it is a chimera, an unrealizable project, or even a reverie.[23] Leibniz gives "utopia" an analogous but even more extensive meaning: he relates it to the idea of the perfect universe, "of a possible world without sin or misfortune." Unconsciously, he compares the utopian, creator and legislator of an ideal imaginary country, with God himself, the great organizer of this "best of all possible worlds." "It is true," said Leibniz, "that one can imagine possible worlds with neither sin nor misfortune and they could be created like novels, utopias, Sévarambes, but these same worlds would be quite inferior in good to our own."[24] Rousseau reproaches the other authors with being utopians. "Your system," he wrote to the elder Mirabeau, "is very good for the people of utopia, but worthless for the children of Adam." On the other hand, he defends himself against reproaches leveled at him for having imagined in the *Social Contract* a system worthy of being relegated "with Plato's *Republic*, the *Sévarambes*, and *Utopia* to the country of chimeras."[25] However, for Brissot, Rousseau's work, which he admires, opens on the most sublime, but in no way chimeric utopia. Thus, he says of Bernardin de Saint-Pierre that he "doesn't belong to this world, he is of Rousseau's. Scarcely have you read a few pages when you believe yourself transported into *a country where utopia is not a chimera.*"[26] Thus,

22

synonyms are used to designate utopian texts. Thus "works whose aim is to present a system of perfection applicable to men as they ought to be and not as they are, works where the prospect of happiness is discovered only in an *inaccessible distance* are called *political novels*."[27] In 1730, Guedeville even invented a neologism to designate the action by which the real is transformed into the ideal. Our social world "will never utopianize itself," he wrote regretfully in his preface to the translation of More's *Utopia*.[28] Even more remarkable: a term was sought to name the specific activity of *producing utopian texts*.

L.-S. Mercier, himself the author of the utopia *L'an 2440*, was a fervent partisan of the massive introduction of neologisms into the language, in order to adapt it to the new life and phenomena that were beginning to see the light. Thus, he proposed the word *fictionize*. "It is not to narrate, to tell a story, fabulize, but, rather to imagine political or moral characters in order to put over truths essential to the social order. *Fictionizing* a plan of government on a distant isle, among an imaginary people, for the development of several political ideas, is what several authors have done who have written fiction in behalf of the science that embraces the general economy of states and the felicity of peoples."[29]

Throughout the century, the works most frequently cited as examples of utopias remain the classic texts of Plato and More. But added to these are the description of the abbey of Thélème, or Fénélon's pages on the kingdom of Salente. References are made rather frequently to a text known today only by specialists, namely Veiras's *Histoire des Sévarambes*. In the Rousseau and Leibniz texts cited above, Sévarambes are synonymous with utopians. Veiras's book is evoked without comment—supposedly known by the "enlightened" reader.[30] Beginning with the Regency, the eighteenth century has a contemporary who is looked on as a model utopian, a political dreamer, who composes chimeric proposals for perfect legislation. He is the Abbé de Saint-Pierre whose *Projet de paix perpétuelle* is most frequently referred to. We shall return to him and to the distinctive characteristics of his utopias; let us cite for the moment only the evidence of the Marquis d'Argenson. "My good friend, the Abbé de Saint-Pierre, also dreams of reforming the State. . . . He writes his dreams and has them printed. . . . With the best possible intentions, he has given several pieces of advice that deserve to be followed; but he attacked generally accepted ideas head-on. He proposed impractical means in order to attain happy ends; he announced his ideas emphatically. . . . All that cast ridicule on his writings and person . . . a good example for those who still want to publish proposals for reform." This bitterness will not prevent the Marquis from creating, in turn, his own similar dreams, which, it is true, he is careful not to publish.[31]

The ways of classifying utopian texts bring other indirect information as much about the diversity of the phenomenon as about the circulation of the texts.

Indeed, in the eighteenth century the definition of the status and character of utopian texts created difficulties not unlike those discussed today. As it happens, taxonomy often implies value judgments. For some, utopias and, in particular, imaginary voyages are only a sub-genre of the novel, of romantic literature. For others, this is "serious" literature, making an important contribution to political and moral thought.

Thus, criticism applied to novels, that newcomer to literature generally thought of as a poor relative, is transferred to utopias. Moncrif reproaches imaginary voyages with magnifying to an even greater extent all the faults common to novels. These narratives have reference only to the "marvelous and the supernatural," and, worse, without "a true contribution of the imagination." Thus, the sole source of utopian novels is "a simple overturning of the principles and customs common to all or most nations; it is the nearly unfounded displacement of some recognized properties in certain beings that are attributed to others to whom nature has refused such advantages. . . . The economy of this Republic, where, under the name of Hounhyins (*sic*), horses get the better of men, is directed toward a similar overturning of ideas. . . . It seems to me that the kind of imagination likely to formulate such contrasts is like the mind characteristic of those able to shine only by taking the opposing view of everything one says; they think they're reasoning, yet all they do is contradict." It is unimportant that a Moncrif doesn't like contradictors and that, in the name of the "natural" and the "rational," in speaking out against the poverty of imagination he reproaches a Swift. Yet, it must be pointed out that Moncrif refers to a wave of interest aroused by this literature, if only to combat it. The public's infatuation with imaginary voyages is explicable, according to him, only by the enthusiasm, both unhealthy and in bad taste, aroused by the odd and the fantastic. Thus imaginary voyages are only a variation on fairy tales or dreams. Beyond these questions of classification and esthetic judgment there is, however, an ideological polemic. If Moncrif reproaches utopias for producing particularly disastrous effects, it is because they are too stimulating to the imagination, orienting it in a dangerous direction. "We are going to know everything, to explain everything, *we will be at will Creators, Philosophers, we will be all that we want to be,* and all because we will be exempt from making a plan and from establishing connections among the parts of our fable, or at least because the links we use will be purely arbitrary."[32] Similar reproaches are addressed to Morelly's *Basilliade* and it is obvious that the vehemence of the attacks is explained by the audacity of the ideas advanced in the work: egalitarianism, community of goods, sexual liberty. "One knows how great a distance there is between the most beautiful speculations of this kind and the possibility of their execution; it is because, in theory, one takes imaginary men who lend themselves with docility to all the arrangements and who second with equal zeal the legislator's views; but, as soon as one tries to realize things, one must make use of men as they are, that is, far from docile, lazy or rather ardently given over to one violent passion or another. The proposal for equality is in particular one of those that appear the most repugnant to men's character; a common state is a burden to them."[33]

In his prefaces, the publisher of the largest collection of utopian texts published during the eighteenth century, Garnier, cites numerous critiques these works have provoked. Moreover, in his edition, he purged certain texts of their most dangerous parts (he censored, for example, the barely veiled attacks against Christianity in the *Histoire de Sévarambes*). In this collection, the imaginary voyages are compared with literature of the fantastic and the supernatural, as can be seen from the collection's title, which gains in expressiveness what it loses in terseness: *Imaginary, romantic, marvellous, allegoric, amusing, comic and critical voyages; followed by dreams, visions and cabalistic novels.* The magnitude of the collection is yet another indication of the interest aroused by utopian literature. Indeed, Garnier's collection includes thirty-nine volumes, published over three years; the edition began in 1787 and the last volumes appeared in 1789. Thus, the last series of these "imaginary voyages and marvelous dreams" and the first revolutionary pamphlets, those dreams and invitations to another kind of voyage, can be read simultaneously, at a time when history is about to go beyond the imaginary. The coincidence is, however, merely fortuitous, only one of those tricks played by history, suggesting symbolisms and parallels that are as facile as they are deceptive. The interplay of social imagination and reality is much more complex; "imaginary voyages" in no way prophesy the Revolution, nor are they in any way harbingers of it. Garnier's collection only offers its readers diverting literature, thanks to which they can venture into the realm of the imaginary and the impossible.

However, and contrary to Moncrif's earlier opinion, these texts are progressively accepted as both diverting and useful. It could be said that the critical reaction turned to utopias' advantage—they are considered useful precisely because in reading them, every reader becomes "a Creator, a Philosopher."

Positive judgments on utopias' usefulness predominate throughout the century, at least in enlightened opinion. Thus Terrasson, in the preface to his utopian novel, will plead the superiority of fiction over history, when the former "is used in the sole manner suitable to a wise writer, that is, with the intention of forming morals." In fact, history alone is "merely a mass of facts that Providence leads to ordinarily hidden ends." That is why the reader of historical works does not find an obvious moral lesson in them—he meets in them too many crimes and villains who triumph over virtue. On the other hand, the account of the history of a virtuous imaginary people, practicing the best legislation, under the reign of a model king, teaches true philosophy and true morality by example. Ch.-P. Duclos goes even further in the apologia for "ideas of imaginary republics," and, in particular, for their educational, political, and moral value. The images of happy peoples make an effective contribution to fighting prejudice and are "at least happy models, *chimeras that are not totally so*. So many things are impossible solely because one has become accustomed to see them as so; contrary opinion and courage often make easy what prejudice and cowardice judge to be impractical."[34] Thus, utopias do not at all constitute literature of escapism; on the contrary, they stimulate reflection and orient the imagination toward the useful. Besides, during the second half of the century, utopian texts are frequently assimilated to serious literature and put on the same footing as political, economic, and social treatises. Their diverting aspect is then considered only an entirely secondary characteristic; the essential is in the ideas advanced. This evolution is revealing, both in respect to the attitudes adopted toward utopian texts and to the public they reach. Thus, utopias are broadly represented in encyclopedias, dictionaries, and collections specializing in political and social problems. Knowledge of utopias is considered a principal element of the political culture of an "enlightened mind."

The analytical table of the *Encyclopédie Méthodique* places all articles on utopias in a special category titled *Theoretical Administration*, where, as the commentary explains, are gathered "the precepts and lessons philosophy took pleasure in giving kings and princes called to head nations, painting the picture of the reciprocal rights and duties of the governed and the governors, the rulers, and the ruled." This section includes, then, political novels of which this dictionary takes note, works whose aim is presenting a system of perfection applicable to "men as they ought to be." In fact, detailed reviews of all the important "political novels" as well as notes on minor texts, sometimes unpublished in French, are found in this section. Moreover, the *Encyclopédie* also includes under this heading texts that are not "novels" but "chimeric proposals," such as Abbé de Saint-Pierre's writings on perpetual peace or Mercier de la Rivière's *Physiocratie*. It is not the form of the exposition of the ideas that counts, but a common orientation of these writings, the search, in an "inaccessible distance" for social happiness and perfect legislation. The majority of the articles in these dictionaries and encyclopedias, moreover, approach utopian texts in a rather particular way. The dream quotient is reduced and the scope of the overall visions of social otherness is minimized. On the contrary, stress is placed on a particular idea of detail whose "utility," the possibility of putting it, at least partially, into practice, is discussed. "Enlightenment today is universal; everyone knows the abuses, everyone indicates their remedies, and this fermentation of the commonweal has already produced a great number of reforms; some are so important that they were not even hoped for at the beginning of the century. Probably, the administrators will stop too soon; too struck by the corruption of the peoples, too frightened of the dangers innovations entail, they will let glaring abuses persist; but the zeal of writers must not be slowed. . . . They will at least have the satisfaction of presenting to sovereigns and to judges the image of order and happiness that societies comprise. The most chimeric proposals on legislation and government ordinarily offer useful views; besides, one likes to see the picture of a happy state, in which one will never find oneself." Thus a fragile compromise is sought between the audacity of utopian views and a prudent pragmatic reformism. If utopian texts offer, on the one hand, a picture of a happy social state that is agreeable but unrealizable, they include, too, a sort of inventory of partial reforms proposed by "theoreticians" for the attention of the too "prudent" administrators.[35]

Against the background of this rather dull and down-to-earth discourse, voices stand out that bring out the weight of the dream as well as its formative influence on minds. Mably, evoking his dream of a society that would conserve liberty and social equality on a long-term basis, does not nourish too many hopes of "seeing in the world what has not yet been seen." But he nevertheless adds that *"these dreams are perhaps our most real good."*[36] Brissot devotes himself to making pertinent observations on the functions of utopias in the formation of the political and social ideas of the Enlightenment. On the occasion of the republication of More's *Utopia*, he attacks the critics who reproach this book with being "full of bizarre and inexecutable ideas." Certainly, "the century when this book was published was not worthy of it and its philosophy was too premature." However, "at the time in which we live," certain of More's ideas have been realized. But, for Brissot, utopias still present a quality he finds essential. Utopias do not only announce "premature truths"; even if they are only reveries, their essential function consists of forming minds for the discovery of the great truths of the century. "*Utopia*, like Plato's *Republic*, served to form our writers. Believe that Rousseau, that Helvétius, had meditated these novels, and the means of arriving at truths was perhaps *to take this pleasant path traced by these political dreamers*." Let us note, finally, the observations of the translator of *Utopia* who, at the time he is proposing a new edition, explains the particularly important role this book can play. When the new edition was published in 1789, it was by no means a fortuitous coincidence; a deliberate intention enlisted the book in the great political and ideological debate of the moment. "All men appear at this time to want to take some steps toward happiness. Troubled nations assemble to deliberate on this great object. . . . Ideas proliferate on all sides on this point; *everyone* wants to be political, a reformer, a *legislator*. And if light—enlightenment—is not always born from the shock of so many conflicting opinions, at least the public wish proves *the necessity of establishing a better order of things*." Thus, More's book will help all those who wish to form an idea of this "better order" for themselves. Even if one doesn't share all the author's opinions, one finds in his work "truths that are of all times and that are good for all peoples."[37]

How many utopian texts were there in the eighteenth century? We have extensively quoted indirect and partial testimony on the magnitude of the phenomenon, to compensate for the uncertainty of numerical data. In fact, the phenomenon does not lend itself to a quantitative approach, even at the most elementary level, that of the number of utopian texts. Certainly, there is no lack of bibliographies of eighteenth century literature or general bibliographies of utopian literature. The problems and uncertainties are elsewhere, arising from the divergency of definitions of utopia. According to whether a particular definition is broad or narrow, the constituent corpus varies from the single to the double or even the triple. More precise figures can be given if we limit ourselves to "imaginary voyages." For the years 1676–1789, there are approximately eighty "imaginary voyages" for the French domain. Variations, by decades, are not significant, with the exception of the years 1750–1759, when there is a remarkable density (sixteen works for that decade out of a total of forty-seven for the years 1750–1789). These figures include neither subsequent editions and printings nor pirated editions. Only such data would provide us with the true magnitude of this literature and its audience. Werner Krauss, after having remarked that in the eighteenth century "utopian literature enjoyed an unprecedented boom," puts forward an impressive estimate: according to him, an average of ten and, in some years, up to thirty imaginary voyages were published.[38]

These figures only present an overall and provisional estimate, one that must be used with caution and that calls for reservations. Every imaginary voyage is not necessarily a utopia. The account of the discovery of an unknown land, of the mores and institutions of an imaginary people occasionally falls short as a utopia, if it limits itself to satirizing contemporary life or to recounting more or less fabulous adventures. On the other hand, however impressive the quantity might be, it cannot hide the mediocrity of the majority of these texts. They are imaginary voyages, to be sure, but how little imagination the overwhelming majority of them show. As we have pointed out, the paradigm proves to be too easy; repetition and the wear and tear of time continually erode it. Some innovations stand out against this rather monotonous background.

L.-S. Mercier transforms the voyage in space into a voyage in time—*utopia* thus becomes a *uchronia*. With Mercier's novel, *L'an 2440*, the new paradigm takes a rather mediocre literary departure, but one rich in prospects and developments to come.[39] Diderot invents a new formula, substituting a sort of "philosophical voyage" for the "imaginary voyage." We are thinking, of course, of the *Supplément au voyage de Bougainville*, where he uses, most freely, the account of a real voyage to project, on a half-real, half-imaginary space, the vision of a social state that alone would correspond to human nature. "I am convinced that there can be true happiness for the human species only in the social state where there would be neither judge, nor priest, nor laws, nor outsiders, nor third parties, nor private property, nor vices, nor virtues, and this state is devilishly ideal." Diderot's example, playing ironically with the traditional formulas of the imaginary voyage, was not much followed and, certainly, it was not easy to imitate. On the other hand, another innovation that appeared in the eighteenth century was to establish itself for the long term, meeting with the greatest success and having numerous effects. We are thinking of the *anti-utopia*, of which *Gulliver's Travels* remains the inimitable model.[40]

The very limited indicative value of the figures we have put forward calls for a further reservation having to do with the definition of utopia as well as the delimitation of its field. In fact, the figure of some dozens of texts is only an overall figure, showing the popularity of a *single paradigm* of utopian discourse, that of the imaginary voyage. We have, however, stressed the fact the utopian idea-images extend beyond this paradigm whose scope is increasingly perceived as rigid and repetitive. The utopian phenomenon gains in richness and in scope outside this paradigm which is very often considered only as a simple literary expedient. Thus our estimate, limited to "imaginary voyages," does not take into account cases where the same author freely uses diverse forms of discourse to express his dreams and proposals. Let us mention only two cases. Morelly's *Basiliade* is an imaginary voyage. But this is not the case with his *Code de la Nature* that, nevertheless, includes the "Modèle de législation conforme aux intentions de la Nature," an exposition of the detailed vision of a perfect society, based on community of goods. But it is specifically the *Code de la Nature*, a text that had, moreover, long been attributed to Diderot, that was widely circulated at the end of the eighteenth century. The other case is that of Restif de la Bretonne. If Restif wrote *L'Homme volant ou la découverte de la terre australe*, an imaginary voyage in which the search for the fantastic and the novelistic aspect prevails over the utopian enterprise, he exercises his utopian inventiveness as well and even primarily in other texts that in no way follow the paradigm of the imaginary voyage. Let us cite only his proposals for reform, such as the *Andrographe*, the *Pornographe*, the *Thesmographe*; the statutes of an imaginary collective farm established in Auvergne (in the *Paysan perverti*); the picture of an ideal community established right in the middle of Paris (*Les Contemporaines*). In both of these cases, the authors pass from one form of discourse to another to express their utopian idea-images (there is, moreover, a whole interplay of actions set up between the idea-images and the type of discourse). But there are numerous utopians—and by far the most important of them—who never had recourse to the paradigm of the imaginary voyage. The Abbé de Saint-Pierre who, in the eyes of his contemporaries, incarnates the model utopian, composed only innumerable proposals for reform and refused any parallel between of his work and novels. Nor is it a novel, but rather the discovery of ultimate truth, the "key to the metaphysical and moral enigma" that Dom Deschamps brings into play in his vision of the ideal society. It is in the course of his reflections on history and legislation that the Abbé Mably gives the sketch of his vision of a communal and egalitarian society.

The more diffuse the utopia becomes and the more diversified its forms become, the less clear are its frontiers, so that the magnitude of the phenomenon escapes a quantitative approach. But it is thus precisely that the utopian invention is established at the very heart of the Enlightenment, that it progressively assumes the role of a relay station between the field of social experiences and the horizon of hopes and expectations, between lived realities and the imaginary future. That is particularly striking in a category of texts that proliferate in the second half of the century and that it would be improper to assimilate as a group to utopias, but that very often take on utopian dreams and visions. We are thinking, in particular, of the numerous proposals for reform in which new legislation, social therapies, remedies to persistent evils, etc., are envisioned. The phenomenon brings to the fore the progressively diffuse character of utopian invention as well as certain distinctive characteristics of this diffusion. Thus it merits comment.

In the abstract the contrast between the utopia and reform is clear. In the utopia, as we have said, the ideal is situated specifically in relation to social realities—the utopian idea-image is disruptive and all-encompassing. The utopia as an ideal type (in Max Weber's sense) does not accept partial and limited arrangements that would only diminish the existing social evil. As we have observed, it calls for a radical rupture with the established society that it refuses to continue; it imagines a new beginning *ex nihilo*. It refuses at the same time to confine itself to alternatives offered by the established order. From the utopian perspective, politics is not at all "the prediction of the present" to repeat the definition given by the last great reformer of the Ancien Régime.[41] On the other hand, a reform does not imply a global vision of social otherness; proposals for reform even exclude any radical rupture, but call for limited and partial changes in the continuity.

This is however only an abstract schema. It is completely operative only in extreme cases that come close to ideal types. In reality, the relationships between utopias and reforms are much more complex and finely shaded; particularly so in the eighteenth century. Indeed, much research, and in particular the works of F. Venturi and P. Francastel, have shown that the ideologies as well as the mentalities of the "enlightened minds" of the *intelligentsia* of the time are marked at once by the aspiration to the utopia and pragmatic attitudes toward the dominant order.[42] A complex interplay of exchanges and amalgams, illusions and confusions between utopias and reform is set up. For some, the most lucid, there is a dilemma: either to refuse realities in the name of the "devilishly ideal" utopia, or else to find, at least provisionally, modes of coexistence with the established order, in order to transform it and turn it against itself. The reforms then seem only to be the most effective, if not the only possible, means of realizing the utopia, of "utopianizing the world." But in the majority of cases, the alternative is not even posed in clear terms. Compromises are sought between the utopia and the spirit of reform, and, according to the case, the former or the latter prevails. Thus hopes are turned at once toward the established power and toward reason conquering the future for the utopia. It is at the borders between utopias and reform that are found the ideological figure and the myth, both ambiguous, of the *enlightened Prince* who would make the inherited power of irrational history the agent that transforms society into an order as reasonable as it would be transparent.

Proposals that claim to draw their inspiration only from their pragmatism, promising the definitive reign of Reason and Happiness are situated at the same borders. Or even other projects that do not hesitate to invoke this reign of reason in order to propose only a minor, limited innovation.

It could be said that utopia becomes a sort of *perpetuum mobile* that set in motion numerous proposals of reform. We shall follow in detail this interplay of opposites and of complements among criticism, utopia, and pragmatism. Let us cite, nevertheless, some examples, in order not to remain in the abstract. The Abbé de Saint-Simon wants only to be a practical and realistic reformer, yet his "proposals" are set up as a gigantic utopian construction. There is nothing of the utopian about Suard; he is a prudent man who has no dream of an *alternative society*, but wants to settle himself as best he can into the existing order, that he would wish more enlightened, more open to enlightened ideas, and, by the same token, more welcoming to the intellectuals who convey them. However, the encyclopedic enterprise and its success awaken in him utopian dreams and hopes that he shares with many other enlightened minds. "What a moment! and of what an era it (the prospectus of the *Enclopédie*) gave promise! What a sublime contrast in all these first-rate minds between a circumspection that made them excessively multiply doubts and increase research, and an audacity that extended or overthrew all limits before their hopes! . . . They presented the genius in tears and on his knees, at times before kings, at others before the peoples, beseeching them in turn to have pity on human nature; they already stipulated the articles of a more legitimate and propitious pact between those exercising the power and those obeying it; it was somehow as though their wishes for the human race showed almost a divine force that would realize them sooner or later on earth; and nearly *drunk with so much hope for the progress of reason, they prophesied a Jerusalem of philosophy that would last more than 1000 years*."[43] Yet another example, that of Restif de la Bretonne. He himself distinguishes between the utopia and reform and considers the latter a means of arriving at the former. Time has not yet reached the maturity required by the realization of the final aim of the utopia presented in *L'Andrographe* or in *L'Homme volant*. That is why Restif proposes to reconcile "the general reformation" with real life and to make it realizable by degrees. "I have never aspired to the happiness of seeing it (*L'Andrographe*) realized, except perhaps at in the time of regeneration. Ah! if one wanted, how many troubles would be avoided. What happy brotherhood would be suddenly established among men. Oh legislators, I repeat, deign to read *L'Andrographe*. . . . It is because we did not yet have hope that our aim was no longer only to give a plan of partial reformation.''[44] And what can one say of the utopian elan that inspires the ''proposal for reform'' conceived by an obscure provincial attorney who promises effects defined with equal clarity and modesty in the title of his work: *L'avant-coureur du changement de monde entier par l'aisance, la bonne éducation et la prospérité générale de tous les homme ou prospectus d'un mémoire patriotique sur les causes de la grande misère qui existe partout et sur les moyens de l'extirper radicalement. . . .* [The forerunner of the total transformation of the world by the affluence, good education, and general prosperity of all men or prospectus of a patriotic report on the causes of the great wretchedness that exists everywhere and on the means of completely eradicating it.] Babeuf, a young, self-taught man, read the work, and found it a bit extravagant, but still full of new and attractive ideas. Following up his reading, he, in turn, proposed a subject for the annual contest held by the Académie of Arras: namely, pondering the theoretical and practical possibilities of establishing an egalitarian society, based on the community of goods. ''Given the present amount of knowledge, what would be the state of a people whose social institutions would be such that the most perfect equality reigned indiscriminately among all of its individual members; that the soil they inhabited belonged to no one, but rather, to all; that, in short, everything was held in common, even including the products of all kinds of industry? Would similar institutions be authorized by the natural law? Would it be possible for this institution to survive and even for the means of establishing an absolutely equal division to be practicable?''[45]

These examples and this evidence, many more of which exist, reveal even deeper tendencies. In fact, the interaction between utopian dreams and reformist hopes contributes to the development of certain ideas that dominate the ideologies, if not the mentalities, of the ''enlightened'' elites. Utopian representations, more or less carefully developed, heighten the expectations aroused by these ideas and thus give them a specific tone. We have already evoked the figure of the philosopher-king, if not of the enlightened despot, who would put his power to the service of the utopia. In the same way, the idea of progress allows history to be thought of as the accumulation of innovations and partial changes that would inevitably lead to the ''Jerusalem of philosophy,'' a new era for all of humanity.

With certain proposals of reform taking over utopian representations, a specific circuit of exchange between the imaginary and political and social realities is doubtless established. However the effects of this are very frequently ambiguous, if not paradoxical. In losing clarity, the utopian representations do not necessarily gain in realism, in the sense that they do not leave the sphere of the imaginary for that of action and accomplishment. As is known, the proposals of the era are only rarely lead to practical realizations—it is the *discourse on reforms* that prevails over the activity of reform. Utopian representations do not always stimulate the will to action, even reforming and limited action. Utopias can be places of refuge and escape in which one settles down to *dream* of reforms and imagine their beneficial results. The repercussions of utopian effects that pragmatism confers on itself is often only the sentiment of nostalgia and crisis. One lives in an enlightened century, at an exceptional time, when with all the proposals of reform social life could easily regenerate, yet nothing changes. The divorce between the imaginary that takes on the appearance of the possible and the real only becomes more pronounced. Therefore utopian representation can still less be considered as the place where, before 1789, a revolutionary political project was being worked out. The utopian who imagines an alternative society is neither a revolutionary nor even a ''dreamer,'' who would create ''revolutionary dreams.'' Utopian representations do not enrich the field of expectations of the pre-revolutionary era either with omens or with horoscopes of political and social upheaval. The historian of utopias is not in the least disappointed by this, provided that he does not mistakenly class the utopia, even spoken of in the future, as a sort of social astrology. On the other hand, he is all the more attentive to the profound transformations, both sociological and epistemological, that intervene in the relationship between utopia and politics during the revolutionary period, a period of rapidly accelerating changes, but also of particularly intense production of hopes and dreams.

These observations on the scope of the utopian phenomenon call for yet another complementary remark. Indeed, one notices that the interaction between utopian idea-images and pragmatic proposals of reform do not lead to utopias put into practice in the sense we have given this term: the foundation of small communities, where the members maintain new social and moral relationships with one another and with the entire society, based on the model of a micro-society where communion is expressed by more or less complete community.[46] As we have observed, in the eighteenth century, this sort of initiative proliferates in England, while America becomes a chosen land for model communities formed by English or German immigrants. In France, it will be necessary to wait until the first half of the nineteenth century to inspire Saint-Simon's, ''Phalastérian,'' ''Icarian,'' and other utopian experiments. This contrast is certainly explained by the fact that in eighteenth century France there is no collusion between utopian idea-images and a messianic or millenarian spirit, whereas the latter was precisely the motivating force of English or American utopian communities in search of paradise on earth. In very Catholic France, the terrain is hardly favorable to ideas or movements of that type. Even when Jansenism, in an exceptional if not unique occurrence, happens to take the form of a quasi-Messianic movement, it doesn't lead to a communal experience, nor does it enrich the social imagination in any way.[47] It is the enlightened mind that takes on utopian ideas and representations and, in a sense, it is on the "lights"—enlightenment—and on their progress, their flourishing as a promise of happiness, and not on salvation, that utopian imagination is fixed.

The utopias that offer a continuation of deist ideas, if not of atheism, in the realm of the imagination would be unable to sustain energies and a will of a religious, sectarian nature. There are many utopias that give a positive response to Bayle's famous question on the possibility of the existence of a society and a legitimate power that will do entirely without any religious foundation. (Let us merely cite one example of utopias inspired by Bayle's question: Fontenelle's utopia *La République des Philosophes*.)

Nevertheless, the absence of utopias put into practice is not necessarily evidence of a flight from reality. Occasionally, the orientation toward a utopia is too rapidly and summarily categorized as an escape. This hasty categorization takes no account of one major phenomenon: the majority of utopian texts are part of the literature of the era that is the most committed to ideological battles. Of course, this commitment is undertaken according to the modes suitable to the utopian enterprise, but how numerous are the utopian texts that only circulate clandestinely! It is yet again when criticism turns toward utopia that it commits itself still further. It then occasionally indulges in the most radical opposition to established society, as the work of Dom Deschamps demonstrates.

Noting the absence of established utopias calls for yet another observation; in fact, if model communities are not formed, at least people dream more and more of putting utopias into practice. There is no doubt whatsoever that after 1760 the description of an ideal society that attracts the most readers doesn't aim at a city located on an unknown island or near the austral lands. On the contrary, it presents a micro-society, a sort of applied utopia, imaginary of course, but localized in the same space-time as that of the reader. We are thinking of the society of Clarens in *La Nouvelle Héloïse*, of the detailed and realistic picture of its social and economic relationships, its religion, its holidays and rites, that put the ideal of communion and transparency into images.[48] Now, the utopia of Clarens and the success it meets with are only the most striking signs of a general tendency. The representations of ideal society move, let us say metaphorically, from the periphery toward the center of the space-time of the authors and the readers. If Clarens remains a sort of island of happiness isolated from the surrounding society, visiting it does not call for the rupture and the disorienting change of scenery tinged with the fantastic that characterize the ideal cities in the imaginary voyages. Let us note, too, that the utopian descriptions that are interpolated in the form of episodes in a novel become progressively numerous. The imaginary, even exotic, city is only a place to pass through, one where the hero enriches himself with new ideas and experiences, to turn himself, thereafter, toward the world he shares with the reader.

The distances between the ideal society and the real society diminish in proposals of reform, as they do in discourse on history-progress. The impossible is no longer at the other side of the world, but within reach, if not of the hand, at least of the imagination. It is quite close to us in both time and space and its realization rests on improvements and actions to be accomplished. Thus Restif de la Bretonne depicts, for example, an ideal micro-society, based on the community of goods, that revives the golden age not in exotic lands but in the very center of Paris. In another text, Restif imagines an ideal rural community established in Auvergne, and expounds the statutes that rigorously regulate the modes of property, family life, living conditions, education, relationships between the sexes, etc.[49] What could be more remarkable than this imaginary vision of an ideal society that claims to draw on a real experience, or rather, what contemporaries took to be the discovery in the heart of France, and not among the Hurons, of the existence of egalitarian and communal micro-societies. Whether misunderstanding or self-deception, the episode is particularly revealing of the reorientation of the utopian imagination we have evoked and it is worth dwelling on it for a moment.

In 1755, the *Journal d'agriculture* published an article questioning the possibility of founding a "singular establishment." The proposal foresaw the union of peasants and artisans in a community of production and consumption. It would be a free association: goods would be shared in common, work planned by a council, and each member would receive a sum of money according to the work done. The community would take responsibility for the education of the children and the organization of the social life and of mutual aid on behalf of the sick and the elderly. The anonymous author refers to the economic principles of monastic life, whose advantages he would like to apply to secular life. But, as this monastic example is hardly stimulating in the "enlightened century," the author evokes another example in support of his proposal, this one quite secular. He announces, in effect, the discovery in Auvergne, in the area of Thiers and Brioude, of peasant communities completely similar to his "singular establishment." The article rapidly calls forth echoes: the *Journal d'agriculture* next published two reports describing these communities in Auvergne in detail. They show the idealized images of what is in fact only the residue of an anachronistic mode of agricultural enterprise by extended families, whose survival in Auvergne was due to a whole combination of local circumstances. This image, always substituted for realities, is taken over by diverse authors of proposals in search of realistic arguments and effective means. In the *Encyclopédie*, the article "Moraves" takes up the good example of these communities in Auvergne in order to demonstrate that it is entirely possible to establish social life on a communal basis, suppressing private property, the source of disorder and inequality. "We are so inattentive to the advantages of communities, and so dominated by individual interest, so little disposed to help one another and to live on good terms, that we regard as chimeric everything we are told of a society that is reasonable enough to share goods and work in common." And yet, "both ancient and modern history furnish several similar occurrences." The author evokes Sparta, "the Esseniens among the Jews," "the Gymnophysistes in India," and "large tribes in Paraguay," as well as the Moravians and their communities in America, England, and the Netherlands. However, while the Moravian brothers are a religious sect, "we have, especially in Auvergne, old families of laborers, who have lived from time immemorial in a perfect society and who might be regarded, with good reason, as the *Moravians of France*. The image of the Auvergne community, of these "Quitard-Pinons who give proof of 500 years of association," is even more embellished than the reports published in the *Journal d'agriculture*. Thus it becomes a model or, rather, a springboard that allows one to "imagine an association of good citizens" whose principles and functioning are expounded with a great wealth of detail. As far as the essential is concerned, the article specifies that the community will be free, benevolent, and secular, "with no monastic observations." The associates will share their goods and each one, by working for the community, will work for himself. The association will be responsible for satisfying fundamental needs in food, clothing, and living conditions, leaving to the associates the freedom to provide for their "arbitrary needs" (tobacco, wine, etc.). Children will be brought up together, in a fraternal spirit. All trades will be practiced, but sciences and, especially, medicine and physics, will be cultivated. Thus, "the order and the good morals that rule in the communities in Auvergne, the great age of these houses and the esteem accorded them in the country prove . . . that an institution that formerly survived during centuries and that still exists nearly under our eyes, is not always either impossible or chimeric."[50]

The good example of the Auvergnats living in community added to ideas drawn from diverse utopian works finally gave support to the proposal for establishing a model community "nine leagues from Marseille." It would be only the first step before the formation of a network of similar communities throughout France. The title of the proposal is as promising as it is explicit: *Maison de réunion pour la communauté philosophe dans la terre de l'auteur de ce Projet. Plan d'ordre propre aux personnes des deux sexes, de tout âge et de diverses professions, pour leur faire passer dans des communautés semblables la vie la plus agréable, la plus saine et la plus vertueuse.* The author, Hupay de Fuvéa, who speaks of himself as a "communist author" in a letter to Restif de la Bretonne, bases his work on the "Moraves" article in the *Encyclopédie* and on the example of the "good Auvergnats," which had become quasi-proverbial. But he also evokes More's *Utopia*, Morelly's *Code de la Nature*, and the experiences of the Quakers and of the Jesuits in Paraguay. Thus the Quitard-Pinons rub elbows with the Utopians in a vision of social otherness that comes close to being idyllic. Everything for its perfect functioning is provided for in the proposal for this community. Harmony and happiness will reign, goods will be shared, and children will be brought up together and in an egalitarian spirit. Few laws or rigorous rules, but many rites and, in particular, holidays and ceremonies that will assure communion and transparency. The proposal is studied in detail: layout of the premises and architecture, schedules, leisure, food, etc. Plato and Rousseau, whose statues would be erected on the central square, would preside over this model life. The proposal had no practical consequences although Hupay de Fuvéa committed himself to putting his land at the disposal of the future community. The proposal is, however, revealing, as much of the diffusion of utopian ideas as of the convergence, if not the mixture, of diverse types of utopian discourse.[51]

Who were the "utopians"? Even if we have a complete list of the authors it does not seem that correlations valuable for a sociological analysis could be established. J. Server's observation seems correct: "if a sociologist wanted to establish a statistical pyramid of the authors, he would soon come to a stop, considering his attempt absurd, so different were the men who, in a few pages, recorded their dream, sometimes the best part of their lives."[52] Several partial observations are, however, in order. It is thus that some common traits can be spotted in the biographies of the utopians of the end of the seventeenth century, such as Foigny, Veiras, Tyssot de Passor: social instability; conflicts articulated, on different levels, with the established order; peregrinations across Europe; links with the Protestant émigré milieu. It is interesting, too, to note that the Entresol, the first English-style club where, under the Regency, politics, and reform were discussed, had a strong contingent of utopians. The Abbé de Saint-Pierre presented his proposals there and met A.-M. Ramsay (the author of the *Voyage de Cyrus*), Fontenelle, who, at that time, it seems, was writing his utopia, *Ma République*, and the Marquis d'Argenson, a cabinet minister who liked political "dreams and chimeras." Let us note, finally, some distinctive characteristics that derive from the very way the utopia is practiced and that merit some further study.

The term *utopian* must be given neither too narrow nor too broad a meaning, as far as the eighteenth century is concerned. Several great names of the Age of Enlightenment can be recognized among the utopian population: Fontenelle, Prévost (the happy isle in *Cleveland*), Marivaux (*L'Ile de la raison*), Montesquieu (*Histoire des Troglodytes*), Voltaire (*Micromégas*, Eldorado in *Candide*), Diderot (*Supplément au voyage de Bougainville*), Sade (the imaginary kingdoms in *Aline et Valcour*), etc. But it would be incorrect to rank all of these authors among the utopians. There is obviously a fundamental difference in the very approach to utopian idea-images of, say, Montesquieu and the Abbé de Saint-Pierre, of Voltaire and Dom Deschamps, of Fontenelle and Morelly. The Abbé de Saint-Pierre, Deschamps, Morelly—we cite their names only as examples—are, so to speak, "serious utopians"; they aim, in their texts, at an alternative society as an objective to be achieved, and some of them even envisage the means and the modes of achieving their proposals. The others, on the contrary, practice the utopia neither as a profession of faith nor as a synthetic way of thinking and imagining the social world; they use it only as a literary device, a narrative framework. To take up Brissot's formula, the utopia is a pleasant path that they chose in order to express their moral and philosophical reflections in an amusing and agreeable way. If we now stop comparing extreme cases, the distinctions between the "play" and the "serious" become much less clear. Think, for example, of the society of Clarens in the *Nouvelle Héloïse* or of the case of Diderot, who recognizes in Dom Deschamps's radical utopia the only state suitable to human nature, but who considers it "devilishly ideal." This fluidity of distinction between the play and the serious constitutes, as does the diversity of the utopian population, sociological testimony the import of which can only be very imprecise. But it is, perhaps, this very lack of precision that makes it interesting. The social motivation of the refusals and hopes, the discontent and expectations, that come to light in utopias are extremely diverse, even contradictory. The utopia, in its diverse forms, permits giving free rein to all these feelings and attitudes, even when they remain rather vague and imprecise. The most unexpected meetings are possible on the paths of utopias. Dom Deschamps finds a zealous partisan of his communistic and libertarian utopia in the person of the Marquis de Voyer, who takes it on himself to find new proselytes among the young aristocratic officers who frequent the château d'Ormes. Rousseau, between two "solitary promenades," imagines his great civic dream realized by the Confederates of Bar, a nobiliary movement marked by a conservative spirit and sustained by a fervent, if not fanatic, Catholicism. The young Babeuf nourishes his social refusal and extends it into the realm of the imaginary by reading an obscure proposal that announces itself as *L'avant-coureur du changement du monde entier par l'aisance, la bonne éducation et la prospérité générale*. It is impossible to find a community of imagination beyond these multicolored varieties. But the fact that certain anxieties and expectations, discontents and hopes are linked to images of the social otherness reveals the orientation of minds: with the utopia, one embarks simultaneously on the imaginary and the social. For some, the utopia will only be a place to pass through, a relay station where they exercise their imagination and their mind, free of all constraints and enjoying the very exercise of this liberty. For others, the utopia will serve as a place for the formation and training of the social imagination as well as of the desire for change.

Nevertheless, utopian discourse, in its diverse forms, remains a discourse of the learned culture, of the culture of the elites. Indeed, one could question the utopian character of the social dreams underlying the peasant revolts of the eighteenth century and, in particular, of the secular dream of a state protective of the poor and that would also be a state without taxes.[53] But if it is a utopia, it could only be an untold utopia, or else, if you will, an abortive utopia in the sense that it is never successfully acknowledged in a developed discursive form and is expressed only in gestures and rites. In the same way, the diffusion of utopian discourse is circumscribed within the domain of the "learned" culture; thus no trace of utopian works is found in so-called popular literature, made for the common people (almanachs, the *Bibliothèque bleue*, etc.).[54]

The rare exceptions to this learned or scholarly character of utopian discourse only prove the rule. The case of Meslier is certainly the most remarkable as much for the originality of the work as for the indirect testimony it gives on the rarity and difficulty of conjunctions between different types of social imagination and of discourse on social otherness. It is from this perspective that the case of Meslier calls for further discussion.[55]

Meslier links, in an original way, two figures that are products of different if not opposing cultural formations. On the one hand, he is a prophet who fleshes out his discourse with secular myths and revolts; on the other, he is a utopian who puts the entire arsenal of a critical philosophy at the service of his social dream. Meslier's utopia is, first of all, the vision of a communal and egalitarian society where men will possess "all the goods in common and will enjoy them equally, all in common, as well; I mean all those of a same place, and of a same territory, so that all the men and women of a same village, of a same town or of a same parish and community all together make up only one family, seeing themselves and considering one another as brothers and sisters." In this *alternative society*, as a result, men will live "together, peacefully and in common, all having but one and the same food and all well dressed, equally well housed, in well set-up, comfortable and heated lodgings, but all applying themselves equally to the tasks at hand." Meslier does not seek this land, where justice, happiness, and perfect equality reign, in foreign regions. The coordinates of this country are those of Etrépigny, the curé's very parish; they are also those of all the other Etrépignys where his word will be heard. Meslier is even more of a utopian in the orientation he gives his materialism and his atheism. The great moral and social dream that dwells within him, like the exceptional character of this dream, is linked to the image of a society without religion or rather, more exactly, to a society that will know no religion other than that "of true wisdom, and of moral probity . . . that of entirely abolishing tyranny, and the superstitious cult of the gods and their idols." Was it not more audacious to imagine Etrépigny, at the end of the reign of Louis XIV, populated by "Godless men" than it was to glimpse a life with neither tyrants nor private property? However, Meslier associates this utopia, nourished with a whole philosophical culture of the elites, with a prophetic discourse that falls within the province of a very different tradition, one close to millenarianism.

This prophetic discourse, it is true, is distinguished from millenarian discourse by the secular and atheistic character of the dream announced by Meslier. However, he remains a prophet in the sense of one who knows and *sees* ultimate truth and who by his words unveils it to others. He announces the advent of a different time, free of all material and spiritual oppression and one that would bring a sort of collective salvation. The word, he affirms, becomes efficacious only if it awakens consciences, and its consequences extend into collective actions. But is it not the distinctive feature of prophetic discourse to want to be an efficacious active word, thanks to the revelation it brings? The prophecy, in calling for action, is nourished by memories and myths, by what is unspoken in the peasant revolts. Thus, Meslier's utopia is not a proposal for perfect legislation, much less a political project. Only the truth of the message and its conformity with the real suffering of the peasant masses allow the hope that the word will not be suppressed and that it will one day inspire the last great revolt.

Such discourse, which conveys at the same time biblical prophetism, the myths of the peasant revolts, an atheistic philosophical utopia, and a communal egalitarianism, can seem heterogeneous, if not contradictory. It nevertheless corresponds to the time and place in which it arose. How else, without having joined the audacity of a utopian to the faith of a prophet, could the radical upheaval of permanent history that Etrépigny was experiencing be imagined?

Because it is the meeting place of opposing cultural formations, Meslier's work represents an isolated if not unique case. Its exceptional character shows, on the one hand, to what extent utopian discourse is circumscribed by the culture of the elites and, on the other, how the admixture of popular culture and learned culture remains rare and difficult in the sphere of social imagination. The conjunction of a similar experience and a sociocultural configuration only recurs, in the utopian sphere, a century later, in the formation of the young Babeuf; and, even there, one might well wonder if the differences of the times and the biographies are not more important than the analogies/similarities. Indeed, only the accelerated time of the Revolution will intensify the circulation of ideas and values, images and symbols that in a specific situation function as so many relay stations for the social imagination in quest of utopia. But even there the movement will be essentially from top to bottom, continually frustrated by numerous obstacles.

II

Utopia and Politics: An "Imaginary Voyage" by Rousseau

*P*oland is not a country *nowhere* and Rousseau doesn't speak of its discovery in a text that could recount sea crossings, shipwrecks, and unknown islands. We will visit countries situated in the imaginary *elsewhere* later, as we will follow the innumerable adventures of their explorers. However picturesque they were, they were nevertheless less rich in surprises and discoveries than those that Rousseau encountered exploring Poland, a country to which he never went.

Rousseau's works present most important and revealing evidence of the changes that the utopian sphere undergoes in the second half of the eighteenth century. Rousseau did not write any imaginary voyages and was careful not to codify his political ideas and social dreams in a proposal for perfect legislation; he even judged the composition of such a code to be too easy a job, within the range of even a law student. Yet, those who considered and still consider, some indulgently, others reprovingly, the author of the *Contrat social* as a political dreamer, a maker of chimeras were, and still are, legion. Was Rousseau utopian? Let us leave aside this debate which has already lasted for two centuries and which is too often short-circuited, degenerating into a quarrel of semantics, words, definitions, and value judgments. Whatever the "real" Rousseau might have been, this debate confirms, if that was necessary, that a utopian interpretation of Rousseau's texts was not only possible, but that it was indeed made. In the case of certain texts, such a reading is in perfect agreement with the explicit intention of the writing. As we have already noted, there is no doubt that the utopian text most read at the time was that depicting the ideal micro-society, the "happy isle" of Clarens. As far as other texts and particularly Rousseau's political works, are concerned the problematic proves to be more delicate and more complex. Certainly, Rousseau himself didn't mean them to

43

be utopian. However, these texts lent and continue to lend themselves to several readings, particularly those that elicit primarily representations of an *alternative society*, a harmonious reunion, in a transparent community of free and equal men. The fact that Rousseau's social philosophy and political thought are not summarized in this vision and that such interpretations are only partial readings, is another question. From our perspective, we will note the sociological phenomenon pointed up by such readings, echoed by both the admirers and detractors of these "chimeras" of Rousseau. Through this orientation of the readings, one notices that the *elsewhere* of the social otherness is displaced. It leaves the places inhabited by expatriates from the time and space of real societies, whose only link with the latter was the thin thread of the accounts of imaginary voyages. In these voyages, as in the proposals for perfect legislation, the *alternative society* and its "elsewhere" had as a condition of their existence the imaging activity that was heralded as having "fictionized" and immediately recognized as such. This was no longer the case with the visions of social otherness armed with, if not clothed in, a philosophical and political discourse. They then underwent a displacement in the imaginary. It is by forcing back the shifting frontiers of the possible and the impossible that the time and the space that would be linked to history and yet be habitable for an imagined and dreamed-of different society are sought. This transformation was not announced only in Rousseau's texts. But what other chimeras had such an effect on the imagination and turned it more toward new paths?

Considérations sur le gouvernement de Pologne et sa réforme projetée was long recognized and read as a marginal writing, if not an occasional work. The text's reputation among "Rousseauists" was no better. It was found frankly embarrassing more than once; it seemed the most confused of all the writings by which the author of the *Contrat social* launched himself into the political domain *sensu stricto*. Despite referring throughout *Considérations* to the *Contrat social* or to *Emile*, Rousseau seemed to contradict and disavow his own ideas. Even more, he seemed to do so by predicating an ill-defined political realism, whose result was a timid reformism, if not ideas that were clearly conservative, and incompatible with his own civic dream of a New City. *Considérations* thus was thought to be evidence of a double failure. While his social ideas and dreams were belittled, Rousseau was thought to have failed to prove himself as far as that famous realism was concerned. From this point of view, his advice to the Polish was found completely disappointing—it lacked a sense of reality and was overrun with "chimeras." It could be said that *Considérations* was blamed for being too opportunistic and for not being enough so, for being riddled with "chimeras" while not being sufficiently "utopian." Moreover, this disconcerting work came within the context of the history of Poland that Mornet, in the course of his reading of *Considérations*, found frankly inextricable.

All of these are difficulties, if not absolute drawbacks. But doesn't the very fact of being difficult and neither well-known nor understood make a work interesting?[1] Other reasons, however, made it necessary to include *Considéra-tions* in our study. First of all, in this text, the manifestation of the movements of the frontiers of the utopia is expressed in a way as original as it is revealing. A political text par excellence, *Considérations* is nevertheless defined by the vision of a New City that tends to situate it not in the vacuum of an imaginary elsewhere, but rather within historical and social realities as dense as they are resistant to dreams. Rousseau is grappling with these realities, as well as with this dilemma: to refuse the latter in order to save the ideal or else to sacrifice the "chimera" in order to transform the real; it is not the first time the author of *Considérations* sees himself confronted by this dilemma and he is not the only one to have faced it during this "enlightened century." Yet, *Considérations* brings him a solution that is remarkable for its originality. Rousseau's reply to those who had reproached him for fabricating chimeras was "they see me in the land of chimeras, but I see them in the land of prejudices." In *Considérations*, the "land of chimeras" gains ground over the "land of prejudices" and it is the "limits of the possible in politics and morale" that are thus displaced.[2] In addition, Rousseau envisages the displacement of these limits as the effect of the action that the chimera, the representation of a New City, is able to exercise on realities. We will pay particular attention to this point.

These are all more or less scholarly reasons for studying *Considérations* in detail. But why hide another, more personal, reason? Among so many voyages to dreamlands, how could I not have chosen to trace the one that led to Poland and at the end of which this real country was enveloped in an imaginary one which made it the chosen land where dream would have its unique chance of taking over from reality.

But let us go on to the text of *Considérations*, which requires a careful and consistent reading.

1
"To Show Routes Unknown to the Modern . . ."

As we know, Rousseau wrote *Considérations* during the winter of 1770–1771 at the behest of Count Wielhorski, the spokesman for the Confederates of Bar, who gave him a file on Poland and its political situation and asked him to give his opinion of the "proposed reform" of its government.[3] But the conditions Rousseau judged necessary before he would take the floor must be further specified, as must the spirit in which he accepted this role of "politician."

"Basically, the institution of laws is not such a marvelous thing that any man with sense and equity could not readily find by himself those that, well observed, would be the most useful to society. Where is the merest law student who will not draw up a code of morality as pure as that of Plato's laws? But that is not the point. It is to so adapt this code to the people for whom it is made and to the things on which a ruling is made, that its enforcement follows from this propriety alone; it is to impose on the people, following the example set by Solon, not so much the laws that are best in themselves as those that are the best he can apply in the given situation. . . . Things having to do with morals and universal justice are not regulated, as are those of individual justice and absolute rights, by edicts and laws; or, if sometimes laws do influence morals, it is when they draw their strength from them. Then they give them back the same strength by a sort of reaction that is well known to true politicians."[4]

Thus the true politician does not draw up proposals for perfect legislation; he doesn't write books that, like *Sévarambes*, can be relegated to the "land of chimeras." He does not exert himself to make systems that, like that of the Abbé de Saint-Pierre, are too good to be adopted.[5] The true politician, then, must take reality into account, which does not mean that he agrees to adapt himself to any reality, no matter what. It is true that it is not sufficient to have

46

invented an ideal code to be a true politician; but it is all the more true that one cannot become one, without being guided by a great moral and social objective.

On the other hand "our politicians believe only the *little things that they do are feasible.*" They want only to govern and they have confidence only in force, fear, and money. "A bad teacher only knows how to flog a student, a bad government official only knows how to have people hanged or put in prison." The best political maxims would be of no use to them, since they inevitably lack imagination and don't believe that they can be applied.[6] The "important government officials," petty politicians, "judging men in general by themselves and those who surround them . . . are very far from imagining what motivating spirit love of country and the élan of virtue can give to free souls" (pp. 1038–1039).[7] They always look at men as they themselves should be seen, that is "as worthless men on whom only two instruments have any influence, namely money and the knout" (p. 1039). And that is why "in all courts, liberty is regarded as a mania of visionaries that tends to weaken rather than to strengthen a State" (p. 1038).

Thus it can be said that the "true" and the "petty" politician both take into account the reality that defines their field of action, but that each one envisions things in a different, if not opposite, spirit. One believes only what he does to be feasible and thus he perpetuates the workings of the political mechanism of which he is at one and the same time the driving force and the product. He never comes to imagine a politics guided by other interests and objectives than those that made him a politician and an "important government official." Naiveté in politics, the error for which Rousseau reproached the Abbé de Saint-Pierre, consists of taking people for something other than what they are. While denouncing abuses, the author of the *Projet de paix perpétuelle* didn't see that they "are based on the very interest of those who could destroy them" and to whose goodwill he was appealing.[8] That is why nothing "is more frivolous than the political science of the Courts; as it has no fixed principle, no certain consequences can be drawn; and the entire beautiful doctrine of the Princes' interests is a child's game that makes sensible men laugh" (p. 1038).

But not all political discourse is inevitably that of the "frivolous science." Certainly the other politician, the "true one," must also "take men as they are" and distrust any system that "would be good for the people of Utopia and is nothing for the children of Adam."[9] But he, too, would be lacking in imagination by setting the limit of the human element where the people themselves, degraded by bad morals and unjust institutions, find it. "When one reads ancient history, one believes oneself transported into another universe and among other beings. What have the French, the English, the Russians in common with the Greeks and Romans? Nearly nothing but their figure. The strong souls of the latter seem to the others exaggerations of history. How could those who feel themselves to be so small think that there could have been such great men? They did exist, however, and they were human beings like us; what prevents us from being men like them?'' (p. 956) Now, these ancient peoples were formed by great legislators. Their actions and their works are so many models for every true politician. Yet these legislators of the ancients didn't have exceptional men at their disposal. On the contrary: Moses formed a nation ''from a swarm of miserable fugitives, without arts, without arms, without talent, without virtues, without courage''; Lycurgus established a people ''already degraded by servitude and its resultant vices''; Numa transformed brigands into citizens (pp. 956–957). In *Considérations*, Rousseau again takes up the exposition he had made in the *Contrat social* of the charismatic qualities of the legislators of the ancients. They were real miracle workers, but it is the great soul of the legislator that constitutes the true miracle and it is by it that he gave proof of his mission.[10] The legislators of the ancients had the indispensable audacity and spiritual strength to transform souls by raising them above themselves, in bringing ''their courage and their virtues to a degree of energy of which nothing today can give us the idea'' (p. 958). It is striking to see how Rousseau stresses in *Considérations* the imagination of the legislators of the ancients that accompanied their works as well as their art of shaping the imagination of their peoples, of orienting it by institutions and apparently frivolous rites that nevertheless inflamed souls, setting them aglow ''with emulation and glory'' (pp. 957–958).

We will return to these ceremonies and rites as well as to their functions. Let us note however that Rousseau, proposing the legislators of the ancients and their political art as an example to himself, does not in any way assimilate his own political discourse in *Considérations* to theirs. That is due not only to the fact that he does not attribute to himself the qualities of a miracle worker, but principally to the distinctive features of their respective words as well as to the historical era when these words were spoken. Indeed, it is characteristic of the legislator's word that it is immediately translated into action or rather that it is the very act that founds the institutions. Thus this founding word is never a discourse *on* politics and *on* institutions, it is never a ''proposal'' or a ''theory.'' The exceptional qualities of a great legislator, in whose soul ''the fire of enthusiasm is joined to the depths of wisdom and the constancy of virtue,''[11] perfectly correspond to a precise historical situation that defines the conditions of possibility of this word-action. The great legislator can only intervene at the dawn of history. If he ''makes the gods speak'' to his people, it is because such a word is still possible, in the times when gods have not yet become mute. There is certainly in Rousseau's work a mythology of the great legislator, the founder of the state and educator of the people, but the author of *Considérations* confines it to a time when the myth itself could still be part of history.[12] This is no longer the case in modern times, an additional reason the discourse of *Considérations* doesn't aspire to substitute itself for that of a great legislator; nor is Rousseau seeking a quasi-mythological hero for Poland. In other words, the legitimacy of the political discourse of *Considérations* is due to the presupposition that the time of the great legislators is past and that, therefore, a discourse on politics is possible.

Does the discourse of *Considérations*, then, follow the paradigm that controls a large part of the literature of the time, namely that of the philosopher-adviser of the prince? This comparison is not unreservedly valid; there are subtle distinctions. Those to whom Rousseau addresses himself in *Considérations*, through the intervention of Wielhorski, are the Confederates, the defenders of the original constitution and of republican liberties in revolt against the abuses of the prince. Their revolt owes its legitimacy to the fact that in a moment of peril for both liberty and the fatherland, they act in the name of the body of the nation. In defending republican liberties they oppose any and all types of despotism, including that called enlightened. Thus, Rousseau does not seek to enlighten the prince but to form an "enlightened patriotism" (p. 905). In the Confederation, Rousseau sees an exceptional institution similar to that of the Roman dictatorship. "Both silence the laws in a pressing danger, but with the great difference that the Dictatorship, diametrically contrary to the Roman legislation and to the spirit of the government, ended by destroying it, and that the Confederations, on the contrary, being only a means of strengthening and reestablishing the constitution that had been weakened by great efforts, can tighten and reinforce the slack authority of the State without ever being able to break it" (p. 998). Rousseau considers this institution a "political masterpiece" and—the greatest praise—even superior to the Roman institutions. Such a unique institution, that concentrates all executive power and suspends the law, can only exist and function thanks to the "generous citizens" who devote themselves heart and soul to their endangered country. The Confederates thus furnish the proof that their souls, like those of the Ancients, are liable to be inflamed with a "truly heroic zeal" (p. 998). They attest to a state of mind that marked Poland's past and that can still, at the present time, inspire the whole nation. The existence of such a state of mind, of "souls still having great force," is the necessary condition of the discourse of *Considérations*. In order for communication to be possible between the person who speaks and those to whom he speaks, those addressed must understand the language used, the language of the country and of liberty, which are inseparable. The latter must grasp the real meaning of the words country and "citizens" that should, however, be erased from modern languages.[13]

Thus Rousseau posits a complicity between himself and his readers, between a man with "singular ideas" in relation to his time and a republic sustained by a singular spirit and one that gives "one of the most singular spectacles that can strike a thinking being" (p. 954). "Perhaps all of this," he says in *Considérations*, "is only a *heap of chimeras, but here are my ideas*; it is not my fault if they are so dissimilar to those of other men, and it was not up to me to organize my head in another way. I even admit that whatever singularity might be found in them, as far as I'm concerned, I see nothing that is not well adapted to the human heart, good, practicable, especially in Poland, as I have applied myself, in my views, to following the spirit of this Republic" (p. 1041).[14] Thus the text takes a particular form: through detailed observations on the institutions and the legal reforms, it is an appeal issued to souls, "to the energy of courage and to the love of liberty" (p. 998). And it is, finally, the activation of this "energy" that is spoken about; Rousseau only proposes to show from a distance "*routes unknown to the moderns* by which the ancients led men to that vigor of soul, that patriotic zeal . . . that are unparalleled among us, but leavens of which are in the hearts of all men; they are only awaiting suitable institutions to activate their fermentation" (p. 969).

It is therefore based on a certain image of Poland and the Polish people that the political discourse of *Considérations* is constructed. We will clarify this image more precisely, but must first take up a very delicate problem, often considered a key problem in the understanding of *Considérations*. One wonders, in fact, to what extent the image on which Rousseau's developments are based corresponds to reality. One would even like to judge the value of *Considérations* according to the answer to this question. This would give rise to a long debate but, in truth, the question seems to us badly posed. There are many essential reservations to it. Were the Poles "really" crazy about liberty and inspired by a patriotism without equal in other nations? Can the complex realities of a people be embodied in an overall image that it creates for itself or one attributed to it by others? And does this image depend on the sphere of knowledge or that of ideologies and mythologies expressed in stereotyped images? Is its function to advance a knowledge or rather to install, in collective mentalities, a set of values and models of behavior grouped around these stereotypes? It is, however, certain that even if *Considérations* is not supported by a *true image*, it is closely akin to a *true myth* and translates a *true* political and social *dream*. The importance of the problem deserves an explanation.

We do not know exactly what the dossier was on Poland submitted by Count Wielhorski to Rousseau.[15] However, there is no doubt that the dossier contained not only information and that it specifically suggested an overall image that the Confederates had given of themselves and their cause. For complex historical reasons impossible to discuss here, the Confederation of Bar was a movement with strong ideological and mythological components. In its ideology that was, in many ways, syncretic and paradoxical, nostalgia for national grandeur was confused with opposition to any attempt to modernize the country, the defense of anachronistic nobiliary privileges was allied with a republican and egalitarian mythology, and Catholic obscurantism was mixed with a patriotic élan. This ideology was translated not only by an abundant political literature, but also was expressed in patriotic poetry and especially in a diffuse feeling of enthusiasm and exaltation that was all the stronger for being nourished by an ardent faith, if not by a religious mysticism. Thus the Confederation generated a whole national mythology concentrated in the image of a heroic, patriotic, profoundly Catholic Poland, attached—to the death—to liberty, ever faithful to its republican past and the enemy of all tyranny.

Rousseau surely had other sources of information (in particular those that came from Ruhlière, then working on his *Histoire de l'anarchie de Pologne*). He also knew the other image of the Confederation found in Voltaire, that of a group of fanatics opposed to their philosopher-king and who defy even the Sémiramis of the North. However, Rousseau doesn't hesitate to adopt as his own the important themes of the mythology of Bar, but not without reservations. Moreover, he lends a personal touch to this mythology, enriching it by associating it with his political theory, thus giving it a certain conceptual coherence. It is thus that *Considérations* contributed to the formation of an image of Poland whose multiple effects on Polish destiny cannot be overstated. The image of Poland stemming from the Confederation will be taken up and amplified in great Romantic poetry, thanks to which it will penetrate the collective mentalities and sensitivities of several generations. *Considérations* too will have its greatest resonance among the Romantics. According to a legend—but every legend has its own truth—Mickiewicz knew entire pages of *Considérations* by heart.[16]

Looking at it closely, one sees that *Considérations* is the meeting place, the place of fusion and interaction, of two imaginary formations, of two "fantasies." Rousseau could only be inflamed by this idealized image of Poland because it was closely akin to his own civic dream, a political and social reality dreamed by himself. This image seemed to him to confirm the existence of a modern people different from the others, with a patriotic energy and a love of liberty that equaled those of the Ancients. In a noteworthy phrase, Jean Fabre defined *Considérations* as the "first novel of national energy."[17] Paraphrasing this formula, it might be said that it is also the last reverie in which the civic energy condensed in Rousseau's political work is expressed. More than any other political text of Rousseau, *Considérations* resists a reading that only looks for abstract reasoning on politics, cold and impartial reflection, or even the application of a system to a given reality. The movement of thought is guided by the dream of a New City, the ideas are inseparable from the images, the word is always an appeal to souls, and the truth attempts to win over hearts. In Rousseau's political work this civic dream very frequently took on a nostalgic tinge. He then turned to a past at the limits of utopia and shut himself up in idealized images of Sparta and Rome. But even in this refuge, he remained, so to speak, in expectation of a favorable circumstance to "raise souls to the level of the souls of the ancients" (p. 961). At the contact of the images that had originated in Poland, this dream is revived and joined to the hope that politics will become something other than the "frivolous science" of the courts, and will find, once again, its true meaning that has been forgotten by the moderns.

2
"If My Ideas Are Extravagant . . ."

*I*t is not our intention to reduce *Considérations* to a pure political reverie. As we have already stressed, Rousseau was wary of falling into a "student's task of composing a code of ideal legislation." To avoid that danger, he spent "six months . . . examining the constitution of a miserable nation,"[18] he gathered information on the political and social realities of Poland and, within the given limits, the seriousness of this documentation can only be admired. On the other hand, Rousseau, in advising the Polish people, wanted to remain true to his political thinking and ideals and especially to the ideas formulated in the *Contrat social*. That is when he faced apparently insurmountable difficulties. There are indeed numerous references to the *Contrat social* in *Considérations*, but it is easy to note several points on which there are at least seeming contradictions between the two texts. To cite just one striking example, the institution of representatives, judged disastrous in the *Contrat*, is accepted in *Considérations*. But even more, the very idea of "drafting a reformation" for Poland seems to contradict the principles defined in the *Contrat* and in particular the exposition of the confluence of conditions that ought necessarily to be present for a people to be "suitable for legislation." The problem calls for closer study as it must be tackled as much for the reading of *Considérations* as for that of the *Contrat*.

Let us first recall in what terms and how rigorously Rousseau defines these conditions. "What people, then, is suitable for legislation. The one that, finding itself already linked by some union of origin, interest, or convention, has not yet borne the real yoke of laws; the one having neither deep-rooted customs nor superstitions; the one that is not in fear of being overwhelmed by a sudden invasion; that, without entering into its neighbors' quarrels, can by itself resist each of them, or, with the help of one of them, repulse another; the one each member of which can be known by all, and where no man need be charged with a burden greater than one man can bear; the one that can do without other peoples and which all other peoples can do without; the one that is neither rich nor poor and can be sufficient unto itself; finally, the one that joins to the substance of an ancient people the docility of a new people."[19] Rousseau cites only one country in Europe that meets all these conditions, namely Corsica, and when he was asked to make a proposal for a constitution for the Corsicans, he thought he had found a marvelous opportunity to apply in real life the fundamental principles of the *Contrat*.[20]

In this context there is no allusion to Poland in the *Contrat social*, nor could it have been otherwise. In fact, the situation in Poland did not meet any of these conditions either at the time the *Contrat* was written or ten years or so later. They were not "a new people" but a quite ancient nation, with old customs and old prejudices; nor was it a small country, but an immense land; Poland was involved not only in "quarrels" but was in the midst of war with nearly all of its neighbors; torn apart by contradictions, she was undergoing a severe political crisis; the society was divided into states, inequality was pushed to an extreme point, and, even worse, the privileges of the nobility were the cornerstone of its constitution. Why, then, did Rousseau take it upon himself to draft a proposal for reform for such a country? Why didn't he himself follow the example he cited with praise in the *Contrat*, namely that of Plato who refused to give laws to the peoples who didn't lend themselves to legislation?[21] And didn't he contradict himself again by proposing to Poland a project completely different than that made for Corsica, all the while referring in both cases to the same principles of the *Contrat social*?

Was Rousseau aware of all these difficulties? It is striking to note that, in defining in *Considérations* "the state of the question," he characterizes Poland's condition as nearly a direct antithesis of the conditions in question in the *Contrat*. Poland, he says, is a "depopulated, devastated, oppressed region, open to its aggressors, at the height of its misfortunes and its anarchy." It is a state so "oddly constituted" that it is hard to understand how it has been able to survive for so long a time. "A great body formed by a great number of dead members, and a small number of divided members, all of whose movements, nearly independent of one another, far from having a common end, mutually destroy one another; that makes much ado while accomplishing nothing; that can make no resistance to whoever wants to breach it; that falls into dissolution five or six times a century; that falls into paralysis at any effort it attempts to make, at any need it attempts to provide for" (pp. 953–954).

Is proposing to "reform" such a country not inevitably a paradoxical enterprise? And could the work that such a proposal would entail be able to remain faithful, if not to the letter, at least to the spirit of the *Contrat social*?

"I prefer to be a man of paradoxes than a man of prejudices," said

Rousseau of himself. And in determining the principal motivating force of his "proposed reform" for Poland, he said: "If my ideas here are extravagant, at least they are quite completely so, for I confess that I see my madness as having all the characteristics of reason" (p. 955). This "extravagance" was indeed necessary in the case of Poland: it could hardly be a matter either of copying the proposal for Corsica or of simply implementing the ideas of the principles of the *Contrat social*. It was to be a singular undertaking, for, in studying the Polish case, Rousseau found it odd and paradoxical, in flagrant contradiction of all political maxims. Poland, he frequently insisted, presents an "astonishing, prodigious" case, "an example unique in history" (p. 971), "one of the most singular spectacles that can strike a thinking being" (p. 954).

Of what does the Polish paradox consist? This "so oddly constituted" state has not, however, collapsed: it still "lives and maintains its vigor" (p. 954). In this Europe where all the states that are in appearance so magnificently constituted, are, in reality, rushing toward their ruin, only Poland "still shows the fire of youth; and it dares to request a government and laws, as though it had just been born. It is in chains, and discusses the means of keeping itself free!" (p. 954). The last phrase recalls the famous formula of the *Contrat social*: "Man is born free and everywhere he is in chains." It is as though Poland were challenging the political condition of man. A storm has only to threaten the country for this people to reveal their distinctive characteristics, for the "Patriotic souls" that were being lulled into a lethargic sleep to awaken (p. 954). Do the Poles not again give evidence of this prodigious awakening of a people precisely by seeking advice from Rousseau on the means of conserving their country and their liberty?

The fact that Rousseau's personal mythology is recognized and reflected in a collective mythology is not enough to explain his being so impressed by the image of Poland, an exceptional, free, and miserable nation. Besides, this image is distinguished by both contradicting and confirming his political theory. The case of Poland contradicts it precisely by its "prodigious" character. The *Contrat social* did not predict that an important European state, with a long past, could escape decadence and that its citizens could maintain and be worthy of love of country and of liberty. But, on the other hand, doesn't the case of Poland confirm the truth of an essential yet unknown principle of "our politics," namely that the true constitution of the state comprises only the laws engraved in the hearts of the citizens and that they have to do with morals, customs, and opinions?[22] Surrounded and threatened by its enemies, Poland nevertheless forms an island where thanks to the spirit of her people liberty is not a "chimera."

The "unique spectacle" of Poland surprises Rousseau and strikes his imagination; he strives too to understand it and to draw conclusions from it for the future. Whence the double query found throughout developments of *Con-*

sidérations: how was this "wonder" possible? And what can be done to safeguard this people in spite of the dangers threatening it?

The first question finds its answer in the fact that the Poles succeeded in maintaining their love of country. "Country" is the key word of the political discourse of *Considérations*, and, it could be said, the key to the puzzle. Its frequency alone is highly significant. Only complete semantic studies of Rousseau's political vocabulary could furnish precise numerical data on this frequency, which is exceptional in relation to the other texts. However, a provisional calculation shows that in the first twenty pages of *Considérations*, the semantic unity *country* is better represented than in the entire text of the *Contrat social*. In Poland and for the Polish, this word has kept its meaning; one can talk to them of the country and appeal to their patriotic zeal. And love of country is inseparable from that of *liberty* and thus we find the key word of all of Rousseau's political discourse. How does it happen that in this era in which only the souls of slaves abound, the Polish have remained free and succeeded in cultivating the love of liberty? What are the factors that gave this particular cast to the history of Poland?

Rousseau sought the answer in what was distinctive and unique in Polish institutions and in their spirit. He did not have many illusions about the Polish constitution: it "was made successively of bits and pieces, like all those of Europe. As an abuse was seen, a law was made to remedy it. This law led to other abuses that then had to be corrected" (p. 975). Rousseau finds no great plan that might have governed this legislation and, something particularly characteristic, makes no allusion to a legendary legislator who might have been at the origin of Polish institutions. And yet, there is "something remarkable and that merits reflection" (p. 975) in these institutions. The weakening of the legislation—the inevitable result of the proliferation of laws—"happened in Poland in a very distinctive and *perhaps unique* way. That is, it lost its force without having been subjugated by the executive power" (p. 975). Thus, the Polish never knew either tyranny or despotism, whence a truly singular situation—"the legislative power maintains its complete authority; it is in inactivity, but without having anything above it . . . nothing dominates it, but nothing obeys it" (p. 957). The legislatorial class, although it has representatives in the Diet and although it is limited to a single faction, the nobility, is nevertheless *continually* present, which is not the case in any other European state. But the political cost, of this conserved liberty, proves to be heavy. If the legislator is not subjugated, it is because the government is without real power and the laws have no force. Thus Poland experiences a distinctive sort of anarchy, one the theory did not foresee. Generally, anarchy is the expression of the dissolution of the state as a consequence of government abuse and its path toward degeneration; in a monarchy, the government degenerates into despotism.[23] Now, in Poland as well as elsewhere, the government, embodying executive power, inevitably shows an inclination to subjugate the sovereign, the legislative power (p. 977). However, too divided and too weak, it didn't succeed in doing so. The anarchy experienced by Poland is not the effect of the abuses of its government but rather of the abuse of their liberty by the Poles themselves. This is clearly the case with the confederations and the *liberum veto*, two institutions peculiar to Poland. It is in them that the spirit of liberty is expressed and yet it is from their abuse that anarchy arises.

How does Rousseau consider these two institutions? The confederations guarantee the inalienable right of the citizens to institute a sort of dictatorship to protect and defend, if necessary by arms, their liberty. Rousseau sees a "political masterpiece" in this "federative form" (p. 998). The confederations must intervene only in grave situations, major crises that endanger liberty and the country. At these times, they alone can rally wills and put patriotic energy and hatred of despotism to work. "Every free state where the major crises have not been foreseen is in danger of perishing with every storm. It is only the Poles who have been able to derive a new way of maintaining the Constitution from the crises themselves" (p. 998). But throughout their history, the Poles have frequently abused this salutary institution to defend particular interests, contrary to the general interest. Thus, the confederations have become one of the causes of anarchy, yet they have preserved the liberty that would otherwise have been forever destroyed (p. 998). The means of saving the republic was at the same time the source of its weakness. A similar argument is valid for the *liberum veto*, that is, the institution that gave each representative the right to suspend, by his vote alone, the work of the Diet and to annul all its decisions. This right, frequently applied, and exploited to corrupt the nation (the Russians, in particular, easily bought representatives' votes in order to paralyze the work of the Diet), is, nevertheless, the expression of the principle of unanimity that "was required, by the natural law of societies, for the formation of the body politic and for the fundamental laws that stem from its existence" (p. 996). Whence Rousseau's practical conclusion: it is inevitably necessary to seek means of eliminating the abuses, but while remaining faithful to the constitution and preserving Poland's originality.

The change proposed to the Poles by Rousseau must, "while *but scarcely* meddling with" the essentials of their laws, be "capable of bringing patriotism and the virtues inseparable from it to the height of intensity they can attain" (p. 961). The restrictive clause added by Rousseau well expresses the embarrassment in which he finds himself in formulating his "administrative reform," for how, in fact, can the laws of an "oddly constituted" state remain untouched, particularly as they lend themselves to all sorts of abuses and imply inequality and social injustice? And, on the other hand, hasn't their effectiveness been proven, in the sense that it is thanks to them that liberty has been preserved?

How can he succeed in this other paradoxical undertaking that seeks to "give the constitution of a great kingdom the solidity and the vigor of that of a small republic?" (p. 970). Rousseau sees but one possibility: begin a reform movement, a "gradual progression" (p. 1020) that would nevertheless avoid the "slightest shock," for that would risk overthrowing a nation in a state of weakness and anarchy (p. 1036). "Extreme circumspection" (p. 955) must be used in tampering with anything. Whence the prudent approach Rousseau imposes on himself in *Considérations*. It is only in apparent contradiction with his desire to transform political and social structures; it only translates the feeling of precariousness of that "Polish wonder," that island of liberty racked by dangers. The Poles must, then, run the risks of liberty and preserve the institutions liable to provoke an odious anarchy (p. 955). It is also necessary that their adviser resign himself to dealing carefully with several vices and defects and not seek ideal laws, but rather preserve those which the Poles will recognize as applicable to themselves, those that "will suit them and . . . have the internal consent of their wills. Loving the country, they will zealously and wholeheartedly serve it. With this feeling alone, sentiment, legislation—even bad legislation—would make good citizens" (p. 961).

The political, economic, and social reforms proposed by Rousseau need not be studied in detail here. However prudent they were for the moment, their final desired objective was no less clearly defined. The "proposed reform" and the "gradual progression" must lead Poland, an anarchic country crushed by social injustice, to become a just and egalitarian community of free men who respect their liberty, a state wherein the entire nation will fully exercise its sovereignty, a "peaceful and happy" state, that "will set a great example to the universe" (p. 1041). Following paths appropriate to herself, however winding and roundabout they may occasionally seem, Poland will thus finally realize the ideal underlying the political discourse in the *Contrat social*. Certainly the formulas expressed in the *Contrat* do not anticipate such a possibility. But did Rousseau not say that "*the limits of what is possible in moral things are less narrow than we think*; it is our weaknesses, our vices, our prejudices that shrink them. The base-minded do not believe in great men; lowly slaves smile mockingly at this word liberty." It is in Poland that the "limits of the possible" are seen to be displaced; it is liberty, that "mania of visionaries" that makes the frontiers of the "country of prejudices" recede and extends those of the "country of chimeras." Why could Poland not join and catch up with the other historic wonders Sparta and Rome, now considered chimeras? Yet what today is only a chimera "was not one 2000 years ago. Has the nature of men changed?"[24]

Thus all the discourse in *Considérations* is based on this vision of an *alternative society* that Poland would have a unique opportunity to realize. To what extent a particular reform was really appropriate to the true situation of the country, to what extent these reforms were practicable and had a chance of leading to the desired results, is another problem not within the scope of our study. At the risk of repeating ourselves, let us stress once again that Rousseau is not grappling *directly* with the political and social reality of Poland; he sees it only *through the image* the Confederates give of themselves as well as their country and its fate. Although Rousseau doesn't accept this image uncritically without reservations and criticism, it is, finally, to it that he adapted his reforms. Moreover, Rousseau further amplifies this idealized image by enveloping it, so to speak, in a second image of his dreamed-of City. Thus, a whole play of mirrors is set up between the utopia and the national mythology, and the contours of the real country are progressively blurred by an imaginary Poland. In other words, it is very easy to show to what degree the image produced by the Confederates deformed reality and to what extent the apologia for the republican spirit, the confederations and the *liberum veto* was an amalgam of demagogy and self-mystification. It follows that the author of *Considérations*, working on these images, is as partial as he is "chimeric" in his proposals. Let us also note, however, that he is scarcely more so, though in a completely opposite spirit, than a Voltaire in his pamphlets against the Confederates. The primary interest of the political discourse of *Considérations* is elsewhere. Their novelty in relation to the other texts on the Confederation of Bar consists of the opening up of the political thinking of Rousseau and of his social dreams to the national phenomenon. How sensitive the author of the *Contrat social* is to these problems! He succeeds in deriving the beginnings of a national ideology from the mythology of the Confederates, just as he recognizes in the national originality and in the values implied by the latter a motivating force to be exploited by the "true politician" who displaces the "limits of the possible."

It could be said that this opening up was imposed by the circumstances and that Rousseau only adapted his theory and language to the present circumstances, but that would be a very simplistic interpretation. And it would still be necessary to explain how such an adaptation of the political thought formulated in the *Contrat social* was possible. All political thought and all political language are neither receptive nor adaptable to any and all problems. Should not the question rather be to what point the political discourse of the *Contrat social* and the social dreams it conveys meet the necessary condition for being the receptacle of the values and myths suitable to national, if not nationalistic, ideologies?

These are all important questions that would call for long discussion. Let us note, nevertheless, that the assimilation of a new problem necessarily encountered difficulties and imposed a flexible approach, one example of which seems to us particularly instructive: the use made by Rousseau of the model of the ancients to outline the Polish "wonder" and to define its characteristics. Indeed this model—one of the main themes of Rousseau's entire work—plays a double role in *Considérations*. On the one hand, the reference to antiquity allows the originality of the Polish situation to be reduced to what is already known; on the other hand, antiquity is evoked to bring out the novelty of this same historical situation. It could be said that Rousseau writes ancient verses on new ways of thinking. *Considérations* illustrates particularly well how, in the second half of the eighteenth century, a certain model of antiquity, associated to a civic dream, becomes the place for a renewal of ideas and values, and yet, how outdated is the traditional opposition between neoclassicism and pre-romanticism.[25] There are almost continuous references to Greco-Roman antiquity in *Considérations*. In order to save their country and make it into the City of virtues, what examples could the Poles follow but the incomparable ones of Rome and Sparta? Thus, they must "grasp the opportunity given by the present event to raise souls to the tone of the souls of antiquity" (p. 961). Yet, they have to sing their own hymn; they must remain themselves, and preserve and cultivate their own "national physiognomy." "It is national institutions that form the genius, the character, the taste and the morals of a people, that make it itself and not another, that inspire in it that ardent love for the country that is based on habits that cannot be uprooted" (p. 960). Despite his references to the ancients, Rousseau clearly sees that the political and historical data are not the same. Moreover, the importance he attached, in *Considérations*, to a model of antiquity other than that of the Greco-Romans, namely that of the Jewish people, is extremely characteristic. Evoking the "great legislators" whose spirits must preside over the reform of Poland, Rousseau quotes, beside Lycurgus and Numa, the example of Moses, stressing the distinctive characteristics of his work. Contrary to the other legislators, Moses was not the founder of a *State* but of a *Nation*, and even a "singular nation." He gave to his people "that durable institution, which has stood up to the test of time, of fortune and conquerors, that 5000 years have not been able to destroy or even to alter, and that still exists today in all its force, even though the body of the nation no longer survives." He prevented "his people from being subsumed among foreign peoples" and it is thus that this nation "so often subjugated, so often dispersed, and apparently destroyed, but always idolatrous of its principles has maintained itself up to this point, scattered among the others without being merged with them, and its morals, its laws, its rites and rituals, survive and will last as long as the world, despite the hatred and persecution of the human race" (pp. 956–957).

As Jean Fabre judiciously noted, the analogy between the Polish people and the Jewish people is one of the keys of *Considérations*, an analogy that will moreover be taken up again by Polish messianism and, particularly, by Mickiewicz.[26] In the comparison, the religious differences of the two peoples are disregarded. The problem is analyzed uniquely from its political and moral aspects, which is even more revealing. Besides, Rousseau practically ignores the religious problem in Poland, as though he was embarrassed by the fervent, if not fanatic, Catholicism of the Confederates, who made it an essential element of their ideology.

In *Considérations*, the functions of the two models of antiquity—Greco-Roman and Jewish—are both opposite and complementary. They conflict insofar as they correspond respectively to the two different hypotheses on Poland's future envisaged in the text. In the first, Poland would succeed in preserving its independence, its status of a free state, thanks to the realization of reforms. The discussions of the "administrative form of government" go in the direction of this hypothesis and Rousseau then refers to the Greco-Roman model, to which he nevertheless adds changes and modifications. But, on the other hand, Rousseau also envisages a pessimistic hypothesis, that of a Poland subjugated by the Russians and no longer an independent state. This hypothesis poses the problem of knowing whether a people can survive the destruction of its state; specifically a *people* and not a shapeless mass of individuals. In other words: how can a people, reduced by arms to submission, preserve its identity, its will to live in common and protect its originality, and thus remain a *nation*, a living organism? It is in this hypothesis that the examples of Moses and the Jewish people are particularly enlightening. "The laws of Solon, of Numa, of Lycurgus are dead, while the even older laws of Moses still live. Athens, Sparta, Rome have perished and have left no children on earth. Zion, while destroyed, did not lose its children. . . . They no longer have leaders and yet they are a people, they no longer have a country and yet they are citizens."[27]

However, the opposition between these two models is relative, for the practical enterprises that result from the two hypotheses are confluent. The condition necessary to the success of the reform is the same as that which would guarantee the nation's survival if the state did not withstand violence.

"In the present state of affairs, I see but one means of giving it (Poland) the substance it lacks: that is to infuse, so to speak, into the whole nation, the soul of the Confederates; that is to establish the republic so strongly in the hearts of the Poles, that it would survive there despite the efforts of its oppressors. That, it seems to me, is the only asylum where force can neither reach nor destroy it. . . . *You will be unable to prevent the Russians from gobbling you up; at least don't let them digest you.* . . . The citizens' virtue, their patriotic zeal, the particular form that national institutions can give to their souls, that is the sole rampart always ready to defend it, and one that no army can overthrow. If you see to it that a Pole can never become a Russian, then I answer you that Russia will never subjugate Poland" (pp. 959–960). Elsewhere, Rousseau is less categorical; he speaks of a "temporary yoke" that will be shaken on condition that love of country burns continuously in hearts.

Whence the advice on which he continually insists: it is necessary to give souls a "national physiognomy," a "national form," the "national force." The word *nation* and its derivatives often flow from his pen. Combined with terms such as "country" or "fatherland," "enthusiasm," "energy," and "liberty," and associated with examples from the ancients, the words *nation* and *national* take on an even greater emotional charge. Nowhere precisely defined, *nation* determines a source from which values originate, a way of being in the world that links the individual to a community and permeates his entire existence. "Every true republican ingests, with his mother's milk, love of country, that is, of laws and liberty. This love affects his entire existence; he sees only the country, he lives only for it; as soon as he is alone, he is nothing; as soon as he no longer has a country, he no longer exists and if he is not dead, he is worse. . . . At twenty, a Pole cannot be another man; he must be a Pole" (p. 966).

But how can politics "reach into hearts" and to what means should it resort in order to infuse souls with patriotic energy and enthusiasm and to transform them into forces that will transform the country as it is into the one it must be in order to "set an example for the Universe"?

3
"They Must Enjoy Themselves in Poland . . ."

"**M**any are the public games that the good motherland takes pleasure in seeing her children play. . . . They must enjoy themselves more in Poland than in other countries, but not in the same way" (pp. 962–963). Rousseau was perfectly aware that such advice given to a country at the height of civil war and whose very existence was threatened by the Russians could only seem extravagant. And yet he was by no means looking for an additional paradox. By insisting on the particular importance of celebrations and public representations for the success of his "proposed reform," he is only developing his ideas on the "limits of the possible" in politics. It could even be said that the encounter with Poland had given him the opportunity to apply a theory and a utopia of the public festival and of its many social functions, underlying all his work, and sketched out in his other writings, particularly in the *Lettre à d'Alembert* and in *la Nouvelle Héloïse*.

If in *Considérations* the problem of festivals and public celebrations takes on such importance, it is because Rousseau brings to the fore the profound affinity by which he wants to join political action to pedagogical action. It is public education that "must imbue souls with the national force, and so guide their opinions and tastes that they will be patriots by inclination, by passion, by necessity" (p. 966). The true meaning of politics is not the art of governing men but that of ennobling their hearts and souls, and the greatness of a true politician is manifested by a system of public education he sets up. Rousseau saw Plato's *Republic*, the work named when one "wants to refer to the land of chimeras," as the finest "treatise on public education ever made."[28] Could it not be said that *Considérations* is Rousseau's great treatise on public education?

Rousseau sees in the public festival a particularly effective means of education, hence the privileged place he accords it in the mechanism of the "proposed reform." The festival is the high time of "patriotic zeal," of that collective sensitivity that must permeate public life as well as daily activities. Expressing this diffuse sensitivity in one single act, the festival is also the instrument of its formation and intensification. The imaginary representations of civic virtues that the festival sets up by its rites and symbols are all means of shaping the souls of those who participate in them. Thus the festival conveys both a political and an educational discourse whose effectiveness is due to its specific language, that of images and signs. It is the only one that is able to bring into play and to orient the action of both the individual and the collective imagination. Some observations must be made here on the distinctive characteristics of this language that make it a privileged means of political communication and action of politics as education or, in a sense, of an education for politics. We will see below that Rousseau's ideas on the imagination and its language will be taken up again during the Revolution, with the attempt to implement a system of festivals for a New City.

Let us note first that Rousseau considers as "the most forceful language" the one "in which the Sign has said everything before one speaks."[29] "The object one displays to the eye shakes up the imagination, excites curiosity, keeps the mind in a state of expectation about what one is going to say and often this object alone has said everything."[30] Although "the language of gesture and that of the voice are equally natural," the latter is nevertheless easier and depends less on conventions. The spoken language also gains in "energy" to the extent that it associates images with sounds and "inserts the most images." This "energy" of the language of signs and images is due to the fact that one "speaks to the heart better by the eyes than by the ears." Thus the language of images is more suitable to "strong souls." "Reason alone is not active; it sometimes holds back, rarely excites and has never done anything great. Always reasoning is the mania of little minds. Strong souls have quite another language; it is by this language that one persuades and stirs to action."[31]

That is why this language imposed itself naturally on the ancients. They used images and gestures as so many symbols to make the virtues and values of their City perceptible. Like the Romans, who paid particular attention to this "forceful language," Rousseau is fascinated by the symbolic if not decorative aspects of their life. "Clothing differing according to the age, the social status —togas, sagums, praetestas, bullas, laticlaves, tribunes, licitors, fasces, axes, crowns of gold, of grasses, of leaves, ovations, triumphs; with them, everything was trappings, representation, ceremony, and everything made an impression on the hearts of the citizens."[32] Thus, they also naturally used this language of signs and gestures at the great moments of their history to express the strongest emotions, like Antony, who had the body of Caesar brought in without uttering a word. This rhetoric managed without the words and commonplaces so abused by the moderns, who have abandoned and even forgotten the forceful language of signs, additional evidence of the degradation of morals and politics. Power whose only hold over men is force and money has confidence only in these instruments. Even kings no longer utilize "the august trappings of their power." The most skilled politicians, however, have always had recourse to this language, although they only exploit it to manipulate men. The Catholic clergy proves its skill when it associates richness of decor and costumes with its rites and adorns the Pope with the marks of his dignity. This is also the case with the government of Venice which, despite the fall of the state, still enjoys, "under the trappings of its antique majesty, all the affection, all the adoration of the people." Rousseau certainly evokes his own memories and the impression the ceremony of the *Bucintoro* must have made on him when he says that it is this ceremony that "would make the populace of Venice shed all its blood to uphold its tyrannical government."[33]

What is the basis of this power of the language of images that gives it such ascendancy over souls that, welcoming it, a people is ready to defend its own tyrants? It would be foolish to seek the explanation in the strength of prejudices that take possession of reason. Those who think that way are themselves inveterate reasoners and do nothing but reduce man to a purely rational, if not reasoning, being, who acts only according to a rational demonstration. This error into which modern nations fall and one which is expressed in their philosophy is particularly harmful in politics and in morality. "In trying to give everything to reasoning, we have reduced our precepts to words, we have put nothing into our actions."[34]

The importance accorded the language of signs and in particular its political use involved all of Rousseau's anthropology. The active principle in man is not his reason, but his heart, passions, and desires; his reason has no direct hold on these motivating forces, so whoever wants to make man act must touch his heart and bring his reserves of passion into play. And there is a specific faculty in man whose flame kindles passions: the *imagination*. The forceful language of signs and symbols addresses itself specifically to it. For Rousseau, as for all the philosophers of the time, the imagination is an ambiguous faculty, veiled and difficult to define other than by its effects.[35] The distinctive attribute of the imagination is to *"transport us out of ourselves"*; it is the imagination alone that permits the passage *from self to other*.[36] Thus it brings into play all the social affections and sets off the complex mechanism at the origin of all social bonds and, consequently, of the passage from the natural man to the social man. "He who imagines nothing is aware of nothing but himself; he is alone in the midst of the human race."[37] The imagination, inactive in the natural man, is always in play in the social man and, in a manner of speaking, it escorts his activities. In other words, no social relationship and, all the more so, no social institution is possible unless man extends his existence in images he makes for himself of himself and others, of his past and his future. The institution of the social implies a permanent effort of the imagination, its interaction with reason and the passions and, in particular, the translation into images of abstract concepts such as virtue, justice, equality, the City, and so forth. Contrary to memory, which only accumulates ideas, the imagination is creative; the images it produces are organized in a complete *imaginary world*, both infinite and unlimited. There is always a gap between the real world, which has its natural limits that man cannot extend, and the imaginary world. "It is *the imagination that extends the measure of possibilities for us either in good or in evil*, and that therefore arouses and nourishes desires by the hope of satisfying them." Either in evil: the gap between the real and the imaginary encourages man to distance himself from his true condition, makes him run after mirages and neglect his present; or in good: man, inspired by images of virtue and of the City-fatherland, extends the "measure of possibilities" for himself and for his Republic.[38]

This digression, if it was one, was doubly justified. We will have occasion later to refer to the theory of imagination and its language that Rousseau passed on to the succeeding generation. But it also allows us to understand that the apparently paradoxical formula *they must enjoy themselves in Poland* is by no means an innocuous phrase. It summarizes a system of public education that appeals to the realm of the imagination and that Rousseau wants to set up in an imagined if not imaginary Poland, so that the attempt "to extend the measure of possibilities" be made there.

Far from proposing to halt the work of the imagination, which would in any case be an impossible task, education aims to give it a slant, to bind it to real objects, to orient it toward the true, the good, the sublime. Emile's tutor attentively follows, sometimes with anxiety, sometimes with hope, the progress of his pupil's imagination. His teaching is in large part devoted to the formation and orientation of the imagination, by frequent recourse to the language of images. The true legislator, the educator of the people, recognizes even more the importance of imagination to the success of his work. First of all he himself must be an imaginative soul. His action is guided by the ideas and images of the institutions he wants to set up and of the people he wants to form. Moreover, he also knows how to guide the imagination of his people and knows full well the force of the language of signs and the use that might be made of it. If necessary, the great legislator effaces himself behind an image, for example, when he "makes the Gods talk" in order to give more authority to the laws. Besides, he dreams of setting up complete social mechanisms that would assure the permanent emission of the images that maintain the activity and vigor of the collective imagination. These images stimulate patriotic emulation and serve as so many models of behavior for the citizens. In this mechanism, at once political and educational, public games and festivals play a prime role. It is within their framework that unanimity, the true foundation of the just and virtuous City, is formed. Moreover, this unanimity *implicates not only the community of presence but also and especially that of the imaginary.* Thus, the legislators of antiquity "sought links that would attach the citizens to the country and to one another, and they found them in particular customs, in religious ceremonies that were by their very nature exclusive and national . . . in games that gathered many citizens together; in exercises that augmented their pride and self-esteem along with their vigor and strength; in spectacles that, reminding them of their ancestors, misfortunes, virtues, victories, interested their hearts, kindling a keen spirit of emulation in them and strongly attaching them to that country that was constantly kept in their minds" (p. 958). Like Moses, who "overloaded his people with rites and particular ceremonies"; like Numa, who was the "true founder of Rome"; because "by those apparently frivolous and superstitious rites, whose force and effect were felt by so few," he had returned "their sacred city" to the Romans (pp. 957–958).

Public festivals and ceremonies are also the pivot of an educational system imagined by Rousseau and one he advised establishing in Poland. For him, education is the "important article" on which all the other articles of his proposed reform are based. Only education can inspire souls with "the national force" on which the fate of the country depends; yet, the educational system established everywhere in Europe produces inverse effects. "A Frenchman, an Englishman, a Spaniard, an Italian, a Russian are all more or less the same man; he comes out of school already shaped for his degree, that is, for servitude" (p. 966). True civic education can only be public and concerns only free men who alone have a common existence.

How can festivals and ceremonies, which are an exercise in public education, orient men toward the City which, although it does not exist, will yet not seem to them a "chimera"? This is perhaps the most original idea of *Considérations*: to represent a social order that does not yet exist but that, by being represented in this way, already establishes itself in imagination. His image thus becomes an agent that modifies realities and extends the "measure of possibilities."

In *Considérations*, Rousseau reworks and elaborates on his utopia of the ideal festival coupled with a sociological theory of the festival that he had explained in the *Lettre à d'Alembert*. We shall discuss them more fully in the chapter on *Utopia and Festivals*. Let us note here only some essential points Rousseau emphasizes in *Considérations*, contrasting the civic festivals that Poland will experience and the theater by which all the other countries are fascinated.

These festivals also will be important spectacles but how different from those of the theater! The two spectacles contrast with each other by their spaces, their spirits, and their functions, in the same way as the social experience that each of them expresses in its own way. The theatrical spectacle is an experience only of "closed-in rooms" whereas the festival of a free people takes place "out of doors," "under the sky" (pp. 958, 963). The theater is a spectacle for the rich, in which participation costs money, where the common people are "always looked down on" and "always without influence"; the civic festival, on the other hand, is, of necessity, free and popular. The theater is cosmopolitan and frivolous; "they know how to speak only of love" there, where one sees "actors declaim histrionically, and prostitutes mince about affectedly" (p. 958). On the other hand, civic festivals are virile spectacles that "must always exude decency and gravity," and where "only objects worthy of their esteem" should be presented for the admiration of the people (p. 964). The theatrical spectacle is only artifice on the stage and a pseudo-catharsis on the part of the audience. Far from giving rise to a communion of ideas and feelings, it only stimulates egotistical interests and corruption, the only "lessons that thrive of all those that there is a pretense of giving" (p. 958). The public festival, in contrast, unites the people with their leaders, it is a "theater of honor and emulation that gives luster to patriotic virtues and fuses souls in a feeling of harmony." Contrary to the theater, the public festival eliminates distinctions among author, audience, actors, producers, and directors. The festival gives free play to the spontaneity of free men. It must be noted, however, that in *Considérations*, to the contrary of what he did in the *Lettre à d'Alembert*, Rousseau stresses the organized and institutional character of the festival. The people must take part, but the ranks must be "carefully distinguished" and the common people not be confused with its leaders, hierarchical subordination thus always being maintained (pp. 963–963). It is a matter of a difference of register and tonalities rather than content. Order is supposed to be spontaneously established, and behind this spontaneity an organizer is always hidden.

All these solemn festivals and ceremonies always play out the same spectacle if they do not follow the same scenario; only the places, the people, and their arrangement change. Each time, it is the people or, it may be said, the nation that gives itself its model image in a spectacle. By applauding the best sons of the fatherland, by remembering the glory of its ancestors, by crowning the victors in noble and virile games, by exalting virtue and liberty, the people always have in front of their eyes their own representation that is at once idealized and normative. The festival starts off the imagination but, by a retroactive effect, the social and moral model, translated into images, keeps this imagination continually occupied and does not allow it to wander off from the moral lesson arranged as a *tableau vivant*. In the symbolic images of what is worthy of their esteem and imagination, the people divide themselves in two, so to speak. They live their own existence on two planes between which a permanent exchange is established. All these guiding images are linked in an educational discourse. But is it not the people who thus tell themselves what it ought to be, who set forth their utopia and who, thus, become their own educator? That is the political masterpiece, although one might wonder to what point the people only take up again and amplify in their collective rites and images the founding word of the artisan of this masterpiece. Is it not he, the "true politician," who is the hidden organizer of all these civic rites and ceremonies?

Thus, it is necessary to multiply the festivals and ceremonies in Poland, representing the free, just, and harmonious City—that will be performed because they are desired, and desired because they are performed.

However opposed they may be to the theater, all these solemn ceremonies imbue the space and the social time with a specific theatricality. Let us make an effort of imagination and follow a citizen walking about in the imagined Poland of *Considérations*. A quasi-permanent setting surrounds him and *speaks* to him. Thus, the Pole wears a national costume and sees only others dressed in the same way. Those he meets often wear identity cards—gold, silver, or steel—the respective inscriptions *Spes Patriae, Civis Electus, Custos Legum*. These distinctions are worn by the "active members" of the republic, who take part in the administration (pp. 1020–1023). He meets others, too, with other distinctive signs, as a man of influence is never allowed to remain incognito; the entire nation observes him, and the marks of his rank or his dignity must follow him everywhere (p. 1007). Note that the absence of any decoration consequently becomes a distinctive sign in itself. . . . Our citizen will certainly come upon one of the solemn ceremonies of which there is no lack in his country. Thus he will attend, for example, public games for children, among whom he will easily recognize those of poor parents who have deserved much from the country; these children wear still other distinctive signs. He will admire the trappings with which these games are organized and will attend this spectacle as a judge, since, along with the other decent men and gallant patriots, he will, by acclamation, award the prizes to the victors (p. 968). Perhaps he will attend a public meeting of the so-called censorial or charitable committee, where the needs of overburdened families, the ill, and widows, are provided for, with funds supplied by the contributions of the well-to-do people of the province. Or this same committee might deliberate on the choice of individuals from all the states whose conduct is worthy of honor and reward (p. 1026). He himself might be distinguished or, at least, might bring this same committee "good information" about those who do good quietly but who are honored in public. It might also be a meeting on the occasion of the ennoblement of several worthy bourgeois or perhaps on the occasion of the freeing of peasants. In that case, our citizen will attend a ceremony celebrated with the greatest pomp and circumstance and all the trappings that can make it "august, touching, and memorable" (p. 1028). These ceremonies will proliferate, like a snowball. And a real avalanche would be necessary to free all the peasants. . . .

Perhaps our walker, not at all solitary, has the opportunity to be out on the day of a posthumous trial of a defunct king. Besides, how could he stay home and miss such an opportunity to show his civic spirit? He will then participate in another ceremony, this one, too, organized with the greatest pomp. Numerous citizens will take the floor to accuse the defunct or else to praise his merits with respect to the country. Propelled by his patriotism, our citizen will certainly deliver a harangue, naturally as eloquent as it is noble and simple, so as to contribute to a just and fair trial, followed by a judgment rendered with all possible solemnity (pp. 1034–1036). The symbolism emanating from all these solemn ceremonies is all-enveloping, and our citizen can never escape the model image of his own good citizenship. Can his dreams and daydreams be other than patriotic and civic? Aren't the landscape, the sky, and the earth part of a setting where civic virtues unite with the idyll? Rousseau doesn't tell us anything about the city planning of Polish cities. It doesn't, however, seem to us to be stretching his thinking to imagine them of moderate size, with straight streets that lead to wide plazas able to accommodate the crowds solemnly assembled. And would it not be necessary to think about building arenas or circuses similar to those of antiquity to give a setting to the public games and equestrian exercises? Should all public buildings not be monuments whose sober and severe facades express the spirit of justice and liberty presiding over these institutions? In imagining these cities we have but to draw conclusions from the theory of the "forceful language of signs" and its profound affinities with the esthetics of an architecture for utopia to which we will return in another chapter.

Thus, *Considérations* does not only envisage a reformed and regenerated Poland. It also establishes the imagination at the very heart of its public life. Let us, however, beware of anachronism. The imagination must indeed be omnipresent and escort passions and desires, but it is by no means in power, as the famous slogan "power to the imagination" would have it. On the contrary, the imagination is bound. It only translates an educational discourse, both political and moral, and communicates it with monotonous insistence. One can wonder whether this will to impose a civic didacticism on the totality of life, both collective and private, does not widen the gap foreseen in *Considérations* between the final objective of the proposed reform and its immediate realization. Indeed, Poland was to remain, during a very long period on the order of several generations, a country where serfdom, social and political inequality, and certain aristocratic nobiliary privileges would continue, though progressively lessening. We have already discussed reasons why Rousseau resigned himself to such pragmatism. All the more significant is the gap between these realities and the collective realm of the imagination, also planned if not programmed. The civic rites, festivals, and solemn ceremonies translate values not yet fully realized in the social and economic areas. In other words, it is in the collective realm of the imagination that Rousseau wants to transpose the vision of the City whose immediate realization seemed impossible to him because it was dangerous to the existence of the country. This City was not, though, to remain in the domain of dreams. This imaginary was to exercise a pressure as real as it was permanent over collective and individual life, and thus have a double effect: on the one hand, to affirm the distinctive national characteristics that make Poland a unique country and, on the other hand, to propel this country toward a social and moral transformation, to guide its "gradual progression" toward the City of liberty and equality.

Rousseau's "imaginary voyage" to Poland is not an excursion to a utopia at the end of which one meets a people with perfect legislation and morals. Nor does *Considérations* limit itself to a reform that would sacrifice "chimeras" to realities confused with "prejudices." The dilemma of pragmatism or chimera was one Rousseau thought it possible to go beyond in a real yet prodigious country where, by love of liberty, men would espouse the dream. Poland was not, certainly, an imaginary country; nor was it the country Rousseau imagined. In *Considérations* the fusion of the utopia and politics does not go beyond the level of a proposal, of a *discourse on politics*. But, making use of the bumpy vehicle of political discourse, utopias themselves embark on distant voyages and it is in history that the exploration of the "limits of the possible" is carried out.

III
Utopia and Metaphysics: Dom Deschamps

"*I* have found the truth with all certainty and I shall perhaps reveal it." These are the terms in which Dom Deschamps announced his "True System" containing—as the subtitle of his work specifies—"the key to the metaphysical and moral enigma." The author did not, however, do what he had announced and his work met with a most curious posthumous destiny. During his lifetime, Dom Deschamps published only two pamphlets and those anonymously: *Les lettres sur l'esprit du siècle* (1769) and *La voix de la raison contre la raison du temps et particulièrement contre celle de l'auteur du Système de la Nature, par demandes et réponses* (1770). These two works were nearly unnoticed—with a few exceptions—by his contemporaries who were, nevertheless, avid for intellectual novelty and polemics. It was only a century later that a scholar from Poitou, E. Beaussire, rescued the work and the personage from oblivion. But then, it was another figure he revealed.

In fact, in the archives of the Municipal Library of Poitiers, Beaussire came upon an extremely odd set of documents, namely a manuscript by Dom Deschamps, *La Vérité ou le vrai système*, which contained the exposition of complex, if not bizarre, philosophical and social ideas. Beaussire saw in it an echo of Spinozism, but was especially struck by the affinities between this work of an eighteenth-century monk and the Hegelianism associated with the socialism increasingly spoken of at the time. Beaussire presented his discovery with ambiguous feelings. Like any true scholar—and he was one—he was proud of his find; he was also proud to be able to show the precedence of a Frenchman over the German systems in vogue. But, on the other hand, he found the systems themselves repugnant.

"What have we found," he wrote, "in this monstrous system that we were pleased to exhume? Materialism and communism presented without disguise, or rather, unblushingly, with, as their basis, a pantheism quite frankly calling itself enlightened atheism. We have no call to pride ourselves on the priority of such doctrines, and if Hegel might have borrowed them from us, the supposition honors us no more than it does him."[1] And of course, if Beaussire names only Hegel, it is because at his time even scholars had not yet heard of that other German named Marx who then was only the author of a few obscure works.

Following this "exhumation," Dom Deschamps again fell into oblivion, especially since Beaussire had not published the texts, limiting himself to quoting numerous extracts as well as fragments of the correspondence. In his *Manual bibliographique de la littérature française*, Lanson still classifies the two printed works of Dom Deschamps under the heading *Adversaires de la philosophie* and *Théologiens et polémistes*. Nevertheless, there was something disturbing about this thought, even as presented by Beaussire, that attracted the curious. Some minor articles as well as fragments of the correspondence are published in reviews. However, it will be necessary to wait seventy more years before the work emerges from the archival dungeons. And yet, *habent sua fata libelli*. . . . The first edition of Dom Deschamps's texts began far from Poitiers, in Baku, in a Russian translation, in 1930. As we have said, these manuscripts had an attractive force. It was in 1907 that a Russian revolutionary and scholar, Zaïtseva, exiled at the time of the decline of the revolutionary wave in Russia, went to Poitiers in search of the manuscript of the *Vrai Système*; it was, in a way, a return to sources. Zaïtseva made a copy of it, translated the text into Russian and, after the October Revolution, wanted to publish it. The Revolution, then in search of a distinctive, characteristic tradition, was seeking ancestors. Interest was naturally concentrated on the utopians, and particularly on those forgotten by the bourgeois culture. But this search for ideological sources, becoming itself an integral part of the institutionalized ideology, would have a turbulent, even dramatic, history, that would draw the researchers themselves into the depths of its vortex. . . .[2]

It was only in 1939 that the texts of Dom Deschamps became accessible to the general public in French, thanks to the edition of J. Thomas and F. Venturi (the latter, at the time, also an exile seeking in history the message of liberty). This was only a partial edition and the circumstances hardly lent themselves to a good reception of Dom Deschamps's work. In fact, the following years were favorable neither to metaphysical reflection nor to dreaming about the *state of morals*. Nevertheless, the texts, once published, broke ground for research that has become progressively more extensive, increasing in scale particularly during the last twenty years. The crowning achievement of this recent career of Dom Deschamps, many of whose texts are translated and published in foreign languages, might be said to be his entry into the Sorbonne, with the course devoted to him by J. Wahl in 1966, as well as the first *Journées européennes d'études sur dom Deschamps* (Poitiers 1972). The importance and originality of Dom Deschamps's work in the evolution of ideas of the last decades preceding the Revolution has begun to gain recognition. And yet we are only at the beginning of in-depth research; the discussion on the "monstrous system" has just begun and Dom Deschamps's work is still awaiting publication.[3]

It could be said that Dom Deschamps went from the antechambers to the great salon of the *philosophes* of the Enlightenment to find himself among his peers although occupying a place apart. What has in fact characterized the recent studies is not only their growing number but primarily the reorientation of their perspectives. There is, increasingly, an attempt to let the work speak for itself, to shed more light on it by situating it in its time, but also to better clarify that era by bringing out the conditions that made possible work that contradicts it. Thus the historian of philosophy is captivated by the originality of "nothingism"—as Dom Deschamps called his metaphysical system—which seems to be the only case of mystical materialism. Dom Deschamps's metaphysical speculation, while opposing the *philosophes*, brings out many of the aspirations and philosophical aspects of the Enlightenment that are often still obscure. It could be said that this work comes to the support of Yvon Belaval's appeal to reread the eighteenth century as a philosopher and finally deign to receive it into good philosophical society.[4] If, for this task, a Diderot, a Rousseau, and a Voltaire are insufficient, and if the philosophy known as "academic" needed a true metaphysician with his own system—well, then, it has all it could wish for, with "nothingism" and reflection on *le Tout* and *Tout*. For the historian of social ideas, and particularly one interested in utopias, the work of Dom Deschamps is fascinating. There is nothing more audacious, in fact, or more radical than that idea-image of the state of morals, of a society with neither private property nor classes, where perfect equality and the community of women and goods reign, and where communal life aims to abolish all the hierarchical structures, the order, the power, the constraints, and the aggressiveness that mark daily life. Beside a Meslier and a Morelly, Dom Deschamps and his works attest to the permanent presence in the ideas of the Enlightenment of an orientation that unites the denial of the existing overall social system and the search for and invention of collectivistic forms of social life in order to embody the idea of happiness, the idea that at the height of the Revolution was proclaimed to be "the new idea in Europe."[5]

For still other reasons, the work of Dom Deschamps and the person himself, as well as his disciples, present particular interest for the historian of collective ideas and mentalities. What a curious case is this, scrambling as it does clichés and received ideas. Here is an atheistic monk who forms a sort of sect, a utopian "communist" who finds his most ardent proselyte in a d'Argenson and who, at the château d'Ormes, preaches his egalitarian doctrine to a Talleyrand and a Dumouriez. A materialistic visionary, a profane apostle, whom Diderot listens to for hours, recognizing himself in his most abstract system and in his reckless utopia. And yet, this monk is opposed to the materialistic philosophy of his time, that of Diderot and d'Holbach, because he finds it only "semi-enlightened." This work seems to knock down the partitions in which the eighteenth century is still too often shut up. In stressing these multiple aspects we are far from letting ourselves be carried away by the enthusiasm of a proselyte of "nothingism." However singular it might be, the Dom Deschamps phenomenon is only an example that proves the rule: that is, that this "enlightened century," more perhaps than any other, demands a most exceptional historical aproach.

We don't wish to prolong this preliminary information about the personage Dom Deschamps and the fate of his work.[6] The latter interests us most particularly because it presents a privileged case for all research on utopian thought and imagination. In fact, where other utopians hesitate, dissimulating their problems and difficulties, trying to accommodate themselves to the received ideas of their times, Dom Deschamps does not prudently avoid any taboo or seek any compromise. He is inspired by the intellectual audacity, united a rationalistic naïveté, suitable in one who thinks he is in possession of ultimate truth, qualities that had so strongly struck Diderot when he met the author of the *Vrai Système*:

> A monk called Dom Deschamps," he wrote Sophie Volland, "had me read one of the most violent and most original works I know. It is the idea of a social state that could be reached by starting from the savage state, passing through the police state, emerging from which, one has experienced the vanity of the most important things, and where one finally conceives that the human species will be unhappy as long as there are kings, priests, magistrates, lawyers, laws, a yours, a mine, the words vice and virtue. Only judge how this work, badly written as it is, pleased me, as I suddenly found myself in the world for which I was born. When I got home, I started to dream about the principles and their ramifications of my stout Benedictine who has just the air and the tone of an old philosopher and I couldn't think of one line that could be deleted from his work, which is full of new ideas and bold assertions. D'Alembert knew it and did not judge it as I do. What bad metaphysicians geometricians are, for the same reason that they are bad gamblers. . . . What will amuse you is the good-naturedness with which this apostle claimed that his system that attacked everything most revered in the world, was innocent and did not expose him to any disagreeable consequences; whereas there was not one sentence that could not have led to a charge of heresy against him.[7]

There is no question of tackling this work in its entirety here. We shall limit ourselves to only three problems and these only in their relation to utopias: the social critique, the revolt against history, and the conjunction of utopian idea-images and metaphysical discourse. The latter, although arid, is particularly interesting. In fact, the work of Dom Deschamps represents a case that is unique in the eighteenth century and is as well one of the rare cases in the entire history of utopias of the nearly total fusion of utopian images and a discourse on being. The *true system* integrates the social imagination and the search for a metaphysical meaning in a single unit.

1
Social Critique and Contestation of History

*I*n proposing a reading of Dom Deschamps that begins with his critique of the established society and goes on to the vision of ideal society and its metaphysical foundations, we are going against the logic of the system that considers moral truth a derivative of metaphysical truth. However, Dom Deschamps himself encourages us to expound his "True System" in this way when he invites us to follow with the human race the educational path he sets out and to become aware of the immensity of the moral evil that gnaws away at it, so that we may become capable of grasping "the key to the metaphysical enigma." In fact, he assures us that only the existence of the absurd requires the exposition of the metaphysical truth, education that would be superfluous for our children if we educated them without false influences. That is all the more so in regard to moral truth: if it were the basis of our morals it would be useless to speak of it. [8] But since these morals remain what they are, let us follow the introductory path that is the most accessible to us who do not yet live in the world of realized truth.

"It is not the state of laws that men need, but the state of morals, the social state without laws. The latter assertion against the state of laws is fully incontestable with knowledge of the first truth that annihilates every divine law and which is the stamp of evidence. It is incontestable, to repeat, that moral inequality and property are, as a secondary cause of moral evil, the cause of all the governments and of all the crimes with which our social state teems. One is finally persuaded that man is evil only because of our social state which is detestable." [9]

Any idea of society that doesn't include the future and, hence, the *alternative society* that it brings, is not only incomplete, false in itself, and the prisoner of false morals: it camouflages the truth. It is only the message about the future that makes the past and present legible and dissipates the appearances of history and brings out its foundation.

Dom Deschamps teaches us that the evolution of history is articulated in three states whose general schema is the following. The *savage state* is the point of departure. It is a quasi-animal state, dominated by physical inequality, *the state of disunity*. Men live there "with no unity other than that of instinct."[10] However, man already distinguishes himself by his faculty of becoming social and reasonable. "If the other animals do not have the faculty we do of becoming reasonable social animals, that is because it is necessary to be in society and in unreasonable society to have it, and they do not have this advantage, which is the misfortune of our days and of our children."[11] Then, the second stage of the human evolution is established: "*the state of extreme disunity in unity* which is our state of laws."[12] Men then go from isolation to group life; they communicate among themselves by making up languages; they invent tools, work, etc. With social life comes the establishment of moral inequality, private property, whose most repugnant form is monogamous marriage, the ownership of women, as possessions, the state and the power, division into nations, wars, etc. Men then create false needs for themselves and embark on vain sciences. But that is not the last stage of human evolution. The human race will go beyond the state of laws to enter the ultimate stage of its evolution, in "*the state of unity without disunity*, which is the state of morals, the social state without laws. It is the latter, to which truth alone can lead us, and from which we are further and further, without ever having been there, that men must live, if they want to be as happy as they have been unhappy until now."[13]

Dom Deschamps even speaks of "three human natures" that would correspond respectively to each of these states: the savage or asocial nature, the unreasonable social nature and, finally, the reasonable social nature.[14] What seems "natural" to us today corresponds only to the savage nature or to our own unreasonable nature—the only ones we know. On the other hand, perhaps what seems to us "against nature" is in perfect accord with the human nature to come. That is, in particular, the case of the community of women, an idea that we find revolting but one that will be quite natural for man once he has attained the state of morals. Thus, man's nature undergoes a transformation in time and it is men themselves who transform it.

Let us note some of the problems touched upon in this summary that require further expansion in the context that interests us.

Note, first, the ternary rhythm that marks historical evolution.[15] Thus, the second stage of the evolution, the state of laws, is a negation of the first, of the savage and asocial state. The state of laws is nevertheless antinomic, the unity of opposites, as it is characterized by "the unity in the disunity." The third stage goes beyond the antinomy and is thus "the negation of the negation." It is not, nevertheless, a return to the savage state. In the "state of unity without disunity,'' sociability is at once preserved and heightened just as the spontaneity and simplicity of the savage state are found there, but they too are transcended at a higher level.

Let us note, next, that this pseudo-dialectic of history makes no reference to any specific historical event. War in general is mentioned, but no real war; the state, but no specific state. No date or specific historical fact intervenes in the course of this discourse. It is, in fact, an *anthropological discourse on history*, and not a *historical discourse*. Dom Deschamps questions the *why* and not the *how* of history.

This abstract character is striking, beginning with the description of the savage state; very cursory, it is limited to explaining the definition of this state as an asocial state. This severe oversimplification contrasts with the curiosity of the literature of the time for detail, eccentricity, and exoticism. Dom Deschamps refers vaguely to ''Caffres'' and to ''Hurons,'' but they are only clichés. The narrative is static; it is focused on the comparison of the savage state with the state of laws. In showing the relative advantages of the former, Dom Deschamps is far from idealizing it. Nor does he consider it the state of nature. As we have noted, the savage state is only ''natural'' insofar as it corresponds to savage and asocial human nature. The narrative takes on more depth and movement when it touches on the problem of the passage from the savage state to the social state. Moreover, Dom Deschamps adopts the problems common to the time, namely, the questioning of origins; he examines in particular the origins of languages, tools, and religion. However, the essential is still the problem of the *reasons* for the passage from an abusive and oppressive state, and not the history of that passage, even supposing that it is hypothetical, to take up the formula given in the *Discours sur l'inégalité* (to which Dom Deschamps refers in criticizing Rousseau's ideas).

The abstract character of this discourse on history is even more striking in the expositions of the state of laws. With the exception of the contemporary era, the state of laws and its history are summarily described, without divisions into specific ages. The references to historical events and situations are rare, if not nonexistent. Dom Deschamps speaks of states, of empires, of kings, but without naming them or giving examples. He accords no preference to an era or a state that could be distinguished from the others, by good or by evil, with the exception, once again, of the contemporary era, the present. Specifically, there are no privileged references to Greco-Roman antiquity, a significant absence at a time when a new model of antiquity was being developed, one rich in utopian potential. The analysis of the state of laws is dominated by synchrony. It focuses on a ''structure,'' on the interdependent relationships among the elements that make a whole of the state of laws, such as tyrannical political institutions; the church that, like the army, only protects the prince from his own subjects; private property, the basis of moral and social inequality, and so forth. (We shall return to these points.) The diachronic approach takes shape mainly with the problem of moral evil, its origins, its manifestations in history, its relationships with human nature—therefore with a set of key problems for the era, one whose antichristian if not antireligious resonance in philosophical literature is well known. Dom Deschamps's opinions on these problems are clear: the origins of moral evil are social and historical; they are obviously a product of secular history, the only one that exists; the state of laws is characterized overall by the growth of evil in its multiple forms.

The synchrony and the diachrony intersect to bring out the present, the contemporary era and its exceptional role. To define this era, Dom Deschamps has recourse to the concept of "century." Along with the "state," it is the key concept of Dom Deschamps's discourse on history, which is articulated into successive "states"; on the other hand, the word "century" is almost exclusively reserved for the contemporary era. It is vaguely defined chronologically: the time during which one lives and of which one is speaking. Thus, Dom Deschamps speaks of "this century," of "our century," and of the "spirit of this century," but he also adds, to characterize it, the adjective "semi-enlightened." It is useless to emphasize the importance of this concept of "century" to the formation of this historical consciousness of the Enlightenment. W. Krauss showed particularly well how it took on a new meaning during the era, how it translated the sentiment of living in an exceptional time, that marked a historical turning point, the beginning of a new era.[16] Dom Deschamps takes up this new meaning of the word, but adds a polemical cast to it: contrary to the opinions of those who proclaim it *the* enlightened century, and even the first truly enlightened century, it is only a semi-enlightened century. Nevertheless, it is indeed an exceptional era on many accounts.

First of all, the century is critical, in both meanings of the word. It is the century of *criticism*. Evil has reached such a point that its manifestations at least are denounced from all sides. Thus, religion is criticized, reform of the state is discussed, the abuses of power are denounced. But, by the same token, it is also the critical century in another sense: that of a *crisis*.[17] The criticism remains purely negative; furthermore, only secondary phenomena are attacked without the essentials of the state of laws being touched on. Thus, the attacks are concentrated on religion, without the realization that it owes its existence to property, the possession of goods and power. Purely negative criticism can only be destructive and the *philosophes* who practice it only destroy, and sow trouble in the state. It is obvious how easy it was to relate this polemic to the traditional attacks on the *philosophes*. All the more so as, in his esoteric writings, Dom Deschamps contented himself with vague allusions to the real content of his ideas, to "positive truth." It is not surprising that Voltaire misunderstood and saw in *La voix de la raison* only one more attack on the *philosophes* who are reproached for preparing "a horrible revolution, if it is not forestalled." He would have been still more horrified, and for quite other reasons, if he had known Dom Deschamps's esoteric comment: "It is by half destroying, as the *philosophes* do, that one sows trouble in the present state; but the same would not be true of total destruction, as its effect would be the unity of men, and only evidence of the common interest would then take effect and not force."[18]

Thus, it is necessary to go beyond criticism by an ever-more-radical criticism. It is necessary that "the destruction be total" for positive truth to do its work or, in other words, the truth about the state of morals is positive only because it entails total destruction. This moral, social, and metaphysical truth finally finds its expression in the work of Dom Deschamps itself. And it is primarily thanks to that revelation that the "century" takes on the true dimension of an exceptional era and the crisis that marks it becomes salutary.

Let us look a bit more closely at the picture of this "century," one in which criticism, both the expression of the crisis it is going through and its ultimate remedy, supports the refusal of history, the basis and product of the state of laws.

Property and social inequality are the principal vices that gnaw away at the state of laws. Property, division into "mine" and "yours," said Dom Deschamps, often passes for a natural thing. This is unjust insofar as, in a savage state, men, like animals, fight among themselves over the objects of their appetites. But the state of laws gave the "vice of property" greater power than it had had in the savage state. The division into "mine" and "yours" spreads to include everything: the earth, housing, food, anything and everything that satisfies the most natural and basic needs and desires. In particular, the "vice of property" took the form of monogamous marriage, which goes against "the natural appetite of the two sexes for each other." Property is, on the one hand, the continuation of the fundamental vices of the savage state, proving that human nature is not yet free of what identifies it with animals; on the other hand, it changes man's nature. "This vice, in the state of law, engendered all the moral vices and all the false passions."[19] Since property is the cause of all tyrannies and all the crimes that are rampant in our social state, Dom Deschamps concludes that man is only bad because of the iniquitous social state in which he lives.[20] Property is the source of the dissension, of the "disunity" that reigns in the state of laws. The effects of man's depraved attachment to property have even changed the nature of some animals. Dogs "are by their function that consists of defending our properties, of all domestic animals, those most related to us, the most proprietorial, and the most disunited among themselves; whence their attachment to their masters and the mockery we make of them."[21]

The "vice of property" is closely bound up with the social inequality that is translated by the division into rich and poor, as well as into states. Property also gave rise to false passions and needs, such that hardly any human penchant or need manifests itself in a pure form. It distorts the natural hierarchy of utility;

thus, those who work in order to satisfy natural needs, those who are truly useful, are also the most scorned. But the most important and most harmful consequences of property are laws and governments. The latter were established to protect the property of the rich and powerful, and also to prevent the "war of all against all," the incessant crimes and conflicts the vice of property gave rise to. On the one hand, law and power are secondary evils in relation to property; on the other hand, the governmental power is interested in the maintenance of property as a source of dissension among men, for only discord, conflicts, and social inequality constitute its raison d'être. The principle of all domination is *divide ut regnes*. There was protest against Machiavelli because he made the practice of this motto public; moreover, "the machinery of domination must be hidden; it would no longer work if men knew about it."[22] The individual morality of the prince ought not, then, to be attacked, as it is inherent in the very existence of power, in the source of evil and disunity.

The very fact of power implies distrust and hatred among the prince and his subjects. Certainly, thanks to laws, there is "some shadow of order" in our morals without which they could not survive. "But this shadow of order exists only in disorder, only in the sphere of a state whose very principle is depraved; and hence, the world as it is. . . ."[23] Concern for maintaining this order serves as a pretext for the existence of the army. But the prince still needs the pretext of the defense of the state for, in reality, the army serves to "hold peoples subordinate to its power and in submission to its laws." The prince provokes wars with his neighbors in claiming reasons of state; in reality, he wants to justify the maintenance of troops that are sufficiently powerful to be used against his subjects. Thus, the source of wars between nations is equally in the existence of laws, property, and power. Dom Deschamps criticizes the Abbé de Saint-Pierre and his proposal for perpetual peace. It is merely a "chimera" because this peace should be based on treaties among kings and on respect for international law. Yet, wars are inherent in the state of laws and its vices; princes will extend, not limit, them. It is not sufficient for us to kill one another on the sea, we will do the same thing in the air, if we find the means to fight there.[24] The essence and the functions of power do not change with the form of the latter, whether the government be a monarchy or a republic.

All power is, then, by its essence, tyrannical, and the tyrant employs in his service the soldier as well as the priest. The fundamental social function of religion, assumed thanks to the church, is to defend the power. The church and the sword are "two states that play the same role, that is the force of the prince against his subjects and consequently against themselves. The church, by the nature of its arms, made to subjugate the heart and mind of the ignorant and subservient man, is the throne's first militia; the sword, which can only subjugate the body, is the second. The soldier must give precedence to the priest, his comrade, and the prince must give him his first protection."[25] Every religion, whatever its content, is sure of its social success as soon as it preaches submission to the power.

Religion can assume its social functions because it is a lie: by exploiting the ignorance of men, it increases that ignorance and, dissimulating the source of the evil, it puts itself at the service of this evil and aggravates it. It is false, as the church proclaims, that human laws are derived from divine laws, human justice derived from divine justice. The law exists only in consequence of sin; it is, itself, a sin. The distinction between "good" and "evil," "virtue" and "vice" is not instituted by God, but by men, and comes from the existence of property and inequality, from the system of laws and its constraints.[26]

The social functions of religion during the contemporary era best explain its origins and content. Religion attributes a supernatural sanction to moral norms and values. It is, moreover, absurd to suppose that there exists a personal God who rewards or punishes in conformity with an eternal justice. It is equally false to believe that the distinction between good and evil is innate and revealed to man by the voice of his conscience (Dom Deschamps is clearly engaging in a dispute with Rousseau). Thus, to the contrary of what the deists affirm, there is neither a natural morality thus comprised nor a natural religion liable to be reduced to this morality. The origins of religion are strictly social: religion is immanent to the state of laws, and human laws preceded divine laws. Following the example of the king, the terrestrial sovereign, men have created a representation of the celestial sovereign, an image maintained by religion and the church. Religion, then, draws all its power from the existence of the state of laws, from the division between "mine" and "yours," from moral constraints and prohibitions. But this very state of laws, especially when it is exercised by a despot, inevitably needs religion: if religious sanctions did not protect property by sowing fear, law, and inequality, the men who groan under the yoke of the misfortunes and vices of the state of laws long would have been free of them. Thus, we find at the source of religion, as at that of all moral evil, the reign of the absurd, of nonsense, in human minds. However, ignorance alone does not explain the longevity of religion, that will exist as long as the state of laws survives. One cannot simply attack a "false state" without attacking at the same time the very foundations of the social system. "It is not morality, it is *politics that constitutes the basis of our morals*, and that politics *inevitably caused by our spirit of laws, is self-propelled without theory's having anything whatever to do with it*, I mean without being basically known either by the kings or their ministers, or the church, or the sword, or the robe, or even philosophers."[27]

The *philosophes* give themselves credit for combating evil: religion, ignorance, the church. However they don't go far enough back to its social origins, for they consider the state of laws the only possible social state. That proves that, far from being the "enlightened century" proclaimed everywhere, it is only a "century of semi-enlightenment."[28] This key concept in Dom Deschamps's vocabulary and in particular in the judgment he passes on his times explains his ambiguous attitude to the philosophy of his era. The *philosophes*, particularly the atheists, attack—with reason—religion, which they treat as an amalgam of prejudices and absurdities, which proves a certain progress of the Enlightenment. Atheism, then, has in common with truth its refusal of all religions, but it stops halfway for, while destroying the idea of a personal God, it does not propose any other metaphysical idea in exchange, limiting itself to doubt or partial truths.[29] Nor does it propose a moral truth: knowing nothing of what the state of morals is or, what is worse, considering it a "chimera," it recognizes the state of laws, the domination of property and vice, as inevitable. Atheism, then, is only a destructive system, a reproach Dom Deschamps levels many a time at "our *philosophes*," and one he directs in particular at d'Holbach's *Système de la Nature*. Atheism refuses the religious sanction to human laws, but thereby removes all moral sanction from them. Not daring to attack the state of laws, it doesn't destroy the causes of evil and crimes, annihilating on the other hand all moral restraints able to attenuate vices. Indeed, in order to ensure the effectiveness of its action, religion has seen itself obliged to preach true moral maxims such as "love thy neighbor as thyself." Religion is full of contradictions: it praises poverty although it defends the rich and powerful; it glorifies the equality of the first Christian communities while supporting inequality and violence. But, just like law and power, religion sees to it that there is at least a semblance of order in the state of laws. To destroy religion without touching the state of laws would be to encourage the extension of vice, injustice, and crime. As long as social and moral evil exist, there will be evil and depraved men. Religion restrains them somewhat, if only with the aid of absurdities, such as the fear of a nonexistent God and a nonexistent hell, or the hope of a reward in a chimerical paradise. Atheism, then, serves only the ambitious, the schemers, and the agitators, and all the powerful of this world will joyously adopt the doctrine that a d'Holbach proposes to them. (Dom Deschamps here agrees with Rousseau's criticisms of the social and moral consequences of atheism, a "doctrine for the rich"). As long as the state of laws exists, neither destroying religion nor revolting against the power accomplish anything, for even the "shadow of order" that exists would disappear. In this sense, the "True System" demonstrates the superiority of theism over atheism, although it combats both at the same time. Contemporary philosophy and particularly the atheism that is being propagated are symptoms of the total crisis, to the brink of which the state of laws has been driven, and attest to the impossiblity of its survival. Dom Deschamps brandishes the fan of the revolution to which this "semi-enlightenment" must inevitably lead. Such a revolution, deprived of any guiding moral idea, would be "the greatest of evils." It could be avoided only by the annihilation of the state of laws and the establishment of the state of morals. It is only with this "happy revolution" that the greatest evil would be replaced by the greatest good.[30]

Indeed, there are no partial means capable of improving the state of laws; even worse, the constant search for small reforms results in a grave evil. By creating illusions, they only hide the crisis. Thus educational reform is proposed in the hope that it will form a new, virtuous, and enlightened man. But it is an illusion to believe that education is omnipotent, and it is another illusion to think that it could raise itself above the social system of which it is a part. Just like all the moral rules it teaches, education is contaminated by the state of laws, its iniquity and madness; it only forces the prohibitions and constraints of laws on natural human needs and aspirations. These attempts lead either to violation of laws or to depravity. This is particularly true of relationships between the sexes. The "stout Benedictine" constantly returns to the latter subject and his criticism of sexual morality is mixed up with certain obsessions it is tempting to call monastic. We have already said that Dom Deschamps saw in monogamy a specific case of the law of property and in every sexual prohibition (including the prohibition of incest) the expression of the state of laws. However, Dom Deschamps was by no means a feminist. Woman for him is merely an object, a "natural good," serving to satisfy men's needs.[31] With particular vehemence, Dom Deschamps condemns celibacy, which he accuses of being against nature and socially harmful. As for sexual perversions, he attributes their cause to the constraints and prohibitions imposed by the state of laws. Thus, in relationships between the sexes, which are the most natural of relationships, all the most odious characteristics of morals particular to the state of laws appear: property, lies, hypocrisy, guile, false passions, and so forth.

Dom Deschamps's social critique is inseparable from his moral critique, and is even subordinate to it. In his "social diagnosis," Dom Deschamps is continually inspired by myths which, if not borrowed from Rousseau, are at least in keeping with the spirit of what is becoming a standard "Rousseauism" of the era. False passions and needs led to the birth and flourishing of arts and sciences useless to man, at the expense of knowledge of the most important truth: moral truth. Relationships among men became more complicated—just look at our language, whose excessive richness is a claim to glory for us and which is used only for idle chatter and reasoning. "It is madness for us to have pushed it (knowledge) to the point we have, and to still try to push it further, as we are doing. . . . We are crammed with knowledge irrelevant to our true happiness." In search of truth and unable to find it, men, "plunged into a sea of prejudices and absurdities," constantly step up their efforts to get out of it, or better, to "get out of themselves, where they find only a chaos they cannot untangle."[32]

Thus violence, contradictory interests, lying, and hypocrisy put us "continually in contradiction with ourselves and one another . . . and keep us always distrustful, behind a mask and in difficulty." The permanent conflict between our natural penchants and our law "puts a mask on each of our faces." We don't know what pure felicity is, happiness that neither the fear of punishment nor the remorse of conscience could disturb, and this uneasiness continually arouses a spontaneous revolt of the mind and heart against the state of laws and its constraints. Social inequality and the over-diversity of morals have destroyed all communication among men. This state of things is manifested—to retain the characteristic theme of Dom Deschamps's thought—in the individualization and differentiation of men, both physically and morally. "It is the extreme diversity of morals that produced the immense moral and physical diversity of men." It is not merely that the king, for example, totally differs from the shepherd as a consequence of the division into social states and the reign of inequality. What is most important is that every difference between individuals, or at least any too extensive difference, is the result of the domination of moral evil and is itself an evil. "Beauty and ugliness, a noble or common appearance, witty or foolish, wise and mad, etc., are only produced by morals like ours, for it is our morals that, very heterogeneous and extremely studied, inevitably bring about a considerable variety in physiognomies, in the flesh, in forms, tastes, temperaments, characters, and minds."[33]

Have we perhaps overly stressed this critique of his century offered by the author of the "true system"? But we wanted to introduce the reader into the climate of that work that allies the most abstract speculation to the most concrete social realities, to allow him better to define the place from where a man who both places himself above his era and commits himself completely and relentlessly to the conflicts that traverse it holds forth. And even so, we have omitted many more detailed questions. Let us try now to reintegrate this whole critical picture of the present into the ternary rhythm sketched above: the savage state —the state of laws—the state of morals.

The state of laws is, as we said, a transitory state. This transitory nature manifests itself in particular in the fact that this state, although social and moral evil are triumphant in it, is a necessary stage for the accomplishment of moral good, for the advent of the state of morals. However, the condemnation of moral evil does not remove all its historical meaning. Dom Deschamps's historical philosophy *is a theodicy without God*. It justifies moral evil not with respect to the intention of the creator, but on the grounds of the function this evil assumes in the search for truth by men (or, to be even more precise, in the preparation of men to open themselves to that truth when it is proposed to them). Humanity can neither persist in the state of laws nor return to the savage state. In spite of all nostalgia for the past, history is irreversible. One sees in it only a mass of absurdities and contingencies, but it is rational and necessary. It seems to bring only suffering and misfortune yet it is the *negativity* of that experience that translates as *positive truth*.

History is irreversible because it is impossible for men, once having set out on the road of socialization, to backtrack. Although Dom Deschamps himself doesn't start on any idealization of the savage state, he is nevertheless sensitive to the manifestations of nostalgia among his contemporaries for this state called "natural." He explains this nostalgia as a secondary phenomenon: it is only a reaction to the real evils of the state of laws from which men suffer. Compared to this cruel reality, the savage state can seem a paradise. However, these ideas are retrograde, "reactionary"—to risk the anachronism—since they sow illusions and divert minds from the idea of the future when men can attain their true paradise. History is equally irreversible in the sense that once moral truth has been discovered and announced, the beginning of the end of the state of laws is already set in action and the "seeds" will not take long to germinate in minds. It is from this double perspective that Dom Deschamps formulates his critiques with respect to Rousseau. He considers him the one who has progressed further than the *philosophes* on the road of truth. Not only has he gone further than others in his critique of the society, that is, of the "state of laws," but he even added a positive aspect to his critique by affirming that man is good by nature and only depraved by his social state. Moreover, he denounced the destructive skepticism of the *philosophes* and the sterility of their atheism. However, Rousseau wasn't consistent enough. He didn't see the defects of the savage state and confused it with the state of nature. He didn't understand what the true social functions of all religions were, and he preached a "pure theism." Finally, he missed the essential: "he didn't see the true state of society after having seen the savage state and our false social state."[34]

Thus the fact that men seize on this dream of returning to the savage state proves their ignorance as well as their revolt against existing social and moral relationships. Their ignorance, because men don't know that their happiness lies ahead of—rather than behind—them, because they don't know the "moral truth" on the future state of morals. But also their revolt, because it is the torments engendered by the state of laws that cause men to idealize the savage state, to forget that it was an animal state in which force and the absurd exercised their uncontested reign. The state of morals, the alternative society, would then be a negation of the negation—a return to sources that is an elevation to a higher, even ultimate stage of human evolution. And this passage has as a prerequisite condition the negative self-education of humanity which takes place throughout its history. Evil and misfortunes, the result of the absurd and ignorance, cause men to seek truth and inspire them with the desire for true happiness. That is the specific course of history and that is the price that the human race must pay for its supreme felicity. Truth can arise from nowhere else; if not precisely from the crisis, from moral and spiritual chaos. Man can come to reason only by absurdity, by the madness that has reached its highest point during this century, inducing men to reflect. And it is only at the moment when reason wins that we will be able to say that we have become more reasonable than the other animals.[35]

It is not difficult to discern a transposition of Christian motifs of original sin and expiation through suffering in this pseudo-theodicy; moreover, Dom Deschamps himself refers to these motifs, particularly that of original sin. He considers them, however, as myths and prejudices or, at most, as a premonition of truth, obscured by the absurd and by ignorance. Men are in no way guilty; the fault, if there is one, is to be attributed to the laws, to ignorance, even to religion itself. Their sufferings aren't the redemption of their sins, but the price paid for their ignorance. The truth is contained not in the revealed word, for it doesn't exist, but in the "True System." It is not for Christ, a mythical figure, to bring salvation to men; it is incumbent on men to attain it by their own efforts and thanks to the truth that has finally been discovered.

Thus the discovery of the "key to the metaphysical and moral enigma" marks the historical turning point. Dom Deschamps speaks of it with the certainty of a visionary who sees once and for all the realization of the truth that he is announcing. He is inspired by an unshakable rationalist faith and by his feeling of having a mission to accomplish for his fellow men. He is an "apostle," as Diderot called him, and it is with the ardor of a lay apostle that he engages in the controversy with the "spirit of the century" that "will be, without contradiction, as much politically as morally, the most essential of all."[36]

Dom Deschamps doesn't situate the ideal society, that of the "state of morals," on any island, nor does any traveler who might have visited it tell us about it. It is a society that nowhere exists, that never yet has existed, but one that must inevitably be realized. Thanks to the discovery of the "key to the metaphysical and moral enigma," an approximate image of it can be given that is within the reach of those whose imagination remains imprisoned by the social state in which they live. This idea-image of the ideal society is not *a fortiori* inextricably bound up with the paradigm of the utopia-proposal. First of all, the state of morals is opposed, by its very essence, to any society founded on any legislation whatsoever. The state of morals, the alternative society, is specifically a social state without laws. Besides, it is not a legislator who is speaking in the "True System." Dom Deschamps is as self-effacing as possible in his discourse. He is not the one who transmits a truth, or, rather, the one through whom *the* truth is revealed. And, indeed, this truth only has recourse to the word provisionally, in order to adapt itself to the present society. With the state of morals, when it is realized, there will no longer be any need for it *to be spoken*. It will then be situated at the level of the lived and not that of the word.

How could this passage from society in crisis to the society of the realized truth be accomplished? Dom Deschamps's answers are numerous, if not ambiguous.

Note that at least once Dom Deschamps has recourse to the paradigms current in the utopias of his time. In particular, he evokes them apropos of one of the modalities of the passage from the discovery of moral truth to the practiced utopia, to the application of this truth. Thus, he proposes "that a man imbued with the true principles recruits ten thousand men and women to cross the sea and come with him to found a new colony in an uninhabited land, one that will have no master; that once debarked, he establishes moral equality and community of any goods, and that he himself starts it by setting an example for the others, keeping only the right to aid the colony in the beginning with his advice and to enlighten it with his knowledge; I respond that shortly these ten thousand transplanted people will live according to his desires, without its being in him, in them, or in their posterity to degenerate. If there were any who resisted, they would certainly be mentally deranged and treated, by common agreement, as insane, to be locked up."[37] The confluent images and ideas of the characteristic myths of utopian literature are obvious: a group transplanted to an isolated island, led by a quasi-legislator, sets up a new life, in total rupture with what it had known. The presence of these themes is revealing—it is testimony of the affinities between the approach characteristic of the author of the "True System" and the utopian thought of his century. The reference to madness is even more revealing—only a sick person, a stranger to reason and human nature, would not accept the state of morals, the ideal society. Yet the paragraph quoted represents only a marginal remark. It is an appeal to set up a social experiment that would prove—even to the most incredulous—the advantages of the state of morals. The very idea of setting up this experiment is clarified by the context in which it is found: *the island* and the *legislator* are only provisional and secondary means. The colony would only be the prefiguration, in a limited space and thanks to the application of specific means, of the social state that one day, by other paths, all of humanity will attain.

Dom Deschamps never links his utopian discourse to a revolutionary proposal for action by the common people. There is no question of the "poor" embarking on a fight against their oppressors, and Dom Deschamps is far from speaking the language of a Meslier. He addresses himself primarily to those who are able to understand the metaphysical truth, cultured people, and preferably, men influential in political and intellectual life, who, for particular reasons, have found themselves in conflict with the existing order. The main thing was to win converts to the truth and to attain, thanks to them, a sort of cultural revolution. It is necessary to turn minds upside down and then the divulged truth will work its way through into real life. Dom Deschamps's intention is not confined to his texts; it extends itself into specific action aiming at founding a quasi-sect, a society of proselytes in the service of the truth and which, following the example of Freemasonry, had had to admit of several layers of initiation for its members.

However it may be carried out, the "happy revolution" must completely annihilate everything the state of laws produced throughout human history. The rupture can only be total and on all levels: knowledge and morality, language and property, and the relationships between the sexes and between man and nature. The state of morals will be the total and radical refusal of human history as it had existed up to that point. As we have said, for Dom Deschamps it is not a question of reforming the established society, of progressively improving one institution or another, of eliminating a particular injustice, of reducing the evil or increasing the good that already exist. By its opposition to reform, Dom Deschamps's enterprise is closer to the ideal model of utopia: the latter is opposed to society in its entirety and aims at a new overall system, while reform seeks partial adjustments, staggered in time. For Dom Deschamps, history as man has known it is the domain of the false and evil, of the uncertain and provisional, of injustice and dissension. Whereas the state of morals, that *alternative society* situated in the future, can only exist as the kingdom of the true and the good, of the certain and the absolute, of justice and unity. And that is why it is necessary to "clean the place out completely"—as Dom Deschamps wrote in a letter to Rousseau.

2
The World of Realized Truth

The vision of the ideal society is founded on the metaphysics of the "True System" and the state of morals must be the accomplishment not only of the moral but also of the metaphysical truth. On the other hand, the utopia, which constitutes the relatively autonomous element of Dom Deschamps's doctrine, explains the metaphysics and serves in some way as its support. The vision of this new society, contained primarily in the second part of the *Observations morales*, is certainly the most esoteric part of the "True System."

What, on the whole, are the distinctive characteristics of this utopia? What distinguishes it, first, is an absolute radicalism and the extremely rigorous—it is tempting to say fanatical—consistency with which problems are solved. It is a vision of society opposed on all levels to the picture of contemporary society and, in this sense, the two images are isomorphic. The state of morals is situated, as we have noted, at the end of history; it will undergo no transformations and will leave no social or moral problem without a definitive solution. The refusal of history that this utopia thus reveals is all the more radical, since the time in which Dom Deschamps situates the state of morals is no longer a *historical time*. Let us be very clear about this: of course, the state of morals *follows*—in time—the other states through which the human race has passed in the course of its history. But, from that point on, it is not a question, in Dom Deschamps's utopia, of setting aside a certain history in order to substitute another history, a new history into which men will be initiated in passing into the state of morals. Dom Deschamps does not oppose to real history a desired history, which would supposedly be the "good" and "true" one. The men of the state of morals will know *no history*; with the state of history it is the *homo historicus* who will be superseded. Deschamp's utopia aims to suppress the historical dimension of human existence and to eliminate the very time of history. The state of morals is, then, the realization of the perfect equality and liberty of which men up to that point had not even had an idea. So they will know no constraint—there will be neither state, nor laws, nor moral pressure. All goods will be held in common and this collectivism will be, so to speak, naturalistic.

Indeed, the elimination of all private property will be the consequence of a literally natural way of life, that is, one *identical* to nature and not only in conformity with its principles. Let us note finally in this overall characteristic a most rigorous anti-individualism closely linked to a no less radical anti-intellectualism. The latter is nevertheless rationalistic, and this seems paradoxical only at first glance. It is only because men will live in the world of realized truth that they will no longer make use of their reason. Indeed, they will have no further need of reasoning.

Dom Deschamps describes the ideal society with a multitude of detail, although he stresses at the same time "that a there is hardly any means other than by comparison with the way we think and live that one can enter into any detail on the way we ought to think and live; this way being so simple that by itself it provides little to discuss about it."[38] Without going further into these details, let us emphasize the development of the characteristic formulated above.

Just like the philosophy of history and the criticism of society that demonstrate the origins and nature of moral evil, Deschamps's utopia, too, is focused on the problem of the suppression of this evil. The state of morals will realize "the natural moral law" that up until now, in the state of laws, men only sensed (in the form of maxims such as "love thy neighbor as thyself," for example), without ever respecting it. The state of morals is a social state, and that is where it differs radically from the savage state. But here it will be a matter of a completely different social nature than in the state of laws. None of the latter's institutions will be preserved and the eternal dream of men, paradise, will come true. It will become a reality in the only place it can truly exist: here, on earth.

The society of the state of morals will be rigorously, authentically egalitarian. The equality established in the first Christian communities, the example excessively and hypocritically praised by the church, only gives an approximate idea of that ideal state. The new equality will be founded on a total transformation of the way of life and social relationships. Cities will be the first to disappear; either destroyed or abandoned, they will fall into ruin. Men will live in small rural communities, in villages, living communally "under long roofs," and without being divided into families. Moreover, men will install their dwellings in the regions with the most favorable climatic conditions, which will make most of their present preoccupations about clothing useless. In these villages, everything will be held in common—wheat, livestock, tools—and the main occupation of the inhabitants will be to work the land and raise animals. Both the disappearance of luxury and the existence of equality will, with a minimum of work, insure sufficient natural products "to satisfy not only the least reasonable animal appetites and needs but to lead the most comfortable life without indolence."[39] A rudimentary industry, mills and forges, will be maintained in certain villages and will serve neighboring communities. There will exist, then, elements of exchange, but reduced to the minimum. Mining and ironwork will be reduced to a level determined by the real needs of the men and they will be minimal. Men "will not kill themselves digging into the bowels of the earth to extract riches that will be useless to them, they will not occupy themselves building and decorating palaces like ours, constructing ramparts and fortresses, smelting metals other than iron which will be useful to them, braving nature on all sides to defend themselves against one another and to destroy one another, studying absurdities throughout their lives and continually doing violence to themselves and their feelings in order to bend their morals to it."[40] Work would no longer be painful and exhausting labor; "nothing would be work to them, because work would always turn into amusement and pleasure."[41] The division of work will disappear, every man will be able to go from one occupation to another, and all will be capable of doing any necessary job. There will no longer be a strict line between work and rest, between days of work and those of celebration, or even between night as the time of sleep and day as that of work. Work will be a pleasure not only because it will no longer be painful, but also because each person will work for the good of all, drawing the greatest enjoyment from this feeling. Each person will, therefore, willingly take on even the hardest work.

Community of goods will also—or even principally—be extended to include women. Monogamous marriage, the source of disunity, crime, and jealousy, will disappear. "Women there would be to men what men would be to women: a common good, without the least unpleasant consequence, the least disunity ever resulting from it."[42] False modesty and hypocrisy will disappear, too. Sexual penchants—the most natural ones, which bring the most natural pleasures—would have no artificial constraints and prohibitions, the source of so much unhappiness. Incest would no longer be forbidden, sexual perversions and prostitution would disappear, and the women "unquestionably healthier, better formed, remaining young longer than ours, without any mystery and without being known as beautiful or ugly, or belonging more to one man than another, would provide an always easy sexual pleasure that would entail no ensuing disgust." We will no longer know mad loves, but neither will we know the despair or humiliations of an unhappy or flouted love. Children will belong only to the community. They will be much more independent and robust than ours: they will raise themselves, once they have been weaned. Neither nurse nor teachers will be in charge of their education: it will be done spontaneously, by their participation in morals. It will be all the easier as, if we inherit from our parents such passions as envy, jealousy, etc., in the state of morals, the children will inherit only natural passions and penchants from their parents (whom they will, in any case, be unable to identify). The suppression of property and sexual prohibitions will lead to population growth, while men, thanks to their new conditions of existence, will become more robust, healthier; they will live longer and stay young longer.[43]

The state of morals would, then, be a social state, but one without any organization, hierarchy, subordination, rule, or constraint. Everything would be spontaneously ordered—but then spontaneity would be, so to speak, de rigueur. It would be a life with neither conflict nor quarrel, neither diversity nor change; on the other hand, it would, in its unity, be the expression of a "happy physical existence" that would be fully enjoyed. "The chagrins and remorse, worries and alarms that kill us would not live under their roofs; that sweet serenity, that natural gaiety, that naive candor and that nice unaffectedness that always have more right to our love than the most brilliant qualities would reign there. Both physically and morally, they would be what it is beyond me to render as it should be, because of the extreme difference there would be in all respects between what they would be and what we are."[44]

Dom Deschamps's words: *"extreme difference"* and *"in all respects"* must be taken in their strongest sense. In his mind, the transformation must focus not only on the external conditions of human existence, but on its very nature: it will be not only moral, but physical as well and, in a certain sense, ontological. Moral existence will be reduced to what it is in its essence, that is, to physical existence. All individuals will be equal and interchangeable and thus would manifest in their social existence what they really are—parts of the "great whole," of the totality of things, material beings of which the universe is composed. It is useless to elaborate here the metaphysical argument on which these affirmations are based. Indeed the criticism of the state of laws as well as the philosophy of history allows us to predict what prospects the "happy revolution" already opens up to individual diversity. Wasn't the latter considered secondary in relation to moral evil, to social inequality, and to complicated and false social relationships? As soon as all these harmful phenomena disappear, in the state of morals, the sources of individualization in the context of the human species will be dried up. One can reproach Dom Deschamps for anything but a lack of consistency. "The same morals (and the same morals can only be the true morals) would make, so to speak, *only one same man and only one same woman of men and women*, I mean that in the long run there would be much more resemblance among us than among animals of the same species that most resemble one another, or among the animals of the forest. . . . People in the state of morals would no longer laugh or cry; *a calm expression would be widespread*, common to all faces which *would all have more or less the same form*, as I have said."[45] It is on this perfect uniformity and interchangeabilty, inscribed in nature itself, that absolute equality will be based. It is thus that the last obstacle to the community of women and the causes of rivalry, hatred, or any ambition to become otherwise, better, more reasonable, or richer, will fall.[46]

This standardization would not be only the effect of identical conditions of existence for all. It would be at once testimony and a demonstration of the realized moral truth. Indeed, only lies can be manifold, only errors and searches for truth can be diverse and different. As far as truth is concerned, it is, *ex definitione*, one and unique, identical in time and space. As for men in the state of morals, it is not sufficient to say that they *will possess* the truth: the possessive relationship evokes property and implies a difference between the subject and the object. And men in the state of morals are distinguished from us "in every way"; they will be perfectly similar because they *will be* the truth, or rather the truth will consist of them. Men, as well as their way of life and their conditions of existence would be identical to the truth—one and unique, eternal and definitive.

In terms of what have individuals differed up to now? Knowledge, thought, morality, language? All these differences will have no raison d'être in the world of realized truth. The arts and sciences will become useless and there will no longer be men "painstakingly making vessels to transport themselves, to transplant themselves, to go in search of food, clothing, furniture, and utensils beyond the seas." The final aim of all sciences developed until now consisted of the search for truth. Thus, it was sought in geometry, physics, and philosophy. This research was not entirely useless, although it accumulated more errors than truth and contributed more to the increase of misfortunes than to the extension of happiness. But it is precisely by suffering errors and miseries that the desire of attaining happiness and truth matured. As soon as the key to the enigma is discovered and known, all other research will become vain. What purpose could it still serve? And, moreover, who would want to undertake it? "In men's estrangement from the way in which they ought to think and live, they are inevitably in a position where they must philosophize and moralize endlessly; but once this way is well established, *everything would be said*, there would be no philosophizing or moralizing; for why would there be, once there was no longer cause to do so?" All the books that have been written are only testimony of the vanity of our research, registers of our miseries. In the state of morals, they would be not only useless, but even harmful—they would have to be destroyed. "To enter into it (the state of morals), it would be necessary to burn not only our books, our titles and any papers but also to destroy everything we call beautiful productions of art. . . . The more one thinks of it, the more one will see that even our most esteemed physics and metaphysics books exist, as do all our other books, only for lack of truth, by our fundamental ignorance and its sad effects."[47] All our books call for one sole book, the one that would prove that they are superfluous. But, as soon as this book is written and as soon as its teaching is put into practice, even this "true book" will become useless. For, it is no longer from books, but from themselves and in their lives that men will draw their knowledge. "There is only one book such as the one I describe that can make men pass from the state of laws to the state of morals. This book, once given and having had its effect, would be good, like all the rest, only for some physical use, such as lighting our ovens. . . .''[48]

Thus, utopian discourse announces its own negation and its own destruction as the effect of the realization of the ultimate message it reveals. The total affirmation of reason is total annihilation: in the world of realized rational truth, any exercise of rational thought becomes superfluous and purposeless. Daily activities, always the same, performed in identical circumstances and with the regularity of natural processes, become mechanical habits. No one any longer thinks out the truth, identical to the way of life. Moreover, any conscience of self, any feeling of the *ego* proves to be uncalled-for. Men ''would not make a study analyzing feelings for themselves, they would limit themselves to enjoying them, and give themselves up to them, with that wise moderation that prevents them from becoming dull and makes them always intense and pleasing.'' The state of morals will be so intermixed with the moral good that justice would reign without anyone's realizing its existence, since there will be no injustice. The latter will be annihilated, including its very concept.[49] Physical ills, death in particular, will, of course, persist, but they too will be accepted without meditation, as part of the natural order. Finally, after all that has been said, it is easy to guess the consequences that ensue for language. In a society where the perfect communion is lived, where men and their days are identical, no one has anything—or hardly anything—to say about himself or others. Why talk if communication takes place in any case without words? And, once again, one can reproach Dom Deschamps everything but his implacable consistency. Would our language be so rich and ''would we be the speakers we are if our first gatherings of people instead of leading us to the most senseless social state had been able to lead us to the state of morals? Animals, organized in a different way than we are, and wisely limited to their needs, don't speak our language and don't talk to one another only to converse; therefore they don't speak, nor are they understood. That is what we have concluded and we don't blush to say so.''[50]

The state of morals will have to resolve all fundamental problems. It will, therefore, also resolve the problem of death. It will assure men of immortality, an immortality understood not as an eternal biological existence, but as the disappearance of any moral sense falsely attributed by men to death, which will then have only its true metaphysical sense. Thus, in the state of morals one will know the *good death* or, if you will, a *death other* than the one that torments men in the state of laws. It would be equality, gentleness, and peace. Fear and illness would no longer accompany death, which ''would be only the evening of a beautiful day, for it would no longer be preceded, as ours commonly is, by a painful illness, by the afflicting sight of a confessor, a doctor, a lawyer, a disconsolate family and all the spiritual suffering that then tyrannize us, contributing a great deal to bringing it about. They (men) will die a gentle death, a death equal to their life, as we will die a bitter death, a death equal to the life we have led."[51] Death will no longer be a source of sadness and regret for the living, since emotional ties will unite interchangeable beings. All men will respect one another and need one another equally, and there will be universal sympathy and friendship. But that is also the reason that particular friendships and relationships, feelings that until now have been substituted for universal communion, will disappear. "They would be attached to one another by the mutual need they would have of one another, but as this need would no longer consist in one man or another as it does in our mores, they would not be attached to any particular man, to the point of envisaging his death as a personal loss, and regretting it. . . . We don't cry for a dead man, but for ourselves, for what we lose in him. And man, in the state of morals, would lose nothing in the death of another man."[52] In this way, the attitude toward death would become appropriate to the metaphysical essence of death. Indeed, in the metaphysical sense, is not death simply, like life itself, a way of being?

"Only that which is physical changes; the metaphysical is, on the contrary, always identical. . . . Death and life are two correlative ways of being, which enter into each another, are part of each other, and which exist through each other." One only lives or dies more or less. "Death lives in us, living by the dead substances we feed on, and life is equally in our deaths, since we are then merely a mass of worms, the most developed of which devour the least."[53]

We have already penetrated into the very heart of Dom Deschamps's metaphysics. And the texts cited have as their context the entirety of that metaphysics. However, before going on, let us note another important question in the understanding of the *metaphysical ethos* of Dom Deschamps's vision of the perfect society.

The effect of ideal and absolute equality, the suppression of property, and the total depersonalization is the disappearance of all conflict and discord in society. Individual interest—if this term still has a sense—therefore becomes identical to the common good or interest. However, the supreme value or the human vocation realized thanks to the "moral truth" does not consist of identification with the community. Dom Deschamps emphatically repeats that perfect equality—and there is no question of another form of equality in the state of morals—is not in nature, *but is nature itself*.[54] Any retreat from nature, implied in words such as "in" or "in conformity with," is suppressed. In the state of perfect equality, man is freed from the burden of his own individuality. The state of morals aims further than the integration of man to a social whole. The community is only an intermediary, however indispensable, for man to identify himself with a totality which is the cosmic whole, nature, the universe—this "great whole" that fascinates the minds of this "enlightened century." "Moral truth, being a purely relative idea, can logically result only from the idea that we also have of the whole or, what comes to the same thing, of order, harmony, unity, equality, perfection, this being the real idea in which one must see every-thing relative and specific that exists.'' All people show a tendency to identify themselves with the whole, with their own metaphysical principle. In the absurd social state, this metaphysical tendency was given a moral character: just as a personal God was created from the metaphysical being, man was required to love this being, to give him the affection of a son for his father. And all of that is absurd. The God of religions does not exist and by ''loving one's neighbor,'' one shows only his natural tendency to identify completely with order, nature, with the whole as a metaphysical being that is ''unity, union itself.'' It is his fundamental unity with things that man finds again and realizes through the state of morals.[55]

3
Utopia and the Thirst for the Absolute

"Nothingism? What is nothingism?" one of the habitués of the château of Ormes and its "philosophical salon" asked after hearing the name the "stout monk" proposed for his system.[56] We will use this neologism, as the term "nihilism," to which Dom Deschamps could justifiably claim priority rights, already has an established meaning and would lend itself to false associations. Indeed, the "nothingist" affirms not "that he doesn't believe in anything" but "that he believes in nothing," in the existence of Nothing as *negative existence*. By no means does he question all morality but, on the contrary, he puts forward a metaphysical system that establishes the definitive, unique, and absolute moral truth.

We have already had a foretaste of the main intention of his metaphysics, as well as of the difficulties his exposition entailed. Dom Deschamps felt that his system was a "precise metaphysical grammar," that is, that he revealed the metaphysical meaning of common expressions and current linguistic distinctions.[57] There is a premonition of metaphysical truth in the foundations of language as well as in current speech. This truth is nevertheless veiled by the distortions language has undergone in the false social state. The *true system* must then be the unveiling of the *key to the enigma* that men sense and toward which they unconsciously aspire. All these references to the current language that were intended by Dom Deschamps to facilitate the reading of his text occasionally make it even more difficult. In explaining his doctrine, Dom Deschamps comes up against several obstacles that have as much to do with the system as with the modes of his communication. On the one hand, as we have noted, his discourse is self-destructive—the bearer of a message that nullifies it. Dom Deschamps must *express* the "truth" in a language that *cannot tell it*. The "key to the enigma'' is in the real life experience of the state of morals, and any and every metaphysical word inevitably distorts it. Dom Deschamps does not only announce a truth of ideas, but also, and especially, heralds one of images, a vision of the social state in which moral and metaphysical truth will enjoy a diffusion that bypasses discourse entirely. On the other hand, this apostle, conscious of the subversive character of his ideas, dissimulates the ultimate truth. Thus he divides his discourse in two: an esoteric discourse and an exoteric discourse. This doubling and the complex interplay between the esoteric and the exoteric are found in all his texts. The first discourse attempts only to awaken minds, sowing anxiety and troubling the conscience of those who, while seeking the truth, in reality only possess it partially since they stopped at *semi-enlightenment*. The other discourse, destined for the proselytes, initiates them into truth itself and it is only with this latter discourse that the unveiling is accomplished, the passage from the apparent to the true meaning, dissimulated by appearances. This whole subtle interplay does not in the least make the reading easier and, since the state of morals has still not arrived, our initiation into nothingism will never be complete.[58]

The many-leveled text lends itself to several readings; this is particularly so of the most esoteric part of the system that deals with nothingism. Thus we note recently that with the exhumation of Dom Deschamps, his metaphysics and, in particular, the concept of *nothing* are beginning to cause much ink to flow. There is an attempt to clarify the thought and enterprise of Dom Deschamps, by referring not only to Hegel but even to Heidegger, to Nietzsche—the list is not complete and the discussion seems only to have begun. A discussion of the totality of problems posed by this vertiginous metaphysics is not, however, within our scope. We will only take it up in its relationships with the utopia and then only insofar as it clarifies the latter and, if necessary, as it proves to merge with the vision of the state of laws.

At the center of this metaphysics is the interrogation on the relationship between the whole—and that implies union and order—and its parts. Now, man is a part of the whole that is the universe, Nature, and what is presented to his senses are the other elements of this whole, things, individual and material beings, that surround him. Contrary to the sensualist commonplaces of his time, Dom Deschamps doesn't consider perception to be a contact with the thing perceived, mediated by ideas and impressions. There is more in the act of perception: the subject assimilates a fragment, an aspect of the perceived object. We perceive a physical object only to the extent that we, ourselves, are what we perceive in that object. Of course, we are not the sun, but we are partially that fragment of the sun that shows it to us. In the most general terms: to perceive, to understand, to know anything at all, is to be to a certain extent what we perceive and understand. This is a question of epistemology, of course, but with implications that go beyond it. C. B. Macpherson has shown how the universalization of the category of *possession* which leads to what he calls "possessive individualism" took place in the epistemology and anthropology of the seventeenth and eighteenth centuries. The individual is considered free to the extent that he possesses the images and ideas, and enriches his impressions and knowledge.[59] For Dom Deschamps, on the other hand, the fundamental, if not unique, ontological relationship established between the subject and the object is that of *coexistence* and not of *possession*. It is not difficult to note that that idea, in its opposition to possessive individualism, corresponds to the aspects of the social vision of the author of the "True System" that have already been discussed.

Man is, then, a sensitive being in permanent relationships with physical bodies, not only in order to know them, but to satisfy his vital needs. But what are present to our senses are also aggregates of things that constitute wholes. Let us take the example of an army (remember that it is a *tropos* in the philosophical education of the seminaries) that, as a body composed of soldiers, suggests the idea of a certain "form," of a union among its parts that make it a whole. And if the example of the army is not convincing, "as a whole insufficiently linked in its parts," let us refer to the example of our own body which is incontestably composed of parts and which nevertheless constitutes a real whole, or even to the example of the globe. By our senses, then, we perceive not only specific beings, but also the "specific wholes" that really exist. In turn, these "specific wholes" compose—as the generality of possible parts—*the universal whole*. "These generalities (like men and trees) are only parts of the generality with the globe of the earth of which your person is a part, and which, with all the other possible globes and their vortexes, produces a generality that is no longer specific, or physical, but universal, metaphysical."

The idea of nature as a "great whole" was a current theme in the second half of the eighteenth century, borrowing its inspirations and different shades of meaning from diverse sources, including Spinoza and Leibniz. Dom Deschamps situates himself in this tradition and attacks head-on the difficulties posed by the problem of the relationships between the whole and its parts. In the philosophy of the Enlightenment this problem was translated into much pondering on the autonomy of this "whole" and, in particular, in relation to the Creator, on the existence of the physical and moral order and on the place occupied by man among the elements of the "great whole." Where others—the Voltaires, the Diderots, the d'Holbachs—evade the difficulties or hesitate, the author of the "True System" has no doubt.[60]

"There is a whole once there are parts," wrote Dom Deschamps, "and this whole is what we call the universe, matter. . . . The whole can exist only through its parts, just as the parts can exist only through it, and each through one another."[61] The universal whole is nevertheless "of another nature than each of its parts, and consequently one can only conceive it, and not see it or imagine it."[62] In this sense, it is a metaphysical, not a physical, being.

How "is [this] universal whole linked in its parts?" That is the stumbling block of all metaphysics, the question to which the "True System" brings the key to the enigma. Different aspects enter into play here and the metaphysics has its consequences for theology (or rather *against* theology and for an enlightened atheism), for morality and, indeed, for politics. First of all, the whole that does not exist outside its parts is uniquely the metaphysical aspect of their physical, material, and sensory existence. But neither do the parts exist outside of the whole and they cannot separate themselves from their metaphysical aspect. Consequently, the universal whole as well as its parts exist only relatively, that is, their existence is relative, the first in relationship to the second, the second in relationship to the first. In this sense, the whole is the cause of the existence of the parts, the parts the cause of the existence of the whole. The whole is then at once "the cause and the effect" or, if one prefers a traditional way of putting it, "the creator and the created." Let us beware of the false analogies suggested by this language which only hints at the truth. The metaphysical being is of another nature than its parts alone to the extent that its totality is irreducible to its elements taken in isolation, without their agreement and participation. The universal whole, nature, is not intelligible to our senses, but rather to reason, or even to a specific sense, the existence of which we are not always conscious of and which is the "special sense of agreement and participation."[63]

This "special sense" thus brings out what "we have strictly in common with all beings." Beyond sensory differences, the world is ontologically homogeneous, and all its parts are of the same nature and participate in the same totality. The being and existence of any body, of each individual thing, depend, then, on all the other things: nature constitutes a continuous chain of beings. That is why there exists nothing absolute *in* nature: no body in nature is autonomous, separated from the others, existing by itself. No property or quality belongs to the parts absolutely—all is relative in nature. Only our senses make breaches in the continuity of nature. On the other hand, nature being the "universal whole" has as attributes all the properties that, seized upon by the senses which isolate, seem mutually exclusive. Taken metaphysically, everything in nature is "more" or "less"—more or less living or dead, free and necessary, past and future. In this sense the universal whole is the unity of oppositions, as well as the complement of each individual being.[64] It is, likewise, in this sense that nature is perfection. But by that must be understood a perfection devoid of any moral characteristic. The latter is only man's projection of his false existence on the universal whole. Indeed, man living in the state of laws adds to two aspects of his existence—the metaphysical aspect common to all beings and the physical aspect that distinguishes the different beings from one another—a third aspect, the moral aspect. Men suffer from moral evil in all its diverse forms and do not recognize it as their own work; thus they have given themselves a God who is supposed to be perfection and will supposedly deliver them from their misfortunes. Yet, in nature, in the universal whole, there exists, at most, physical evil, if by this term one means the relativity of each individual being, that "more" or "less" that falls to his share. Thus, death is a physical evil and even that is completely relative because there is no rupture between death and life in nature. The whole that incorporates the individual beings is the *maximum* and the *minimum* at the same time and it is only in this sense and in relation to its parts that it is perfection.[65]

The universal whole, the aggregate of all the individual beings, is rational. By that Dom Deschamps does not mean that any creative intention can be discovered in it nor that a spiritual existence can be attributed to it. We say that the universal whole is rational, because the metaphysical aspect of the existence of things, that which makes them homogeneous, can be grasped only by reason and not by the senses. Indeed, all sensory knowledge implies the action of one thing on another, and the comparison of one thing to another. And nothing can act on the universal whole, on the aggregate of all beings, and there is no reference system outside of it. "The aggregate of the physical, by which I mean the universal whole, can only fall under the understanding, under the sense of agreement and participation, since it is absolutely true that it neither has nor can have any point of comparison outside itself, but uniquely in itself."[66] When we consider anything at all, in light of what distinguishes it from others, in light of its *esse tale*, that is, in light of its sensory properties, we then conceive it as a physical being. On the other hand, once we consider that same thing—and this is equally true of man—in light of its *esse*, of what it has in common with all beings, we see it metaphysically, and speak of it from the point of view of the intellect.[67] Whence the predominance of metaphysical knowledge over all the other sciences, including mathematics. Sciences in fact are always relative: they refer to the testimony of the senses, they bear only on some characteristics of the *esse tale*, of the "secondary existence." Metaphysical knowledge is, on the other hand, purely intellectual and absolute, and it bears on the "primary existence" which disregards any difference among things.

Thus the "True System" leads to the predominance of the homogeneous whole over the differentiated multiplicity of its parts. In the strict or metaphysical sense of the term, "nothing in nature is a thing on its own or independent; nothing in nature is individual except for one or another of our senses."[68] That is why there is an element of appearance in any sensory perception (but, on the other hand, as that was in question, every sensation is also a means of identifying with things, of going beyond the completely relative character of the individuality). For each of the individual beings, the universal whole is the absolute term of all its possible relationships. Thus, the metaphysical homogeneity of nature is shown through the diversity of all the "physical and sensory properties" of all these "more" or "less" predicable things. But, at the same time, the uniformity of all things, their belonging to the "whole," is shown in the tendency peculiar to each of these things to unite with, to identify with the whole. By its nature, each individual being strives toward the perfection of the whole, that is "to enjoy everything that is possible," to unite the beings with himself, to concentrate them in him. For in nature there are no privileged beings; there is, in her, no absolute center. From the metaphysical point of view, all beings are absolutely equal and the whole is the same in each of its parts; it can, then, be said of each thing that it is the center of the whole and is identical to the whole. It is precisely that capital truth that men sense in the dictum "the center of the universe is everywhere."[69] And it is that tendency of each thing to identify with the whole that Descartes and Newtons reveal by discovering the force of gravitation or indeed the tendency of each body to move itself with a uniform movement along a straight line. Metaphysicists, too, sense the same universal tendency when they discuss the harmony and order reigning in nature; likewise theologians when they attribute to each being a tendency to unite itself with God. But nowhere, perhaps, does this tendency manifest itself with greater force than in the most powerful of the pleasures experienced by man—in sexual pleasure.[70] Indeed, the sensory manifestation of the metaphysical essence of man is his natural tendency to think wherein each thing might satisfy his desires fully, so that his cohesion with the world would find expression in a way of life that would assure his pleasures, his happiness. If men realized this tendency, their existence would become identical to their metaphysical essence and, without differing in any way from other beings, they would at the same time be their center; their life would be identical to nature itself. Such is the consequence of the metaphysical nature of man and that is why the moral truth, which is that of the state of morals, is a direct implication of the metaphysical truth, or rather it is that metaphysical truth lived by man with his fellows in a happy community.

Morality and the search for happiness, inferred up to this point from man's aspiration toward God, are only the presentiment of the metaphysical truth, obscured and weighed down by ignorance and prejudice. "Any part at all, considered metaphysically, is considered in what it has absolutely in common with whatever other part, as a part of the whole. Now, once it is considered in this way, it is absolutely equal to all the possible parts that are the whole and, consequently, to the whole; whence, it follows that it is the whole. Thus, each thing in effect centers other things."[71] As this tendency is universal, there is no reason to consider man a privileged being in relation to his fellows. All that singularizes a man, all that separates him from his fellows and prevents his pleasure is contrary to his "primary existence." Equality and the enjoyment of a common happiness prove to have a metaphysical basis.

We have not yet introduced the category from which the name of the "True

System" derives, the category of "nothing." Up to this point, we have presented our "stout Benedictine" not as a "nothingist," but rather as a "fullist," if we may be permitted to coin an additional neologism in order to avoid the association linked to the term "totalitarian." The "nothing," on the other hand, brings to the fore another aspect of the "universal whole."

The "great whole," nature, the universe, is in a certain sense the logical synthesis of individual beings, but one having a real existence. It expresses aspects of being such as finitude, extent, temporality. As we recall, this whole is a relative being in the sense that it depends on its parts, having no existence outside them. It exists then in itself, but not by itself. It is a determined being, but *omis determinatio est negatio*. The Spinozistic inspiration of Dom Deschamps's metaphysics had never been as clear as it was in this issue. The finite, extensive, temporal, determined, and relative being postulate the infinite, inextensive, timeless, and absolute being. The universal whole is the affirmation of these parts: all the characteristics common to its parts can be attributed to it. "The whole is a purely relative being and consequently doesn't exist at all per se; the whole is the unity of its parts."[72] But the dependent being implies the independent being as well as its characteristics. If all the positive characteristics could be attributed to the universal whole, it would be necessary to attribute to the absolute and independent being uniquely and exclusively negative characteristics. The absolute is therefore the negation of the generality of the finite beings, the negation of the whole that encompasses all possible beings as its parts. The absolute is therefore *nothing*, nothingness.

We can try to clarify this speculative development by taking another approach. The universal whole must, specifically, by virtue of its universality, include everything in itself. It must then equally contain in it its own negation; now the negative can only be an aspect of the existence of the whole, it can have no autonomous existence in relation to "the aggregate of all possible beings." Thus the *nothing* is an aspect of the universal existence, in some way the negative aspect of the universe. "The nothing is not the result of the finite beings, but the infinite. . . . It is not time or the result of time, but eternity. . . . It is the being that exists by itself and of which one can only deny what one affirms of the other beings. . . . It is no longer the sensory or the result of the sensory beings, but nothing, nothingness itself which is uniquely and which can only be the negation of the sensory."[73] Nothingness not only denies the sensory world, but it affirms it, for the infinite implies the finite, eternity implics temporality. Thus, it is the very principle of the whole, of the totality that encompasses all possible sensory and finite beings. In this sense, it is the term *whole* that is perfectly suitable and it is uniquely minds unversed in metaphysics, and that content themselves with "semi-enlightenment," that would draw back from this obvious conclusion: *nothing* and *everything* are identical. Moreover, men have long sensed this truth that they expressed in their ordinary speech, saying, for example, that "all is nothing." They sensed it even more once they tried to talk of God, the being they considered All and Everything, and about whom they never succeeded in saying anything positive. . . .

Thus we have followed this approach to its ultimate conclusions and the least that can be said is that it is not lacking in speculative audacity. And even so, we have simplified it, without pointing out all its subtleties. . . . This metaphysics, the attempted clarification of which has had recourse to Hegelian dialectics or even to the Heideggerian concept of "nothingization," seems more intelligible to us, at least historically, as soon as the Christian God appears as a negative reference. Indeed, Dom Deschamps combats the "absurd" representation of the personal God to whom infinity, eternity, and supra-sensory existence are attributed. As the conclusion to the absurdities that dominate the state of laws, men have additionally endowed this God with moral qualities and have thus instituted him as the source of eternal justice, of moral and legal norms and constraints. Such an idea of God procured a sanction for the state of laws, the reign of property, social inequality, tyranny, and oppression. On the other hand, the "True System," which is an "enlightened atheism," brings to the fore the absolute that is the basis of the state of morals, that *alternative society* that we already know.

The opposition does not however exclude isomorphism. Atheism that claims to be enlightened does not content itself with following the freethinkers who purely and simply deny the existence of God and, hence, of any absolute. The false social state rested on a false idea of the absolute. The state of morals, while refusing the God of religions, must, so to speak, realize the promise of the absolute and rest on the true absolute. This atheistic absolute is, of course, the absolute opposite of God, but is second to him in nothing—is not less "solid" metaphysically than he, nor less rich than he in attributes. It could be said that Dom Deschamps's atheism is "enlightened" in the sense that he attempts to clarify the whole theological and scholastic heritage that he takes on. As the author of the "True System" formulates it: "God," I said, "is the all in all, is the finite or the perfect and the infinite. Indeed, I would say *non est deus ad imaginem nostram phisicam et moralem*. But one must ask no more of me: for with that exception, I say *est deus*; I say that he is a being who according to the way of envisioning him either relatively or not, is the finite or the infinite, the one or the unique, the whole or everything, the sensory taken metaphysically or nothing."[74] Thus it is striking, for example, that the ternary construction— the sensory and individual beings, the universal whole and All—is isomorphic to the traditional religious representations and, in particular, to that of the Holy Trinity.[75] It is moreover sometimes impossible to decide when the theological references have to do only with the exoteric discourse and when they serve as the framework of the esoteric discourse.

Thus, Dom Deschamps unifies two intellectual approaches that for his contemporaries, for the *spirit of the age*, were incompatible, if not antithetical. On the one hand, he makes the ideas and philosophical and social orientations characteristic of the Enlightenment his own, but on the other hand, he pushes them to the extreme, using a reference system and conceptual tools that he took up during his eccclesiastical training.[76] This fusion would certainly not be possible without the most radical calling into question of the social order added to the fervor of the social imagination in search of an *alternative society*.

Thus the "key to the metaphysical enigma" leads to a sort of *mystic materialism* or, if you will, to a *materialistic mysticism*. Indeed, the paradoxical aspiration of a mystic is found in the "True System": to effect the blossoming of the individual and of his person by his annihilation, by his resorption into the absolute. However, for this atheistic and rebellious Benedictine, this absolute is nothing but "the aggregate of all sensory beings," of material bodies, and it is only here on earth, in an ideal community that fuses with nature, that man can transcend himself. The utopian vision is thus pushed to the limit where it merges with a metaphysical project, but at the same time, it is the aspiration toward utopia that is revealed as the motivating force of the search and of the metaphysical fervor. The realized utopia is thus charged with satisfying the thirst for the absolute.

Let us however abandon this domain of the absolute where every word has the solidity of a rock and withdraw to the moving sands of history. But is it not the most stable if not the unique support of the solidity of every absolute?

The question was posed whether, with the exhumations of Dom Deschamps's work, the face of the eighteenth century wouldn't change.[77] The discussion is still open, but we don't think this would be the case. Nevertheless, it is by no means our intention to detract in any way from the originality of this work or from the intellectual audacity that inspired it. By the very challenge it sends to the spirit of its age, it brings precious testimony of the historical conditions in which it is situated as well as of the intellectual and social realities it confronted.

Situating Dom Deschamps's discourse in relation to the ideas that made his time "the enlightened century" is a delicate problem. On the one hand, indeed, one is struck by the fact that all that vertiginous metaphysical speculation, all that heavy "nothingist" system and its conceptual tools go against the intentionally anti-systematic and anti-metaphysical spirit of the philosophy of the Enlightenment. On the other hand, it is nevertheless striking that the "True System," despite the accumulation of the "everythings" and the "nothings," rejoins, in a paradoxical and singular way, the intellectual and moral preoccupations of the era.

The reactions of contemporaries to what they knew of the "True System" conform to this duality of impressions. Let us recall Diderot's enthusiasm after his meeting with the "stout Benedictine" as well as the passages of his texts to which we have referred and which bear witness to a convergence of questions and even of certain answers between the author of the *Rêve de d'Alembert* and that of the *Vrai Système*. On the one hand, numerous reservations about Dom Deschamps's work are well known—those, for example, of Voltaire and d'Alembert, of Rousseau and Robinet. The correspondence that has been preserved proves that it is not solely a matter of a polemic on the subject of a particular thesis, or of misunderstandings having to do with the "exoteric" language. One clearly senses that these correspondents are embarrassed by something in his very way of thinking and of formulating his ideas. He was reproached for practicing scholasticism and "Scotism," for constructing chimerical and omniscient systems instead of studying facts, as d'Alembert wrote, or instead of studying the laws most useful to man, as Rousseau advised.

It is, however, necessary to go beyond these divergences and ambiguities to find a common basis of preoccupations and hopes, of problems and aspirations. It is at that level, and not at that of responses made into systems, and of doctrines that inevitably diverge, that an undoubted unity of the Enlightenment becomes apparent. We have noted that the "True System" takes on a whole set of questions and oppositions that persist in the enlightened mind. Dom Deschamps reproaches his contemporaries for their lack of intellectual and social courage, but he concedes, all the same, that his "age" is further advanced along the road to truth than the others, having reached "semi-enlightenment" and "half-truths." Does he not, in the very counterarguments that he brings to his "age," share the hope of the intellectual elites who produce and convey the "Lights," "the Enlightenment," and who are impatient to see their time finally enlightened by the sun of reason and freed from the yoke of prejudices? Dom Deschamps is not the only one of his time to have the certainty that the "key to the enigma" provided by "full knowledge, total enlightenment," must inevitably join metaphysics and morality. It is by no means peculiar to Dom Deschamps to give moral and social implications to the most abstract philosophical questions, to associate them, on the one hand, to the feelings of malaise and crisis of the existing social order and, on the other, to the search for rules and expedients that man ought to devise to live with happiness in a happy society. Diderot's evidence is doubly revealing, because he recognizes himself in Dom Deschamps's metaphysical and social dream and lets himself be carried away by him and because of the fact that he considers only a *dream* what to our secular prophet could only be the revelation of ultimate truth.

We are not attempting to compare the "True System" with one doctrine of the era or another, or to reconcile it with any of them. However, on the level of the history of ideas and mentalities, one finds, beyond the divergences of the systems, an affinity among the main schemes of intellectual curiosity and the social imagination. On this same level, it is quite revealing that Dom Deschamps's work is not limited to his texts. As we have said, it is extended into a very specific action that aims at founding a more or less secret society, a circle of proselytes initiated into the "key to the enigma"; by the propagation of the truth, one "would give impetus" to a "blissful revolution." It is well known that the intellectual climate of the society that was soon to become the Ancien Régime was marked at the time by quests for an ultimate truth that allied, often paradoxically, the naiveté of a militant rationalism to social reverie, as well as to an esotericism that often verged on mysticism. Do "the metaphysical academy" of the château of Ormes, its initiates, and their discussion not still bring us evidence of this collective phenomenon? This godless monk, "this displaced being, and for that very reason all the more interesting,"[78] as one of his contemporaries said of Dom Deschamps, is certainly, if only by his extremism, a figure who situates himself in a marginal intellectual and social group; the same may be said, from still other points of view, of his protector, and of this restricted group where he finds, if not an audience, at least curiosity for his "monstrous system." But every marginal group is not possible during every era; every society engenders its own marginality whose malaise, preoccupations, and modes of rupture reveal the state of the society itself. Through the abstract figures of the philosophical discourse, one finally finds evidence of a whole blocked society where the muddled feelings of unrest favor the ideas that explore the domain of the impossible. And how striking the correspondence still is between the "social landscape" that takes shape against the background of moral and philosophical criticism of the "state of laws" and the social realities of this small corner of Montreuil-Bellay as they are presented by contemporary historians.[79]

It is by looking social reality in the face that Dom Deschamps turned against it, and it is by confronting it that he imagined the great social and moral upheaval, the "happy revolution," that will actualize the "key to the metaphysical and moral enigma." The conviction that a truly enlightened age could be nothing other than collective happiness, the audacity of the social vision of Dom Deschamps, as well as his intellectual audacity, are part of the "spirit of this century" that the author of the "True System" so criticized, although it was his own.

IV
Utopia and the Idea of History-Progress

"**I**t is left to the spirit to establish the best legislation, and consequently to make men as happy as possible," wrote Helvétius in 1758. It is true that even the novel of this legislation has not yet been written and that many centuries will elapse before the fiction of it is realized; but, arming oneself with the patience of the Abbé de Saint-Pierre, one can predict after him, that "everything imaginable will exist."[1]

Forty years later, in a pamphlet that fits in with the great social and political debate that marked the eve of the Révolution, Sylvain Maréchal called for a radical transformation of society. Setting himself up as a lay prophet, he announced the imminent triumph of equality and liberty, of the peace and innocence of happiness rediscovered. "All this," he said, "is only a story at the time I'm telling it but, I say truly, *it will be history*." To give prominence to the idea that this time of a new history was already established, once and for all, Maréchal gave as the publication date of his pamphlet: *Year one of the reign of Reason*.[2]

The imaginary which becomes reality by espousing history, and history which is renewed by realizing the "novel"—these two approaches are characteristic of the encounter that takes place during the eighteenth century between utopias and the idea of progress. A meeting between the images of an alternative society, at odds with the social realities to which it is opposed, and the idea of history, considered as a purely human work and as the series of innovations that, by their cumulative effects, assure the collective future a continuity and a finality. A meeting too of different, if not opposing, discourses. One is defined by the nonexistence of the ideal City in question; the other attempts to be the faithful translation in words of a real process of history of which it unveils the true meaning, hidden by its convolutions. However, the two approaches were, so to speak, complementary; one necessarily led to the other. For those utopians who

113

refuse to satisfy themselves with dreams, the idea of history-progress offered an exceptional opportunity to give their dream an executory force: history found itself charged with assuring the transformation of the "political novel" into collective reality. On the other hand, the ideologies of progress did not seek only to interpret the past but also, if not primarily, to clarify the present as well as foretell the future. Thus they implied the more or less detailed image of a better society situated in that future and epitomizing in itself the finality of the historical evolution.

Affinities are noticeable between the two approaches and the two discourses but so is an interplay of opposites by which their distinctive characteristics are shown. To simplify matters, one could say that the encounter between utopias and the idea of progress is a double movement: utopian discourse assimilates the themes peculiar to the idea of progress, by transforming them; on the other hand, historical discourse adapts and modifies utopian themes.

There is no question of following this double maneuver here; we will limit ourselves to bringing out several examples of this interaction between utopias and history. Thus we will first touch on visions of the history found in the "imaginary voyages" and the proposals for perfect legislation—the other *history* that then appeared as *the promise of utopias*. We will then pass on to another phase, to the writings in which *utopias are announced as the promise of history*. It is, finally, starting with the debate over the revolutionary calendar, a remarkable example of revolutionary discourse on history, that we will examine the exchanges between the images of the New City and the collective attitudes toward history. At that time, utopias translate the hopes and expectations with which the lived experience of a historical change surrounds itself, but they intervene, as well, in the revolutionary experience that changes the collective modes in which time is lived.

1
History: The Promise of Utopia

Insular History and Alternative Histories

In the works that espouse the two most frequent paradigms of utopian discourse of the era—those of imaginary voyages and proposals for the best legislation—the rupture between the image of an alternative society and social realities has repercussions on attitudes toward history. Thus, the image of an ideal history is opposed to history as it was made (or, more precisely, to the ideas and images of history that function in the historical science of the collective mentalities of the era). On the other hand, this same image is a reflection of the ideal City that succeeded in dominating the collective conditions of its existence—in other words, that can never be surprised either by its destiny or by its evolution.

The accounts of imaginary voyages give numerous examples of these ideal histories.

Let us note, first, that the imaginary *space* spoken of in this sort of narrative is opposed to the *time* of history. Indeed, it is obvious that the long trip across the sea made by the narrator points up not only how spatially isolated the country he is going to describe is from his native land and, hence, from the cultural and social universe of his readers; but the topographical rupture also points up a rupture in time. The history of the imaginary country was not that of the readers, i.e., ours. Thus the narrator will often have difficulty explaining to the Utopians (let us use the word in its generic sense to designate the inhabitants of diverse countries described in the imaginary voyages) the march of his own history, such as the wars of religion and their causes. Let us also note that in the structure of the narrative the time required for this long voyage to Utopia takes on the double function of assuring both the continuity and the rupture between the time in Utopia and that of real history. It is thanks to this journey that the passage not only from one country to another becomes possible, but also that from a real historical experience to an imaginary one. On the other hand, the time of the journey, although rich in adventures and episodes, is, so to speak, historically hollow in the sense that it is a "private" time of the narrator, as much in relation to real history as to imaginary history. In other words, all these adventures only emphasize the fact that the world the voyager will discover is cut off from the history of the world from which he left. As the narrative continues, this break becomes more and more obvious—it is the very condition of the existence of the imaginary country.

These utopias of space are not, however, devoid of all historical reference, which could even be said to permeate the narrative in two complementary ways. First of all, the "real" history, that of the narrator and the readers, is presented negatively. The Utopians have succeeded in escaping from this history and that is why they have not known either our evils, our vices, or our injustices. Thus the historical experience brought by the voyager is quasi-useless to them. The Utopians have no need to know "our" history to clarify their social life. The latter is understood based on itself and is closed in on itself. On the other hand, the narrative implies that the reader can and must refer to the imaginary history to clarify the social realities known to him: hence, his judgment of the latter could not but be all the more severe.

Whence the presence, positive this time, in certain narratives, of history, in the sense that the narrator tells the imaginary history of the utopian country. The word *histoire*,* moreover, frequently appears in the titles of imaginary voyages and with a double meaning—that of "a true narrative, which is coherent, and linked by several memorable events" and that of "fabulous but plausible narrative, either made up by an author, or disguised."[3] Thus in the *Histoire des Sévarambes* a whole portion of the narrative is devoted to the "Histoire des lois et des mœurs des Sévarambes." The latter "is the subject of several volumes" and the narrator has taken it upon himself to extract for the readers "only the most remarkable parts and those most essential to the history of this happy people."[4] The Sévarambes date events by their own calendar: "they count their time by dinermis, that each contain seven solar revolutions." According to "our calculation," it was in 1427 that "these peoples established their principal era." It was then that Sévarias, aged 32, went down for the first time into the "austral lands," later becoming the first king of the Sévarambes and founder of their government.[5] The narrator gives a rather detailed account of this history, beginning with the life and admirable actions of Sévarias himself and then passing in review the reigns of his successors: Khomédas, Brontas, etc.[6] In other narratives, the imaginary history leaves out this sort of detail, limiting itself to a simple sketch of a few major events. Whatever the richness or poverty of detail,

*Translator's note: *"Histoire"* means both "history" and "story."

however, nearly always, behind the events, the same key personage is found. It is the great legislator, the "incomparable legislator," who, "thanks to his unique wisdom," and after having "recognized from what sources the misfortunes of society are derived," gives his people the perfect legislation that makes them happy.[7] This personage (as well as his founding act or, if you will, his founding word) marks the turning point—the beginning of a model history. He likewise incarnates its rupture with the history which was experienced only by us, the non-utopians.

Accounts of "imaginary historians": unimaginative accounts. The fact is not due to the lack of imagination of a particular author. The series is too long, the phenomenon too frequently repeated, even in authors not thought to lack, so to speak, an imagination for events, when they describe the adventures and shipwrecks of their heroes, or social imagination, when they speak of new institutions. A Restif de la Bretonne, for example, had given ample proof of his imaginative powers, yet his history of the Mégapatagons, the perfect people inhabiting the austral lands, and discovered by the flying man, is no richer than many other utopian stories.[8]

The relative poverty of the historical imagination is actually due to the very finality of the narrative. It doesn't propose to its readers that they live *another history* but that they experience intellectually and in the realm of the imagination *social otherness*. What imaginary voyagers explore is the possibility of thinking up and freely imagining alternative societies, based on values, beliefs, and social hierarchies which differ from our own, and which, nevertheless, are in perfect harmony with human nature and the physical and moral order of the universe. The possible, that is, the thinkable, as well as the different, are thus seen extended into the imaginary, or rather, translated into images. The game of the possible and the different is what the imaginary voyagers practice and it is into this game in which liberty of thought and imagination are exercised that they draw their readers. These utopias, for instance, bring imaged responses to the famous question posed by Bayle about the existence and functioning of a society of atheists. Paraphrasing the title of a famous work, much appreciated at the time, it could be said that it is on the *plurality of social worlds* that the authors of the imaginary voyages establish a dialogue with their readers.

It is indeed difficult, if not impossible, to situate these imaginary societies in relation to our historical time. That is not because of the absence of chronological indicators which, on the contrary, are frequently abundantly provided, as we have seen, for example, with the Sévarambes. And yet the history of the Utopians is neither the one we might hope for nor even the one we have missed; in fact, we have neither past nor future in common with it. These narratives of imaginary societies do not suggest that the real societies are going to orient themselves toward the models they present; nor do they tell us that in the past a reorientation of our history, similar to that which took place in the imaginary history, would have been possible. Nor do these texts present the beginnings of what is now known as "historical fiction," that is, a narrative that refers to the imaginary consequences and repercussions of historical events.[9] The utopians do not even live a history parallel to ours; it could rather be said that they are situated in a *time that is superimposed on our own*. The fact that they use a different calendar—we pointed this out for the Sévarambes, but it is repeated in several other utopias—seems revealing. Certainly, synchronizations can be established between the utopian calendars and our own, but these do not suppress the difference. The time of these societies, even when they are not located on islands, *is an insular time, confined to itself.*

The visitor to the imaginary country (and with him the reader of the narrative), thus finds himself before a ready-made, finished, completed history, whose meaning is transparent, for the utopians as well as for himself. The discourse on history in the utopia is moreover the same as that to which his own historical readings have accustomed him. The utopians speak new and unknown languages, much more rational than ours, but they have not invented new ways of writing history.[10] In their annals, the reader finds familiar figures and events—the births and deaths of kings, the acts of their reigns and even, occasionally, wars. However, these actions are only signs analogous to those he knows; their meanings are different. History in the utopia is a purely human—not providential—work; it is that of justice, virtue, and happiness, not that of crimes, discord, perpetual wars, and religious persecutions. He finds in it nothing that constituted the eras of his own history. The history of the utopians derives from a founding act and word that deploy their rationality in time and take hold of the reader.

Presenting a transparent and rational imaginary history was only an intellectual game. But the practice of this game was neither gratuitous nor without social consequences. Comparing and contrasting the transparency and rationality of the imaginary history with the annals of real history was calling into question once again the values conveyed by the latter as well as the resultant social justifications. And it is in this sense that the insular histories told by the imaginary voyagers are just so many *anti-histories*.

The same founding word, if not the same personage of the great legislator who opens the time of history to rationality, is found in the utopia-proposals. It is thus that we find them again in the *Prince ou les délices du cœur* by Morelly. This is in many ways a curious book, not least because it is situated at the borderline between the utopia of space and the utopia-proposal, indeed, even bordering on a treatise on the education of the prince (which shows moreover that in utopian discourse the combination of several paradigms and the passage from one to another are made rather easily). In a framework furnished by an imaginary country vaguely situated both geographically and chronologically, an ideal prince, in a discussion with his advisers, expounds on the principles of a policy that makes the interests of the state coincide with the happiness of its citizens. The exposition of the art of governing takes shape, and is extended into the development of laws, which thus form an ideal, yet applicable, proposal for legislation to transform social realities as they exist.

In other proposals, there is only the underlying presence of a "good prince" who would set in motion the transformation of the social life. The proposals are then just so many appeals to a virtual great legislator who would personify at once the rupture in the history and its continuity. Rupture since by virtue of the true and just principles that inspire him, he must, in realizing the "project," transform and reorient the present. But continuity, too, since the good prince can only take on this mission insofar as he is a product of history as it was: it is history that furnishes him his titles and qualifications, as well as his powers and his possibilities of action. This can be seen with the European princes of the Abbé de Saint-Pierre's *Projet de paix perpétuelle* who were to meet to establish an alliance and an international institution destined to open a new era in history, by eliminating wars forever. All the mechanisms and the system by which this institution functioned are presented in the *Projet* with an overabundance of detail. The Abbé de Saint-Pierre was not seeking ideal princes; he only wished to show princes as they are that his proposals only expressed their true interest. (Rousseau will point out that it would still be necessary that the prince, having to choose between "self-interest and the true," agree to put his power at the service of reason.)[11] In the following chapter, we will return to how the Abbé de Saint-Pierre attempts to reunite the utopia and history in a sole discourse. Here we will only point out a revealing trait. The Abbé who, to his century, was an exemplary utopian figure, had not the slightest doubts about the realism of his proposals. It is sufficient that truth be brought to the fore for it to impose itself sooner or later. Once the prince is persuaded, the reason embodied in the proposal will become a compelling and imperative force to him. His acts then cannot but translate into facts the true discourse and thus transform the revealing word into the founding act of a new reality.

Without seeking to analyze the multiple attitudes the utopia-proposals take toward history, or even trying to review them summarily, let us limit ourselves to a general observation. The paradigm manifests much more flexibility than that of the imaginary voyage and in its substitutions are found many attitudes toward history that are appreciably more varied. To give but one example of this variety, let us look at another text by Morelly, the *Code de la Nature*, which will be quite important in the history of socialist utopias (the text, moreover, was long attributed to Diderot; Babeuf, who assimilated several of the ideas in the *code*, took it for the latter's work). The *Code de la Nature* expresses, on the one hand, attitudes toward history not without similarity to those that were predominant in the accounts of imaginary voyages. But on the other hand the utopian discourse in it refers to a much richer philosophy of history, all the more remarkable for combining the idea of historical decadence with that of a possible progress. Degradation is judged inevitable if history remains abandoned to the forces that have controlled its course up to that point. But history is also an open field of possibilities: the realization of the proposal for ideal legislation would allow for changing its course and installing an *alternative history*.

Nor does the text lend itself to a coherent interpretation. It is divided into parts whose organization is not well defined by the structure of the work as a whole. A polemical work, the *Code* opposes to the critics of the "chimeras" of the *Basiliade* (an imaginary voyage in which Morelly told of a happy country, without private property, state, or a repressive morality) an overall reflection on history as well as a *Modèle de législation conforme aux intentions de la Nature*. However, the way the two parts are linked together does not emerge clearly.[12] Without entering into a detailed analysis, we will limit ourselves to suggesting a reading, solely in the context that interests us here.

The reflection on history and the proposal for ideal legislation are complementary in the sense that both bring responses to the *same problem, that of evil*. Thus the proposal seeks to answer the question of knowing *"what is the situation in which it is nearly impossible that man be depraved, or wicked, bad, or, at least, minima de malis."*[13] A remarkable formula, the perfect formula of a whole orientation of utopian research. For Morelly, this question imposes itself on man as the most urgent because of the oppressive reign of moral evil. It is up to reflection on history to respond in its turn and to say what the origins of evil are and what are the reasons for its persistence. Such questioning of history is necessarily part and parcel of any criticism of it. Indeed man only degrades himself in the course of his history; this history, then, is to be eliminated or remade.

At the dawn of their history the peoples come up against—to risk using anachronistic terminology—the difficulties of their demographic growth. The more numerous the population became, the more the bonds and primitive sentiments "of fraternal unity" were relaxed; it thus came about that the authority of the fathers was weakened. These physical causes to which must be added the dispersion of the population finally "broke nearly all community among men," whence the quasi-dissolution of their sociability. The resultant dissensions, troubles, and wars imposed on men the necessity of giving themselves laws. They then, however, came up against "the predicaments and the difficulties of a new establishment." All the legislations instituted were defective and the legislators—including Solon and Lycurgus—"didn't correct any disorder. The laws that brought only palliative remedies to the evils of humanity can be seen as basic causes of the regrettable consequences of their bad cure."[14] To the original primary disorder were grafted the vices and evils that had been getting progressively worse for "seven thousand years": private property and the resultant social inequality, oppression and despotism, false religions and false moralities. In a certain era, it was easy to prevent evil by a true and just legislation, in conformity with the intentions of nature. Perhaps even today there are still nations that "find themselves in a disastrous equilibrium . . . ready either to fall into barbarity or to draw closer to the laws of nature, if they are fortunate enough, to grasp the propitious moment."[15] There are, however, forces opposed to all change and that is as true of social forces—that is, of men in whose interest it would be to have the evil persist and to keep private property, false religion, etc.—as it is of moral forces, the most powerful of which are intellectual inertia and the sway of prejudices.

Has history, then, brought nothing positive to man? The response is qualified, if not ambiguous. Perhaps all these disastrous lessons that men have inflicted on themselves throughout their history were indispensable so that they could learn "how unreasonable" was any society not in conformity with the intentions of nature. But the experience of evil is incapable, by itself, of causing it to disappear. In order to succeed in doing so, it is necessary to know where the error originates and, in light of this, to decompose this "institutional morality, to prove the falseness of its hypotheses . . . the opposition of its means and their ends; in a word, to demonstrate in detail the defects of each part of this monstrous body."[16] To start on this reform "of the defects of politics and morality," it is necessary, unconditionally, "to give the truly wise complete freedom to attack the errors and prejudices sustaining the spirit of property." Once "this monster has been struck down," it will no longer be difficult to have the people adopt laws that keep men "from being wicked and the dupes of their errors."[17]

The *Modèle de législation conforme aux intentions de la Nature* is given as an appendix to this critique of history and society. Yet, between the critique of history and the model legislation there are both rupture and continuity. Rupture because the critique does not, by any means, lead to the imminent realization of this proposal. On the contrary, Morelly himself states that it is "unfortunately only too true that it would be impossible, in our time, to form such a republic."[18] But continuity is also found, on several levels. First of all, the proposal demonstrates that the problem that consists of finding "the situation in which man would be as happy and as beneficent as he can be" is a *resolvable problem*. This solution does not require either an imaginary island or a people cut off from our history as a condition and a setting. The utopia and the critique of history intersect. The first brings "complete proofs" to the second since it defines "the fundamental and sacred laws that cut off the roots of vices and all the evils of a society." Besides, the analysis of history shows that it "would have been easy for the first legislators" to institute such laws. Nowadays, it is "*nearly* impossible," but does this nuance not also express a hope and does it not suggest that it is not completely ruled out? Morelly defends himself for having "the temerity to claim to reform the human race," but he nevertheless proposes to formulate those truths men have missed in the course of their history. And yet one can even wonder whether Morelly proposes his *Modèle* as the sole and unique solution that can be given to the problems that torment humanity. Does he not, rather, advance it as an example, as one of the solutions that can be imagined once one is inspired by the "true spirit, neglected, unknown or misunderstood, from time immemorial, of the laws [of nature]."[19]

Be that as it may, the utopia is defined by reference to history. It is in historical time that it unveils the possibility of existence of an alternative society that would give body to what had been only the object of dreams. This alternative society is not intended as the continuation of man as he had been formed in and by history, to whom the utopia opposes the normative concept of man. The utopia seeks to free society of its past; it is installed in history only to imprint new beginnings on it, to make it start again from zero. With a new society, it seeks to inaugurate an *alternative history*.

It is significant that Morelly passes over historical knowledge in silence in the chapter of his *Modèle* dealing with question of arts and sciences. He foresees, however, the developments of the natural and technical sciences as well as of poetry and painting (or, at least, of certain types of poetry and painting, those judged useful for society and for its morality). The essential aspect of the knowledge of the past of pre-utopian history, as it were, is reduced to the lessons given by moral philosophy; the rest is only dross to be eliminated, if not a vain pursuit that, like metaphysics, can only "lead minds astray." The citizens of the ideal City will know only one history, that which the Supreme Senate will compose by combining the accounts of the "actions of the leaders and of the citizens worthy of being remembered." These moral and patriotic annals will constitute "the body of history of the entire nation" and will cause a past that deserved nothing better to be forgotten. It is, however, easy to note that while radically refusing the past, the utopian City adopted the most traditional functions of historical discourse. With the annals of the New City, historical discourse changes its object, certainly. It nevertheless remains the receptacle of the collective memory and merges with an edifying and didactic discourse that develops, confirming the values and principles at the root of the social order, and thus contributing to social cohesion. It is a discourse that can be qualified as "monumental" in the sense that it can be perfectly translated into a series of monuments that would be just so many images disseminating edifying examples and moral lessons to the people.[20]

Let us go on to the last text based on which we shall examine another variation of history in the utopia, in which we are more closely interested here.

Progress in Utopia

Jean-Sébastien Mercier's *L'An 2440*, published in 1770, certainly marks a new phase in the history of utopian literature although it is not the first novel about the future. The author's method is known: substituting *time* for *space* in an imaginary voyage. The method will later be used frequently and often more ingeniously than it was by the author of *L'An 2440*. Far from being a masterpiece, this book is distinguished neither by its originality nor by the richness of its political or social points of view. But perhaps because of its very mediocrity, certain themes emerge with particular clarity. Thus, one can grasp in a real-life situation, so to speak, the modifications undergone by that paradigm of utopian discourse, the imaginary voyage, as a result of the combination of utopian representations with the idea of history-progress.

First, the schema of the narrative. The narrator falls asleep and has a long dream, in which he finds himself, at the age of 700, in a city which is no other than that in which he had fallen asleep, Paris. It is, however, a new and surprising city to him and he rushes off to explore it. He walks about, becoming acquainted with the places and mores, laws and architecture, religion, and morality of this twenty-fifth century society. The narrative paradigm of the utopia of space and its constituents are easily recognizable: the narrator, who comes from a society and a civilization that are those of the reader, finds himself confronted with unknown and alien social realities. So he makes a tour of this new society and, as has been judiciously noted, the narrative space recalls that of a museum where paintings are hung, side by side.[21] Mercier, in fact, seems rather like an amateur collector, who specializes in a sole genre and a sole style of painting—only educational canvases that translate sublime moral and political truths into speaking images. The contrast between the reality discovered and the reality already known, as well as the confrontation between the two, would give rise to surprising effects.[22] It seems pointless to enter here into the details of this ''dream, if there ever was one'' for we still have to reexamine certain details and aspects of this future society. Let us stress, rather, the effects of the substitution of time for space.

As has been frequently noted, *u-topia* has been transformed into *u-chronie*: the New City is situated in an imaginary time. To a certain extent, the functions of time in this narrative are similar to those assumed by space in the other imaginary voyages we have already traced. The time elapsed, the seven centuries, isolates the imagined society in question from the time of the real society in which the act of reading takes place.

However, it is obvious that time assumes different functions as well. Let us note, first, that in *L'An 2440* it is a matter of a historical time and even of a characterized historical time. Of course, the precise date in the title is without great importance (Mercier was born in 1740 and so, adding seven centuries, he arrives at the year 2440). What is, however, worthy of attention is the fact that the year 2440 is not in just any future but in one that belongs to *progress*. And the idea of progress informs the representation of time, of the succession of the centuries of which this future is the culmination. This is brought out by the contrast with this other time intervening in the narrative and that might be called the "private" time of the narrator. In his dream, he sees himself as 700 years old, which leads, in the course of the tale, to several supposedly funny episodes. However, this "private" time is slack time, "hollow" in imitation of the "hollow" space we mentioned when speaking of the imaginary voyage in space.

During these seven centuries the narrator did nothing but sleep. Neither his personality nor his ideas evolved, while historical time was rich in events and consequences. However, if time marks the rupture between present and future, it also translates the link between them, for the eighteenth and the twenty-fifth centuries are part of the *same history*, that of progress. Surprising and exotic effects are indeed found in the text, but here they are due to the historical evolution. The narrator doesn't find himself under distant skies, but in really and truly well-known locations—the Pont-Neuf, the palace Louis-XV, in front of the Louvre, in Montmartre. Familiar and yet unrecognizable places. Actually, it is the time of progress that governs the imaginary space: Paris has undergone enormous transformations thanks to time.

We shall return to this renovated space in another chapter. But let us note, here, that this renovated Paris is inhabited by new men: man measures up to his city and vice versa. Let us note, too, that, contrary to the case of the utopia of space, changes here are not limited to a single country, to an isolated City. The narrator has no need to travel to ascertain this fact. By reading newspapers, he learns that changes similar to those he notices on the spot have taken place throughout the world. Prejudices have been destroyed; reason, enlightenment, and with them liberty and tolerance triumph in China as in South America, in Lisbon as in Warsaw (where those mad Confederates whom Rousseau tried to shelter from time have certainly been forgotten). All of humanity is swept along in an irresistible movement. The utopia linked to the idea of progress breaks with insularity in the sense that its time asserts itself as that of *universal history*.

A dialogue is begun between the hero of the adventure and the twenty-fifth century Parisians, and surprise is shown on both sides: the former is surprised by the innovations and by their magnitude, the latter astonished that a long bygone social reality was nevertheless possible. However, if truth be told, the surprise is not so great, despite the contrasts between the two eras. The narrator, transported into this distant future, gets his bearings rather easily. Actually, what he finds there are *his own ideas*, that is, the advanced ideas of his century, then considered unrealizable, that have been implemented. So the impression of the fantastic and the extraordinary does not come from the invention of daring and unknown ideas, but merely from overturning the relationship between an imagined reality and the ideas broadly held by enlightened readers.

Nor is the surprise very great on the "Uchronians' " side. The meeting with this visitor from the past actually only confirms their ideas on history. What is imagined in the narrative is not only—and not really—a historical evolution, the course of history during these seven centuries, but also and especially the existence of a new historical conscience, new attitudes toward history engendered by this evolution. On these two levels the essential themes of the ideology of progress are put into images. And this transposition is particularly revelatory of the way in which the idea of progress is assimilated by a utopian narrative. The imaginary history—that of events, so to speak—is just barely sketched in. We are told that a "great revolution" took place at an unspecified date.

Let us not misunderstand the sense of the word: *revolution* keeps the meaning it has taken on over the centuries: it is merely a change, not a violent upheaval. It was carried out easily, "effortlessly, by the heroism of a great man." The credit is due "the philosopher-king, worthy of the throne because he disdained it, more jealous of the happiness of men than of the phantom of power, fearing his posterity and himself."[23] It is thanks to him that the change took place with neither catastrophe nor civil war. In any case, the country was already ripe for that transformation, for two reasons. First, despotism and its resultant evils had reached their peak; in pseudo-retrospective descriptions of them the reader could easily recognize the France of his time. Then, too, the men of those times were already sufficiently enlightened to glimpse the reforms and the new institutions based on liberty and justice, in spite of the "lights which were only a twilight."[24] From this sketch it is not clear if this great turning point had been ineluctable or if, on the contrary, the country had faced a dilemma: degradation or decadence, following the example of the Roman empire, or else the triumph of enlightened ideas and the advent of a new era. Be that as it may, "the happiest of all revolutions had reached the point of maturity and we are gathering the fruits"; a change of institutions took place and because of that, "everything lives, everything flourishes."[25] Similar changes took place in other countries and the figure of a great legislator who set this change in motion reappears everywhere. In Russia, the credit is due Catherine II, who not only made her country that of liberty and tolerance, but also took it on herself to do the same for Poland, which is not, of course, the Poland imagined by Rousseau in his *Considérations*. Elsewhere it is imaginary princes who introduced these reforms. However, everywhere the prince only executes what enlightened reason imposes: his acts and his words are second in relation to it. He suppresses the political obstacles and, thereby, society changes, mores and tastes, morality and religion. History is no longer marked by slow progression, but really and truly by progress, an irresistible inclusive movement whose finality rests on the actualization of the great values that compel the perfecting of the human spirit. Each and every historical phenomenon and event appears only as one manifestation and one aspect of one single history which, by its innovations, eliminates evil and makes good increase—signs whose significance is given by and with the unfolding in time of the perfectibility of the human species.

As stated, this great mutation also embraces the historical conscience. The attitudes of the Uchronians toward the past complement the history-progress in which they participate and of which they are the products. And it is striking that this conscience or, if you prefer, this imagined historical mentality is *selective* to the point of being discriminatory.

The narrator retraces for us his visit to a high school. History has little weight in education because of the severe judgment the men of the twenty-fifth century have made of their past. "They (children) are taught little history because history is the shame of humanity and each page is a tissue of crimes and folly. God forbid that we put these examples of thievery and ambition before their eyes."[26] They were not satisfied with making history fall into oblivion, they remade it and rewrote it. In the king's library, visited by the narrator, "a concise excerpt, painting the centuries with broad strokes and showing only the personages who truly influence the destinies of empires" was substituted for innumerable history books. Omitted from this abridged history were "reigns marked only by battles and examples of violence. It was necessary to suppress them and to present only what could honor man."[27] There are two reasons for the choice of this method. Books on history handed down by the past are, with few exceptions, worthless: first, the men of yesteryear knew so little of human nature that they wrote only lies and made only puerile reflections. Second, this list of crimes that was history could only have harmful effects on the morals of the new men. The essential social function of history, a subsidiary of morality, is to furnish positive examples, worthy of imitation. Thus history is like poetry and painting in that they are all paraphrases of the didactic discourse that embraces social life in its entirety. Historians, like poets, are "bards, extolling great actions that make the human race illustrious; their heroes are chosen wherever courage and virtue are encountered."[28] Thus, the new history of humanity is summarized in a sort of moral and patriotic chronicle.

Visiting the king's library, the narrator was struck by its poverty. He learned that a particular process had been applied to it: works and authors whose prejudices or immorality could only have shocked the new spirit had been eliminated. "By unanimous consent we assembled all the books we have judged either frivolous or useless or dangerous on a vast plain; with them, we formed a pyramid similar in height and width to an enormous tower; it was certainly a new Tower of Babel. . . . We set fire to this frightful pile, as a sacrifice offered in atonement to the truth, to good sense, to true taste. The flames devoured torrents of both the ancient and the modern foolishness of men." Thus the library includes only "the books that escaped the flames. They are not numerous, but those that remain have deserved the approbation of our century."[29] Neither Herodotus, nor Anacreon, nor the "vile Aristophanes" are found there; Lucretius has been eliminated, except for a few pieces of poetry, because his "physics is false and his morality is dangerous." Among the moderns, a great number have disappeared: Malebranche, the "visionary"; the "sad Nicole and the pitiless Arnauld." No *Lettres provinciales*, and even the learned and erudite librarian commits anachronisms when he speaks of that obscure affair of the Jesuits and the Jansenists. Besides, "that crowd of theologians known as fathers of the church" has been "returned to the nothingness from which it never should have emerged." "Time, the sovereign judge," has also imposed "cuts" in the works of Montaigne, Descartes, and Voltaire; it was necessary to suppress certain pages in order to preserve the rest. On the other hand, the complete works of the Abbé de Saint-Pierre, "whose pen was weak but whose heart was sublime," had been kept. "Seven centuries had given his great and beautiful ideas suitable maturity. It was those who had scoffed at him for being a visionary who had embraced pure chimeras. His dreams had become reality."[30]

Let's not take this vision of books burned on a pyre and purged works too seriously. Mercier is not an Orwell before the fact. He is a predecessor neither of the Ministry of Truth, nor of those who burned books in Berlin, nor of those who purged them in the libraries of Moscow. Mercier is only indulging in an intellectual game that his readers find as amusing and innocent as he himself does. The author of *L'An 2440* is, after all, only exploiting a well-known literary device—charging a reader who visits a library with criticizing the books on its shelves.[31] The innovation lies in the fact that this time, it is history-progress, "time, the sovereign judge," and its proxy, enlightened power, that are charged, so to speak, with the material execution of the judgment of the literary and philosophical critique.

But precisely because it is only a game, certain principal schemas of the social imagination encounter fewer obstacles in it than they would in several other cases, for example, when this imagination is joined to a reflection that attempts to be scientific and seeks to clarify history, the past as well as the future, in light of the idea of progress (we are thinking in particular of Condorcet's *Esquisse d'un tableau historique des progrès de l'esprit humain*, a work to be discussed in the second part of this chapter). During the Revolution, Mercier will set himself up as a prophet who foresaw everything, beginning with the destruction of the Bastille. He will, however, immediately add how disappointed he was by the real course of events that had surprised and surpassed his social imagination.[32] In reality, Mercier's work is not in the least prophetic, nor is it particularly imaginative. It merely translates his faith in progress into images. This faith is as sincere as the idea he formed of the historical evolution, once it had been opened to this indefinite progress, and is simplistic and naïve. The direct translation of abstract ideas into images, associated with the search for satirical and didactic effects, in no way enhances the literary and intellectual qualities of the book, but for the same reasons is most precious evidence. Indeed, certain attitudes toward history, implied by the linking of the utopia and the idea of progress, are seen in it, so to speak, in the rough.

Progress in utopia is intended to be a rupture with the past. Once it has succeeded in making values and what ought to be coincide with social realities, history returns to square one, or, if you will, begins again from *true* beginnings. To paraphrase the well-known formula of Marx—it is then that the *true* history of man begins and all that preceded it can be considered only a prehistory. But on the other hand, historic discourse, bound up with the utopia, can grasp this rupture only as the privileged moment of a continuity. The mutation, crowning the historical evolution that made it possible, thus brings to the fore the finality of history. Thus, the discourse on the New City proves to be that which bears in itself the key to the enigma of history and which clarifies all its dimensions: the present that engenders the future, but also the "true" significance of the past. The New City is thus set up as the sole legitimate heir to this past, but also as its sovereign judge, the only one authorized to legitimize it by a verdict that makes a ruling on what deserves to be retained by the collective memory.

It will not be necessary to await the year 2440 for this attitude to prove to be sociologically operative; we will find it again, militant and conquering in year II of the Republic, when the new calendar will consecrate *the time that opens a new book to history.*

2
Utopia: The Promise of History

"*T*he leading idea of the Age of Enlightenment is not that of progress, but that of Nature. The recourse to the idea of Nature can translate a mental attitude the exact opposite of the one expressed by the theme of Progress; there remain, nevertheless, serious motives for considering the goddess Nature as the mother of the god of Progress."[33] The utopia was one of the midwives who assisted at the birth.

The assimilation of utopian images and themes was one of the conditions of possibility of the formation of certain historical discourse. This was notably the case of those who nourished themselves with the ideology of progress and who "projected the cult of change and innovation on all eras and all civilizations."[34] In this projection, the vision of another and better social future was closely interwoven with the mythological and scientific reconquest of the past. The thought that man's happiness can and must be at the end of his historical evolution proved to underlie the interrogation of the past. With the opening of history on the utopia, the study of the past thus discovered a new vocation, eliciting change and innovation, the continued *progress* of reason, as the leading idea and the pivot of history. In the eighteenth century, it is still rare to speak of Progress with a capital P, although discourse centered on *progress*—that has been, and remains to be, accomplished—is gaining more and more coherence and unity. It establishes itself as global discourse that summarizes the orientation of history and that joins the past to the present and the future. The reconquest of the past was meant to be necessarily rational and scientific, and it is only in the same spirit that the ideology of Progress could approach the future. Thus it is the very time of history, the object of a science, that was to appear as the producer of the utopia. The images of another City and another history situated in the time of history-progress and integrated into a scientific discourse are no longer taken as dreams and aspirations, but as *predictions* of a future endowed with all the prestige of science. Thus, discourse on history-progress is formed in a contradictory enterprise—it advances utopian themes and images in dissimulating them, it accepts them as *truths* while attacking them as *chimeras*. In other words, one only recognizes oneself in the chimeras of yesterday on the condition that they be accepted as the realities of tomorrow. The social imagination is accepted only in disguise—that of the progress of reason in history if not that of the reason of history in progress.

Thus the fusion of utopian images and a historical discourse in a global discourse and in a myth of history-progress could only be accomplished by putting the traditional paradigms of utopian discourse back into question, and by the formation of an *anti-utopian utopia*. This process was only beginning during the Age of Enlightenment. The two examples we have chosen—those of the Abbé de Saint-Pierre and of Condorcet—seek only to show, on the one hand, the difficulties this fusion must come up against and, on the other hand, the functions of the utopia in the formation of a historical myth.

The Abbé de Saint-Pierre:
History as a Pretext for Utopia

In the eighteenth century, the Abbé de Saint-Pierre is generally thought of as an exemplary utopian. Voltaire called him *Saint-Pierre [Saint Peter] of Utopia* and made him the preferred target of his sarcasm. "He thought he had perfected Plato's republic and Salente's imaginary government. . . . He thought he was the reformer of the human race. He called his perfected election system an anthropometer and a basilometer . . . and calmly continued to enlighten and govern the world. He published a prescription for making dukes and peers useful to the State; he decreased all pensions by one of his edicts, settled all trials, allowed priests and monks to marry and, having thus made earth happy, he busied himself with his *Annales politiques*."[35] The target was much too easy and opportunities for mockery were not lacking. For instance, of his proposal, *Moyen de rendre les sermons utiles*, the ridiculous charge was made that it was a: *Projet pour rendre utiles les Prédicateurs et le Médecins, les Traitants et les Moines, les Journaux et les Marrons d'Indes*; while another proposal—how to make Dukes and Peers useful—was parodied as the *Projet pour rendre utiles les Ducs et les Pairs et les Toiles d'Araignées*."[36]

The personage made people laugh and how could it have been otherwise? The Abbé's faith in his principles and in his proposals was as naïve as it was unshakable. In addition, he tried to establish them immediately, if not in public life, then at least in his private life. Thus he was the subject of numerous anecdotes. The author of the *Observations politiques sur le célibat des prêtres*, he therein demonstrated how this institution was not only useless but even harmful to population growth. But he did not, however, limit himself to criticizing it or even to proposing how to reform it. Since the establishment of this reform—as of all the others—was a long time coming, he decided, it was said, to have pretty female servants and to fulfill with them, to the best of his ability, his duties to society. Furthermore, to be faithful to another of his major ideas, he had all his illegitimate children learn a useful job. His works are boring, badly written, infinitely repetitious with the same ideas and the same arguments. When they were criticized for this, he asked for examples; when they were quoted, he concluded, extremely self-satisfied, that his method had proved to be both excellent and effective. Did the quotation of his repetitions not show that the ideas advanced in his texts had been retained?

Beyond the anecdotes on the perfect utopian, we find more qualified opinions. Certainly, no one took up the Abbé's innumerable proposals on his own account, nor those that formed the three pillars of his "chimera"—the proposal for perpetual peace assured by a pact among the principal European states; the proposal for polysynody, that is, the limitation of the royal power by the councils surrounding the prince; and the proposal for a perfected system of elections that, by a sort of contest, assures the most gifted and virtuous people access to all offices. Still less recognition was given to the hundred or so proposals that were, so to speak, incidental. They went from the improved *taille* to the reform of spelling, from a new educational system to the *pédiposte* that would have assured regular mail delivery in Paris. Following the example of those mad inventors constantly in search of patents, the Abbé was obsessed with perfection in politics and in morality, and never discouraged by his failures. Rousseau grasped the spirit of these "reforms" quite well: "It is the Abbé de Saint-Pierre's policy always to seek a small remedy to every specific evil, instead of going back to their common source and seeing whether all could all be cured at once."[37] But Rousseau also takes on the defense of the Abbé and particularly of the utopian dimension of his work. The "routine foolishness" and the ignorance "that can only measure the possible by what exists" easily dismiss "new views of reason with those trenchant words *proposals in the air reveries*." If the Abbé de Saint-Pierre's proposals are impracticable, it is because the abuses that he wants to eliminate are "based on the very interest of those who could destroy them" and it is, nevertheless, to these "influential persons" that the Abbé appeals. Thus, he reasons "like a child" about the means of realizing the things he wants to establish. However, noted Rousseau, "it is important that this book (*Projet de paix perpétuelle*) exist. . . . Let it not be said that if his system has not been adopted, it was not good; let it be said, on the contrary, that it was too good to be adopted; for the evil and the abuses from which so many profit are introduced by themselves; but what is useful to the public, is hardly introduced except by force, given that individual interests are nearly alway opposed to it."[38]

Montesquieu ironically situated his work in the wake of that of the Abbé de Saint-Pierre, and bitterness is mixed with this irony. "Among the Greeks and Romans, admiration for political and moral knowledge attained almost cult status. Today we esteem only the physical sciences, we are uniquely concerned with them, and political good and evil are to us a feeling rather than an object of knowledge. So, not having been born in the century when I ought to have been, I have decided to make myself the partisan of the excellent man, the Abbé de Saint-pierre, who wrote so much during our era about politics, and to establish in my mind that in seven or eight hundred years, a people will come to whom my ideas will be very useful."[39] The short phrase of Cardinal Dubois often flows from the pens of those writing of the Abbé's proposals: *They are the dreams of a good man.* D'Alembert quotes it in his *Eloge de l'abbé de Saint-Pierre*, but he insists on adding a comment: "Would to God, nevertheless, that those who govern might sometimes dream that way." He wonders, further, whether, with the advent of Turgot, the greatest dream of the Abbé de Saint-Pierre was not realized, that of the "disintestedness and generosity he preaches everywhere to influential men." D'Alembert particularly emphasizes the Abbé's faith in a future that, for him, could only be that of the "more or less belated progress of the enlightenment in all genres and all states." He kept this faith against "so many causes united to hinder people becoming enlightened, of which the principal one is the despotism that he (the Abbé) saw as the born enemy, the necessary and vigilant enemy of knowledge and enlightenment." What enlightened mind would not see himself in this message? But, on the other hand, did the Abbé not push reason to the point of madness by attempting to rigorously demonstrate this future progress? Did he not ridicule them by calculating the time "when every prejudice, every error, every foolishness of men had to end"? He did not hesitate to predict that a time would come when, to borrow his own words, *"the simplest Capuchin would know as much as the cleverest Jesuit."* Thus he is somewhat similar to that learned mathematician who pushed "the finesse of arithmetic to the point of determining the precise year of the end of the world."[40]

Let us recall again accounts in which admiration for the intellectual courage of the Abbé de Saint-Pierre prevails over reservations, which are all the more interesting because their authors refer to collaboration with the Abbé at the Club de l'Entresol. The Abbé was one of the dynamic forces behind this breeding ground of ideas, where politics was mixed with utopian discourse, where the aristocratic spirit of revolt against the despotism of Louis XV joined the philosophical spirit, where Montesquieu met Bolingbroke, and where Fontenelle rubbed elbows with the Marquis d'Argenson. We have already evoked the latter's words: he speaks of his "good friend who dreams of reforming the state." The Marquis recognizes himself in him all the better as he, too, has a penchant for "building castles in the air" (what an odd predisposition to utopias and utopians in that family—another d'Argenson will be the disciple and patron of Dom Deschamps).[41] Bolingbroke's evidence is no less revealing—and it is useless to specify that in this case, as in that of d'Argenson, it is a matter of statesmen who have rich personal political experience and who, additionally, make the enlightened ideas their own. And Bolingbroke's recollections of the Club de l'Entresol and the Abbé's activity of that period show the same strong mixture of irony and admiration. "It was as though he had suddenly found himself, there, in a country he had long and fruitlessly hoped to see. His systems, which are known to the public, show nothing but offices of discovery, public lectures. For a long time, he has embraced with all his might that science of political philosophy that was so cultivated among the Greeks by the Platos, the Dions (Chrysostome) and so unknown and nearly insulted among us. . . . He communicated to us all his unprinted works, asking for written criticism which he always answered, unfailingly satisfied with his own objections."[42] Let us, finally, recall that the utopian inspiration of our good Abbé, if not exactly the same ideas, are to be found in one of Fontenelle's texts, titled *Ma république*, that seems to date from the same period, that of the activity of the Club de l'Entresol.

Let us explain the sense we attribute to this evidence, of which there is a great deal more. It is not our intention to "rehabilitate" the Abbé de Saint-Pierre nor make of him "our contemporary lost in the eighteenth century," to quote the title of a thesis written on him.[43] It is as easy to scoff at his proposals as it is to present them as anticipatory ideas, misunderstood and underrated in his time but later realized. We do not, however, think that the proposal for perpetual peace is the forerunner of the Holy Alliance or the UN; nor do we seek in the plan for making celibacy useful a portent of Vatican III. The spelling proposed by the Abbé is certainly a model of rationality in relation to that of his time and of ours; the *pédiposte* is, perhaps, a most effective means of remedying the current French telephone situation. The Abbé de Saint-Pierre's work is not clarified either by the supposed "realizations" of his ideas, examples of which might be dug up throughout the centuries, nor by the rationality of his proposals, as perfect as they were sterile. If we have accumulated evidence on his work it is not because we seek to rescue an underestimated genius from oblivion in order to bring to the fore the fact that he is a witness to *his* century. The good Abbé's utopian enterprise is doubly revealing—first, by the maniacal turn taken on by the belief in complete rationality by which social life would be affected in his proposals, and then by the reactions provoked by these "dreams of a good man."

Indeed, a sort of embarrassment and perplexity, dissimulated behind a laugh, is to be noted in the testimony cited. That has to do, in part, with the character of the man himself. Certainly he lends himself to mockery but on the other hand, his good faith, his naïveté and, particularly, the strength of his principles and his intellectual courage are disarming. Excluded from the Académie for his criticism of the despotism of Louis XV, he never went back on his word; ridiculed for each of his proposals, he was never discouraged and never disavowed his absolute faith in human reason and its power of improvement. But isn't this same sort of embarrassment also seen in attitudes toward his work? How characteristic it is that despite considering him a model utopian, and denying the least claim to practicality in his proposals, criticism is nevertheless qualified by adding that his century was not yet mature enough for them.

The Abbé did stray, of course, but like a "good man," one who takes men as they ought to be and not as they are. "If some of our zealous philosopher's views suppose in human nature a degree of perfection that it will perhaps never attain, the discrepancies and the misunderstandings, for which the author might be reproached, but never with bitterness, must teach his fellows that the virtuous man aspires in vain to do good, if he does not have that *enlightened patience* that can await its moments; and that with the most praiseworthy intentions one can do harm to the truth . . . in rushing to show it before the proper time."[44] Does that absence of "enlightened patience," which in the Abbé is expressed by an avalanche of proposals, not risk compromising the real progress of the Enlightenment? The Abbé presented his proposals as simple reforms, as reasonable as they were easy to accomplish. But does he not, thereby, compromise as "chimeric" the very idea of rational reform? The gratuitous proposals of the Abbé, to which it was impossible to give any practical results, were inspired only by their obvious usefulness. But do they not, at the same time, also discredit that key idea with which the *philosophes* wanted to impregnate the social and political realities of their times? While distrusting this "zealous *philosophe*," were his critics not, themselves, *impatient*? Did they not bitterly reproach their era for delaying too long in putting "enlightened ideas" into effect? And who among the *philosophes* did not toy with the idea of his own little reform proposal? Does the Abbé's utopian élan not express a whole dimension of the Enlightenment, but in its own way, that is, by exaggerating it? Do the Abbé's excesses not resemble a caricature in which one refuses to recognize oneself because it reveals more than one would like to admit?

It is by this almost caricatural cast to the idea of progress in the Abbé de Saint-Pierre that it seems particularly striking to us. The Abbé's reflections on progress have occasionally been considered an important link in the formation of the idea of Progress in the eighteenth century or even as an anticipation of the theories that were to triumph in the nineteenth.[45] It must be admitted that this time it was greatly tempting to establish a connection between the discourse of the Abbé de Saint-Pierre and that of a Saint-Simon or a Comte. It was particularly so for those who projected, so to speak, the "progressive" schema on the history of Progress. In fact, the Abbé was vigorously opposed to any providentialistic theory of history or even to that of cycles. The unity of history is only given with *Progress*, the rational innovations that arise and inevitably accumulate. Moreover, this *progress* in the arts and sciences is only the partial manifestation of a global movement that traverses and orients history. The latter is articulated in stages or eras, according to the acceleration of this movement; it increases in goodness and in rationality. The scientific discovery of this evolution and of the laws that govern it is itself a manifestation of that Progress and is essential to its growth. Thus, *the golden age lies before us*, etc. However, the affinities of these formulas with those that will form the basic structure of the myth of progress one century later are only apparent. Paradoxically, the Abbé de Saint-Pierre only formulated his theory of Progress because he is a *latecomer*, because he did not succeed in renewing either the conceptualization of history or the paradigmatic forms of utopian discourse. The encounter between history and the utopia is only made to the extent that the former serves as the screen on which the Abbé projects his innumerable proposals. History has no depth, no specific resistance: at every moment it lends itself to being infinitely reformable. Progress is thus assimilated to one further proposal; discourse on history is only the meeting place, where all the possible proposals become implanted. History, then, is only a pretext to the utopia. For fear of anticipating our conclusion, let us examine things more closely.

There are no texts of the Abbé de Saint-Pierre that do not mention Progress either explicitly or implicitly. All his writings intend to contribute to the improvement of society and all are based on the idea that this movement of "improvement" is obligatorily imposed on his contemporaries. In his texts, the Abbé effaces his word behind that of *universal reason* (we shall return to this concept below). He only expresses the progress that it has accomplished. Speaking of this progress, the Abbé still relies, in great measure, on the problematic characteristic of the quarrel between the ancients and the moderns. The superiority of the moderns over the ancients is the point of departure of his reflection on history, and the false authority of the ancients is considered the greatest obstacle to Progress. While accepting modernity as an autonomous value, the Abbé nevertheless goes beyond the problematic of the quarrel on several important points. To him, the superiority of the moderns is not a problem but is, rather, a self-evident fact.

He does not content himself with Fontenelle's famous formula: we can equal the ancients because Nature remains identical to herself and the trees in our countryside are today as tall as they ever were. For the Abbé de Saint-Pierre, a law as much of history as of reason manifests itself in the succession of centuries, because *reason has a history*, namely that of accumulated knowledge, of new discoveries, etc. The discoveries of human reason lead naturally to the belief that, supposing that it grows from century to century, in the majority of states, unless it encounters new obstacles, the oldest centuries would have to be seen as the least enlightened; but is it an evil if it is a truth that is important to society?[46] Thus, it is not surprising that "our mediocre scholars have twenty times more knowledge than Socrates and Confucius''—it is an almost natural consequence of Progress.

The fact that this superiority of the moderns does not yet sufficiently manifest itself in all domains disturbs the Abbé and constitutes, in his eyes, a grave problem. If his century goes far beyond the ancients in the sciences, why is this not equally so in morality? The search for an answer to this question marked a turning point in his life in opening to him the double vocation of utopian and apostle of Progress. A young provincial, the Abbé de Saint-Pierre came to Paris around 1680. He was interested at first in the sciences and mathematics, while reading philosophy—Descartes, Malebranche, but certainly also Spinoza—and frequenting salons. It could be said that he followed the classic curriculum in the *republic of letters*. His friendship with Fontenelle and the reading of his first texts led him to the study of morality with the intention of making it into a true science that would contribute to the growth of happiness and the reduction of evil. But the true turning point came with his passage from morality to politics. In an autobiographical essay, the Abbé summarizes that evolution: "After different readings on the different means men take to increase their happiness and diminish their evils, he noticed that the greatest part of happiness and unhappiness came from good and bad laws. . . . It was this persuasion that determined him to apply himself henceforth to the study of government, to try to discover the means of forming wise rules and making good establishments that sufficiently engage men by their individual interest to work constantly and ardently to procure the public interest. . . . This reflection, that often came to his mind, persuaded him that *morality was not the most important science for the happiness of men, but that it was politics, or the science of government*, and that a wise law could make incomparably more men happy than a hundred good moral treatises. Thus, with the aim of becoming more useful to society, he dropped the study of morality for that of politics."[47] Does this evolution—from science, through morality, to "politics"—effectuated by the Abbé in ten years not foreshadow, in its broad outlines, the path the *philosophical spirit* will take throughout the eighteenth century? However, those who will themselves follow this "political" path will not fail to disavow the Abbé de Saint-Pierre to prevent their ideas and proposals from being confused with his "chimeras."[48] And how could it be otherwise, when the Abbé, obsessed by a feeling of consequence, pushed to the extreme the idea of the priority of politics over every other reflection? It was not enough for him to regret that politics lacked a Descartes or a Newton; he went so far as to deplore the fact that Descartes and Newton had been mistaken in orienting their genius in a bad direction. "It is a great loss for the French nation that among human knowledge, Descartes in France and, thirty years later, Newton in England, these two powerful geniuses, did not choose the two sciences that were the most important in increasing their own happiness and that of the human race, in order to go into them more thoroughly and thus to make their work more useful, to others as well as to themselves. . . . Why did they neglect to improve morality and politics and to carry these two incomparable sciences further than our moralists and politicians who have made so little progress in two thousand years compared to the progress that has been made in that time in the arts and in the other sciences? It must be that despite all the penetration and extent of their mind they didn't perceive the infinitely superior importance of the science of morals and the science of government, that is, of the science of the good and the bad, of happiness and unhappiness."[49]

Certainly, it is a "misfortune for humanity," but, in spite of his awareness of this fact, the Abbé does not reproach either Descartes or Newton for it. Nor, finally, can error be imputed to them. On the other hand, the Abbé shows his modesty. He gives himself no credit for having more advanced ideas in this regard than the greatest geniuses of the past. Do Newton and Descartes not share their negligence with respect to politics with all those of their times? Did they not learn in school that the natural sciences are the most useful and admirable? Is it not, after all, comforting that reason, through the Abbé's voice, became aware of this error so quickly? Is this not remarkable evidence that, over a very short period, human reason made enormous progress and that now we will rapidly repair the damage, make up for lost time and attack the essential problems, morality and politics? The Newtons of politics will not take long to appear.

Nature continuously produces a certain number of geniuses—of the ten thousand men who came into the world at the same time as Descartes "in the primitive inhabitants of Africa, of Asia, of America . . . there were one hundred or only ten . . . who were born with similar organs to his for the most sublime ideas of the intellect and for a facile, distinct, and durable memory." Now, "these primitive Descartes . . . remained limited to the small circle of rough knowledge" because "The reason of the human race" had not made sufficient progress in their country at that time. That explains why the other Descartes, *ours*, in a manner of speaking, devoted himself to mathematics and why the Descartes to come will involve themselves in politics and thus will insure the progress of that science and, in its wake, the beginning of a new era of the history of the human race.[50]

The golden age is not behind us, but before us—the idea and the formula were the Abbé de Saint-Pierre's before being Saint-Simon's. We are, so to speak, approaching the beginning of the golden age—this metaphor only summarizes a reasoning that attempts to be rigorously scientific and to clarify the evolution of the human race, its past and future as well as the present time, an epoch that marks a turning point. The Abbé thus recasts an old analogy that compared history to individual life and thus assigned different ages, from infancy to old age to death, to various peoples. This analogy is valuable only if a difference in dimensions is taken into account. "We can consider the human race as a composite of all nations that have been and will be on earth and assign to it diverse ages, as we assign them to Socrates, and suppose that a century is to the human race at the age of ten thousand years what a year is to a man at the age of one hundred; with this major difference that the mortal man ages and weakens in his organism and loses his wisdom, his reason and his happiness by the great number of years and by the dependence that God, by his will and a general Providence, put between the human spirit and human weakening; whereas the human race, being immortal by its perpetual and infinite succession, finds itself at the end of ten thousand years more prone to increase readily in Wisdom, in Reason, and in happiness, than if it were only four thousand years old."[51] Human history seen from this point of view is the history of progress, linear, indefinite, and calculable. This is demonstrated by "history, philosophy, and experience," which teach us that "men began really by ignorance of the arts and by being, consequently, in poverty and misery." The progress that they have accomplished in history is demonstrated and measured by the "augmentation of important truths that have been newly demonstrated or newly noticed by our experiences which are the equivalent of practical demonstrations." And there is no doubt on this point: the progress in all domains is immense. One has only to compare "the portion of the human race that is the most civilized and the most enlightened of the age of Plato and Aristotle," that is, Athens, with the "most enlightened Nations of this century," that is, France and England and, in particular, with "the portion" that lives in the capitals. If one compares, for instance, the political and moral works of Aristotle and Plato with those of Bodin or Bacon, it is obvious that "Bodin's *Republic* is far superior to Plato's *Republic* . . . because Bodin benefited from what Plato taught him, he benefited from the knowledge and the experiences of those who followed him, as well as from his own reflections."[52] Two consequences are drawn from these observations—one that concerns the past and the other having to do with the future. It is a grave error to think that the human race is becoming increasingly degraded. On the contrary, the "universal Reason of the human race" is only in its infancy and the same is true for happiness. Therefore it is necessary to turn the traditional schema—situating "the golden age" at the beginning of history—upside down. That is merely the "iron age," the era of war, of each against the others (the Abbé had read Hobbes). Among the most civilized nations, the age that succeeded this one was the *bronze age*, that is, "a less rough enforcement of law and order, a greater number of good laws and the beginning of the arts that are most necessary to avoid the inconveniences of the seasons and to diminish life's needs." At the present time, Europe is in the process of living the *silver age*, an era "still partially attached to the bronze age," but which, on the other hand, *already heralds the golden age*. Wars, which always cause devastation; the defects of institutions; the prejudices that still hold sway over minds—all of that has to do with the *bronze age*. But, this *enlightened era* has seen an unprecedented acceleration of progress. In order to definitively enter the *golden age* we need only "some wise reigns in our European States, for once Europe has arrived at this golden age, at this sort of Paradise on earth, it will shortly bring into it all the other peoples whose only interest is, as is ours, to diminish their ills and augment their good in this life. . . . Such will be the admirable effects of the new plan of Government that the Kings and Republics can easily implement."[53] Of course, obstacles to the progress of wisdom and happiness exist. Their existence explains why the human race took so long to follow this road, why it stopped from time to time, or even fell back. The major obstacles are civil wars and wars between states; superstition, that which puts its trust in supposedly miraculous revelations and that which bows down to the ancients in the belief that our ancestors were wiser than we are; finally, the fear of "those who govern the States" that moral and political progress can bring their power into question. However, the obstacles cannot definitively stop progress; in history, "natural causes" that increase reason are always at work. The remarkable acceleration of progress during this last century is due to the action of causes that the Abbé carefully systematizes. The growth of commerce and industry produces more wealth, from which it follows that an increased number of people have the leisure to think, to write, and to read; the growth of the sciences teaches them to reason more soundly, frees minds from the authority of the ancients, and contributes to the development of the practical arts; the invention of printing as well as the establishment of the academies and of lectures on the sciences "have made discoveries more communicable," thus contributing to the improvement of education; finally, the growth of cities, particularly the large capitals that "can never be too big or too populated," played the greatest civilizing role because the cities form the privileged place for communication among men and for the exchange of ideas.[54] As more obstacles are removed, as these factors will all act more and more simultaneously, the more progress will be accomplished and the more rapidly people will advance along the path of wisdom and happiness. "The progress of human reason can never be too great. . . ."

Thus a schema of a "system of progress," if not of a theory of history-progress, with its essential elements, is set in place.

The utopia would seem to integrate itself perfectly into this system in the sense that it appears as the inevitable result and culmination of a historical process. However, things present themselves differently if one does not dissociate the ideas from their context and from the word that gives them body. Certainly the Abbé de Saint-Pierre marries the utopia to history, but in such a way that discourse on history can only be based on utopian proposals. The history-progress is only posited in terms of a utopian proposal. It is almost as though it is still a "chimerical proposal" and that is how the Abbé's contemporaries will classify it, with the good Abbé's other proposals for the *pédiposte*, the reform of spelling, etc. In this sense, as we have said, the Abbé seems rather a latecomer than a precursor. To better explain what we mean, let us take an example. Let us study one of the Abbé's texts, as it was really written and published.

Let us belatedly admit it: up to this point, in all our quotations we have betrayed the good Abbé because we have not respected the *letter* of his texts. We transcribed them and the effect of this transcriptions nullifies an entire dimension of the text. The transcription reduced the text to the ideas it conveys; whereas any discourse and, hence, any text is historically and socially at once richer and poorer than the "pure ideas" that can be elicited from it. The writings of the Abbé de Saint-Pierre are a particularly odd and even picturesque example of this play of opposites and complements between ideas and writing, which is at work in any text. Let us, then, quote some lines on progress as they were written.

> Causes naturéles qui ont contribué à augmenter la Sajesse, la Raison et le Bonheur du janre humain depuis cent cinquante ans, malgré les guerres: l'augmantasion du comerse maritime a produit plus de richesse; car les richesses donnent du loizir et multiplient les auteurs et les lecteurs. . . . L'augmantasion de l'étude des Mathématiques et de la Fyzique dans les Coleges nous a anseigné à raisoner plus juste. . . . L'augmantasion de l'art de l'imprimérie a randu les découvertes plus cominicables et fait beaucoup plus de savans.[55]

> Natural causes that contributed to the increase of the Wisdom, Reason and Happiness of the human race for 150 years, despite wars: the increase of maritime commerce produced more wealth; for wealth provides leisure and multiplies authors and readers. . . . The increasing study of Mathematics and Physics in schools taught us to reason more soundly. . . . The advances in the art of printing made discoveries more communicable and led to many more scholars.

The Abbé expounds his ideas, making use of his new spelling. His proposal to reform spelling was supposed to make it more rational by making it more phonetic. The new spelling, freed from the authority of the ancients and from traditional rules, was to be simpler, easier to learn. The new way of writing would thus become at the same time a manifestation of, and an important factor in, progress. To accelerate the implantation of this improved spelling and to demonstrate its utility, the good Abbé both writes his own texts and has them printed using his new system. It is easy to see that in transcribing the Abbé's texts we disfigured both the discourse and the message. In fact, we substituted another *narrator* for *the one who speaks*. The one who speaks in the original texts announces himself and establishes himself in his discourse as a *maker of proposals*. His spelling invites and engages the reader to participate henceforth in an *alternative*, a *different* writing and discourse, opposed by their perfect rationality to the absurd ones that are dominant, justified only by prejudices. By the very manner in which history-progress is spoken of in this text, it shows itself to be closely bound up with an overall proposal for improvement which orders the discourse in its entirety. The new spelling gives a hint, partial though it may be, in the present, of the epoch that must inevitably arrive after some centuries when "la Raison Humaine Universelle aura pris un tel acroissemant qu'excepté les petits anfants tous les hommes . . . seront conduits, non seulemant par raisonemant mais ancore par la coutume, par la mode et avec plaisir à la pratique journalière de la Raison et seront tous par conséquant beaucoup plus heureux de cette vie qu'ils ne sont présantement. . . ." ("Universal Human Reason will have so increased that except for small children, all men . . . will be led not only by reasoning but by custom, by the prevailing fashion, and with pleasure, to the daily practice of Reason and consequently will all be much happier with this life than they are at present.")

Of course, all this is just one more of the Abbé's "oddities." However, this affair of the new spelling only extends to the point of caricature an approach that is distinctive of the Abbé when he begins to write history. For the originality of his historical works is due to his attempt to join the utopia and the idea of progress in a historical narrative. This ends in a failure that is most revealing of the difficulties such an enterprise faced at the time. The Abbé was not the only one to encounter them—all he does is bring them to the fore.

Among the historical works of the Abbé de Saint-Pierre, the *Annales Politiques* are probably the most noteworthy. Published in 1757, posthumously, the book met with a certain notoriety (three editions in ten years).[56] The *Annales* focus on nearly an entire century (1658–1740) and propose to the reader an "immediate history," one of burning political and ideological topicality. Most striking in the book are the severe judgments of the reign of Louis XIV, judgments that contrast greatly with those the reader found in Voltaire's *Siècle de Louis XIV*. "Although there is no comparison," said Grimm, "between the Abbé de Saint-Pierre's slow, calm good sense and Voltaire's genius, I would not hesitate to give the preference to his *Annales* over the *Siècle de Louis XIV*. In the latter I see almost throughout only a panegyrist who is all the more dangerous for being seductive and who praises as beautiful and great many actions that a refined philosophy scorns and condemns."[57]

In fact, the Abbé remained faithful to the ideas that had cost him his seat at the Académie. In the *Annales*, he gives himself up to a systematic critique of the king and of his politics and he does not mince words in his conclusions. "The fact that poets, orators, poor historians and subjects of Louis XIV during his reign propose him to posterity as a model of a perfect king is very natural. But read, after his death, this precious monument, this memoir of the late M. Desmarets, and one will then judge if the benefits he procured for his subjects during his seventy-two year reign much surpassed the ills he caused them. Then one will judge if peoples had great cause to regret him and, consequently, if he is a model of a perfect king. One can indeed, in truth, give him the nickname Louis the Powerful, Louis the Fearsome (for none of his predecessors was so powerful or made himself so feared). But the least clever will never give him the nickname of Louis the Great and will never confuse great power with true greatness. . . . The fact is that this great power, unless it is used to procure great benefits for men in general and for one's subjects and neighbors in particular, will never make a man very estimable."[58]

However the *Annales* is not a pamphlet against Louis XIV. The Abbé de Saint-Pierre intends to be a historian and he gives an account of the major events in France as well as in other countries. His value judgments on the king and his politics are an integral part of a certain historical discourse that intends to be both objective and didactic. Actually, the Abbé follows the leading ideas of "critical and philosophical" historiography. Contrary to traditional historiography, focused on famous men, wars, battles, philosophical *history* must be concerned particularly with the "morals" of a nation, its institutions, its public felicity. In basing his work on documents, evidence, or even on personal recollections, the historian must beware of any flattery and elicit moral truths from history. It is in this sense above all that history can be useful—in teaching enlightened politics and morality, in linking maxims with facts, in teaching healthy philosophy by examples (as Bolingbroke, the Abbé de Saint-Pierre's friend, put it).

It is useful, then, only because it is didactic—it teaches a morality and a politics for the use of all its readers "in order to make them more useful to the country." But this teaching is particularly addressed to princes, to those charged with political responsibility. History offers them models of "true greatness" to imitate, but it teaches them, too, to avoid the faults and errors committed in the past.[59]

For the Abbé, all these preoccupations converge in a single interrogation that was to guide the historian's enterprise, namely the one having to do with the progress accomplished by the *Raison Universelle du genre humain* in the period studied. The generations to come will study and judge the past based on their superior knowledge, and according to the contribution that a given epoch made to progress. This is also the sole valid criterion for the historian who studies his own time and it is from this ideological perspective—to bear witness to the progress accomplished and, hence, to contribute to the progress to be made—that the Abbé situates his own discourse. "Before writing" he said, "of the principal events that during my era increased or diminished the good fortune or the ill fortune of my country, I thought it to the point to give an abridged description, not only of the kingdom in the state in which it finds itself at present in 1735, but also to say something of our morals, our customs, our principal establishments, our principal rules and regulations, so that several centuries hence readers can more easily see the progress that universal reason has made in my country from our time to theirs along the road to felicity.''[60]

Thus, according to the methodology and the philosophy of history of the Abbé de Saint-Pierre, it is the idea of progress that, by clarifying events, their concatenations, and their consequences, was to ensure the unity of the historical narrative. However, in practice, it is the opposite that occurs—the narrative bursts apart, splitting itself into two opposing discourses. One is a discourse on the progress that *could have* been made if the diverse ''proposals for improvement'' had been applied; the other has to do with history as it was really made. The second situates real history outside the time of progress (or, if you will, in the time of progress *manqué*); the first situates progress outside real historical time and transfers it into the time of the utopia.

Each chapter, covering a year, reproduces the same schema with a monotony equal to the consistency of the good Abbé. Thus, first the principal events of the year in question are set out. The list is limited: the important political decisions, wars, peace treaties, events of the court, etc. Then come more or less successful ''portraits'' of the personages, as well as philosophical and moral reflections. Then, the ''reforms'' accomplished or initiated—that, perhaps, the most original part of the work—thus the important edicts of Colbert, the establishment of the Académie of sciences, the new taxes, etc., are discussed. But, in order to measure the progress accomplished, the Abbé follows up on what could and ought to be done. All of that, of course, could be found in the *proposals* of the Abbé himself. He is, then, in large part summarizing his own work—the proposal for universal peace, for improved elections, for the fixing of the rate of the *taille*, etc. It is only with these proposals that the prospect of real progress is seen in history. . . . All would have turned out otherwise, if. . . . The peace of Utrecht and that of Aix-la-Chapelle would have been durable, if the king had followed the proposal for perpetual peace; the king would have had good advisers if he had applied the ''improved system of elections.'' The reform of the Académie in 1713 would have been effective and useful if they had established an Académie that ''obliges authors to show the reader the growth of human reason in the arts and the sciences and to indicate what could be done better to further improve that same human reason. I speak about this at greater length in the proposal for improving the académies.'' Thus his proposals are expounded and they represent a third of the work, grouped in a series that parallels the events and forming a proposition of a history that is an alternative to the real history that failed. The Abbé explains the advantages of this method in which he sees an excellent argument in favor of progress. ''What more suitable way to persuade the reader to implement them (the proposals for improvement) than to make him feel that, if they had been established all this time, misfortunes wouldn't have befallen either the kings or their subjects.''[61] The good Abbé hesitates not at all to apply the same method to the furthest eras. Thus he explains that Romulus wouldn't have been put to death if he had only had the wisdom to have his senate elected according to the rules of the "improved system of election."

Looked at closely, history is only a pretext for the utopia-proposal. Despite his wish to bring the utopia closer to history, the former does not in the least appear as the great promise of the latter. It is, however, only on that condition that the idea of history-progress could rejoin and stimulate a collective mythology. In the good Abbé, progress is seen confined in an abstract and rationalistic discourse on an *alternative* history that would have been that of the realization of his marvelous proposals. Moreover, how significant is it that the Abbé de Saint-Pierre limits himself to the most traditional form of historical discourse, that of annals, which his contemporaries have more or less given up! The idea of progress does not contribute in any way to the renewing of historical discourse; as if there were a block preventing the passage from discourse *on* progress to that which organizes events into a narrative on historical evolution. Between the utopia and history, the link is not made by Progress which would orient history toward the utopia, but by the *utopian*, who judges history based on his proposals. The good Abbé only proposes the dream of a history that would be rationally managed by important government officials (chosen, of course, according to the rules of the improved system of elections) and they would implement the proposals developed by the Newtons and the Descartes of politics (meeting, of course, in an Académie of political and moral improvement).

Condorcet: Utopia as a Realization of History

L'Esquisse d'un tableau historique de l'esprit humain, a posthumous work of Condorcet, marks an important stage in the history of the utopia as well as in that of the idea of progress. It is remarkable for two reasons—first as the result of the reconciliation between the utopia and the idea of progress that had been worked up to throughout the eighteenth century, and second, as the point of departure for a specific utopian discourse wherein the utopia is spoken of solely by means of the history that engenders it. The philosophy and the idea of history expounded in the *Esquisse* are not our concern here. In our context, the vision of the ultimate epoch of history to which the progress of the human mind leads is what interests us. Three points are particularly revealing of the way in which the junction of the utopia and of the discourse on history-progress operate. The *alternative society* is situated in the *time of history* and, notably, in the future; the vision of that society is presented as a *scientific prediction*; the utopian discourse takes on a mode that could be paradoxically called *anti-utopian utopia*. Our discussions will focus on these three problems.

"It is a historical tableau of the progress of the human mind that I am attempting to sketch and not the history of the governments, of the laws, of the morals, of the mores, of the opinions that have successively occupied the globe.''[62] In announcing his enterprise Condorcet specifies what his historical procedure will be and what sense he gives to his work. ''This tableau is therefore historical as, subject to perpetual variations, it is formed by the successive observation of human societies at the different epochs they went through. It must present the order of these changes, present the influence that each instant exercises on the one that replaces it and thus show, in the modifications the human species has undergone, endlessly renewing throughout the immensity of centuries, the course it followed, the steps it took toward truth or happiness. The results that it presents will then lead to the means of assuring and accelerating new progress.''[63] Thus the historical narrative is articulated in ten epochs of which nine cover the past (which goes back to a hypothetical ''state of nature''), as well as the present, which is the time in which the narrator and his discourse are situated—that of the Revolution. (The principles of periodization are not, however, very clear and we pass over the problems their definition would pose.) On the other hand, the tenth epoch is that *of the future*, of the *future progress* of the human mind. Thus we are in the presence of a discourse that links the future to the past and the present by integrating them all into the same history.

This integration can only be accomplished by means of a whole play of correspondences between the historical discourse and its object. At most, it initiates a projection of the characteristics proper to this discourse, which intends to be *universal, homogeneous, and continuous* about its object, that is, about history and its time. Thus the different peoples and their civilizations are considered only as variations, distributions in time and space of one same and unique process of evolution which has ''the human species'' as its subject. All historical phenomena would then be able to be situated with regard to one another on the same axis which is that of ''progress'' and all would be of the same nature in the sense that they all fall under the same law, that of the improvement of man. From this point of view, making the history of the future is a plausible and justified enterprise. Basically, it is only a question of following a process analogous to that practiced in studying a people hitherto unknown or in integrating newly discovered events into a global discourse on the history of humanity. In all these cases, it is a question of finding how the same universal and constant laws of history order phenomena unknown up to that point. Moreover, the extension of the historical discourse on the future attests to the new progress accomplished by the human mind and can only accelerate its rate. With the ''prediction'' of the future, historical discourse confirms itself as ''scientific'' or, if you will, it is scientific discourse that thus affirms itself as universal. ''If man can predict the phenomena whose laws he knows with nearly total assurance; if, even when they are unknown to him, he can, based on past experience, predict the events of the future with great probability, why would the enterprise of tracing, with some verisimilitude, the tableau of the future destinies of the human species, based on the results of its history, be looked on as a chimeric pursuit? The only foundation of belief in the natural sciences is the idea that the general laws, both known and unknown, that regulate the phenomena of the universe are necessary and constant; and for what reasons would this principle be less true for the development of the intellectual and moral faculties of man than for the other operations of nature? Finally, since opinions formed based on past experience on objects of the same order are the sole rule of conduct of the wisest men, why would one forbid the philosopher to support his conjectures on that same basis, provided that he attribute to them no certitude greater than that which can be derived from the number, the constancy, and the exactitude of observation?"[64]

Let us note, in passing, the assimilation of historical discourse, notably that bearing on the history of the future, to the discourse of the natural sciences—a point to which we shall return. Let us further note reservations about the validity of such a history—it would not go beyond the level of conjecture and probability. However, this is, in truth, merely a standard clause. The assurance is "nearly total" and it would be possible to arrive at the same degree of certitude as in any other science. Certainly, Condorcet does not venture into prognostications about dates or predict where and how the events will come about. What he does describe are the general orientations of evolution, its important stages and the duration their realization would entail.

Thus, Condorcet proposed making a historical *prediction*. Yet it is easy to remark that this exposition is organized around a *vision*, around the image of an alternative society, situated in the future and contrasting with the state that humanity had known up to that point throughout all its history. The very language, nourished with a whole revolutionary rhetoric, takes on a visionary turn. "It will then come about, that moment when the sun will no longer shine on earth on any but free men, who recognize no master but their reason; when tyrants or slaves, priests and their stupid or hypocritical instruments will no longer exist except in history where attention will be paid to them only to pity their victims and their dupes, to support one another, by the horror of their excesses, in a useful vigilance, to know how to recognize and squelch, under the weight of reason, the first germs of superstition, if ever they dared to reappear."[65] Thus, the utopia is confused with "the history of the tenth epoch,"[66] and is *told* in a quasi-historical discourse. This "history-utopia" will follow three directions, which converge: the disappearance of inequality among peoples (which implies that one day the "distance between the barbarity of the African peoples and the ignorance of savages" and "the state of civilization achieved by the most enlightened and freest people, those most emancipated from prejudice, the French and the Anglo-Americans" will evaporate); the progress of equality in the same people; the moral improvement of man, the rationalization of his institutions, the consequences of which will be the disappearance of prejudice, the growth of collective happiness, and the elimination of conflicts between the individual and society.[67] It is then that the "sun will shine only on free men." We will return to the social choices implied by this vision as well as to the moral and social values it shows. Let us note particularly, for the moment, the presence of several themes with a long utopian tradition, such as, for example, perpetual peace (but whose "realization would be assured by institutions better devised than those proposals for perpetual peace that occupied the spare time and consoled the soul of some philosophers"—an allusion to, among others, the Abbé de Saint-Pierre),[68] or, again, the idea of a universal language, based on the language of the sciences, which would insure perfect communication among all men and all peoples. This perfectly rationalized society would be totally transparent to its citizens, which would necessarily cause the convergence of individual interest and the common good. Thus for this society the very notion of history would take on a new meaning—its history could not be other than that of the growing conjunction of virtue, happiness, and truth. "The further man advances toward this perfecting of peoples, the less necessary the great virtues will become to him; thus the aim of morality, of the social art must be to make them useless and not to make them useful. . . . We have seen elsewhere how the institutions directed toward this latter aim, far from being able to attain it, have only denatured man, raising him for an instant only to thrust him into a deeper abyss. Here, on the contrary, if the aim is once attained, however imperfectly, there is hope not only of a durable good, but of greater progress. . . . Men cannot become better without seeing the route of justice progressively smoothing out in front of them. It has been said: Happy are the peoples whose name makes no noise in history and often they have owed their obscurity only to the uniformity of their misfortune. One could one day say: Happy are the people among whom good actions are so common that there are no opportunities for performing great actions, and whose history no longer presents acts of heroism, because all that is honest is easy there and because the perversity that renders great sacrifices necessary is there unknown."[69]

Certainly Condorcet's utopia does not lack themes specific to it, such as, for example, the idea of making use of probability theory to secure, through a sort of mutual insurance fund, the elimination of poverty. But the true originality of this utopia does not stem from one particular theme or another. Even the themes that were traditional, if not hackneyed, were put together in a new way: they are brought together in a global image of the free, just, and happy City by means of the idea of historical progress. At all its levels, this new society is only a rendering into idea-images of history-progress and of its multiple effects. This history-progress is not reduced to abstract pronouncements on the perfectibility of humankind and is not dissipated in diverse "proposals" for reform as was the case with the Abbé de Saint-Pierre. It constitutes the pivot of the "tenth epoch" and of its history, the acceleration of the previously overly slow march of humanity on the paths of progress which are those of the growth of individual and collective happiness. The "tenth epoch" is presented neither as a dream, nor a desire, nor a "proposal" that defends its realism: the vision of the City has all of human history as well as the "constant and necessary" laws that order it as surety for its "certain hope." The unity of the historical account of which it is a part and the fact that this epoch succeeds precisely as the tenth to the preceding nine have the effect of making the past, the events that have taken place, serve, so to speak, to guarantee that these other events that have not yet occurred, but which are already shaping up, are necessarily inscribed in the march of time.

Yet the structure of this historical discourse is such that the "tenth epoch" is the condition of its unity. In other words, it is the utopia as a vision of the ultimate stage of history that guarantees the certitude of all the affirmations on progress and its laws: the "tenth epoch" is the pivot on which the entire account rests and revolves. Of course, it only intervenes at the end of the account and is only presented as the result of an induction. But it is precisely the final point that clarifies the point of departure as well as the path followed. Condorcet explicitly makes of this reference to the "final point" the principle of his historical method. "It is in arriving at this last degree of the chain that the observation of past events, like knowledge acquired through meditation, becomes truly useful. It is in arriving at this term that men can appreciate their real claims to glory or enjoy, with a sure pleasure, the progress of their reason; it is only there that the veritable perfection of the human species can be judged. This idea of relating everything to this last point is dictated by justice and reason; but while it would be tempting to see it as chimeric, it is not."[70] It is for the gaze situated in the "tenth epoch" that history becomes transparent and it is thus that the account of the past is not in search of its meaning, but becomes the pronouncement of a sense revealed by History itself. Of course, the "law of perfection" intervenes throughout the account and is referred to in order to elucidate events, to bring out what is "essential" and thus to affirm the unity of history. Nevertheless, until the eve of the "tenth epoch," until the events that render its advent inevitable, no fact takes on its true sense. If one stops reading at the eighth epoch which, in Condorcet's chronology, corresponds to the Renaissance, and all the more so if one goes further back, to the seventh and to the sixth, which are those of the Middle Ages ("that disastrous period when we will see the human spirit rapidly descend from the height to which it had risen and the ignorance that dragged on for too long afterward, here ferocity, there a refined cruelty"),[71] then in all those epochs, all is far from being decided. Despite the affirmation that the "law of perfection" infallibly rules over all history and at each of its stages the account remains hesitant, he doesn't exclude the possibility of decadence or even of a cyclical movement. But this is excluded beginning with the ninth epoch and becomes completely unthinkable in the future that it announces.

With the "tenth epoch" history will no longer experience twists and turns or accidents—every event will be only a manifestation and confirmation of the "law of progress." All ambiguity will be removed from history and this transparency that is already foreseeable sheds new light on past centuries. Condorcet draws up a whole program of renewing the study of history by taking on the leading ideas of "philosophical" historiography. Up to that point, "only the leaders had been the focus of historians' attention." Hence, what had been left in shadow had been "the most important part of the history of men . . . the most obscure, the most neglected part for which monuments offer us so little material," that is, the history of "the masses," of the "most numerous portion of each society."[72] Now, with the "tenth epoch," these "masses" are going to emerge from obscurity, to enjoy the lights and happiness and become the principal factor of progress.

Thus, the utopia of the future is the accomplishment of history and the revelation of its ultimate significance. That does not mean that history will stop, that it will not know new developments. On the contrary, it is only the beginning of a new history, of an *alternative history*. If "humankind" is not going to know an "eleventh epoch," that is not because its progress has stopped. It is only in that epoch that the indefinite character of the progress of the human spirit will fully manifest itself. The human spirit "continuously growing from century to century has no term. . . . The perfection of the order of society inevitably leading to a no lesser perfection in morality, men will continually become happier insofar as they become more enlightened. . . . Let us dare to envisage, in the immensity of the ages to follow us, a happiness and enlightenment of which we can form but a vague and indeterminate idea."[73] This *alternative history*, that of combined happiness and enlightenment, can but confirm, perpetuate, and amplify the principles and values that are at the foundation of the "tenth epoch." Humanity will no longer have to get lost, to seek its road, and to make choices. Any change will only be an improvement and continuation of what has been acquired, and never call it back into question. Once "the obstacles between man and truth have been lowered,"[74] the framework of all ulterior development is fixed—progress can engender no counter-finality, but can be only a confirmation of itself.

Thus, there is a play of rupture and continuity between the past and the future. Rupture because the very time of history changes and history will no longer know this succession "sometimes of progress, sometimes of decadence" that marked it up to that point. Continuity because "the tenth epoch" is the crowning achievement of all that has been accomplished before, and which is only a sort of "prehistory" of the human species. Now, this interplay is possible only thanks to the event which in itself combines both rupture and continuity. It is the last of history as it was experienced, but also the first and founding act of the new time opening on History. It is the *Event* that is situated at the frontier of time. The "last epoch" is that of which "the French Republic comes to mark the opening, placing its origin with so much glory among the last storms that error roused amidst its darkness, and the first rays of the calm reign of truth."[75] For Condorcet, the *Event* is the prerequisite condition for his discourse and it is there that he situates the place from which he speaks. "I have the good fortune to write in a country where no fear, no hope, no respect for national prejudices can cause any general truth to be suppressed or disguised and they are the only ones of which it might be a question in a subject that embraces humanity in its entirety. . . . The rapid movement that the French Revolution transmitted to spirits, breaking stronger chains, could not leave its weak links. . . . There is a country where philosophy can offer free and pure homage to truth . . . and it is the only one where the historical tableau of the progress of the human spirit can be traced with total independence." Condorcet envisages consecrating this exceptional and founding quality of the Revolution by introducing in the *Esquisse* a new system of dating, that is, "in relating all dates to our Republican era." That gave, for instance, the following chronolgy for the "fourth epoch": "it extends approximately from the year 2700 to the year 2100 before the French Republic and encompasses about 550 years, from Lycurgus to Aristotle."[76]

As we have said, the combination of the past and the future in a continuous historical account has, as a necessary condition, reference to science. It is because history is raised to the level of a science and uses scientific methods that the future is within its domain and not of that of dreams and desires. In other words, discourse on the past as well as on the future are only specific cases of the same scientific discourse. Condorcet insists many times on this mutation that is arrived at with his *Esquisse* and that can allow him to distinguish his vision of the future from chimeras. For him, there is no question of giving full sway to the imagination, but, rather of rigorously demonstrating, following a method which had been proven in the study of the past, that certain conditions will necessarily be brought together in the future and that, with that, new possibilities will be open to humankind, whose actualization itself becomes necessary. It is only in "examining the progress and the laws of our improvement that we can even know the extent and the term of our hopes."[77] To predict the rapid development of the sciences and their beneficial effects on social life as well as on public happiness it suffices to put oneself "in a country where general enlightenment and the knowledge of the rights of man do not allow of fear that public happiness might ever be founded on equality of ignorance and stupidity. . . . I can demand these conditions, since it is a question of the progress of the human species, freed, at least, of its grossest errors."[78]

Condorcet's procedure sometimes takes a turn that makes one think of what is nowadays known as *futurology*. This is the case, for instance, when he discusses the major orientations of future developments in the sciences or when he launches his important idea of "social mathematics": applying probability theory to demographic, economic, and similar problems.[79] And how, at present, can we not be impressed by the perspicacity and topicality of his remarks on the obstacles progress might come up against and that the combined efforts of the sciences must circumvent or eliminate? "Bringing one's attention to bear on the general economy of societies, one quickly perceives that the natural limits of their progress are those of the reproduction of the substances necessary to the needs of men, and that, among these substances, *foods and fuels are those that threaten to reach that final limit the earliest*. Means of directing fire so as to produce the same effects with less consumption would then be numbered among the discoveries to which the destinies of the human species are attached."[80]

We must not, however, be mistaken about false and anachronistic analogies. Condorcet is by no means a "futurologist" before the fact. The procedures of contemporary futurology are at opposite poles to those at work in the *Esquisse*. The contrast between the enthusiastic optimism inspiring the *Esquisse* and the pessimism marking the majority of contemporary "futurologists" is only a minor phenomenon—the fundamental contrast is on another plane. Futurology originates in the crisis proper to the kind of global vision of the future that refers to the ineluctable march of history and, in a sense, it is the expression of this crisis. Insofar as futurology seeks to establish itself as a science it refuses specifically to formulate "predictions" whose object is the evolution of "humankind" in its entirety, bearing on an indeterminate future and envisioning only a single schema of evolution, without alternative models. Condorcet did not by any means substitute science for the utopia. His originality, if not his greatness, lies elsewhere. He succeeded in joining the utopia to history in making use of a certain idea of science and of a discourse on progress which professed to be scientific. Thus, the utopia sprang from history—it became its great promise guaranteed by science. It does not seem to us to be of great interest to verify Condorcet's "predictions," to confirm his "clairvoyance" in certain cases and to point out his flaws in others. From this point of view Condorcet's case is not different from those of other utopians—his social imagination proved to be at once too rich and too poor when grappling with realities. What we find noteworthy, on the contrary, is the complex play, which could be called a play of mirrors, by which the analysis of the past and the vision of the future reciprocally supply each other with "proofs" and thus become linked in a discourse presented as scientific. Condorcet's predictions on the progress of the sciences, education, the arts, etc., as well as their social effects, finally merge with the vision of the New City, that of realized happiness. "Does the improvement of laws, of public institutions following the progress of the sciences, not have the effect of bringing together, of identifying the common interest of each man with the common interest of all? Is the aim of the social art not to destroy this apparent contradiction? And is the country whose constitution and laws conform most exactly to the wish of reason and nature not that where virtue will be easier, where temptations will be the fewest and weakest? Do the progress of civilization, of industry, without entailing either dependency or the humiliation of misery, not bring men close to that state where all will have the necessary enlightenment? Do the well-being that follows the progress that all useful arts make, in basing themselves on a sound theory, or the progress of just legislation, which is founded on the truths of the political sciences not dispose men to humanity, charitableness, and to justice? Will not what, up to this point, has always been, merely a chimera finally occur—national, kind, and pure morals, formed not of proud privations, hypocritical appearances, reservations imposed by fear of shame or religious terrors, but by freely contracted habits, inspired by nature, admitted by reason?"[81] The questions are only rhetorical and the answers can only be affirmative. With them, "proofs" accumulate that it is only by "examining the progress and laws of the improvement [of the human species] that we can know the extent or the term of our hopes."[82] The predictions thus are based on the *law* that secures the unity of history. Contrary to the chimeras, they are justified by the latter's constant and necessary character. But on the other hand it is obvious that this very law, that of the undefined improvement of the spirit and of humankind, is undemonstrable other than by its extrapolation on the future, that is, other than by the utopian vision of an *alternative society*, where the opposition between nature and society will disappear, thanks to "the social art that will fulfill its aim, that of extending to all the enjoyment of the common rights to which they are called by nature."[83] All the predictions support one another to attest to the idea of progress that can, at bottom, only be liberating. If, in the course of history, it proved, occasionally, to be oppressive, that was due only to chance incidents, to the tenacious persistence of prejudice, of fanaticism, of bad laws, etc. Thus, the *Tableau des progrès de l'esprit humain*, which presents itself as a synthesis of history, as a rigorous and scientific generalization of historical occurrences, is in fact only a *form of assimilation, as ideological as it is selective, of the past*. Actually, the continuity of history is only developed in the discourse according to a certain scale of values and concepts by means of which aspects of the past labeled "retrograde" or "marginal" are rejected. But how could this selection be justified without the underlying reference to that alternative future, where the values taken up by Progress will fully manifest themselves, without hindrance, in the harmonious and transparent City?

As we have said, the leading idea of this unitarian history is that of progress that does not engender a counter-finality. But this could not have been argued otherwise than with the vision of an *alternative history*, to which men would no longer submit, but, rather, one which is consciously made by and for themselves and which then would no longer experience all the misfortunes that had marked it throughout. Thus, the utopia is put at the service of a certain idea of history. But reciprocally this idea of history owes its vigor to the utopia whose realization it promises and for which it vouches.

In our time, when the mythology of progress is dying, it would be easy, even too easy, to retrospectively draw out the anthropological postulates, the a priori ideologies, the social choices that order the idea of progress as well as Condorcet's utopia and which are hidden by his pseudoscientific procedure. Both the utopia and the philosophy of history are based on a definition of human nature that implies its indefinite perfectibility; both adjust this amelioration to the growth of goods, of knowledge, of techniques, etc. Consequently, in the utopia, the *maximum* of this growth is confused with the *optimum* of the human condition or, if you will, this optimum is identified with the indefinite growth. This is based on another a priori, namely that of the harmony that could be said to be platonic among truth, happiness, and virtue. The accumulation of knowledge and its widest social diffusion must necessarily lead to the increase of happiness and virtue. The most enlightened men cannot but become better from those points of view, and this new man produced by history corresponds to the New City, the social and moral setting of his existence. Yet another a priori makes possible the conjunction of the utopia and history, namely the affirmation that men in their history pose only problems they are capable of resolving. Thus the history will encounter no insurmountable obstacles or impasses. The manifestation of new needs brings about a condition whereby means of satisfying them will be sought and found. "The cause that brings about the need produces at the same time the means of obtaining it."[84] (It must be noted that this idea is frequently encountered throughout the nineteenth century, in numerous social theories and philosophies of history, even in those that are opposed in their political choices and ideological options, but share faith in growth-progress; it is, in particular, vigorously affirmed by Guizot and by Marx.)

Thus history is seen as reduced to a single one of its dimensions, namely that of innovative mobility, with cumulative effects. Its inert forces are only considered secondary phenomena which will be progressively eliminated by the very march of Progress. Whence the privileged place accorded in historical discourse to times and periods of historical acceleration as well as to the events that convey them. Note that Condorcet envisages a sole model of "perfectibility," namely that which merges with the historical evolution of the western world. This model and the values it implies are thus imposed as a norm universal to any possible historical evolution and, in particular, to that which peoples who are still "barbarian" or "savage" must still undergo. Nor is there any contradiction between this "oppressive" model of progress and the courageous and humanitarian positions that Condorcet, one of the prime forces behind the *Société des Amis des Noirs*, took against slavery as well as against a certain particularly brutal colonialism.[85] Is progress not liberating and universal by its very essence, does it not promise the same radiant future to all who follow its paths?

The utopia of the *Esquisse* is perfectly concordant with the social positions of Condorcet. The city of happiness and of perfected man was to be a liberal republic, where the role of the state is limited to guaranteeing and protecting the rights of the citizens and, in particular, that of freedom of expression, and to encouraging scientific progress and assuring its diffusion thanks to a whole system of public education; a society founded on private property, keeping a certain social inequality while moderating it. This social perspective intersects with Condorcet's political options, in particular those of the Revolutionary period. His utopia, contrary to those of the Jacobins or even of the *"sans-culottes,"* of the militant popular minorities, extends, on another plane, the political conflicts of the moment. Nevertheless, there is no question here of considering these utopias as reflections of the conflicts in which they participate. One might even say the opposite: at least certain political options were possible only because they were made according to the respective utopias, because the opposing forces saw politics and power as instruments with which to establish the New City once and for all. That is particularly valuable for Condorcet who was merely a mediocre politician.

What, then, finally, remains of the scientific character of this utopian discourse so vigorously opposed to "chimeras"? Of course, strictly speaking, the utopia and the idea of progress combined neither demonstrate nor prove anything. Condorcet's utopia is only "scientific" in the sense that it accords a privileged role to the sciences as well as to their diffusion in the formation of the new man and in the constitution of the City of the future. It is "scientific," too, in the sense that it draws on a universal science of man, a sort of anthropology that would found the laws that base the evolution of man on human nature, laws valuable for the past as well as the future.

But Condorcet's utopia is "scientific" in still another sense, one whose future proved richer. If, indeed, this utopia "announces the future," that is only insofar as it gives evidence of a new mode of utopian discourse, which is making a way for itself. The term "anti-utopian utopia" would, perhaps, be most suitable to it.[86] The utopia refuses to be an imaginary game or the expression of desires and expectations; nor does it have recourse either to an ought-to-be or to the precepts of abstract and supertemporal reason. Of course, one frequently heard utopians proclaim the realism of the proposals—this was the case, for example, with the Abbé de Saint-Pierre or Morelly. Nevertheless, in this new mode of utopian discourse it is a question of something other than the *possible* realization of a dream: it is the very practice of social dreams that is refused. The "anti-utopian utopia" takes on several traditional utopian themes and, in particular, that of a history that would no longer be the effect of chance and would never deviate from the paths traced by the New City. But these themes and images are incorporated into a universal discourse on history, an object of science, a discourse, then, that by its very structure tolerates them only in making them travesties of history and science, in formulating them as non-dreams.

This paradigm dominates by far the most important part of the utopias of the nineteenth century. It is at work in Saint-Simon and the Saint-Simonians, in Fourier and Comte, and also in Marx and several Marxists. Marx's work might even be said to be a borderline case. It is well known how careful Marx and Engels were not to offer too elaborate an image of the communist society of the future, and how insistent they were on the fact that that society was to be the rational and scientific work of future generations and not that of social visionaries. Yet Marx's work conveys a whole vision of that society; most often it is only just below a historical, economic, and political discourse—but more often than one might think, it explodes, so to speak, at the surface and then reveals itself to be rich in idea-images.[87] Moreover, does Engels not draw up the universal image of the New City, where "the government of people makes way for the administration of things," where "the State is not abolished, but dies out," where "men become the masters of their own socialization," where "the leap of humanity from the reign of necessity into the reign of liberty" takes place, etc.? All of these are classical utopian themes advanced in the text in which it is "demonstrated" that socialism is no longer a utopian but a scientific object, that it is no longer a dream but a historical necessity.[88]

We have not emphasized this new paradigm making its way through Condorcet's texts. It is nevertheless noteworthy that in his work the anti-utopian utopia keeps its links with the traditional modes of utopian discourse, particularly with that of the proposal for perfect legislation, with a reference to an ideal country. Thus, among the works preliminary to the *Esquisse* is found a fragment titled *Sur l'Atlantide, ou efforts combinés de l'espèce humaine pour le progrés des sciences*, which presents a detailed proposal for a sort of international Academy of sciences, a "general meeting of the scientists of the world in a universal republic of sciences, the only one for which the proposal, like its utility, is not a puerile illusion."[89] Condorcet refers explicitly to Bacon's *New Atlantis*, of course, but one is equally struck by the affinities with a similar proposal of the Abbé de Saint-Pierre. The author of the *Esquisse*, however, stresses the differences between his project and the "chimeras" that inspired it. "This is," he concluded, after having given a résumé of Bacon's ideas, "what a creative spirit dares to conceive of during an age still covered with the darkness of a superstitious ignorance, what for a long time seemed merely a philosophical dream, what the rapid progress of both societies and enlightenment today give hope of being realized by future generations and, perhaps, by ourselves." In fact, to imagine this realized "chimera," one has but to put oneself "in a country where general enlightenment and the knowledge of the rights of man do not allow of fear that public happiness might ever be founded on equality of ignorance and stupidity."

And the existence of such a state can reasonably be supposed, not as a dream, but as a hypothesis with sufficient basis, "since it is a question of the progress of the human species freed at least of its grossest errors."[90] Condorcet's expositions, which we have only rapidly summarized, point up both the continuity and the rupture between the two modes of utopian discourse. Nothing is more typical of the traditional utopian enterprise than the reference to an ideal country as a condition for the realization of a rigorously rational proposal of a perfect institution. But it is progress—both that already made and that to be accomplished—that is charged with making this country come about and hence, with transforming a dream, a "chimera," first into a hypothesis and, then, into reality. All things considered, it is the time of history, the producer of innovations, richer and richer in new potentialities, that takes on itself, so to speak, the task of inscribing the dreams and rational hopes in reality.

A striking correspondence between this philosophical idea of the time of history and the lived experience is found in Condorcet's work. The author of the *Esquisse* is particularly sensitive to the utopian potentials of the history in which he participates. It could be said that he only lives his time by giving it utopian extensions. That was already striking at the time of his collaboration with Turgot. Turgot's personality, as well as his ideas and, notably, the idea of conceiving of universal history as continuous progress, profoundly marked Condorcet. But when Turgot, at the time he was in office, made Condorcet his close collaborator, the opposition between the two became obvious. For Turgot, politics has its own exigencies, and, as he says in a remarkable phrase, it is *the art of predicting the present*. Thus, he considers that the "philosopher politician" can only modernize his country and advance progress by partial and prudent reforms (and it is well known how audacious this prudence was). Condorcet, on the other hand, is impatient. For him, power is only an instrument in the service of the utopia and politics merely an opportunity to open the present to the future of progress.[91] This propensity for the utopia becomes more intensified during the Revolutionary period and the *Esquisse* is the ultimate evidence of this. The Revolution and its "rapid march" bring definitive proof that the passage from a "philosophical dream" to reality is through historical change. This certitude also merges with and expresses the experience and hopes of Condorcet-the-politician or rather Condorcet-the-legislator, the author of the proposal of the Constitution and especially of the *Mémoires sur l'Instruction Publique*. It is noteworthy that entire pages of these *Mémoires* anticipate the *Esquisse*. Condorcet conceives of his proposal for a "system of public education" in relation to the future—he made it to "prepare nations for the changes that time must bring."[92] Many of the ideas that proliferated in pre-Revolutionary utopias and that had become commonplace are found once again in his proposal. However, this proposal fits into history in another way: the word intends to be the founding word of a new reality. The utopia is enriched by a political experience coupled with illusions; the proposal, once it is put into words, has every chance of becoming actuality. Would a favorable vote not transform it into an institution? Revolutionary political practice makes history receptive to the most daring ideas. The future perfected man in the New City is still to be accomplished—but is already emerging and history, propelled by the Revolution, can only tend in that direction, and at an ever-accelerated pace. "Can one not sense what immense distance separates us from the term of perfection that we already perceive in the distance, whose genius smoothed out the route it opened to us and toward which its indefatigable activity draws us, while an even vaster space must disclose itself to the eyes of our nephews? Is it possible not be struck, as well, both by all that remains to be destroyed and by all that a future, however imminent, offers our hopes?"[93]

The *Esquisse* also expresses another aspect of the lived experience of the Revolution, the encounter between history and the utopia. It is a dramatic text whose rhetorical style, with its overly elegant and elaborate phrases, barely conceals the haste and tension with which Condorcet wrote it. Condemned along with the Girondinist *députés*, seeking a safe hiding place, abandoned by many of his friends, Condorcet writes hurriedly, fearing that the guillotine will prevent him from finishing his work. The text is marked by current events; it is also a political text not lacking in polemical anti-Jacobin accents and one in which Condorcet attempts to justify his own positions.[94] But the most important evidence and the most revelatory testimony about the time of the Revolution in the *Esquisse* is not in the topical polemics. It teaches how the utopia, assimilated as an innermost truth, allows of *living* the Revolution, as the herald of the great promise of History. That does not, of course, suffice for *surviving* the Revolution, as the fate of the book, which will only be published posthumously, attests. However, it is by honoring history with the utopia as with its ultimate meaning, that Condorcet gives meaning, as well, to his own existence grappling with the realities of history. "How much," Condorcet wrote at the end of his vision of the *tenth epoch*, "this tableau of humanity, freed from all its chains, removed from the influence of chance, as from the authority of the enemies of its progress, and proceeding with a firm and sure step on the road of truth, virtue, and happiness, presents the philosopher with a spectacle that consoles him for the errors, the crimes, the injustices still sullying the earth and of which he is often the victim! It is in the contemplation of this tableau that he is repaid for his efforts toward the progress of reason, toward the defense of liberty. He then dares to link it to the eternal chain of human destinies; it is there that he finds the true reward for virtue, the pleasure of having created something good and durable, that fatality will no longer destroy by a disastrous compensation, by bringing back prejudice and slavery. This contemplation is for him an asylum, where the memory of his persecutors cannot pursue him."[95]

By the drama it conceals as well as by the originality of its ideas, the *Esquisse* is an exceptional and personal work. But, on the other hand, it fits into a broader context and is part of a longer series; it reveals the utopian dimension of the Revolutionary mentality and, in particular, the utopian dimension of Revolutionary discourse on history.

3
"Time Opens a New Book to History . . .": Utopia and the Revolutionary Calendar

During the Revolutionary era, the exchange between the lived realities and utopias, representations of a New City, became particularly intense.[96] We are barely aware of the influence of the imaginary on the political projects of the era and particularly of the utopian dimension of Revolutionary mentalities. Social and political motives merge with and interpenetrate dreams, and representations of the sought moral and social ideal. Of course, too frequently that does not go beyond the level of the word—of discourse, of proposals, of reports, or even of decrees which there is not even the attempt to carry out. But does this avalanche of words structured by Revolutionary rhetoric not express in its own way an important aspect both of the realities and of Revolutionary illusions and myths? Does it not express as well the lived experience of those who, for the first time, have access to discourse on society as a whole, on power, politics, etc., as well as their faith in the power of the true word, the foundation of reality? And was this faith not a product of the Revolutionary experience itself?

The reform of the calendar is particularly revealing of the Revolutionary attitudes toward the time of history bound up with the utopian élan. Indeed in the proposals for a Revolutionary calendar two discourses—on the New City and on history—merge into one. The representations of the City, giving material form forever to the Revolutionary ideals, occur as a prerequisite both to discourse on history and to that on temporality in general. It is almost as though the utopia were launching out to conquer time.

Let us recall, first of all, and only briefly, the important stages of the reform. At the time the Republic was proclaimed, on 22 September 1792, a decree of the Convention established that henceforth all public bills and certificates would be dated "year I of the French Republic." Another decree, of 2

January 1793, stipulated that the year II of the Republic would begin 1 January 1793. In the meantime, the Comité d'Instruction publique was charged with preparing the revision of the calendar and with "presenting, as soon as possible, a proposal on the advantages to France of the accord of its Republican era with the common era." As early as the end of 1792, a working group, composed of Romme, Dupuis, and Ferry, in collaboration with Lagrange and Monge, was set up to prepare this project. Gilbert Romme presented it to the Comité d'Instruction publique on 14 September 1793; on 20 September, on behalf of the Comité, he reported on it to the Convention. A vote was not taken on it until 5 October and put into effect beginning the following day. However, the Convention only adopted the principles; it did not rule on the naming of days and months and sent this question back to the Comité. A committee composed of Chenier, David, Fabre d'Englantine, and Romme discussed several proposals and finally, three weeks later, Fabre d'Englantine presented a proposition to the Convention which this time accepted it forthwith. The Republican calendar remained in effect for twelve years, two months, and twenty-seven days, until 1 January 1806, the date when Napoleon definitively abolished it (the coronation of the Emperor is nevertheless dated according to . . . the Revolutionary calendar, 11 frimaire of the year XII). During this entire period, these principles remained unchanged; the modifications apply to the system of "Republican festivals." In germinal of the year X, an article of the law regarding the reorganization of religions made Sunday once again the day of rest for civil servants. The ruin of the calendar was consummated 15 fructidor of the year XII when the Senate adopted, without discussion, the reestablishment of the Gregorian calendar.

It is not our intention to go further, here, into the rather tortuous history of this reform. Aulard, and more recently Cobb, stressed the audacity of the enterprise. It "was truly of great importance to the Revolutionaries for there is nothing more Revolutionary than wanting to change mores and habits." In that sense, the new calendar was "the most sensational innovation of the whole Revolutionary period," since it aimed particularly at "profoundly changing the personal life of all Frenchmen and Frenchwomen."[97] We know that the reform comes within political and ideological contexts as diverse as they were complex: the rise of the Jacobins and the Terror; the dechristianization (or, to use the formula of Cobb and Plongeron, the dechristianizations) movement and the accompanying debate on religion; the reform of weights and measures issued in conjunction with socioeconomic needs and the will to imbue the totality of social life with a rationality that would make it transparent to itself; the most audacious proposals for a new system of public education, and so forth. We will return to some of these points but it must be noted that the reform, as well as the debate it provoked, become the place for the conjunction and crystallization of diffuse ideas and attitudes. The feeling of having entered an exceptional era links up with the determination to make this turning point irreversible; the will to take over time intersects that of radically transforming the collective ways of living time. Daily and continuously, time must reveal only its *true meaning*, that is, that of the time of the New City. Thus, beyond diverse, if not divergent, proposals, a fundamental convergence is to be seen—time is thought and imagined in relation to the moral and social values that the Revolutionary City wants to install permanently in history. Of course, these utopian representations and images are often imprecise; references to the same values and key ideas often hid the divergences between political and ideological orientations. If the reform of the calendar was imposed as a historical imperative, it was precisely because the City founded on Revolutionary values already was and would become even more *different* than all those that had existed in history. With the new man created by the Revolution, a new era was established. In the debate about the calendar both history and the utopia are the indirect objects of a discourse—only spoken about when something else was brought up. But is this kind of evidence not invaluable for the study of mentalities, and, in particular, of attitudes toward history?

Gilbert Romme, one of the architects of the calendar, found, using Revolutionary rhetoric, the strongest formula for expressing the spirit of reform: "The Revolution retempered the souls of the French; it formed them daily according to Republican virtues. *Time opens a new book to history, and in its new march, majestic and simple like equality, it must engrave with a new tool the annals of regenerated France.*"[98] But what is this "new book" of history? And what will "time" inscribe in it?

The word "new," reiterated forcefully and insistently, expressed the major preoccupation and the leading idea of the reform. The latter must mark a *rupture* with history as it has been up to that point and solemnly affirm the *irreversibility* of that rupture. The old calendar and its nomenclature are only the expression of history as it was lived, or rather, suffered, before the Revolution. "The common era was born among an ignorant and credulous people and in the midst of the troubles that preceded the fall of the Roman empire. During eighteen centuries it served to fix the duration of the progress of fanaticism, the degradation of nations, the scandalous triumph of pride, and vice, and stupidity, the persecutions and the disgust to which virtue, talent, and philosophy were subjected under cruel despots, or that were practiced in their name. . . . The common era was that of cruelty, of lies, of perfidy, and slavery; it ended with royalty, the source of all our evils. . . . The [old] nomenclature is a monument of servitude and ignorance to which peoples have successively added the mark of their degradation."[99]

Thus is it necessary to oppose to this "monument of servitude" a system that would express justice and above all equality. A new system, as rational in its principles as in its symbols, must be opposed to the old calendar, as irrational and imbued with prejudice as the time of history whose march it fixed. The rationality and transparency sought, while attesting to the advent of a new history, that of free peoples, had inevitably to rejoin nature itself—the time of the heavenly bodies and the succession of seasons. Is the fact that the very day of the abolition of royalty and of the establishment of the Republic fell on the day of the equinox not a symbol of reconciliation between nature and history? It is a happy coincidence, indeed; yet how could one not be astonished at this "too striking and perhaps unique accord in the annals of the world, among the movements of the heavens, the seasons, the old traditions, and the course of events offered by the Revolution? Revolutionary affectivity and language were too sensitive to symbols, to "speaking images," for imaginations not to be struck by this double beginning in which regenerated nature joins with renewed history. The theme is therefore widely exploited. When Romme speaks of it, the rhetoric in search of a "language of signs" that would directly touch "hearts" seems to orient him and carry him toward a double mystique, of nature and of history at the same time. "On 21 September 1792, the last day of the monarchy and which is to be the last of the common era, the representatives of the French people, meeting in a national Convention, opened their session and proclaimed the abolition of the royalty. On 22 September, this decree was proclaimed in Paris; and the same day at 9:18:30 A.M., the sun reached the true equinox, entering the sign of Libra. Thus, the equality of days and nights was marked in the sky at the very moment when civil and moral equality were proclaimed by the representatives of the French populace as the sacred foundation of the new government. Thus the sun cast light on the two poles at the same time and then, successively, on the entire globe the very day when, for the first time, the torch of liberty, which is one day to cast light on the human race, shone, in all its purity, on the French nation. Thus the sun passed from one hemisphere to another the very day when the populace, triumphing over the oppression of the kings, passed from the monarchic government to the Republican government. The French were entirely restored to themselves during this propitious season when the earth, made fruitful by the influences of the heavens as well as by labor, lavishly gives her gifts, magnificently repaying the industrious man for his cares, his fatigue, and his labor. . . . This combination of circumstances imprints *a sacred character on this epoch*, one of the most distinguished in our Revolutionary annals and one which will doubtless be one of the most famous in the festivals of future generations."[100]

The will to break with the past and the profound feeling that this rupture is possible only thanks to the "souls retempered" by the Revolution intersects with the desire to affirm the present and its élan toward the future. The reform intends to be complete—it is not enough to begin counting time beginning with the first year and first day of the Republic. Of course, it is obvious that "the years when the kings oppressed us can no longer be counted as a time when we lived."[101] Yet it is necessary to go further and set up a new system which would be the expression of the very spirit of the New City. Now, this New City claims to be educational, and intends to transmit moral and civic discourse continuously. The calendar is considered the privileged, quasi-unique instrument for the transmission of this discourse. It alone can bring it to all the citizens every day or even every hour. A whole "political anthropology" and particularly a whole theory of the imagination and its social functions intervenes in the debate about the calendar. In his report, Fabre d'Eglantine emphasizes the "influence of images on human intelligence" and his argument is inspired by a certain vague sensualism as well as, or even particularly, by Rousseau's reflections on the role that the imagination and the "forceful language of signs" have to play in the City.[102] "We conceive of nothing except by images; in the most abstract analysis, in the most metaphysical combination, our understanding can apprehend only through images, our memory only leans, only rests, on images." Even without entering "into metaphysical analyses . . . the doctrine and the experience of priests" present striking examples of this "ascendancy of images." "Long familiarity with the Gregorian calendar has filled the memory of the populace with the considerable number of images which it has long revered and which are still today the source of its religious errors." Thus it is necessary to draw lessons from this. If it is desired that "the method and the whole of the new calendar penetrate easily into the understanding of the populace and engrave themselves rapidly into its memory, "it is necessary *to seize people's imaginations and govern them*." In addition to this "anthropological" argument, Fabre d'Eglantine uses another, more sociological one: is the almanac not the most read and the most ordinary book of the common people?[103]

Thus, with the new calendar, time will be *secularized* at least in the sense that it will be rid of all the "fantastic objects" that are the saints and patrons. "To govern the imagination" is to reorient it, to turn it toward other objects. That must be done daily but also and especially on days of festival, those times strong in collective affectivity and sensitivity. The debate on the calendar inevitably interferes with the one on Republican festivals since it is the new calendar that was to define a framework for the "system of celebrations."[104] First of all by eliminating the old holidays and festivals and, particularly, *Sundays*. This ideological preoccupation, interwoven with dechristianization, was coupled with another, more down to earth one: to diminish the number of public holidays and increase working days both for the citizens and for the country.[105] But dechristianizing time was only the negative and destructive part of the enterprise. What they sought to install with the new calendar was a *speaking time*, charged with images and symbols which were linked together in moral and social discourse.

For the architects of the reform, that harmonized perfectly with another objective: to promote a time that would be, so to speak, "neutral," so that the measure of its length would be the most "natural" and, hence, the most rational and scientific one. The two directions of the reform—making time "neutral" and charging it with symbolism—proved to be complementary. Indeed, by its "neutral" and "scientific" character did time not take on a whole set of values? Freed from "prejudice," did time not become transparent to reason, to rationality, and to the simplicity of nature? "Old" time would contribute to the diffusion and the domination of fanaticism and tyranny. Ought not the new time to radiate the universal principles of reason, that rationality with which all dimensions of life would henceforth and forever be imbued? And was this rationality not necessarily inextricably bound up with the principles of liberty and equality?

The reform of the calendar came within the scope of a far-reaching venture of rationalization that was to affect the totality of social life. It had been conceived, in particular, as the extension and culmination of the reform of weights and measures and had been inspired by the same principles as the latter. "You have undertaken," said Romme to the members of the Convention, "one of the operations that are most important to the progress of human arts and minds and one that could only be successful in a time of Revolution: that is to get rid of the diversity, incoherence, and inaccuracy of weights and measures, which constantly hamper industry and commerce and to take, in the measurement of the earth itself, the unique and invariable pattern of all new measurements. Arts and history, for which time is a necessary element or instrument, also ask of you new measurements of the duration of time which would similarly be freed from the errors which credulity and a superstitious routine have transmitted to us from centuries of ignorance."[106] Thus, similar preoccupations are found in the ideological justifications of these two reforms: simplicity and universality (the latter went along very well with a nationalism tinged with Jacobinism), the idea of conformity to nature and, hence, to science.[107] For some, such as Condorcet, Lequinio, and Cloots, the two reforms already portended a third, even more important one, which would abolish differences in languages. Would a universal language, rid of the irrationalities of individual languages, not impose itself as the extension and "natural" consequence of the reforms that had just changed secular ways of measuring and, hence, of living space and time? Moreover, in combating patois (accused of being "instruments of counter-Revolution and of federalism") did the Republic not do the same thing it accomplished by suppressing seigniorial measurements and patronal festivals?

The ideological relationship between the two reforms was strongly felt at the time (the Convention decree of 18 germinal year III calls the metric system "the *Republican* system of measurements," by analogy to the calendar).[108] Both are inspired by similar hopes for their social effects. It was expected that they would initiate the people into the sciences and morality, transform hearts, minds, and souls—and do all of that very rapidly. Moreover, the ideology is heavily weighted and the utopian component is stronger in the reform of the calendar than it is in that of measurements. In fact, contrary to the case with measurements, the Republican calendar was only most minimally based on economic reasons. As we have seen, Romme, while establishing a connection between the two, was quite aware of this difference. The former weights and measures, he insisted, "hampered industry and commerce"; it was only "the arts and history" that called for the new calendar. . . .

The rationality of the new calendar rested on two principles. First, "to make the Republican year conform to heavenly movements," and, second, "to measure time by more exact and more symmetrical calculations," by applying the decimal system most broadly.[109] Thus, since "reason demands that we follow nature rather than drag ourselves servilely along the erroneous trail of our predecessors, the year "will begin in future at midnight, the day of the true autumnal equinox for the Paris observatory."[110] We have already brought out the symbolic value of that date. The year is composed of twelve months of thirty days each instead of being divided "into unequal months of twenty-eight, thirty, and thirty-one days." The last five days of the year form a special "corpus," to whose use we shall return below. Every four years, a day would be added to the end of the year, starting with the third one of the Republic, "as many as necessary so that the Republican year will conform to heavenly movements."[111] The months are divided into three equal parts, of ten days each, instead of weeks which "did not exactly divide either the months or the year or the lunar months." The use of the decimal system is carried even further. The former division into hours and minutes was irrational and "made calculation difficult." Henceforth, the day will be divided into ten hours, each hour divided into *tenths*, and each *tenth* into *hundredths*.

"Thus, the year will be composed of 12 months and 5 days
  or of 36 and a half periods of ten days [*décades*]
  or of 365 days
  or 3650 hours
  or 36,500 tenths of hours
  or 365,000 hundredths of hours."[112]

The above table points out the harmony, the clarity, and the symmetry of the new system, as well as the system of equality governing it. The "Instruction sur le calendrier" stresses what is implicit in it as well as its practical value. Thus, one can "easily know the day of the moon, when one knows it is the first of the year." There is nothing simpler. Each lunar month is approximately twenty-nine and a half days; that is, half a day less than the Republican month. And, at the beginning of the third year, the moon was twenty-seven days old. Thus, one has only to "add to this number as many half-days as have passed in the month, and then what day of the month it is; then subtract twenty-nine and a half days and you will have the day of the moon."[113] The correspondences among the new hours and the old are a bit complicated, but not too difficult to remember. Each hour of the new division is the equivalent of two hours and twenty-four minutes of the old; two-tenths are the equivalent of fifty-seven minutes, thirty-six seconds, or one old hour, less two minutes and twenty-four seconds; two-and-a-half-tenths are exactly six old hours, etc. A brave and enthusiastic Genevan citizen presented the Comité d'Instruction publique with an ingenious watch, with two dials, and which allowed one to pass rapidly from one system to the other (an invention that was all the more opportune as Genevan watchmaking was in a serious slump at the time).[114] The architects of the reform, as well as the members of the Convention, were nevertheless aware that the change to a decimal system of hours and minutes was most difficult to accomplish because of "the changes it would require in watchmaking and which could only be done successively." But they did not find that the difficulties, that is the production of new watches and clocks and the elimination of the old ones, would be excessive. In fact, the obligatory aspect of this point of the reform was postponed only a year.[115] It was, however, to be rapidly abandoned and the "decimal watch" was to remain a technical curiosity.

Such was this time, each fraction of which, *"décades,"* tenths, and hundredths, attested to the triumph of reason and measured the passage of time by the clock of the Republic. But was this time not to announce the history to which its march opened "a new book" and cause it to be lived in still another way?

The principles adopted did not determine the nomenclature worthy of the "French and Republican calendar." Romme expressed the common opinion in noting that the new nomenclature could be "neither celestial nor mysterious." This was, however, only a negative principle and with the search for a positive formula a vast field was opened to the imagination.

We do not know the details of the discussions of the Comité d'Instruction publique about the nomenclature. However, a table bringing together seven different projects which were certainly the subject of the preliminary debates was found among Romme's papers. The document is as odd as it is revealing: it is precious evidence of the roads followed by the social imagination of the time.[116] Three basic principles can be drawn in the proposed systems (which certain of the proposals combine, for that matter):

a. The system of simple enumeration, e.g., days: first day, second day, etc.; or primile, bisile, trisile, etc. Note the proposal that keeps the old names for days, while deleting Sunday and that, after Saturday, proposes, for the end of the *"decade,"* terredi, Herscheldi (!), Cieldi, and Soldi.

b. The system of "moral" names. Thus, one of the projects proposed the following names for days: the Days of the Virtues, Spouses, Mothers, Children, the Plow, Commerce, etc. For the months, one of the proposals suggested the signs of the Zodiac.

Another proposal alternated the civic virtues with the seasons and agricultural work (the months of equality, sowing, rest, ice, justice, flowers, liberty, fruits, etc.).

c. The system invoking history.

The nomenclature, to use Romme's own words "is completely drawn from our Revolution, of which it presents either the principal events, or the aims, or the means."[117] Romme, himself, was the author and he presented it, in the name of the Comité d'Instruction publique, to the Convention. Both this proposal and the way in which it was presented are worthy of further study. In fact, in it, the utopia is joined to myth and the attitudes toward history it reveals are distinguished by their extremism.[118]

The order of the months of the Republic	The French, tired of fourteen centuries of oppression, and alarmed at the frightening progress of corruption, an example of which was both provided and brought about by a court, which had long been criminal, feel the need for a
7th from 21 March to 19 April	*Regeneration*
	The resources of the court having been exhausted, it convokes the French, but their
8th from 20 April to 19 May	*Assembly*
	is their salvation. They name representatives whose courage irritates the tyrant. They are threatened; but reassembled at the
9th from 20 May to 18 June	*Jeu de paume*
	and under the protection of the people, they take an oath to rescue the people from tyranny or to perish. This oath resounds throughout France, everywhere people arm themselves, everywhere they want to be free.
10th from 19 June to 18 July	*La Bastille*
	falls under the blows of a
11th from 19 July to 17 August	*People*
	sovereign and incensed. The numbers of the malevolent increase, treason breaks out, the court forms conspiracies, representatives faithless to their oaths sacrifice the interests of the nation to sordid views, but

12th from 18 August to 16 September	*The Mountain* always faithful, becomes the Olympus of France; surrounded by the Nation and in its name, the National Convention proclaims the rights of the people, the constitution and
1st from 22 September to 21 October	*The Republic*
2nd from 22 October to 20 November	*Unity*
3rd from 21 November to 20 December	*Fraternity* are the strength of the French and
4th from 21 December to 19 January	*Liberty* by a sovereign act of national
5th from 20 January to 18 February	*Justice* which causes the head of the tyrant to fall, is forever united with holy
6th from 19 February to 20 March	*Equality*

Thus, the calendar sets up a time-narrative account. The annual cycles take up and reaffirm a history, always the same and enclosed on itself. This time-narrative account nevertheless opens the new era, and defines its framework. The years that are to succeed in the history can only confirm the values and principles incarnated in the memorable events of the Revolution; the latter as well as their heroes are thus transformed into symbols. And the history, that of the years and the ages to come, as well as the New City, emanated from the acts that have been accomplished in this founding time. Thus, the time of history is conceived and imagined as that of the utopia on the move—freed of hazards and hindrances, it can only be the rational time of a wished for and desired history, that of the New City that will never stray from the path it has set itself. But the events and their extensions which are spoken of in the time-narrative account are raised above all historical temporality. In and by the return of the annual cycles they are established in the domain that is no other than that of myth and the sacred, of "*holy* Liberty" and of the "*holy* Mountain," of Time, a "dechristianizer," of course; but also time *making sacred* in the sense that it replaces the sacred in the realm of history and politics.

The time-narrative account is also taxonomic, classifying time. The succession of events taken up in the annual cycle composes at once a table of values and a moral and civic code. "This nomenclature alone," said Sergent during the debate at the Convention, "has the rare advantage of clearly classifying the

Revolutionary ideas that men must hold dear." Thus, the "eloquent nomenclature," to take up Romme's formula, made time speak or even transformed it into a speaking time. The two discourses—moral and civic discourse and discourse on history—coincide to the point where they merge. Of course, historical discourse was solely concerned with the events of the Revolution. But was it not the only history in which the New City recognized itself fully, the only one it accepted as its own?[119] "It is necessary," said Romme, "that each day recall to the citizens the Revolution that made them free and that their civic feelings be revived in reading this eloquent nomenclature."[120]

Romme's proposal nevertheless gave rise to numerous doubts, for both practical and ideological reasons. Did the "Revolutionary and moral" denominations not simply come within a hair's breadth of being ridiculous? The assembly "laughed and applauded" when one of its members remarked that "every day is a spouses' day" and not only the second day of the *"décade"* as was stipulated in one of the proposals. More serious arguments were also advanced. Did the moral and Revolutionary appellations not "overload the calendar with emblems," symbols that could, in turn, become "the object of a superstitious cult?"

Were they not in the process of *"religionizing* our Revolution?"* In fact, the populace "is always inclined to one superstition or another; it always seeks to realize the metaphysical ideas presented to it." Were the signs and symbols associated with memorable days not in danger of being transformed into so many "sacred objects" which new impostors would exploit? Ought they not, then, to be satisfied with the ordinal denomination? Indeed, the latter combined two advantages—that of being the simplest and that of being "natural," as "numerical order is that of nature." Romme, defending his proposal, refers to the future, to the "new book" opened by time. By contenting oneself with the numerical order, he replies, "you do not imprint on your calendar the moral and Revolutionary cachet that would make it go on into the coming century." But this reference to posterity gave rise to still further doubts and objections.[121] How was this future to be thought of and imagined—in the perspective of the "French nation" or in that of a "universal Republic?" With the ordinal denomination, said Duhem, "your calendar, which would only have been that of the French nation, will become that of all peoples. . . . As a philosophical calendar, it will be able to become the basis of the Universal Republic." One still wonders whether the future, the march of time, will not call into question the traditionally honored values and events of today. Certainly, a history able to stray from the path opened up by the Revolution is unthinkable. But is the Revolution finished, has it reached the term of its greatness? Does it not engender progress whose term is unforeseeable and ought not the calendar take this fact into account? "The Revolution has by no means reached the term indicated by philosophy, and yet it has already presented memorable epochs that the legislators would find it agreeable to consecrate; but who can answer them that those they will inscribe will be the greatest that it will have produced? . . . Will the [moral] tableau be judged as such by our posterity whose ideas will be healthier and whose morals will be purer than those of the present generation?"[122]

The Convention hesitates, goes back on its first decision, and finally accepts Fabre's idea of "giving each day the name of plants then produced by nature and of useful animals." Whence the proposal drawn up in detail by Fabre in collaboration with J.-M. Chénier and David, which was finally adopted. The nomenclature set out to join civics to the utilitarian, while referring to a vague "agricultural and rural" ideology. "Our basic idea was to consecrate the agricultural system by the calendar and to lead the nation back to it, by marking the epochs and the fractions of years by intelligible or visible signs taken from agriculture and the rural economy. . . . We believed that nothing that is precious to the rural economy should escape men and the meditations of every man who wishes to be useful to the country."[123] Thus, neologisms were invented (a very fashionable pursuit at the time) to name the months. On the other hand, for the names of the days, the principle of the ordinal denomination was retained, while inventing still more "poetic" neologisms that were easier to work with (primdi, deodi, etc.). The calendar substituted plants, animals, tools, and so forth; e.g., the goat, the plow, for the patron and other saints. The almanac based on the new calendar thus presented a sort of small encyclopedia, both civic and agricultural, for the use of the people.[124]

The calendar and its nomenclature were not, however, totally cleared of Revolutionary history. It reappeared for the last five days of the year—those that the calendar did not place in any month—and that were reserved for festivals. In preceding proposals their denomination had caused problems—they had been called *épagomènes* or *complementary* days. Fabre found that "this word was merely didactic, and consequently dry, mute to the imagination." Therefore, he proposed fabricating yet another neologism, a denomination "that would have a national character capable of expressing the joy and the spirit of the French people, five festival days that it will celebrate at the end of each year. We felt it possible and above all right, to consecrate by a new word the expression *sansculotte*, which would be its etymology. . . . We therefore call the five days collectively the *sansculottides*." The four-year cycle Romme proposed to call the *Olympiade* was called the *Franciade* and the day added at the end of each fourth year, the sixth *sansculottide*, "will be dedicated to celebrating the French Revolution which, after four years of effort and struggles against tyranny, led the French people to the rule of equality."[125]

The reference to history is present in yet another way and in a different context in Fabre d'Eglantine's ideological argument. Of course, the neologism *sansculottide* consecrates the major force of the Revolution and the regenerated French people. But is it truly a neologism and does the word not consecrate the return of the people to its true origins? "Research, as interesting as it is curious, shows us that the aristocrats, claiming to demean us by the expression *sans-culotte*, did not even deserve credit for the invention. In earliest antiquity, the Gauls, our ancestors, were proud of this appellation. History show us that part of Gaul, thereafter called *Lyonnaise* (land of the Lyonnais) was called *la Gaule culottée, Gallia bracata*; consequently, the rest of the Gauls up to the banks of the Rhine was *Gaule non-culottée; from that point on, then, our fathers were sans-culottes.*"[126]

So we have come full circle. The brave *sans-culottes* renew their relationship with their ancestors, the free Gauls. Beyond ages debased by tyranny and prejudice, the Republican calendar joins the mythical time of the origins of the nation to that opened by the Revolution in order to establish there, definitively and forever, the New City.

Let us note yet one more voice in this passionate debate on the calendar. It does not come from the Convention, but is that of citizens Blain and Bouchard, teachers at Franciade (formerly Saint-Denis). Their initiative is all the more remarkable as it is inspired by a certain idea of history-progress. Of course, for them, too, the New City is defined above all by its rupture with the past. But must the calendar not attest, as well, to the fact that the new era opened by the Revolution aims to be the end result of the history that preceded it. Consequently Blain and Bouchard again take up Sylvain Maréchal's old idea of peopling the calendar with great men, benefactors of humanity, substituting their names for those of the patron and other saints. They add to them, of course, the martyrs of liberty, and so, in their *Almanach d'Aristote ou du vertueux républicain* Confucius is placed side by side with Marat, Washington with Le Pelletier, Gutenberg with Chaulieu, dividing up among themselves the days of which they become the secular patrons.[127] As a consequence, the Revolution and its City reveal themselves as the only legitimate heirs of the history of humanity. The calendar makes the idea of history-progress into an instrument for the assimilation of the past. Of course, this assimilation can only be selective if not repressive. The collective memory must be purified of the disastrous memories of tyrants and impostors. But were the latter not something other than an anomaly of history? Its true course and its true meaning are put into images and symbols in the succession of great figures, from Socrates to Chaulieu, that the calendar organizes for the use of the "virtuous Republican."

Construct the New City, "retemper souls," open the new era—how could all this be done while leaving intact the old, the past, the former, the "ci-devant"? The great struggle "begun between the peoples and the kings" did not only engage the present and the future; it inevitably involved the past. The calendar reform translates the same will to break with the past (if not to make history start again at zero) that found its expression in the famous decree of the 18th of the first month of the year II on the destruction of the symbols of feudalism.

What was the old calendar if not a "monument raised to tyranny and prejudice?" And it is to be noted that at the same session when the Convention decreed the new nomenclature, Romme, in the name of the Comité d'Instruction publique presented a report on the abuses that were committed "under the pretext of eliminating the signs of feudalism or of royalty, printed books or manuscripts." Romme was not content with denouncing a particular excess that he quoted as an example. He attacked a whole ideology of systematic destruction and even wondered whether it was not the work of the English and of aristocrats who were thus plotting against the Republic. However, it was not in London or Coblentz that a zealous Republican presented to the Comité d'Instruction publique the proposal "for the purification of French bibliography," that is, of all libraries, beginning with the Bibliothèque Nationale. Urbain Domergue, head of the bibliography department, has a vision of a new library far more audacious than that of Mercier in *L'An 2440*. The two come together, however, in the utopian *élan* that inspires them. The project proposes continuing and very rapidly finishing the bibliographical works begun under the Ancien Régime, bringing to them, however, "a fundamental reform that calls for all the attention of the Comité." Indeed, it is necessary to "bring the revolutionary scalpel into our vast book depositories and cut the gangrenous limbs off the bibliographic body." The authors of the bibliographic plan conceived before the Revolution "joined to the prejudices of the moment the prejudices of their profession; the frenzy of accumulating books made them collect equally carefully Marie Alacoque and Voltaire, the *Guide des pécheurs* and the *Contrat social*, pitiful lawsuits of novices against monks and the lawsuits of the people against the tyrants! Twenty years were insufficient to gather all that "despotism wrote that was revolting, that superstition wrote that was absurd, or that pettifoggery wrote that was unjust." But the "Revolution commands" and it is necessary to go quickly. Let the education of the populace, "the crucible that must distinguish knowledge from the foolishness that had usurped its place" include "all knowledge that improves man . . . all that genius has borne forth for the happiness and the glory of peoples." The conclusion is compelling. "The bishop of Rome puts the *philosophes* on the index of fanaticism, let us put the theologians on the index of Reason. . . . Let us remove from our libraries the bloatedness that is a presage of death; let us leave them only the *embonpoint* that announces health." Consequently they are going to set up a jury, composed of "Republican *philosophes* who see with their minds and spirits and who see with their hearts," to initiate the great purge. But the proposal goes even further and one cannot but admire its shrewdness and Machiavellian cunning. It is not content with eliminating the "venomous books"; it wants the Republic to profit doubly from its doing so. First of all, useless books can be sold abroad, thereby procuring the money so needed by the Revolution. Then, too, once the books are sold, will they not poison the minds of its enemies and thus contribute to the final victory? "We are properly sending to the scaffold any counter-revolutionary author or accomplice; I vote for their deportation. *Let us cast out, into the bosom of our enemies*, the poison of our books of theology, of mysticity, of royalism, of oppressive legislation; and while our phalanxes bring destruction among their satellites, *let us bring to a peak, by means of our books, the vertigo and delirium sown in their minds*; and such is their blindness that they will pay quite dearly for a lethal present. . . . Objections that such a wish was offensive to humanity were in vain. The eager purchasers of these books would not be the populace composed of men, but kings, nobles, priests, and their agents, who are not on the same level as men; they are above it by their pretensions and below it by their insanity.'' The ''Republican library'' nevertheless admits that it is necessary to preserve one or two copies ''of all the productions of human foolishness; either as objects of curiosity, or as historical monuments. It is thus that the botanist places in his herbarium, among great numbers of salubrious plants, the aconite that causes death.''[128]

It is the attitude that prompts this sort of proposal that Romme attacks, with recourse to both the Revolution and history. Books must be preserved, all books, and for many reasons. Of course, ''our libraries teem with elements that attest to the villainy of kings. The history that flatters their pride is none the less the history of their crimes.'' Thus, books and manuscripts ''imbued with the feudal spirit . . . are so many exhibits in the great trial, which is of interest to all of humanity, and which is adjudicated by the French.'' Sovereign and legitimate judges of the past, peoples are, as well, its descendants and heirs. Does justice not demand the recognition that it is the progress of the mind and spirit and, in particular, of philosophy, ''that gave birth to the Revolution and that, alone, can transmit its benefits to future generations.'' And, before the Revolution, ''the most forceful writers, to whom we owe the Revolution, while making formal sacrifices to the prejudices of the times, proclaimed daring truths. . . . To burn their books today for what is bad in them would be to soil our Revolution and to call down on us the scorn of all peoples.'' To have confidence in the Revolution is to trust in the future, in the march of time, of which the New City has definitely taken possession. Consequently, ''we must preserve everything, leaving it to time and to philosophy to purge our libraries, as for the past five years, the latter has been doing to our laws and morals.''[129] Is this purificatory time of a desired history not again that of the utopia on the move?

The new calendar lasted only twelve years and the obvious question is why the reform was not, after all, successful. With recastings of the ''system of festivals,''[130] the calendar survived Thermidor and the Concordat, and even Napoleon's coronation took place on 18 ventôse of the year XIII. Of course, with the Empire, it became absurd to count time beginning with year I of the Republic. But could they not, for example, set year I in 1789 (after all, Napoleon kept the celebration of 14 July!), or else, for the purpose at hand, advance it by twelve years? The principles of the new calendar could also have been kept, while "debaptizing" (or, rather, "rebaptizing") it, from "Republican" to "decimal," as was done with "Republican measurements." The failure of the "Republican calendar" is particularly striking when one compares its results with that of the other reform, of weights and measures. Yet the two "systems" were, so to speak, twins, and were inspired by the same state of mind. One sometimes wonders whether the contrast between the two historical destinies was not the result of the particularly abstract nature of the new calendar. One remembers, accordingly, that it often led to absurdities. While professing to express "the universality of nature," it proposed, for instance, the name *fructidor* for the month that, beyond the tropic of Capricorn, was the season of snow. But does the history of the twin reform not show that all these factors played a minor role? It is not because we are definitively established in the metric system that, retrospectively, it seems to us to have been particularly easy to adopt. We must not forget that it nevertheless took more than a century for it to become imposed on mentalities in France, that it was adopted in Germany only in 1868, in Russia in 1918, and only recently in England. W. Kula did an authoritative analysis of the innumerable difficulties and resistance the establishment of the metric system encountered—or, rather, its imposition by force. It came from above, imposed by the government, if not by bayonets. It only took the withdrawal of the French army from Italy or Flanders for these countries to return to the traditional weights and measures. In Geneva, the new calendar was adopted before the metric system. The "Republican measurements" were not at all felt to be less ideologically charged or less "abstract" than the new calendar.[131] Was the metric system at least more "rational"? This is doubtful, and one wonders what abstract "rationality" is being referred to. It is useless to stress either the fact that the continuation of the decimal system does not facilitate the teaching of modern mathematics in school or the operative advantages of the duodecimal system. It snows in Alaska during the month of *fructidor*. But do the inhabitants of the Congo question the etymology of the words "March" or "January"? To what natural and lived time do these names correspond there and, for that matter, here?

It is necessary, it seems, to seek the reasons for the failure elsewhere. The Republican calendar was, certainly, more "rational" than the Gregorian calendar and it was no less so than the metric system. However, the reform of the calendar did not satisfy needs analogous to those to which the abolition of the former measurements responded. Indeed, contrary to the diversity of the weights and measures, the Christian world utilized a single and, in that sense, universal calendar (with the exception, of course, of those countries that had kept the Julian calendar). It is only in this sense that the "unity" and "universality" the Revolutionary calendar aimed at proved to be "abstract" and more ideologically charged than was the case with the metric system.

The Revolutionary calendar did not suppress the diversity of measurements of time—it only imposed, by force, an *alternative* unity to the one that already existed.[132] Last but not least, this unity that they wanted to destroy was profoundly rooted in sacred time and particularly that of festivals and Sundays. The reform of weights and measures, on the other hand, did not in any way touch on religious feelings. The sacralization of time finally won over even economic imperatives. Let us not, in fact, forget that the new calendar increased the number of working days, which was particularly opportune at the time of nascent capitalism. But this increase was merely illusory—all evidence agrees on the actual persistence of Sundays as festivals. When it came right down to it, only public servants applied the Republican commandment of resting on the tenth day.

Whatever the reasons, the new calendar always remained "Republican." It proved to be less resistant to history, to its march and its inertia, than that "monument of tyranny and superstition" against which it had been set up as another monument, that of victorious reason and liberty, established in time, but to stay there eternally.

V
Utopia and Festivals

"**T**he chamber of inventions will be composed of three hundred members; it will be divided into three sections. . . . The first section will be composed of two hundred civil engineers; the second, of fifty poets or other literary inventors, and the third of twenty-five painters, fifteen sculptors or architects, and ten musicians. . . . This chamber will present a work that will consist of a proposal for public festivals. These festivals will be of two kinds: *the festivals of hope* and *the festivals of remembrance*. These festivals will be celebrated successively in the capital, in the principal towns of the departments, and in the principal towns of the cantons, so that capable orators (who will never be very numerous) can spread the benefits of their eloquence. In the *festivals of hope*, the orators will explain to the populace the works projects that have been decreed by Parliament and they will stimulate the citizens to work with ardor, making them feel how their lot will be improved when they have finished these projects. In the festivals dedicated to *remembrance*, the orators will take it on themselves to make the populace know how preferable its position is to that in which its ancestors found themselves."[1]

Institutionalizing creative invention and having festivals invented as a public institution—this double enterprise expressed in the above words of Saint-Simon is not specific to the author of the *Nouveau christianisme*. Indeed, it could be said that the utopians always had a soft spot for public festivals, celebrations, and festivities, and rare indeed are the imaginary visions of society that dispense with representations of great or solemn occasions. On the other hand, utopian visions are quite frequently found in actual festivals, which spontaneously secrete, so to speak, utopian aspirations and images that include the idea of the inversion of the social universe and translate into lived experience the image of an "upside down world." The medieval carnival and the "feast of fools" so authoritatively analyzed by Bakhtine,[2] the strange bloody carnival of Romans, in 1588, studied by E.

177

Le Roy Ladurie—all examples among many others in which symbolic rites and languages express and bring to life in festivals the dreams of a different society. In Romans, the revolt of the lower classes coincides with the carnival, and the festival is transformed into a "long series of symbolic demonstrations, a sort of psychodrama, of tragedy-ballet, whose actors have acted and danced their revolt, instead of discoursing on it in manifestos." Ladurie reminds us, too, that popular revolts frequently took on the air of "great social saturnalia," whose dominant theme was social otherness imagined as an inversion of the social world, as a permutation, among rich and poor, of ranks, status, spouses.[3]

The eighteenth century represents a particularly important chapter in the long history of the relationship between the utopia and festivals. With the ideas of the Enlightenment and especially with the invention and the practice of Revolutionary festivals, the old affinities were renewed and several particulars of the problem changed. On the one hand, the narratives of imaginary voyages exploring countries in the utopia abound in images of the occasions and festivals that are celebrated there; on the other hand, a remarkable phenomenon is observed—the critique of traditional festivals as well as the search for new forms and expressions of celebration supply imaginations with new utopian resources. This new reflection on festivals, as they are and as they ought to be, takes on a utopian orientation. Thus, the utopia of the festival is formed; the idea-image of the ideal festival becomes a sort of screen on which are projected the dreams and models of an alternative society. With the institution of the Revolutionary festivals, the relationship of the festival to the utopian idea-image becomes even closer and a whole play of interaction is established between the imaginary and the real. The Revolutionary festival is particularly permeable to the utopia. It is the privileged place of the renewal and the exercising of the collective imagination, one of whose pivots is the representation of dreams and social hopes. Consequently, more than one rite of the Revolutionary festivals is an imaged transposition of the principles and values of the desired New City. Moreover, latent utopian aspirations find appropriate modes of expression in the symbolic languages of the festival. The high point of new sensibilities, the Revolutionary festival is also an arm in a combat in which the overthrow of the relationships of force and domination in the symbolic domain is at stake. The utopia presented under the specific modes of the festival and amplified by its portrayal, becomes militant, if not conquering. The utopian representations intervene directly in the organization of the time and space of the festivals, guiding the imagination of their organizers. However, if the utopia and the festival are articulated on each other in Revolutionary festivals, the history of the latter is also evidence of the oppositions that exist between the two phenomena. The Revolutionary festival is, like any festival, a universal social event, to use Marcel Mauss' phrase, and it can be reduced neither to a set of images nor to a utopian discourse.

We can take up only certain aspects of these complex relationships, using only a few examples as our basis for study.

1
Festivals in Utopia and the Utopia of the Festival

"*I* know quite well," said Restif de la Bretonne of his "proposal to implement a general reform of morals and thereby of the human race, that such a project could be accomplished only by the nearly impossible convergence of all the wills of which a Nation is composed. But at least, like Plato, Thomas More, and the Abbé de Saint-Pierre, I shall have the satisfaction of having presented a Novel of virtue and happiness to men. Would that they change my novel into a veracious history." And yet, he added, it is always useful to "present to men as in a magic mirror the image of a felicity which they cannot attain."[4] Images of festivals could not be absent from these "magic mirrors," for a double reason. First, the detailed images of an *alternative* society necessarily imply representations of festivals different from those of reality—counter-festivals, so to speak, in which the nature of the imaginary City, its religion, its morals, and its institutions would be expressed.

Second, as we have already remarked, a specific feature of the utopian enterprise is to imagine individual and collective relationships and behaviors as so many rites. And the more social life, in its entirety, is thought of and imagined as ritualized, the more important the festivals become.

Even without his *Andrographe*, Restif invents several festivals, such as those of winter and summer, which one spends a week preparing for and which culminate in communal meals eaten in large buildings built expressly for this purpose. In his proposal for the Bourg d'Oudan collective farm, Restif gives detailed prescriptions for festivals. "Entertainment will be public and therefore honest." Thus in winter "the people's entertainment will be in the large dining room and in the common barn; the lighting will be provided by the lamps that are now used in the streets of Paris." Among other festivals, there will be marriage festivities that will last for three days; and in cases where "the most

179

deserving subjects of the two sexes are not mutually chosen, the marriage festivities will last four.'' These solemn occasions will be preceded by festival-assemblies of the members of the ideal commune during which ''the girls and men to be married during the year'' will be designated. The following day, at another assembly, the merits of the candidates of both sexes will be examined, and prizes will be awarded. ''The first prize will be that of morals; combined with the prize for plowing, it will give the right of choosing a mistress.'' But this right ''belongs only—and ought to belong only—to men.'' On the other hand, the girl distinguished by the assembly as the most virtuous and the best worker will have the right ''to organize the girls' entertainment throughout the year.'' At Oudan, Sunday is retained and the mass is celebrated; however, the priest is charged not only with reading the Bible to his parishioners but, additionally, with explaining Buffon's *Histoire Naturelle* to them. In this happy communal life, the useful is always, in daily life as well as during festivals, linked to the agreeable and the good is associated with the beautiful and the true.[5]

Morelly, in his *Code de la Nature*, invents a whole new system of festivals and celebrations that marks, on the one hand, the rupture with the Christian tradition and, on the other, expresses the moral and social values that control the egalitarian City of justice and communal happiness. This new system is based, first of all, on a new structuring of time, a new calendar. Indeed, in the City, ''the number ten and its multiples will be the terms of all civic division of things and persons; that is, all enumerations, all apportionment by classes, all distributive measurements, etc., will be divisible by ten.'' So, Sunday is abolished; every fifth day is given over to public rest and the year is divided ''into sixty-three equal parts'' (a day of rest is added in leap years). Thus in the City, where private property is abolished, people work less and rest more; there are in all around a hundred official holidays. The festivals, like time, are devoid of any religious significance. Purely civic, these occasions give a rhythm to time in which work and public life succeed each other. ''Public festivities will always begin with a day of public rest and last for six days, including that. The festivities will be celebrated immediately before the beginning of the first toil before the first day of the harvest, after having gathered and packed the fruits of all kinds and at the beginning of each year; during the latter festivals, marriages will be performed, the city and corps leaders of the year will in turn take on the duties of their offices.''

In the imaginary voyages, the festivals are recounted with a great abundance of more or less picturesque details. Among the Sévarambes, who practice the cult of the Sun, that ''luminous globe'' is the object of the great annual festival. Before the celebration, the fires in all homes are extinguished. At the high point of the festival, ''they light with the rays of the sun, with burning mirrors, combustible material that has been placed at one side of a pyre, or firebrand, that is made in the temple courtyard. In this way, the fire smoulders for several hours and then, during the night, it sets the whole pyre ablaze, which creates a great flame to which everyone comes to light lamps. . . . It is thus that they get new fire, for the whole year, instead of using that of the preceding year, which had been extinguished everywhere.'' The other great annual occasion is that of Sévarision, which is celebrated in memory of the arrival of Sévarius, the founder of the city in the austral land. The cult of the Sun is linked to that of the power, the government. In a ceremony that is as sublime as it is dazzling, the people and the magistrates thank the Sun for having sent Sévarius to ''draw them forth from their crass ignorance and make them the happiest nation in the world.'' The festival lasts for days, which are spent in pure merrymaking, untinged with anything sad or lugubrious. The same is true of the marriage festival, Ospar-enibon, which is celebrated four times a year, for a period of five days each. It is as simple as it is touching and the marriage ceremony is not performed with more ado for the prince than it is for commoners, with, of course, the sole exception that the prince himself chooses the woman he wishes to marry, while the other men, in contrast, are chosen by the women. Let us skip the other festivals—their abundant details only bear witness to the perfect harmony and happiness that radiate, like the sun, in this happiest nation in the world.[7]

We again come across festivals when, following brave M. van Doelvelt, who, having suffered through the shipwreck that is more or less obligatory in this sort of voyage, debarks on the isle of Ajao, whose inhabitants make up a true republic of *Philosophes*. There are no religious festivals for the Ajaoians since they do not believe in the existence of a God and yet, ''without a Divinity, without the fear of an eternal future . . . the morals there are purer and the laws better observed than in any other country.'' There are, however, other ceremonies and distractions, which are all ''entertaining, restrained, and honest'' so that they perfectly express the spirit of this Republic. So every year at the end of the fourteenth moon the Ajaoian army, composed of married men between twenty-two and fifty years old, gathers. In a kind of military esplanade, near Lake Fu in the province of Lamo, these troops pass in review before the highest magistrates. In this country where mine and thine are unknown, these magistrates, like all the others, in fact, are elected and thus, during festivals, the people gather together with their own leaders. Then, ''they celebrate certain military maneuvers, for which there are honorary prizes. These festivities last for seven days, after which each new Magistrate assumes the duties to which he has been elected before leaving the city or the village.'' Moreover, only men attend these festivals—the women stay at home and ''clean it during their husbands' absence.'' Our traveler is not in the least shocked at this quite philosophical custom. What he finds particularly striking is the difference between the Ajaoian ceremonies associated with the most important moments of the life of the individual—that is, birth, marriage, and death—and those he knew in Europe.

Any religious symbolism that could hide the true sense of these events is absent—everything about them is at once simple and solemn, clear and functional. Take marriage, for instance. In Ajao "it is ordained, on pain of infamy, that every young man, having reached the age of twenty, marry." The law is the more readily respected as it perfectly suits the Ajaoians, among whom, thanks to a good upbringing, education, and the choice of food, "there are none who are languorous or disabled, or *refrigidis et malefactis*." So, when a young man reaches his twentieth year, "he casts his eyes over the women with whom he wants to spend the rest of his life," and it is, in fact, *women*, as each Ajaoian has two wives. "This choice is usually made during the days set aside for diversion and recreation at each new moon." Afterward, when the declaration has been accepted, the "novice in love" pays his respects to his mistresses in visiting rooms, which are "rather similar to the parlors of the nuns in Flanders, except for the grill. There, a discreet Cupid takes pleasure in shooting all his arrows into these young and tender hearts." Before the marriage ceremony, the mother (or rather the respective mothers) presents the girl to her future husband—she is only dressed in thin gauze so that he can see "all the beauties that nature put on the body of her daughter." Let us pass over all the other details of the nuptial ceremony—it is as completely transparent to the significance that nature and pure morals give to sexuality as is the gauze that garbs the future bride.

Nor if one undertakes a voyage in time rather than in space will one miss festivals. In Paris, in the year 2440, to which we travel with the narrator of L.-S. Mercier's book, the old religious festivals are supplanted and there are only civic festivals "which relax the populace without leading them to libertinage." The legislator who "knows the human heart" always leads it to virtue by the path of pleasure, by festivals, feasts, festivities, hymns, and dances. Therefore this society of the future also celebrates an initiation ceremony that corresponds to what was formerly the first communion. How moving and instructive it is for the initiate as well as for the audience and one might see the influence of Pascal, but an enlightened if not an expurgated Pascal. A young man "surrounded by a zealous crowd," whose movements depict joy, is led into an observatory in the middle of the night when "the army of the stars shines in all its brilliance." There, suddenly, "a telescope is put to his eye." The young man "gazes at the infinite abyss" with the greatest emotion and then he is brought a microscope and thus finds himself in front of the other infinity. "The young man, moved, astonished, retains the double impression that he got at the same instant; he cries with joy . . . his words are but a hymn of admiration. . . . On the days devoted to praise of the Creator, it is an edifying spectacle to see the numerous adorers of God on our observatory, all fallen to their knees, their eyes gazing and their spirits given over to prayer, casting their soul along with their glance toward the maker of these imposing miracles."[9]

Numerous other examples of holidays, festivals, ceremonies, and solemn occasions encountered throughout imaginary voyages might be cited. But are the places to be visited worth the travel? Beyond the diversity of formulas, there is a common content of ideas and even of images. The festivals everywhere display the peculiarities of the morals, of the institutions of the dreamt societies; but they also express the characteristics common to the majority of these societies—their transparency and their rationality, the perfect alliance between feelings and reason, as well as between nature and social life. The more "complete" the utopia, the more it aspires to encompass all social life and give a detailed description of it, the more it invents festivals, ceremonies, and solemn occasions. The idea of happiness that presides over this discourse on perfect societies easily espouses the images of the festivals that are to be manifestations of it. In this specific case, the general tendency characteristic of the evolution of utopian discourse in the eighteenth century is once again confirmed. The formula of the imaginary voyage is becoming more and more hackneyed because of its rigidity, its paradigmatic fixity. It is a facile, perhaps too facile, genre— which explains its dangers: the repetition, imitation, the absence of individuality, and monotony that mark the majority of these texts, despite the apparent diversity in the accumulation of picturesque details.

The repetition is due, too, to the fact that the majority of these texts do not particularly attempt to break new ground, but content themselves with returning to, and adopting as their own, the criticism of traditional festivals made by the *philosophes*. In fact, the majority of the descriptions of festivals in utopias only translate into more or less vivid pictures, the conclusions imposed by that criticism.

The eighteenth century, or, rather, the culture of the elites of that century, had a passion for celebration. The image of this century fabricated by a certain historical tradition forged of this century is well known—joyous, frivolous, and carefree; it is futile to stress its falsity. Nevertheless, in reaction against the cliché, this aspect of the "enlightened century" has sometimes been neglected, and it is forgotten that the taste for amusement, distraction, and diversion, is an integral part of the culture of the Enlightenment. We shall return to this question below; suffice it to note here that, although diversions are frequently superficial and frivolous, the passion for play in which one flees or goes beyond overly rigid mores or overly pious and constrictive morality is, itself, completely serious. Does the taste of the enlightened public for imaginary voyages not show, in its own way, the same need? They are tired of the ceremonial festivals of the Court, as pompous as they are boring. They are seeking out, and experimenting with, new diversions, *fêtes pastorales* and *fêtes champêtres*, for instance. But these "*fêtes*" are also the object of an ideological battle that the *philosophes* are undertaking on several levels. So, traditional religious festivals are criticized. They are so numerous, they only incite the populace to idleness; so full of prejudice, they impress the crowds with their pomp and obscure symbolism. For the same reasons, the philosophical criticism distrusts popular festivals in which, only too often, all that can be seen is superstition and excess. To the life of idleness, whose symbol is the life of festivals, they oppose the life of labor and virtue of the *honnête homme*. Consequently, they think of new ceremonies which would be suitable to an enlightened or even natural religion and which would reward virtue and work—festivals that are so exemplary, restrained, and moralizing that one wonders what was truly festive about them.[10]

The renewal of the social imagination does not come so much from the festivals in the utopia as it does from the *utopia of the festival*, from the exploration of the potentialities of the festival as a social phenomenon. In fact, the festival lends itself particularly well to use as a "magic mirror" which reflects the social life that is dreamed of and imagined. In the same fashion as the utopia, the festival is a quasi-island, with its own space and time that take it beyond daily life. A universal social event with many levels and dimensions, among which the degrees of coherence are variable, the festival groups participants in a quasi-autonomous totality. The play of its languages and rites results in the association of the social values and models present in the festival with the individual and collective behaviors, with the arrangement of the participants in time and space and to the allocation of their respective roles. In relation to the "everyday," the festival is established as a social "elsewhere," a *heterotopia*.[11] Its time and space exist in conjunction with the imaginary—in the festival they are not lived in their positivity, but with all the partialities of the imagination.[12]

In order for the festival to offer archetypes to the utopia, it must be considered a *model of sociability*—then the new formulas of the festival opposed to those that already exist become prefigurations of a whole *alternative* society, dreamed of if not desired, imagined if not thought out.

It would take too long to examine how the discourse on festivals in the eighteenth century was enriched by utopian elements and how the images of the festival become receptacles for utopian ideas. Let us merely refer to two examples of this undertaking to "utopianize" the festival.

The first to command attention is, naturally, Rousseau's. Let us merely add some remarks on the utopia of the festival and its educational use to what we have already said in the chapter devoted to Rousseau. What he passed on to the succeeding generation was, on the one hand, the model of the ideal festival and nostalgia for such a festival. But, on the other hand, it was also a complete philosophy of the festival if not a theory of its specifically political application, particularly in a system of public education. That generation will enter into the Revolution armed with both that model and that theory and will apply both of them to the conceptualizing of the experiments of new forms of festive activity. As we shall see, the Rousseauistic formulas become constant references, if not commonplaces, during the Revolutionary period.

Rousseau was particularly sensitive to the utopian potentialities of the festival, and references to the latter are ever-present in his work. Consequently, we find the image of the "primitive" festival celebration in the second *Discours* and in the *Essai sur les origines des langues*; in the *Nouvelle Héloïse* we find the famous harvest festival, the "magic mirror" of the ideal society of Clarens; the *Lettre à d'Alembert* offers us the idealized image of the popular festival on the *place de Saint-Gervais* in Geneva, as well as a theoretical reflection on the festival, taken up again and further developed, as we have noted, in *Considérations sur le gouvernement de Pologne*. Rousseau gets the most he can out of the assimilation of the festival to a model of universal society. In other words, for him, not every festival is possible in every society and each society invents and gives itself those it deserves. The ideal one can only be spontaneity and transparency, communion and open manifestation of joy. His formula is summed up in the lines of the *Lettre à d'Alembert*, which were so frequently taken up and harped on in Revolutionary discourse on the subject. "Is no entertainment, then, necessary in a Republic? On the contrary, many spectacles are necessary. It is in Republics that they are born, it is within them that they are seen to shine with a true air of celebration. To what peoples is it more suitable to assemble frequently and to form among themselves the pleasant ties of pleasure and joy, than to those who have so many reasons to love one another and to remain forever united? . . . Let us not adopt those exclusive entertainments that regrettably shut up a small number of people in an obscure den; that keep them fearful and inactive in silence and inaction; that offer to the eyes only barriers, swords' points, soldiers, distressing images of servitude and inequality. No, happy people, those are not your festivals! It is outdoors, under the sky that you must assemble and give yourself up to the pleasant feeling of your happiness. May your pleasures be neither effeminate nor mercenary; let nothing that smacks of constraint and self-interest taint them; may they be as free and generous as you; may the sun shine on your innocent spectacles; you will form one yourself, the most worthy it could shine on. But what will be the objects of these spectacles? What will be shown? Nothing, if you like. With liberty, everywhere crowds prevail, well-being also prevails. Plant a post crowned with flowers in the middle of a plaza, assemble the people there and you will have a festival. Do something even better: present the spectators as a spectacle; make them the actors themselves; have each see himself and love himself in the others, so that they may all be the more united because of it."[13]

It is useless to emphasize the series of oppositions that structure this text: open space/closed space; transparency/obscurity; liberty/constraint; spontaneity/passivity; communion/division. These oppositions demand two types of spectacle, but also two types of society that correspond to these spectacles and produce them. Is the final formula on the transformation of spectators into actors who collectively present themselves as a spectacle not a metaphorical transposition, on the mode of a festal rite, of the fundamental act of the social contract that transforms isolated individuals into a sovereign people ruling over its own destiny? And does the assembly of the people gathered in the plaza, under the shade of an old oak, and unanimously deciding on the laws it wishes to make for itself, in the *Contrat social*, not recall the image of the people gathered in celebration?

The model of the ideal festival goes hand in hand with a sociological and political theory of the festival. In fact, the festival can become a means of political and ideological action and Rousseau insists on the fact that every "true politician" knows the effects of festivals on souls and, particularly, on the imagination. The ideal festival establishes in the imagination the values of which it makes a spectacle in its rites and in its symbolic language. The spectacle of the festival is normative: everything in it is at once real and symbolic, every image is a lesson, every tableau a narrative. Each of its signs and each of its gestures evokes something besides itself, namely a collective reality, an affective *élan* toward liberty and the fatherland. As we have noted, in *Considérations*, the civic festivals, while contrasting with the theatrical spectacle by their spirit, mark the whole of public life with a certain theatricalization. Each citizen is, at least potentially, an actor and plays his role in this spectacle which has the City as both object and setting.

The festival, of course, reflects the people, but as though in a magic mirror. There is always a *gap* between the realities of daily life and the imaged representation that the people gathered in the festival make of themselves and give to themselves. This could be said to be a *significant* gap—the populace gives itself, in and by the festival, a model of itself. Of course, it it the populace that speaks to itself in the festival. But does the skillful educator not owe it to himself to exploit this gap and to turn the workings of the festival to good account by a hidden organization, dissimulated behind spontaneity and transparency? (We must not forget, for that matter, that an organizer is never absent from the narratives in which Rousseau recounts the spontaneous festival. He hides behind the words of the narrator who, by his discourse, arranges the festival as a *tableau vivant* and offers it as such to our gaze.) The festival can become a powerful means by which uniform and common impressions are transmitted to all participants. Thanks to the play of symbols, the festival is a rite of unanimity and fraternity which results in souls merging together in a common enthusiasm. These "souls" thus rise above themselves and, thanks to the imagination which is guided if not controlled, enlarge the realm of the possible in politics. Thus we see the educational effect of the festival and the major role incumbent on it in any system of public education. The spectators are not merely transformed into actors, but exercise an educational activity on themselves. Here may be seen the double social function of the festival: it is stabilizing because it reproduces and amplifies the fundamental values on which the social order rests (this function particularly marks the festival at Clarens); but it is also *mobilizing*, stirring people to action because it awakens and orients energies (this is the use that Rousseau recommends in *Considérations*). Not only are we given the utopia and a theory of festival, but also methodical rules of an action to be exercised on "souls" in order to make them assimilate certain political ideas and certain models of behavior, or, to state it briefly and to take the risk of using an anachronism—a rough sketch of a theory of *propaganda*, which the politicians and ideologues of the Revolution, rereading Rousseau, will not be slow to discover, and they will plant more than one picket to get the festival under way.[14]

Let us go on to the other of our examples, that of Boullée, the great visionary architect. We will devote a whole chapter to his work, to his unfulfilled architectural dreams, to the search for a social order that would take them on. In his work, the utopia is associated with a specific language, namely that of a monumental architecture, or rather this visionary architecture has reference to the ideas and images of social otherness as a prerequisite condition. It could be said that Boullée's visions call for a social order or at least an ideal power that would be susceptible to self-recognition in this architecture. And we find in Boullée a variation of the utopia of the festival conceived as a model of sociability and as a means of civic education. Certain convergences with Rousseau's idea are quite striking, as a matter of fact. Rousseau does not speak of the architectural settings in which the civic festivals he dreams of in *Considérations* are to take place. But, if one had to imagine it, one would inevitably think of the new formulas for great arenas like those of antiquity, whose simple and sober style would correspond to the noble sentiments of the people who would come there to enjoy themselves. It could be said that Boullée's course is backward. The architect imagines a gigantic arena, a new Coliseum that could hold more than three hundred thousand. This colossal monument to which we will return below is only functional on the condition of becoming the setting, the framework, the architectural formula of a type of festival different from the traditional royal festival. Consequently, the architectural dream espouses the utopia of the ideal festival, which curiously merges with the one of which Rousseau had dreamed.

"It is not always by fear of punishment that men are held back or successfully turned away from doing evil; it is also by offering them a powerful attraction that dissuades them from evil. What might this attraction be? National pleasures. Yes, national pleasures. Everything that is offered to our senses is referred to our soul. It is a principle according to which the spectacles of a nation should be managed and, if this were to be the case, it would doubtless be a great means of forming and maintaining good morals. The legislators of antiquity recognized and made use of this great resource. It is in this political and moral view that the Greeks and Romans instituted their festivals. . . . The proposal for a circus presented here is conceived to fulfill moral and political views. . . . Imagine three hundred thousand people gathered as in an amphitheatre, where no one can escape the gaze of the multitude. A unique effect would result from that order of things: that is that the beauty of that astonishing spectacle would come from the spectators, of whom it would be solely composed."[15]

The coincidence of Boullée's ideas and those of Rousseau is striking and all the more remarkable as the architect does not have reference to the author of the *Lettre à d'Alembert*. Based on his evidence, he himself had conceived these "patriotic views," and it was only afterward that he learned that the same ideas were to be found in a scholarly report on *Les jeux du cirque considérés dans les vues politiques de Romains*, a report written by Abbé Brottier, an erudite antiquary. Who influenced whom matters little, however—hypotheses about "influences" conceal more than they explain. The problem that presents itself in any case is to know how it happens that one comes to be influenced by one idea rather than another. What is particularly striking in the examples given is the convergence among art, politics, and the utopia, which merge in the search for a new formula of celebration of the festival which would be the place where the new man is formed, thanks to the renewal of the collective imagination. "Let the general plan of the legislator encompass the great project of bringing the populace to obedience toward the laws and the practice of social virtues through the agency of the fine arts," said Diderot, thinking of festivities; as well, "one will quickly see all the forces of genius being deployed to fulfill this great aim; one can expect to see the rebirth of masterpieces and of masterpieces that, in all likelihood, will be superior to those of antiquity."[16] Let us note, finally, that the search for new formulas of the festival is based on a certain idea of language, namely of a language susceptible to *perfectly translating* ideas and moral values into appropriate signs. These signs will then be linked in a metaphorical discourse which, to use Paul Ricœur's apt formula, would join the *sense* to the *senses*.[17] Art and politics thus converge along with the utopia in the search for a lucid symbolism capable of molding souls.

When the Revolution felt the need for new forms of festivals, celebrations opposed to those of the Ancien Régime, of festivals that would make the great promises of the New City live collectively, it did not have far to seek: in the utopia of the festival it found ready-made models.

2
Utopia in the Revolutionary Festival

"**D**oes there exist," Rabaut de Saint-Etienne asks himself in December 1792, "an infallible means of communicating without delay, within a short time, to all the French at the same time, uniform and common impressions, whose effect would be to make them, all together, worthy of the Revolution; of liberty, that right of justice which is frequently converted into iniquity; of equality, that fraternal tie which is so easily changed to tyranny; and of that simple and noble elevation of heart and soul to which the human race has been brought for the past four years, in the mortal combat that has been undertaken between all truths and all errors? This means undoubtedly exists; it consists of the great and common institutions so well known to the ancients, who were able to arrange that on the same day, at the same instant, everyone got the same impressions through their senses, their imagination, their memory, through reasoning and through all the faculties of man, and through that enthusiasm that could be called the magic of reason. . . . One must distinguish between public education and national education, or civics. Public education enlightens and exercises the mind, while civics must form hearts. Public education requires schools, high schools, academies, calculations, methods; it is enclosed within walls. Civics calls for arenas, circuses, gymnasiums, arms, public games, national festivals, fraternal competition among all ages and sexes, and the pleasant spectacle of the assembled society; it calls for space, the spectacle of the fields and of nature."[18]

Rabaut de Saint-Etienne's exposition is a good example of a double utopia that inspired Revolutionary discourse on civic festivals, namely that of an ideal festival as well as that of the New City and of the people who are worthy of it. In fact, in this discourse, we again find the idea-image of an ideal festival that encompasses all of man and all men; it is the scene of complicity between the natural and the social, just as it develops in a time and space that are projected

189

toward the utopia. On the other hand, this vision of the civic festival rests on an ideal representation of a people united by the ties of fraternity and equality, whose enthusiasm is considered a source of permanent receptiveness. The ideal festival and its organization are then merely the expression of the spirit of this people, the scene where the spirit catches its breath. The people, when it is equal to what it ought to be, never produces conflicts, contradictions, false appearances; consequently the festival can only be transparency and harmony. The dream of the festival is possible only on the condition that it be celebrated by a dreamed people and the ideas on the educational functions of the civic festival are a link between the two utopias. Thus, within the Revolutionary discourse on the festival, a play of mirrors is established between the images of a model festival and the model of sociability that the latter implies. (We shall find this again, not only in proposals for festivals, but also in the accounts of the progress of real festivals.) The present is explained and reveals its significance for the future that the festival allows to be already imagined and felt. "The imposing and pleasant spectacle of assembled humanity," the festival is at once reality and anticipation—what has been momentarily lived in it is the harbinger of a transtemporal state, of a Revolution that will definitively take place "in heads and hearts, as it has taken place in conditions and in the government."[19] The pedagogical intention of the festival is considered only the expression of the people's will to have what is and what ought to be coincide, the real and the possible, the individual and the social. Manifesting this will already prefigures that "new people whose morals are in harmony with the laws," and that joins "to the happy enthusiasm that characterizes it, equality and above all fraternity, that nice, pleasant feeling, the first law, the unique happiness of society."[20]

The Rousseauistic inspiration of this double utopia is obvious. Rousseau's ideas on festivals are assimilated to the point that they become so many commonplaces and clichés in reflections on civic festivals as well as in the arrangement of the decor of actual festivals. It would, however, be distorting the utopia of the Revolutionary festival to consider it only an extension of an ordinary ideological discourse, even of Rousseau's. The search for formulas of new festivals as well as the significance that ought to be given them was sustained above all by the lived actual experience of the first Revolutionary festivals.

The festival is itself an aspect of the Revolutionary phenomenon and it expresses an essential dimension of the formation of Revolutionary affectivity. The affinities among the Revolution, the utopia, and the festival are intertwined in the very depth of the lived experience of a great Revolutionary day. Experience that is necessarily collective—one does not enter into the Revolution all alone: one lives it with *some* and against *others*, in the human warmth of a crowd in the process of discovering itself as a collective reality, in an experience rich in intense emotion, which generates dreams and hopes that mark the scope of collective expectations. The individual feels himself sustained and transformed by collective emotions and forces beyond him; the time lived seems to immobilize itself or rather eternalize itself in this unique moment when the beginning and completion seem but one. "The Revolution is for many this sensation at once brutal, vague, and exhilarating, that it's all up with the old traditional social restraints: the new world to be built also goes through the renunciation of the old world, in everyday details. Whence the atmosphere of a permanent festival that every Revolution exudes, at least at its beginning."[21]

It is not a question of confusing the Revolution with its festivals, and still less of confusing the festival with the Revolution. Nevertheless, the interplay of a whole network of correspondences, of formal and symbolic relationships, makes it possible to relate them to one another. The aspiration to the exceptional affective climate of a "topsy-turvy world" which would be the beginning of a new social universe is a component of the Revolutionary myth. How remarkable it is, as a matter of fact, that in the time under study a certain mythology of the festival is sustained at the same time by the denial of a social system felt to be oppressive and the desire to prefigure in the festival a collective affectivity and sociability suitable to the universal action of social regeneration which is so slow in coming.[22]

In 1789, festivals were not invented according to preconceived formulas but, rather, were formed starting with gatherings of people who moved into an unaccustomed social space and took possession of it, who lived the positivity and hopes of the moment. The collective presence then transformed itself into a richly promising symbolic spectacle, turned toward the future. It could be said that the preliminary sketch for a Revolutionary festival preceded the first great Revolutionary day. On the eve of the opening of the Etats Généraux, 4 May, an immense crowd gathered in Versailles to attend the ceremony. "Beginning in the morning, the people were in the streets. Windows, rented at an exorbitant price, were filled with a crowd of the curious, who had rushed there from all over." The ceremony, the splendor, the decor are all those of a Régime that will not take long to become the "ci-devant," the former, the Ancien Régime. Mass is celebrated with Veni Creator, the king arrives in a ceremonial car preceded by the heralds dressed in their coats of violet velvet strewn with gold fleurs-de-lis, equerries, page boys on horseback, and so forth. The intentional aspect of the festival was emphasized primarily by setting up the spectacle of a social hierarchy. Different dress had been imposed on the *députés* from each state. The Third Estate was dressed in jackets and trousers of black wool, with a short coat of silk and cloth and a muslin tie; the nobles, in contrast, were wearing outfits adorned with gold and hats with white plumes. Public opinion immediately described this symbolism as "gothic" and, what is more, a large number of the spectators made no effort to hide their hostility toward it. Moreover, the entire mode of presence of the populace no longer content with admiring the splendor and the decor and with being part of it, and actively showing its preferences and its reservations, gives a new tone to the festival and rapidly takes on symbolic value.[23] Or rather, this active presence bears witness to a mentality in search of a new symbolism that would increase the value of the events experienced. How many symbolic gestures—a whole war of symbols, it could be said—between this festival on 4 May and the day when the positivity of an event—a badly defended fortress and the crowd that attacks it—is inscribed in a context that makes it the sign of something other than itself, the symbol of the beginning of a new epoch. In this context the image of the seizure of the Bastille had to become the object of an attention and discourse that sought to give a synthesizing sense to the succession of events, and this sense had necessarily to be projected toward the future in order to serve as explanation to the present. The day of 14 July ended more in fear and uncertainty than in joy. But three days later there was the festival. "Imagine," a young *député* of the Third Estate, who was little noticed at the time, writes to a friend, "a king in whose name the entire capital and the entire nation were made to tremble on the preceding day, crossing in the space of two leagues, with the representatives of the nation, an army of citizens drawn up in three lines, among whom he can recognize his soldiers, hearing the cry of *Vive la Nation*, *Vive la Liberté*, on all sides, a cry that struck his ears for the first time. The immensity of the citizens who seemed massed on all sides, who covered houses, hills, the very trees that were along the route. . . . I saw monks wearing the cockade that the inhabitants of the capital sported. . . . Those women who decorated the windows of high, magnificent buildings and whom we met along the way and whose applause and whose patriotic transports added so much sweetness to this *national festival*."

However, this royal visit to Paris on 17 July, whose exceptional character had so impressed the young *député* from Arras, had been planned according to the old formula. How characteristic it is, indeed, that to prepare for the entry of the king into Paris, the authorities of the city and Bailly in particular, feverishly sought out descriptions of the entry of Henri IV. The ceremonial—the greeting of the king at the gates of the city, the handing over of the keys, the solemn mass, the traversing of the city—had only to imitate the latter. But the old rites and gestures had become invested with new meanings—and new symbols, in particular the cockade, prevailed. But above all, it is the casting of roles that changes with this omnipresent crowd, that raises cries and slogans by which it affirms its new identity and proclaims itself a Nation. The royal entry finds itself transformed into a "national festival."[24]

Thus, in the autumn of 1789, we witness the "spontaneous generation of festivals and, toward the summer of 1790 when preparations are under way for the Fête de la Fédération, a great portion of the ritual of the new festival is invented."[25] The federations played the determining role, as is known, in this collective invention. The old ritual is mixed with the new: before the altars of the country, masses are celebrated, but so, too, are the first civic baptisms, the old flags are dominated by the new, and above all by those of the National Guard. The festivals are only *offered to the populace*. The notables and the national guards are placed at the center of the festival whose social character, especially during the autumn of 1789, is rather ambiguous. It must not be forgotten that at the same time the "great fear" is spreading, culminating sometimes in "wild celebrations" reproducing the secular rites of the peasant revolts. In this context more than one local festival of the federation took on the air of a counterfestival of order opposed to anarchy.

Nevertheless, the enormous impression made by the federations, the first Revolutionary festivals, and the enthusiasm they arouse is incontestable. The attendance is as large as it is spontaneous. The popular crowd adheres to the festival; it succeeds more or less, depending on the case, in diminishing the gap between itself and the national guardsmen and giving the formalities of great occasions the air of popular festivals. The festivals are organized around new symbols which are inseparable from them and with which they familiarize the masses. The festival thus becomes the "high and rather privileged point of a diffuse sensitivity that imbues all of daily life."[26]

This sensitivity that had a multitude of nuances and degrees of clarity and intensity is extremely rich in utopian potentialities, in social dreams and hopes nourished in the lived experience of the crisis of an entire system, a crisis in its values and its structures, its social hierarchies and its prohibitions. A. Mathiez, from his own perspective that magnified the religious, if not messianic, components of Revolutionary mentalities, brought out quite well the place that fell to the utopia in the field of expectations with which the Revolutionary experience was surrounded: "It is patriotism, the messianic expectation of Regeneration that inspires souls in 1789, the conviction that the Constitution will make all iniquities disappear not only from French soil, but from the face of the earth, absolute confidence in the omnipotence of human Reason, profound belief in indefinite progress, the imminent vision of a golden age, placed in the future and no longer in the past. . . . By Country was meant not a dead entity, a colorless abstraction, but a real and durable eternity, a mutual desire for the public good, the voluntary sacrifice of private interest to the general interest, the renunciation of all provincial, local, personal privileges . . . . The liberty of which one proclaims oneself the 'idolater' is not a sterile, neuter, indifferent liberty, but it is the faculty to realize the profoundly unitarian political ideal, the means of building the future harmonious and fraternal City."[27] The rites and ceremonies of the festivals lent themselves particularly well, if not to embodying, at least to presenting the image of what the sought-for triumph of liberty and virtue, of equality and the nation, of fraternity and happiness could be.

The "spontaneous generation" of festivals gave birth, on the one hand, to *utopias of the festival* and, on the other hand, revealed to the politicians and ideologues the power that symbols and ceremonies exercise over souls. The spectacle of the first festivals strikes the imagination of artists as much as that of politicians. For the former—for a David, a Chénier, a Gossec, a Quatre-mère—what a unique opportunity to realize the dream of a pathetic and mon-umental art, which would express intense emotions and form hearts and minds! The very absence of material means—time and money—stimulates the imagi-nation and orients proposals for festivals and settings toward the utopian. In fact, it was easier to rapidly give substance to dreams of a monumental art using cardboard and plaster than it was to construct from stone and sculpt in marble (all the more so, as a technique for the construction of such décors was available—it had, in fact, been established and perfected by the Menus Plaisirs for the great royal festivals). The contradictory constraints—to go quickly while striving for the monumental and the colossal—came, as a matter of fact, from the political evolution: the more events accelerated, the more changes accu-mulated, the more they wanted to situate them not in the provisional and relative, but in the durable, if not in the eternal and absolute.

Thus we have not only visions of festivals, but also theories and ideologies of festivals. In fact, it was rapidly realized, particularly after the enormous success of the Fête de la Fédération and it political exploitation by La Fayette, that festivals not only translate a real need to express a new sensibility, but that they are also a particularly effective instrument for influencing and orienting it, for impressing crowds, if not for manipulating them.

Mirabeau was the first, it seems, who with his habitual political intuition insisted on the novelty of the problem and launched the key formula: "seize the imagination!" He based it on a whole applied politico-philosophical anthropol-ogy. Man, as a sensitive being, is guided much less by "general principles that necessitate meditation to be grasped in all their aspects, than by imposing objects, striking images, great spectacles, profound emotions." Theoreticians have not taken this "very important" consideration, "so fertile in practical truths" suf-ficiently into account in "making their calculations on the progress of enlight-enment and on the rapid and certain effects they supposed them to have." And it is not sufficient to "show man the truth; the capital point is to inspire him with a passion for it; serving him in basic necessities is little, if one does not take over his imagination." If this "new consideration" is rigorously applicable to individuals, it is even more so "to nations taken collectively." Good orga-nization of national festivals is the most important and most effective means of "fulfilling this political and moral objective." Public education, as distinguished from schooling which is limited to dispensing knowledge, has as its prime object the guiding of the imagination and necessarily includes festivals. The example Mirabeau evokes in support of this is the Fête de la Fédération.[28]

Rousseau's themes and formulas on the imagination and its political func-tions are readily recognizable here but, as we have said, at the time they had become clichés. On the other hand, it is striking that beyond an abstract discourse are found specific, if not technical, problems of the "good organization of festivals." These are sometimes formulated in quasi-technological language, as, for instance, in this formidable formula of Cloots, who is wondering about the opportuneness "of guaranteeing the Republic *exclusive trade in the raw materials with which public opinion is formed.*"[29] Festivals could be said to be compared to a factory that "fabricates public opinion" with that "raw material" that consists of the images of the dreamed City.

If there is a contradiction between this "technological" attitude toward the festival and the utopia of the festival, there is complementarity as well. All things considered, both translate the same practice. The "spontaneous genera- tion" of the festival was not possible without the objects of social dreams, of that fraternal and harmonious City toward which all hopes are borne, being put into images. But the practice of the festival is also that of its *organization* and, hence, of the training of its *organizers*. The more the festivals multiplied and the broader their scope became, assembling hundreds and even thousands of people, the more they required preliminary scenarios and the elaboration of certain techniques for carrying them out. The festivals set up as "national," as an institution of public education, implied an organization on a countrywide scale and, hence, the activity of the supreme organizer which could only be the government. The utopia and bureaucratic technology combine with and hide behind each other in the ideological discourse that seeks to conciliate the different aspects of the festival, to justify the multiple roles and functions imposed on it, to define their finality and above all to insure the passage from isolated, more or less improvised festivals to a "system of national festivals."

"Assemble men, you will make them better; for men gathered together will strive to please one another, and they will only be able to do so by the things that make them estimable. Give a moral and political purpose to their gathering, and the love of honest things will enter their hearts with the pleasure; for men do not see one another without pleasure. Man is the greatest object that exists in nature; and the most magnificent of all spectacles is that of a great people assembled. . . . *A system of national festivals of course would be at once the sweetest fraternal tie and the most powerful means of regeneration.* Have general and more solemn festivals for the Republic as a whole; have individual festivals for every place, which are days of rest and which replace what circum- stances have destroyed. Let all aim at reawakening the generous and noble feelings which are the charm and the ornament of human life, enthusiasm for liberty, love of country, respect for law. Let them draw their interest and their name from the immortal events of our Revolution and from the most sacred objects, dearest to the heart of man; let them be embellished and distinguished by emblems analogous to their particular object." The orientation of all this "system of festivals" toward the utopia is explicit: according to Robespierre, it is a question of implementing the indispensable means for "successfully bringing about the masterpiece of society,'' the formation of the "new man.''[30] The Rousseauistic themes and formulas (which are once again evident), to which Robespierre was particularly sensitive, allowed him to rethink the historical experience of the Revolutionary festival and to associate the utopia of the festival to the social utopia and both of them to the power, the government. In fact, does this discourse, which is as sentimental as it is grandiloquent, not have as its second, and barely concealed, object, the government, the supreme organizer of this "system"?

The change from sporadic festivals that responded only to the needs of the moment to a "system of festivals" was essential for ideological reasons as well as because of political constraints, which were, in any case, inseparable from them. The "system" is considered an integral and most essential part of the education in civics that they wanted to establish most rapidly. For some, it was only to consolidate what had been gained by the Revolution; others saw it as a means of insuring the continued progress of the Revolution, its march toward its final aim, the City of social happiness, "a new idea in Europe." The religious conflict and the progress of dechristianization made a new system of festivals an urgent imperative. Indeed, more and more, the *national festivals* took on the significance of counterfestivals in relationship to Catholic ritual. With the introduction of the Republican calendar, they could not wait any longer. As we have seen, under the pressure of the moment, a "system" was improvised, in great haste, expressing the meanings with which it was desired to charge the restructured time. This system, which was intended to be definitive, was but the first. After Thermidor, they did not delay in getting rid of its utopianism, which had become more and more bothersome, the festival of all those "sansculottides," the remembrance of events they would like to have forgotten.

We cannot evoke the entire ideological debate dealing with festivals, nor can we examine the innumerable proposals that accompanied the birth of the "system of festivals." Let us point out only two common elements. First of all, the proposals have a share in the mythology of the festival and reproduce it. Because they have lived the exhilarating experience of the first festivals, because they have repeated with such energy and grandiloquence the accounts of ideal festivals, the ideologues and politicians have come to believe in the limitless possibilities of "taking over the imagination" with the aid of festivals, and have come to believe, too, in the infinite possibilities of fabricating them, of prescribing and organizing enthusiasm and the imaginary. It is, then, striking to note that in these proposals the imagination is curiously married to the bureaucratic and systematic spirit. The proposals aim to establish a system of festivals defined in the text of a law, divided into articles and paragraphs. They thus take the form of a discourse at once administrative and taxonomic on the values and norms that are already to command the imagination and, hence, social life in its entirety. Thus, they do not tire of inventing festivals. Everywhere, certainly, are to be those of liberty, of equality, or even those that are to commemorate the great events of the Revolution. But why not a festival of visible nature? Why not those of man's companion animals, of printing, of the fraternity of mankind, of the improvement of the language? Or even a festival of misfortune when "misfortune and unhappiness will be honored, the misfortune which humanity cannot entirely banish from the earth, but which it relieves and solaces with respect?" A festival of Love? Or even of Justice and Good Fortune?[31]

3
From the Broad Fresco to the Autopsy Report

*U*topian intentions and representations intervene in the discourse on the festival—proposals, theories, systems—but also, and above all, in the very practice of the festival.

Between the utopia of the festival and the real festivals, there are both convergences and conflicts. Real festivals are fashioned after models of the ideal festival but, on the other hand, the scenarios and, to a greater extent, their realization, had necessarily to be adapted to the constraints of time and space in which the real festival was taking place. The space of the revolutionary festivals is commanded by the vision of a space that is, so to speak, doubly transparent. It could be marked by no significance contrary to that lent it by the festival; it could never be an obstacle to the sight of the actor-spectators who were supposed to have the festival, both in its entirety and its individual elements, permanently before their eyes. In reality, this vision battles against insurmountable difficulties. In the large cities, it comes up against obstacles of the historic city—its space is *already* charged with meanings, marked by the monuments and the history they evoke, in flagrant contradiction with the regenerative message of the festival. The streets and broad, straight avenues are lacking, the plazas are too small for enormous crowds. In small towns, how can the space be found to create a setting worthy of the festival? The calm sky, a frequently dilapidated altar of the country, a tree of liberty in no way resembling an "old majestic oak," both set up in the middle of a village square, only worked well in rhetorical discourse.[32]

Similar contradictions and tensions are found on other levels. Thus, in the utopia of the festival, nature is not presented as a benevolent mother looking out for the happiness of her children, but is only the setting or even a sacred witness. The time for the festival could only be permanently fine weather—only the space of a blue (or starry) sky, under a soft and caressing sun. Yet, as is

198

well known, on the day of the Fête de la Fédération, it rained terribly. While situating itself in historical time, the utopia of the festival assumes it only by sublimating it in symbols and in a ceremonial that tended specifically to suppress all uncertainty in the celebrated event, and to situate it in a universal and timeless order of values. Even death exists in the utopia of the festival only by its denial, by ceremonies and symbols that proclaim the immortality of men and their actions. The time of the utopian festival, then, closes in on itself; it is reduced to the succession of symbols and the unfolding of the ritual; it conveys but a single meaning and the latter can only converge with the double civic and moral lesson given by the festival. However, in real festivals how frequently this sought transparency of the time of the festival is only shadow and opacity which conceal the ambiguities and the conflicts of the time of history!

As the message, both noble and simple, of the festival touched hearts directly, it had to be explained in a symbolic language and in a ceremonial that would strike the imagination so as to "take it over." There arose, then, a tendency to overload the symbols, which became ever more refined and complicated, in and by which the festival attempted to tell its own simplicity and its own transparency. The utopia of the festival rests on spontaneity, on the free transformation of the spectators into actors who are their own spectacle. Nevertheless, even in the utopian narrative recounting only pure spontaneity, an organizer is always present, if only in the execution of his word glorifying spontaneity. In the real festivals, the more they wanted them to be educational and the more numerous the crowd became, the less spontaneity was accepted as anything but an element of the order, and then only on the condition that it conform to the scenario that had been established in advance. Last but not least, the festival requires the presence of the people who made it into the "most beautiful and most sublime spectacle." It requires, as well, the participants' assent to its message and symbolism. Were the latter not only supposed to explain what the populace had already felt to be its own truth? But at the same time, the festival was intended to be educational, bringing a moral and civic lesson to its participants, if not imposing it on them. And, above all, it was necessary that the participants come to the festival, to form the countless crowds that brought it to life.

So as not to remain in the abstract, let us take the example of a festival in which the interplay of these convergences and oppositions between the utopia and reality is particularly striking. We are thinking in particular of the Parisian festival of the Unity and Indivisibility of the Republic, celebrated on 10 August, 1793. It is, as a matter of fact, a festival as curious as it is noteworthy. It owes its particular features and its élan both to the historical circumstances and to the imagination of David, who was the author of its scenario. The precarious situation in which the Montagnard Convention convoked a "republican meeting" is well known—externally, the debacles of the war, aggravated by Dumoriez's treachery; internally, the Vendéens, that incomprehensible popular revolt for ideologues and militant minorities, prevailed over the troops. "Federalist rebellions" broke out in Lyon, in Marseille, in Bordeaux; Toulon was in the hands of royalist insurgents. In the capital, the weeks preceding the ceremony were particularly tense. The 14 July was not celebrated—Marat had been assassinated the preceding day and his funeral took place on 16 July with the massive participation of the populace (David was given the responsibility of giving a setting and an artistic framework to the funeral). Food shortages were becoming more acute and whole sections were in a state of unrest. Under this pressure, the Convention voted, on 27 July, for the law against monopolizers and hoarders, and the day prior to the festival the law on "public granaries" was adopted. A brochure spread the rumor of a plot aiming to "set Paris to fire and the sword from around 10-15 August." Among the Jacobins the question was raised: Had the Lyonnais rebels not grasped the opportunity given by the festival to infiltrate the capital "with traitors and plotters?" Under these conditions, the Convention wanted the festival on 10 August to be both reassuring and stirring. The festival did not commemorate only the fall of the monarchy; its essential object was the solemn acceptance of the new Constitution and, in that sense, it is a portentous festival. The festival was, at one and the same time, to dispel and bring to the fore the dangers threatening the Revolution. They could only be temporary; it is the triumph of the Republic, solidly based on its constitution and opened on the future, that was to be celebrated. But what had already been gained as well as the promised future had to be defended against their enemies, both old and new. The very terms "unity" and "indivisibility" under the sign of which the festival was placed had an obvious political meaning and clearly designated the enemies to be combated and conquered. Delegates of the primary assemblies of all the departments were invited to the festival. Several groups of *fédérés* arrived with wagons loaded with foodstuffs for starving Paris. Barely ten days after the festival the levy en masse was to be decreed.

In the history of revolutionary festivals, that of 10 August 1793 is situated, so to speak, at the border between "spontaneous generation" and a "system" enclosing and fixing the festival. The ceremony is conceived as a unique event, a response to a concrete situation and to the emotions to which it gave rise. But, on the other hand, although no "system" was yet in place, a whole ritual had already been established based on the "matrix" of the Fête de la Fédération of 1790. Festivals, then, were threatened by repetition and lassitude. For that of 10 August, David wanted to innovate, while avoiding a rupture.

"Do not be surprised, Citizens," he said in his proposal, "if I have drawn away from what has been common practice up until today. The genius of liberty, as you know, does not like shackles; success is all; the means of attaining it are immaterial." Artistic means, certainly, but material means, as well. David asks the Convention for half a million *livres*; he will be given only one hundred and twenty thousand. They want the wished-for moral effects at less cost, and there really is a lack of money.

David *sees* the festival—his proposal is indeed a text inhabited by a vision. He conceives it as at once a gigantic fresco projected on the city and a collective psychodrama played out by an enormous crowd. The scenario anticipates everything: setting, symbols, roles to be played by the participants. It even forecasts emotions: here will be happiness, there a profound, moved, silence, and elsewhere "our mutual feelings will meet in tender embraces."[33]

The festival begins by assembling on the site of the Bastille where "some of the ruins were still confusedly spread." It was still night. "The French, gathered together to celebrate unity and indivisibility, will rise before dawn." Successive directives advance the hour of assembly from five to four in the morning, "that is, to sunrise, which is strictly necessary to the spirit of the festival." In fact, the time and place converge in the spirit of the beginning. "The touching scene of the gathering is lit by the first rays of the sun and the accomplishment of the regeneration of France is thus associated with the rise of the day star, which makes Nature quiver with joy." To the rising sun is joined "a song that expresses the return of the light." The beginning of day, but also the beginning of History. It is here, at the Bastille, that it started anew with the luminous time that opened a new book to it. This symbolism of the beginning, of darkness, obscurity, and light, can escape no one. In any case, twenty or so inscriptions "placed on the stones of the Bastille" are there to recall that other time, that dark and tyrannical time of suffering and injustice. So, one can read, going from one stone to another: "an old man bathed this stone with his tears"; "this stone was never illuminated"; "hell vomited forth kings"; "my children, my dear children"; "hell vomited forth priests"; "I no longer sleep"; "my faithful spider was crushed before my eyes. . . ." Daybreak, the dawn of history, the beginning of the festival.

The latter links, in a "harmonious whole," two formulas: that of the procession crossing the city and that of the gathering of the populace in a vast open space. The itinerary followed—the Bastille, the boulevards, the place de la Révolution, the Invalides, the Champ-de-Mars—is approximately that which had already been utilized in other festivals (that of Fédération in 1791, the festival of the soldiers of Châteauvieux). It has the advantage of bypassing the historical center of the city, impracticable because of the narrowness of the streets, but also because of the "monuments of tyranny" marking it, which contradict the spirit of the festival. On this route, there are five "stations," including the points of departure and arrival. They are the high points of the festival, acts of the psychodrama.

Let us look first at the order of the procession, for there is one and it is most rigorous. The places assigned to the participants give them a symbolism and strictly prescribe their roles. This procession "of a nation restored to liberty and returned to nature" is divided into three groups. At the head, the popular societies that carry the banner with the eye of vigilance "opened on the clouds which it penetrated and which it dissipated; a reassuring and threatening sign of the vigilant guard from which no traitor had escaped or could escape." Then comes the National Convention, preceded by the Declaration of the Rights of Man and the Constitution inscribed on tablets. The *députés* are surrounded by "a light tricolored ribbon which links the envoys of the primary Assemblies to one another." Each of the members of the Convention carries a bouquet of wheat and fruit in his hand; the envoys of the primary Assemblies carry "a pike, the symbol of liberty against tyrants, in one hand; an olive branch, the symbol of peace and fraternal unity among all the departments of a single and indivisible Republic, in the other." (The distribution of the bouquets, pikes, and olive branches was provided for before dawn, in a place and according to modalities set by a directive.)

But it is the third group that incarnates "the idea of the festival by which its organizer imprinted its finest characteristic." This third group is "composed of all the respectable mass of the sovereign power." Here *spontaneity* and *equality* reign. "There is no order drawn; there is no longer any division of people or of civil servants. . . . Everything here slips away, everything comes together, becoming one and the same." Let us however look at this attentively, letting nothing escape our glance. This "respectable mass of the sovereign power" has a place to itself and by no means will spontaneity extend beyond it. Of course, there is "no prescribed regularity," but directives indicating that participants will not walk "ten abreast" and that "the tricolored pennants carried at intervals will show, when they are raised, that it is time to march and, when they are lowered, that it is time to stop," will be respected. And then, in this "respectable mass," all individuals "useful to society will be *indiscriminately* merged, although characterized by their *distinctive insignia*. "The *procureur* of the Commune will be "on the same row" as the blacksmith, one carrying a scarf, the other a hammer in his hand; the judge is beside the mason, one wearing a feathered hat, the other holding his trowel. The white gives his hand "to the Black African," this time they wear nothing, so to speak, as their "distinctive insignia," but the color of their skin. "In this social and philosophical confusion where everything gave the sight and the sentiment of sacred equality, the eternal stamp of creation, and the first law of Nature," in this mass that in itself already formed a moving spectacle, still further representations were in play. Here, on a trailer, "the students of the Institution of the Blind make the airs of their joyous songs ring out." There, it is the nurslings of the orphanage, carried in white rocking cradles, who "announce that the Republic is their mother and the Nation their family." Still elsewhere, a venerable old man and his wife, placed on a wagon and pulled along by their children.

In its march and by this very march, advancing from one station to another, the *procession tells itself a story*, recounts a history, while representing it at the same time. This account is on many levels: it is the story of the procession itself, but also that of the Revolution, a profane history but also a sacred one, an account of the past, but an anticipation of the future as well. "Five times, in the space that it was to cover, this august pomp came to a halt and each station presented monuments which recalled the finest acts of the Revolution, or ceremonies that consecrated it or completed it."

At the first station, the Bastille, is the *time of beginnings, of regeneration*. "The history of the infamies of despotism, which prompted painful, moving impressions in souls, along with the consolation of a profound and meditative joy" was read on the stones that had been "mutilated by the axe of liberty." But then eyes turned from the periphery toward the center, toward the fountain of Regeneration where rose the colossal plaster statue of Nature, represented by a nude woman, in the Egyptian style. From the numerous breasts that she was pressing with her hands "two streams of pure and abundant water, images of her inexhaustible fertility, poured forth into a vast basin." The president of the Convention recites "a kind of hymn": "Sovereign of the Savage and of enlightened Nations, O Nature, this immense populace assembled at the first rays of day before your image is worthy of you, it is free. It is in your breast, it is in your sacred springs that it recovered its rights, that it was regenerated. After having traversed so many centuries of error and servitude, it had to enter into the simplicity of your ways to find liberty and equality again." Then he fills a cup of antique shape with the regenerative water that "falls from Nature's breast" and drinks from it. Then he passes the cup to the elderly men, one from each department, in the order "determined by alphabetic chance." (There was difficulty in designating the eighty-six venerable old men because the preceding day, at the Jacobins, the envoys of the primary assemblies had been admonished for having failed or forgotten to delegate their "elderly agents," despite urgent and repeated notices from the organizers of the festival.) Each of the eighty-six elderly men feels the need to express his emotions in one sole phrase, as concise as it is sublime. The last, whose "white hair floated in the winds, seized with a prophetic spirit, cries out: O France! Liberty is immortal; the laws of the Republic, like those of Nature, will never perish." Then they sing "the air dear to the children of Marseille stanzas analogous to the ceremony"; each time that the cup passes from one hand to another, they give each other the republican and fraternal kiss, cannons sound, and "the electric movements of a solemn joy join" with their noise.

At the second station, the Boulevard des Poissonnières, it is the *time of combat* that is recounted. A triumphal arch represents the days of 5 and 6 October, 1789, when "one saw woman, who had become intrepid with the sentiment of liberty, drag cannons along and in a manner of speaking lead the men where it was necessary to attack tyranny.'' Under this arch which, by its beauty, surpassed the masterpieces of ancient Rome and Athens, ''these courageous women represent themselves in the middle of the monument of their glory,'' seated on the cannon carriages. (We do not know where and how the organizers of the festival recruited these representative women or how many they were.) The president gives each a fraternal embrace, places a laurel crown on each head, and the procession, which they have joined, turning their cannons around, gets under way again ''amid universal acclamations.''

The place de la Révolution is marked by the third station—it is *the time of the Revolution on the march, purificatory and victorious over tyranny*. The very spot recalls the death of the last tyrant (the guillotine had been removed for the festival) and it is here that the statue of Liberty is erected. ''As the daughter of Nature, she appeared through the leafy shade of the young trees with which she was surrounded. It is to this divinity that the love of the French offers tributes.'' From the branches of the poplars are hung red caps, garlands of flowers, pencil drawings that recalled the prodigious moments of the Revolution, verses ''found more beautiful because they all expressed but one sentiment.'' However, these offerings do not suffice and ''still another sacrifice to the Goddess was necessary.'' They go on to ''the great purification of an empire by fire.'' With a torch, the president lights an enormous pyre, ''covered with combustible materials,'' where the throne, the scepter, the armories, all the ''odious trappings of despotism'' disappear ''in the crackling noise of the flames amidst the acclamations of more than eight hundred souls.'' Then three thousand birds of all species fly off into the heavens wearing thin streamers around their necks on which are written these words: *We are free, imitate us*. Two doves took refuge under the folds of the statue of Liberty and set up their home there. ''They remained faithful to this sacred monument. Superstitious antiquity would be jealous of such a trait . . . but the true oracles of the French people are its reason and its rights, quite superior to all political charlatanism.'' Still, however good a rationalist one might be, how can one prevent oneself from reading the happiest portent for the Republic in this sign drawn by Nature herself?

The fourth station was in front of the Invalides. It is, certainly, ''a monument of the pride of a despot.'' Nevertheless, it is already ''improved by benevolence and national sovereignty.'' And then, it is only a setting for the gigantic statue of the *peuple Hercule* crushing the monster of federalism and *beating it* down with its club (both the giant and the monster are in plaster). The historical time recounted by the procession and the moment at which the procession recounts it meet—this is the *time of the last combats*. Of the recent victory over federalism, ''that new monster no less dangerous to liberty than is tyranny,'' and of the combats still to be fought, whose result is already prefigured by the statue. ''Contemplating these emblems rising in the air to a great height, the populace recognized its force and its triumph.'' And so that they not misunderstand, "the images under which it and its history were retraced under their own eyes became the text of the discourse that the president pronounced on that occasion."

It is at the last station, the Champ-de-Mars, that the past and present culminate in the *future* or are even transcended in the successful outcome of the story recounted of the history. While the crowd covers the esplanade, the first group of the procession makes an entry that "offers to the eye, to the imagination, and to the soul one of those sublime and touching lessons the idea of which only liberty can conceive and the spectacle of which only liberty can present." A tricolored ribbon is suspended from two columns and a level is suspended from the ribbon. Those who form the head of the procession penetrate into the esplanade "only after having bent over or, rather, raised themselves under this level, a tangible allegory of equality, an emblem of what makes the unique greatness of man, of what alone prepares real and lasting prosperity for him." It is then that the final act takes place, which makes this festival and this instant "the greatest epoch of Humankind." The president, "having attained the highest point of the altar of the Country," having the eldest of the departmental administrators at his side, from that height, as if from the veritable holy Mountain, published the vote count of the primary Assemblies of the Republic and proclaimed the Constitution, "the only Constitution, since peoples have existed, that gave a liberty based on equality and which made fraternity a political dogma, to a great empire." The continuously repeated artillery salvoes and "a million voices converging in a single shout send the joy of the earth up to the heavens." It could be said that both of them, heaven and earth, are joined by this solemn act that establishes the New City, that "Republic that Humanity charged with its cause and which must save the Universe" forever. Some rites are still to be performed. The eighty-six departmental administrators who, during the march, each held a pike, place all these pikes in the hands of the president of the Convention, who gathers them into a single bundle, held together by a ribbon in the colors of the nation. The ashes of the defenders of the Republic are placed in an antique-style funerary temple. This is the final homage and the final appeal: "May the Republic triumph, this Republic which, all alone, stands up to all tyrants, to all the vile passions, to all peoples who dishonor themselves."

"Such was the march, such were the objects and tableaux offered to the gaze of the sovereign people in the inauguration of the French Republic. Never had liberty appeared more august to eras and nations. The populace was great and majestic like it." The people had gathered before dawn; it is past noon. They begin to eat "seated fraternally on the grass." It is a "frugal banquet"; each shares, mixing "with that of his brothers the food that he himself brought" (the directives are specifically insistent on this latter point. Contrary to the customs of tyrannical festivals, nothing is offered to drink or eat, none of the gifts that were as degrading as they were contemptible. And there was, above all, a terrible lack of provisions). Then, on a vast theater, the principal events of the Revolution are presented in pantomimes. One of these spectacles takes up and represents the ceremony that has just been completed: the procession, the stations. Thus, by a play of mirrors, the festival is reflected in itself; the time lived and the time recounted converge, opening and closing on each other.

As regards the history, the festival tells its story in symbolic language. It is useless to stress the fact that in this gigantic production everything is intended to be symbolic: time and space, setting and costumes, each and every step and gesture. Everything is a sign. The programmed spontaneity is only the sign of spontaneity; the festival in its entirety is only the sign of the people in festival. That statue of the *peuple Hercule* is the emblem of the "respectable mass of the sovereign power." But would an opposite reading not be equally justified? Is this "respectable mass" not merely a sign whose meaning is in the colossal statue? It is useless as well to insist on the excessiveness of these symbols, however numerous the emblems and rites we have omitted. The ceremony of the "republican and fraternal kisses" is repeated a good dozen times—millions of embraces in series, to be graphed according to their emotional intensity, by a scrupulous historian.

This linkage of symbols forms a coherent discourse whose orientation toward the utopia of the New City is intended to be obvious, if not aggressive. What is affirmed, and set up as a spectacle, is a dreamed Revolution definitively triumphant over enemies and difficulties. In a time and a space that are themselves "utopianized," it establishes its great principles and values for eternity, incorporating all of humanity, regenerated and reconciled with Nature.

We have only spoken of the symbols *present*. But another symbolism, of which this festival is totally devoid, is conspicuous by its *absence*, which has an enormous symbolic charge. The priests and their superstitious cult were only rarely explicitly indicated. But in the crowd, everyone had in his memory those other very recent revolutionary festivals which were announced by the ringing of church bells and during which mass was celebrated. Was the festival, by recounting in its march a history of regeneration, by stopping at the stations where hymns were recited and songs were raised to heaven, not a negative replica, either deliberate or unconscious, of those other processions that, in fourteen stations, told another story? Those processions had been forgotten by no one. Barely two weeks before the festival of 10 August, scuffles had broken out in Paris because the Commune had tried to prevent the procession of Corpus Christi with its habitual splendor. By opposition to the time evoked in the religious processions, that celebrated by this festival was defined as *secular*. But from another point of view how can we not recognize the *sacred* inherent in it? Was it not the regenerative and purificatory time in which the Revolution was to accomplish the task, with which humanity had charged it, of "saving the universe"? The New City was the great promise of the time. The transfer of the sacred into the time of secular history, proposed or imposed by the scenario of the festival, announced the great wave of dechristianization. Some weeks later, this time will be institutionalized with the adoption of the republican calendar and its system of festivals.

The symbols muddled up with one another formed an inclusive and omnipresent discourse whose redundancies further reinforced the wished-for aggressivity. Nevertheless, superfluous inscriptions and discourses that took up and commented on all these "vigorous signs" were added—as if their force and effects on the imagination were doubted, despite frequent reaffirmation.

However wordy it already was, this festival could not do without a narrative which would recount it once again, from its beginning to its end. Whether in the future, as in David's proposal, or in the past, as in the accounts that only repeat the initial scenario, such a narrative proves to be indispensable to the final success of the festival. That is not only because of the necessity of explaining symbols that were overly refined and complex; there are more profound reasons. The festival, in its totality and in all its individual elements, was intended to be transparent—readable, visible, and audible for each of its participants, its actor-spectators. But in the reality of the festival there was no place from which it was materially possible to embrace it in its entirety, from which it could offer itself to the view as a whole which harmoniously combined the innumerable signs and gestures spread out in an enormous space and during several hours. In other words, the festival does not fully affirm itself, does not attain, so to speak, the plenitude of its being, if not in a second narrative which recounts it specifically as absolutely transparent. But such a narrative account was itself possible only on condition that it followed a gaze wandering freely about in the imaginary *elsewhere*, that place where the utopia of the festival encountered no obstacle. But then in this narrative account the real festival itself is no longer anything but a sign to which the imagined and programmed ideal festival gives its true meaning.

The festivals differ from one another; contrary to the spectacle, whose performances are repetitious, every festival is unique. Each festival has its particular physiognomy which depends, in part, on its "affective temperature," the collective sensitivity that inspires it. Also, the number of participants has a lot to do with this and the civic festival, in particular, calls for a relatively large throng as well as a certain "population" density in the space—an indispensable condition for the individuals to be able to enter into contact with one another and for them to feel themselves sustained and transcended by the collective presence. It is, however, obvious that it is not the scenario alone, nor the number of participants alone, who make the festival—how many examples do we know from both yesterday and today, where the gathering of thousands of people did not succeed in the least in lending even a festive air to a sad official ceremony. The festival, when it comes right down to it, really stems from the way in which it is experienced and lived by its participants. "This solemn day," said Mercier of the Fête de la Fédération, "was like an electrical experience. Everything that touched the chain had to feel the shock; it was great, it was universal."[34] This "shock," an essential factor of the festival, is also its most ephemeral, its most subjective and variable aspect, and hence the one most difficult to determine. It is here that the interrogation on the presence and role of dreams and social hopes in the emotional climate of different festivals comes up against a major difficulty. How can the state and the intensity of the social imagination at work, its orientations and its ambiguities, be defined and delimited? How can its dreams of an alternative society, dreams which espouse the reality in this unique event where the real itself existed only coupled with the illusory and the imaginary, be reconstructed?

The mass of available documents does not necessarily facilitate the task. The quantitative data furnished in contemporary accounts cannot even be relied on. Large popular gatherings are difficult to count and evaluations are still more uncertain when they translate the emotions of the spectator, his way of seeing and experiencing the festival. How many were at the festival of 10 August? Two hundred thousand? Eight hundred thousand? "The entire populace of Paris?" Was the million mentioned in a report anything but an additional metaphor? And then again, how can one go from this quantitative data, itself uncertain, to the qualitative study of the spirit of a festival and of its utopian components, assessments of which are vague, and particularly suspect of being impressionistic? Just as the festivals are overloaded with symbols, the narrative accounts of them abound in grandiloquence. As we have noted, the latter is both revealing and misleading. Revealing insofar as it attests to the presence of the utopia of the festival as well as to the use of a certain language of the sensibility that is becoming almost standardized at the time. But, on the other hand, the projection of the utopia on actuality, as well as the standardization of the language, conceals the affective climate of the festivals. If we believe the narrative accounts, particularly those of the newspapers and official documents, all the festivals become more and more "simple and sublime," all are inspired with the "sacred fire of enthusiasm," the populace always are its "greatest" or its "majestic and moving" ornament. Nor do "electric movements of solemn joy" ever fail to occur.

One is struck by the monotony of this type of evidence which, moreover, contented itself with embellishing the official scenarios with adjectives. A small detail is often more instructive than long pages. Such as, for example, these stanzas improvised during the Fête de la Fédération, when nature failed to fulfill the symbolic function its organizers had wished it to:

> Ah, ça ira, ça ira, ça ira
> En dépit d'aristocrates et de la pluie;

Ah, ça ira, ça ira, ça ira
Nous nous mouillerons, mais ça finira.

It'll be okay, it'll be okay, it'll be okay
In spite of aristocrats and the rain;
It'll be okay, it'll be okay, it'll be okay
We'll get wet, but it'll be over.

Or:

Que'qu'a me fait à moi, d'être mouillé
Quand c'est pour la liberté.[35]

What do I care about being wet
When it's for liberty.

However, the collective affectivity of the revolutionary festivals is most frequently concealed under the false transparency of the words and symbols that speak of it. It is, therefore, necessary to approach them as one does the trompe l'oeil decors so well liked at the time and whose reality was in the very illusion they presented. And yet the historian would so like to take the elements apart, put them back together, and then look at them anew, while frequently changing his point of view. . . .

Nevertheless, through the mass of evidence an evolution is clearly outlined, although its roads are winding, with chutes and ladders, gaps, falls, repetitions, and reruns from one festival to another and from one locality to another. It is obvious that the political and ideological content of the revolutionary festival as well as its social characteristics change in relation to the evolution of the Revolution. At the Montagnard epoch, the festival has its principal support in the spirit inspiring the militant minorities, massacred or dispersed after Thermidor —which does not, however, mean that the history of the festival is reduced to the political and social history of the Revolution or that it is a simple reflection of it. Indeed, once born of "spontaneous generation" and then institutionalized, the festival has a relatively autonomous evolution. Its utopia, its symbols, and its mechanisms acquire a certain historical inertia. The political and administrative power cannot manipulate the festival without respecting its specific structure and its internal workings. Throughout its long history, the revolutionary festival, while translating the social, political, and ideological conflicts into its own languages, conceals them at the same time behind the illusions that it disseminates. Finally, the festival wears itself out in its own contradictions, and succumbs under the weight of its own myths, institutions, utopias, and symbols.

Great is the distance traveled by the festival between its explosion in autumn

1789, the great psychodrama of 10 August, 1793, and those spectacles of years V-VII of the Republic to which the reports of the administration of a commune of Périgord bear witness. The festivals take place then "in compliance with the order of the Directoire" of such and such a date: they combine "the municipal administration with the totality of its members, all the public employees of the canton as well as all office workers and all wage-earners of the Republic." The scenarios are prescribed in detail by official orders and "the local administration in its entirety" does its best to carry them out. So, on 1 vendémiaire year V, "in compliance with the order of the executive Directoire of last 13 fructidor," they assemble at 8 A.M. for the anniversary of the founding of the Republic. The president gives "the starting signal" to go (in the words of article 2 of the order) to the altar of the country. There, the constituted authorities are placed "according to the order indicated by the program of the festival, the populace lined up surrounding the tree of Liberty." Then comes the reading of the first article of the draft of the constitution and of the Declaration of the Rights of Man. "The profound reverence that followed this reading is the indubitable characteristic of the respect and admiration that those in attendance could not help feeling at the memory of the sacred principles of which they had just been reminded." Then the president makes his speech, which was "burning with patriotism," and takes an oath of "hatred of royalty and anarchy, and attachment and fidelity to the Republic and the Constitution of Year III and at that moment the assembly became the perfect echo of the voice that was pronouncing it." Then they practiced once again the "songs that love of Country had inspired" and the festival ends by "general enjoyment under a calm sky" as well as a "fraternal banquet where equality and concord presided over frugality." "For lack of pecuniary means," the ceremony is made without the required pomp, but substituted for this is "the effusion of the hearts of those who attended." Thus all the workings of the festival are in place and we omit numerous details, such as the stanzas to ancient Rome read on 23 Thermidor of the Year VI, or the twenty-four elderly men provided with white sticks who got together on 30 ventôse for the festival of the sovereign people.

There is but one element lacking. In fact, the enthusiastic reports scarcely hide the fact that the populace supposed "to be lined up surrounding the tree of Liberty" has missed the appointment. "Despite the frequently reiterated invitation of the municipal administration, the participation of those attending the national festivals is almost always reduced to the members of the authorities, so that it is impossible to give splendor to these epochs that call up such fond memories to true Republicans." "The festival of this day (1 vendémiaire, Year VII) showed the effects of this harmful indolence and ended by the public employees' wishes to see our legislators take effective means to give to these festivals all the interest that they might present." The ceremony of the replacement of the first tree of Liberty that withered between 1789 and Year VI, solemnly celebrated on 10 pluviôse ("in compliance with the law of last 24 nivôse") thus takes on a symbolic sense that is exactly the opposite of the festival's intention. And that is despite the assurance given that "the new tree rises majestically, that its still tender branches contain the productive sap that seems to be awaiting germinal to give the first sign of life. . . ."

In the general lassitude, there is only one person, the elementary school-teacher, citizen Petit-Bregnat who, with inexhaustible energy, composes from festival to festival songs and stanzas "analogous to the subject of the festival and apt to inspire ardent love for the Republic." It is certainly also he who writes these reports, combining in their flowery style the exactness of a public servant and the patriotic enthusiasm of a poet whose muse is never absent. "Everyone was still casting his thoughts into that happy future that peace promises to us, when citizen Petit-Bregnat reproduced in Republican couplets the sentiments expressed by the two orators, for his muse inspired him with hatred for kings and with the benefits of peace."[36] His phraseology, in which all the clichés of the utopia of the festival are to be found, is doubly revealing both by what it conceals of the reality of these ceremonies and by its evidence of the illusions the festival programmed by the order seeks to disseminate. Good citizen Petit-Bregnat—why would we doubt the sincerity of his sentiments?—seems to be the last who is still inspired by the radiant utopia, in the colorlessness of these festivals that are more and more devoid of living content. Did he suspect that in his enthusiastic reports he was in fact drawing up so many autopsy certificates, postmortem examinations of the Revolutionary festival?

4
Models of Festivals and Speaking Sensibility

*T*wo sets of observations are called for here by way of conclusion, one which has to do with the ideal models of Revolutionary festivals, the other with certain particularities of the language of these festivals.

Michelet's famous pages that recount the Revolutionary festivals are uneven, as much because of their expressive force as because of their pertinence. Michelet's historical genius is here all the more at ease as the Revolutionary festivals lent themselves particularly well to his imagination, which made history live again while nourishing itself on history. Besides, these pages also owe much of their strength to Michelet's own personal utopia of the festival, one that was marked by the author's profound nostalgia for the Revolutionary festivals he had not known, and by the repulsion with which lugubrious memories of imperial pomp had left him.[37]

There is, of course, no question either of imitating Michelet's historical and literary genius, or of taking up his language and his own symbolic repertoire. The major interests of his works for contemporary analysis of the collective psychology of Revolutionary festivals and, in particular, for questions concerning the utopian components of the affectivity that underlies them, seems to us to be elsewhere. What we today find particularly striking in these pages is that there are *two ideal types of Revolutionary festivals* to be found in them. If fact, found in these pages are, on the one hand, the model of the "hot" festival, the scene for the expression of a creative spontaneity; a nearly perfect correspondence is set up between the ideal project of the festival and the manner of collectively living its rites and symbols; the collective affectivity is characterized by a strong utopian component; the time is lived as that when "everything is possible" and the social imagination is oriented toward a social elsewhere, toward a world different in its values and norms. On the other hand, it is the model of the "cold" festival, which is only a bureaucratic institution utilized as an instrument of political and ideological action and where there is a divorce established between the intentional aspect of the festival and the collective way of living it, where "nothing is produced" although many things happen; the rites and symbols are therefore reduced to purely decorative functions and do not in any way stimulate the social imagination; the utopian component of the collective affectivity is minimal or nonexistent; tolerance for spontaneity remains very weak.

It is useless to insist on the fact that no real festival is perfectly in conformity with either of these two models. As we have already noted, there are no festivals which would do without a minimum of organization and, hence, of organizers; besides, the greater the crowds of participants, the more vital is the necessity of a certain technique, if not of a certain technology, that is substituted for improvisation. The symbols and rites are not invented on the occasion of each festival; they are taken up again, just as there is an attempt made to reuse their settings. Besides, one can expect that even at the time of the progressive degradation of the festival, citizens like Petit-Bregnat are still to be found who, prisoners of a utopia and a mythology of the festival, do not tire of their enthusiasm, carried away by their own emotions and their own words, for lack of other resources. As we have already seen, a complete ideology of the festival, largely taking its inspiration from Rousseau, contributed to a self-mystification. That whole dialectics of the people as object and subject of the festival promoted the illusion that the discourse pronounced at the festival was not at bottom anything but the word addressed by the participants to themselves, and that order wanted, if not imposed by the organizers, was only the expression of the popular will for order.

Thus, the explicative value of these two models, as of every ideal type, is limited, and it is not the same for both of these models. Nothing could be simpler than finding festivals that seem to have been copied from the model of the bureaucratized festival; how rare, on the other hand, are the festivals that combine all the elements of the other model, that of the "hot" festival. Let us, however, beware of confusing the ideal types of festivals with the *sociological* characteristics of one real festival or another. A festival might be perfectly programmed and exploited by the power that *offers* it to the people and this offer, if it satisfies a real affective demand, might be accepted with true enthusiasm. The festival then reinforces that enthusiasm and reforms it. Was this not, after all, the case of the Fête de la Fédération in 1790, that matrix for great Revolutionary festivals. Let us beware, even more, of a procedure which is nevertheless very much in vogue, which assimilates the model of the spontaneous festival to the popular *and* Revolutionary festival or which, rather, makes this model the link between them. This procedure is as simple as it is reassuring, at least for some. The historical realities, on the other hand, are a good deal more complex. As we have said, at the time, popular festivals are to be found, which in certain respects are close to the model of the spontaneous festival. Such as, for example, the festivals that occasionally explode during the "great fear" when, after having burned the "papers" in anger and joy, they bring barrels from the wine cellar of the château. But the Revolutionary festivals, in the historical and not the mythological sense of the word, did not at all aim to prolong or continue these "savage festivals," celebrated as they were on the modes of the secular ritual of the peasant revolts. But the other popular forms of festive activity, in no way "subversive" or violent, are not taken up either in the practice or the theory of Revolutionary festivals. They subsist during the Revolutionary period beside the Revolutionary festivities, occasionally, if not frequently, in conflict with them, rarely, if not exceptionally, in symbiosis with them. Thus, whether and to what degree the Revolutionary festivals which were supposed to impress the masses had other than temporary effects on popular mentalities remains an open question. And it would be necessary to pay strict attention to not confusing the "people," however multiple the populace, with the militant minorities grouped in popular sections and societies, which carefully worked out their own specific rites. If the Revolutionary festivals were the scene of certain cultural admixtures, then the process was as contradictory as it was complex, and the circulation from "high" to "low" predominated.

This complexity of the social functions of the Revolutionary festivals, if not their ambiguity, is particularly striking in the symbolic and metaphorical language that served as their support. That leads us to the second point of our remarks. We have stressed the fact that the festivals are, on the one hand, the privileged scene for the initiation of the masses into the new Revolutionary symbolism and that, on the other hand, they furnish a setting and symbolic support to the powers that establish themselves and seek to stabilize themselves.

We have already said that the "spontaneous generation" of the festival was produced simultaneously with that of Revolutionary symbols. The Revolution is, at its beginning, an "immense and nearly universal explosion of sensibility";[38] it is, as well, that of signs by which this sensibility is expressed. The social dreams and hopes, frequently vague and contradictory, seek to become crystallized, and are in search of a language and modes of expression that would make them communicable. Moreover, they are found in imaged signs, collective rites, and the spoken language; the latter tends to translate the ideas into images by the play of rhetorical figures and metaphors. The symbolic language is particularly appropriate to assure a mode of communication to the masses who seek to recognize one another and affirm themselves in their actions. In fact, Revolutionary actions presuppose not only a collective presence and at least the germ of structuring, but also a community of social imagination and, hence, the use of a language specific to it. Marx's pages, in which he opposes the French Revolution, disguising its actors in the costumes of antiquity, to the proletarian Revolution, whose actors need no disguise, are well known. But on no path of their history, not even on those of Revolution, whether bourgeois or anything else, do men go naked. They need signs and images, gestures and costumes, to communicate with and recognize one another along the road. Abstract concepts and principles only become guiding ideas insofar as they are capable of becoming nuclei around which the collective imagination is organized. The extent of their imaginary aureoles makes them gain in emotional diffuseness. Thus, the formation of the symbolic Revolutionary repertoire and its diffusion are a complex social process. The implantation of these symbols and their war against the old ones (but also the syncretism of both, which was quite frequently the case, especially at the beginning of the Revolution) are all Revolutionary *events*. One is mistaken about their impact if one sees in them only a setting in which one seeks to situate some Revolution or other, as pure and transparent as it is mythical.

The Revolutionary festival was a privileged scene of both the establishment and the exercise of the multiple functions of this symbolic language. It is in this language that the images of the New City fuse with the founding myths of the Revolution and are expressed with "force and energy." In other words, the double character of these festivals—that of being *festivals* and that of being imbued with a *Revolutionary sensibility*—converges in the predilection for a certain symbolic language.

That being the case, it is nevertheless still necessary to question the linguistic foundations of this sensibility and, in particular, to see whether it does not follow rules of expression already in place with a certain language of sensibility that had been formed prior to the Revolution, in the second half of the eighteenth century. In other words, the question that must be considered is whether the renewal of the collective imagination necessarily entails the alteration of the rules that govern the linking of these new signs into a discourse. This is a vast problem that would call for an in-depth study; we will return to it, taking up a specific example in our chapter below on visionary architecture and city planning. Let us, for the moment, limit ourselves to noting that in the second half of the century numerous manifestations of new means of expression of sensibility are observed. There is a delicate distinction in definition between what is called the "reawakening of sensibility" at this time and what could be called the establishment of a specific code of sensitive language. It seems, though, that sentiments and feelings must not be confused with the rules that govern their modes of expression. What in fact is being carefully worked out and developed at this time in the culture of the "enlightened" elites is a *speaking sensibility*.

It is well known that "sensitive souls" cry abundantly in novels and on the stage; but we have a great deal of evidence that they do the same, shedding torrents of tears, in daily life. These tears are by no means feigned. One cries because feelings must manifest themselves by outward signs; the tears are true, but they are tear-signs by which one speaks to others and by which people recognize one another, among friends; and that is by making a spectacle of oneself, putting oneself forward as a *tableau vivant* of friendship. One not only feels deep emotions while looking at ruins—either historical ruins, ruins artificially constructed, or even trompe l'oeil painted ruins—but one begins to cry in admiring them. There is, then, a whole tendency to express and theatricalize sensibility, to give it as a spectacle to oneself and others. One also ponders the language particularly privileged for the expression of feelings, a language whose sign-symbols would be quasi-transparent with regard to their signifieds and which would thus assure perfect communication. That amounts to saying that affections must quite "naturally" lean toward a certain repertoire of signs in order to "speak" in this way. This pursuit has reference to a whole philosophy of nature and morality, but also to the idea of a "speaking" art, one thus conveying, thanks to its languages, a moral message. Thus there is an attempt to translate this message into "speaking images" or even into "imaged words" and, hence, art is considered a privileged means of the formation of souls—leading back to ideas about the educational functions of art. There is also an attempt to explicitly specify the rules that govern this language of feelings in writings on "speaking art" (this is notably the case of those that deal with visionary architecture, and which we will come to in the following chapter), as well as in linguistic debates of the origins of languages.

The Revolution was, certainly, the time of strong emotions. However, the exuberance of symbols marking festivals in particular, the penchant for rhetoric, a certain theatricalization that imbued all of political life—all these phenomena of which the Revolutionary festival became the high point—do not seem explicable only by the intensity of the emotions experienced. It was still necessary to resort to another language to express and communicate emotions, expectations, and dreams. And this language was none other than that of speaking sensibility. It is thus that a paradoxical effect is reached: in order for a festival to express the aspiration to simplicity, transparency, and spontaneous unanimity, it is overloaded with symbols which are more and more "speaking," complicated, and refined. Thus one might well wonder whether the secondary effect of the festivals was not the democratization, in the sense of a rather large social diffusion, of a certain language of sensibility, a language which was not, however, of their own invention.

Of course, symbols are "speaking" only when they are supported by a community of imagination—otherwise, they have a tendency to disappear from the collective life or even to be reduced to purely decorative functions. Those that were signs of the dreams of a New City then become their mortuaries; and festivals, in which they were brought into play, are no longer anything but their cemeteries.

VI

"A City Named Liberty": Utopia and the City

On 12 floréal of year V of the Republic, One and Indivisible, F.-L. Aubry, a surveyor-geometrician, publishes a brochure in Douai. In it, he expresses his ideas on the Monument to the Glory of the defenders of the Country, the erection of which had been recently decreed by the Legislative Body. As a good patriot, he can only admire the object of this monument and necessarily approves the principle behind it. "All hearts have already dictated eternal gratitude for our brave Republican Soldiers who saved the Country and Liberty." Yet this will not suffice. "The glory and the happiness of the French People" requires that an edifice be erected which "constantly reminds all the French that they won Liberty over all the kings and tyrants of all of Europe."

The surveyor-geometrician dreams of a very specific monument, which must "in no way resemble those that have been erected from pride and hypocrisy; it must even be remote from these so as not to be confused with them." That is why no large city can lay claim to this "Eternal Monument of French Recognition" and even Paris can hardly escape this stricture. Is it not, in fact, still "soiled with the emblems of pride and despotism, such as the hypocrisy of the kings, the priests, and the nobles? Certainly, Paris "was able to gain liberty." But was the city not, as well, "the source from which came the blows that were to overthrow it?" And what could be said of other cities? They are without Paris's merits, yet everywhere in them are found "emblems of the old yoke of the French" and each of them had had "their conspirators."

For its setting, the monument calls for a place that has never been soiled by history, after the example of liberty, which purified time. Thus the monument ought to be erected in a place that is itself "pure and free," in which the original purity of nature would harmonize perfectly with the cause defended by the soldiers of the Republic. However, Aubry does not propose that the monument be erected in the fields, or even on a mountain. Is not liberty, which is part and parcel of nature, at the same time a work of the men who won it forever in shaking off the yoke of their past? It is in an urban space that the surveyor-geometrician dreams of his monument. But this space must be singular, different from all others. A work of free men, entirely constructed and laid out by themselves, would it not perfectly incarnate the spirit that inspires them? Thus, the monument must be erected *"in the middle of a New City consecrated to Liberty."*

The author is conscious of both the novelty and the greatness of his idea. But, "however new and great it might be," it nevertheless proves to be eminently practicable. The proposal will surprise only "tyrants and slaves," whose degraded souls lack greatness and imagination. On the other hand, the "French Genius" will easily recognize it as worthy of it. The City-Monument will be "the guarantee of the happiness of the people" who will find in it the most perfect expression of its own greatness and of the "sweet emotions of the love of Liberty."

How is it imagined, this New City named Liberty? It is a city-symbol which, by the very organization of its space, speaks to spirits and inspires hearts. Constructed in the form of a circle, its privileged place is its center, where the Monument is erected. This will be "a colossal Pyramid which will have as many sides as the French Republic has levied victorious Armies." On each side of this pyramid, "the glorious exploits of the Defenders of the Country will be consecrated in inscriptions" and the "flags taken from the enemy will be adapted" there as well. The project is inhabited by an obsession with the center—the center of the city must also be the center of France. The city named Liberty will be erected "in the center of the French Republic, in a National Wood, spacious enough for a New City to be erected and for provisions, resources for its new inhabitants, to be found there, without having to take any property away from any individual." The center therefore performs a double symbolic function. The values incarnated in the Monument radiate from it over the entire country; but it is also the center, the seat where all the noblest sentiments inspiring the hearts of all patriots are concentrated. By a "happy coincidence" it is charged in yet another way with symbolic significance. Indeed, "the apparent center of the Republic, since the union with Belgium, is *approximately*, the former District of Saint-Fargeau." And this area was "the asylum of Leppelletier, who was assassinated for having voted the death of a tyrant, for having served the cause of the people, in a moment fraught with peril."

Why did Aubry, as a good geometrician-surveyor, content himself with choosing this "center," which was only "approximate," even taking the annexation of Flandres into account. Was he a native of that region and, hence, inspired by local patriotism? Or did he find in this specific area the "National Wood" that belonged to no one and that lent itself particularly well to furnishing the setting for his dream? Be that as it may, "the soil, the site, everything is beautiful there,'' and that beauty is associated with the useful since the place is situated ''among several navigable canals at the center of commercial communications of the interior.'' Thus, from all angles, the place proves to be ideal. ''The pyramid and the city of Liberty must rise freely, near Lepelletier's asylum, because this spot is the center of the French territory, because Lepelletier died for the cause of Liberty, because the Region offers all the beauties and all the resources that free men like to contemplate and must find.''

A symbolic city, a monumental city by its location, but also thanks to its other particular characteristics. In this city there would be no neutral space that was not charged with moral and civic values. Thus, each principal street would lead to ''one of the faces of the Pyramid and would bear the name of an Army, such as the *rue d'Italie, rue du Rhin*, etc.'' Moreover, the ''communicating streets would bear the names of the Generals, of the Soldiers, who were particularly worthy of National Recognition.'' The capital would not be moved to the city of Liberty, it would remain in Paris. But beyond its symbolic and monumental functions, or rather thanks to them, the New City would have a completely special role to play in the life of the country. In fact, Aubry foresees that the city of his dream will serve as the ultimate refuge during the epochs that are most important for the country. The Corps Législatifs, the Directoire, the Government Ministers will have reserve locations there, so to speak. They will seek refuge there ''when Liberty is threatened, when the Country is in danger; they would be able to leave it only after the danger.'' Aubry can already imagine the solemn moment when ''arriving in this City, the Députés, the Directeurs, the Ministers, will go to take their oath at the feet of the Pyramid, invoking the spirits of the Defenders of the Country, to perish under its ruins rather than to betray the People and Liberty, rather than not to defend them against their enemies.''

How big would Liberty be? Who would live there, besides high-ranking civil servants? And what would its inhabitants do while awaiting the solemn moment of the patriotic oath? Aubry's proposal leaves us unsatisfied or, if you will, leaves our imagination a clear field. His own imagination contents itself with dreaming of an urban space that is only a sort of stage set waiting for a civic ceremony.

We have found no trace of the surveyor-geometrician F.-L. Aubry other than this proposal that he handed down to us. But is this quasi-anonymity not precious in the sense that it eliminates any reference to the individual in the dream? However personal the dream, in which the extravagant is closely allied with the obsessional, it nevertheless clearly shows the conditions of possibility which are of course situated beyond the individual. There is a certain poverty of imagination even up to and including the quest for the grandiose and for grandiloquence—the imagination works only with the ready-made elements it finds.

We have said that the proposal, by its perfunctory character, leaves a clear field for our imagination; this is, however, only partially true. Is it not, in fact, easy, too easy, to complete this vision of the New City? The streets within it can only be wide and straight; access will be marked by monuments—for example, triumphal arches or even a sort of replica of Ledoux's gates. It would be necessary to think about providing the city with a temple of the enlightened religion, let us call it theophilanthropic, which would be erected on a plaza linked by a broad avenue to the central square. And how could there not be fountains—symbols of life and purity—on crossroads and squares?

It could be said that this city, reduced to a monument and a setting, haunted by the symbolism of the center, and itself centered on a colossal pyramid, that sacralizes virtues and the government at the same time, is only an involuntary pastiche. Despite the precise coordinates indicated by Aubry, it is tempting to locate Liberty elsewhere than in France, namely in Utopia. In fact, this New City and the organization of its space are isomorphs to the city found in utopian novels and proposals throughout the eighteenth century. We are speaking, specifically, of isomorphism and not of influences. To nourish his imagination, Aubry had no need to read and consult utopian texts. His proposal is only a repetition, a revival, on a monumental scale, of a space and a style he could have known from innumerable Revolutionary ceremonies and festivals, their setting, their arrangements, and so forth. The city named Liberty is only one of many pieces of evidence of a double movement: that of the utopian imagination to conquer urban space and that of dreams of city planning and of architecture in search of a social framework in which they can materialize.

1
The City in Utopia

Sévariade, the capital of the kingdom of the Sévarambes, with whose mores and history we are already somewhat familiar, is located in the center of an island thirty miles in circumference, in the middle of a large river. This island, in turn, is approximately at the middle of the lands belonging to the nation. The capital makes its contribution to the population of these lands as the number of its inhabitants increases. In fact, the Sévarambes have a maxim that the population of the capital must never surpass a certain limit. So Sévariade has approximately 267,000 inhabitants. In the land of the Sévarambes, other cities following Sévariade's example are to be found, although they are smaller and less beautiful. As far as the capital is concerned, it could be said that it is the most beautiful city in the world, whether one judges it by its location and the fertile soil surrounding it, or one considers the beauty and salubriousness of the climate, or the magnificence of its buildings and the good maintenance of law and order one notices in the capital. We can trust the narrator's judgment on this point: he has traveled a great deal and seen a lot before having debarked among the Sévarambes, in the austral lands. But we can judge for ourselves, as well.

The island where Sévariade is located is surrounded by a thick wall which fortifies it all the way around and thus protects it from all enemies. The city is square in shape and although we are not told its area exactly, this is not too difficult to calculate. The capital is conceived according to a rational, clear, and simple plan, which is rigorously followed, and which makes this the most regular city in the world. It takes about an hour to go on foot from the periphery to the center of the city, where the palace of the Sun, the residence of the king, the wise Sévarminas, is situated. Let us, for the moment, pass over the marvelous architecture of this palace, while noting that it, too, is located in the middle of a spacious square onto which several very straight and extremely wide streets open.

If our narrator were initiated into the jargon of modern city planning and not only into the language of the Sévarambes (and not particularly well specialized in this field although he is perfect in several other respects), he would have told us that the urban space of Sévariade is laid out according to a fundamental unit of the habitat. The capital contains, in fact, 260 *osmasies*. An urbanistic unit, the *osmasie* is, at the same time, the fundamental socioeconomic unit of the Sévarambes. As we know, the latter know nothing of private property and each osmasie works in common. The products of this work go into a public store where everyone stocks up on supplies of everything he needs. A system of stores allows for the redistribution of surpluses as well as for each osmasie's being able to procure the products that it cannot secure for itself by its own industry. And each osmasie, composed of more than one thousand people comfortably accommodated, inhabits a square building, with a façade of fifty geometric feet, with four doors opposite one another and a large court in the middle of the building. Thus each osmasie forms a quarter that is at once opened on the city and centered on itself and particularly on its interior court which forms a large square and where the public store is located. All the houses have four stories and are built of a kind of marble or white stone.

Sévariade is a city conceived for the well-being and convenience of its inhabitants. Although it is frequently very hot (located at a latitude of 42° south), there are fountains, shade, flowers, and gardens to be seen everywhere. It could even be said to be a city-garden. Thus, greenery surrounds the city since there are fields and meadows on the island and, as the island is completely surrounded with strong walls, it could easily be taken for a city. But even in the city proper there is greenery everywhere, and this greenery is its greatest ornament. In fact, in every street there are iron pillars which support wide balconies decorated with beautiful vases filled with earth, in which grow diverse flowers and bushes, making so many gardens against the windows. At the interior of each osmasie, similar balconies and gardens are found, all around the court. Greenery has even been planted in the court itself, where there are a fountain and a spray of water. The balconies protect the city dwellers from the rain and sun. In summer, cloths are hung over the streets, making them all the cooler as the air circulates freely in this city of wide avenues.

An ingenious system insures the abundance of water indispensable both for the greenery and for the cleanliness of the city. The water comes to the roof of each house, which allows for extinguishing fire should this be necessary (it does not seem, however, that Sévariade was ravaged by a single fire). From there, the water is distributed by diverse pipes, into the courtyard fountain, baths, different offices, and finally all the apartments. (Can one reasonably conclude that with this abundance of water and advance technique of piping it, the Sévarambes also have an invention similar to that made in Europe in 1625 by J. Harrington, an aristocrat-philosopher, and have succeeded in transforming lavatories into water closets within each of the apartments? At the time of our account, this invention, however paramount its importance for the evolution of the big city and for its salubriousness in particular, is a very recent technical novelty.) The same system of water distribution permits frequent street cleaning, which is, moreover, all the easier as the streets have been re-covered with paving stone.

The principal ornaments of the city are the palace, the temple of the Sun, the large amphitheatre for public celebrations, and the fountain basin. The palace, that radiant center of the capital and of the whole country, is of dazzling beauty. It is square like the other buildings, and has a façade of no less than 500 geometric feet and a circumference of two miles; it is completely built of white marble, ornamented with different architectural pieces; it has twelve doors on each side which are placed "one opposite the other so that one can see through the whole palace." Besides these doors, the main entrance is formed by a colossal portal which has 244 bronze and marble columns on each side and several orders of pillars above, mixed with diverse figures and statues. In this magnificent palace, all the orders of architecture are admirably well observed and our narrator—let us trust him yet again—has never seen anything that could approach it. If we lack a less cursory description of this edifice, which was so rich and majestic, it is only because such a description would fill whole volumes. And, as our guide frankly admits, it would call for people more skilled in art than he, to be worthy of fulfilling the task.[1]

To know Sévariade is to know all the other cities of the Sévarambes. They are all built on the same square plan, respect the same principles, and only differ by their size. But, this is likewise true of the other cities of Utopia, situated other than in the country of the Sévarambes, which resemble one another to the point that after having visited one of them, one has the feeling of having seen them all. Nevertheless, to use the formula consecrated by that famous guide who arranges the itineraries for millions of tourists, as well as the use of their imagination, these cities, if they are not worth the trip, nevertheless are worthy of a detour. It is only infrequently fascinating, but almost always instructive. And that is true not only because of the repetitive elements but also because of a detail that distinguishes each of them: in one case, the shape of a plaza; in another, the architecture of a building, or else a technical invention.

Leliopolis, the capital of the kingdom of the Féliciens, is built at the mouth of a river and, by its site, is somewhat reminiscent of Marseilles. The city is of the same size as Paris, with approximately 600,000 inhabitants, but what a great contrast there is between the two. One is struck, above all, by the perfect regularity that prevails there. The streets are wide and so straight that one has the impression that they were laid out with a ruler. They open on spacious plazas, in the middle of which are fountains and public buildings. No wall encloses the city—it is open to the fields that surround it. The two banks of another river that runs across it are set up as splendid promenades. To facilitate communication in the city, several bridges have been constructed across the river, which is about the same width as the Seine. There are no houses on these bridges, which is very practical for their users, and which adds to the beauty of the city by opening broad perspectives on both sides of the river. The streets are covered with white and red paving stones, which are very strong and easy to wash. Thus, moving about in this city is easy and the beauty of the surroundings makes it truly enjoyable.

All the houses are constructed of marble, which is found in abundance in the country (which is, besides, quite rich in alabaster; diamonds and rubies are also easily found there). The architecture of the houses is nearly uniform, although the residences of the important people in the state are more sumptuous and distinguished by their beauty and exterior richness as well as by their particularly luxurious interiors. The economic and social system of the Féliciens is different from that of the Sévarambes—private property is respected. Nevertheless, no one there is poor—there are only people who are richer than others. And since, as we know, it is not riches that make for happiness, everyone there is happy. Leliopolis, like the entire kingdom, lives in the time of progress. The expansion of the sciences, the arts, industry and commerce allowed for decorating the whole city as well as the individual houses. Their splendor, their luxury—always useful as it allies comfort and beauty—greatly surpass everything that can be seen in European countries (once again, we can trust our narrator who is, once again, a seasoned traveler). The houses are surrounded by gardens; and the city extends—for ten or twelve miles—with innumerable pleasant and well-cared-for country houses. The most important monument in the city is the Royal Palace which, by its architecture, is worthy of the enlightened and benevolent king who inhabits it. This palace is not in the center of the city but is, rather, situated at one end of it, on a hill that dominates it, surrounded entirely by magical gardens, which descend in terraces. Once again our guide assures us that it would take whole volumes to describe the beauties and all the splendor shining forth from this edifice. Other beautiful cities are to be found in Felizia, but it is the countryside that most particularly strikes the travelers—the stone houses, with beautiful gardens, grouped around a central square, the scene of festivals and games.[2]

In order to visit Selenopolis, it is necessary to make a detour by way of the moon; or, more exactly, it is necessary to go to the other side of the moon. In fact, on one of its hemispheres, one can find nothing that at all resembles earthly cities. The capitals everywhere are dirty; one runs the risk of being run over by vehicles; theaters resemble prisons; the promenades, formerly splendid, are like cesspools; the streets are narrow and winding; the air is unhealthy; and the water, in the few fountains, is not drinkable. It is only on the other hemi-sphere, on a continent that corresponds to the American continent on earth, that one discovers a different universe.

Selenopolis is located three miles from the sea, to which it is linked by a large canal. It is laid out according to a strictly even square and each side measures twenty-four *stades*. The principal street, called avenue Royale, crosses the entire city and ends on both sides with triumphal arches of simple but noble and majestic architecture. These triumphal arches are the entrance gates into the city, as it is surrounded by a wall. Thus the city, in all its beauty and splendor, opens itself to the traveler as soon as he enters it. The other streets are as straight as the avenue Royal and, although not so wide, they are at least twenty-four *toises*, not including the colonnades bordering each street on both sides. These colon-nades have a double function: they reserve paths for pedestrians and thus insure their safety, and the arcades they form protect them from the sun and rain. The façades of individual houses are all uniform and regular, but numerous public edifices—temples, schools, and the like, as well as fountains, lend variety to the architecture. Thus, the ensemble is harmonious without being boring, as the uniformity is not pushed too far. (The narrator is very sensitive to this aspect of the architecture—he disliked the château of Versailles, seen from the garden, particularly because of its monotony.)

In the middle of the main street and, hence, in the middle of the city, is a spacious square from which eight wide streets lead, in turn, to other similarly shaped plazas. The central plaza, called the place Royale, is composed of six separate buildings, all of sublime architecture. The most majestic is the royal palace, distinguished by its magnificent colonnade. The other edifices situated on the plaza—the arsenal, the court, the city hall, the theater, the Scholars' Palace, and the seat of the Academies—are all of the same height, but each is constructed in a slightly different style. On the balustrades along these buildings, appropriate statues symbolically express the purpose of each building. In the middle of the plaza is an equestrian statue—that of the reigning king. This statue is, in a manner of speaking, removable. Certainly the love of the people for its just and enlightened king calls for the statue to be located in the most prestigious spot in the city; but, on the other hand, reason deems it impossible to make a new place for each king in a city where every inch must be properly utilized to avoid falling into disorder. And what of the enormous expense that that would entail? So, at the death of the king, his effigy is removed and placed in a special rotunda. But that is done only on condition that the defunct king had contributed to the happiness of the people—otherwise, he is forgotten. On the eight other plazas, obelisks and pyramids were erected; also there were the statues of the great men deserving of the recognition and gratitude of the country. These latter statues are not removable, and famous warriors rub elbows with scholars and artists.

All the houses are of marble, stone, or brick—the city is never in danger of falling victim to a fire, all the more so, as it doesn't lack for water, thanks to the aqueducts that transport it into every house. The well-to-do have all installed baths in their houses and even sprays to water the gardens. For the less well-off, public baths have been set up throughout the city, with separate ones for men and women. They are open all day, they are free, and there is abundant clear running water. Thanks to an ingenious system of streams, the streets are regularly washed.

Cleanliness is also insured by sewers installed in every house, as well as canals and a central main sewer (large enough to be maintained and cleaned without difficulty) by which refuse is sent out to sea. And another detail, extremely important in a large city: to prevent stench in the streets, small discrete cottages were built in several areas so that urgent needs can be satisfied, and these, too, are continuously cleaned by a technical installation. The air is thus always fresh and salubrious, all the more so as on every marketplace, which are all spacious and convenient, a pit cleaned by water coming from a large fountain is to be found. The slaughterhouses are outside of the city, as are the cemeteries and hospitals. Nevertheless, in each section of the city there is a small hospital serving only urgent cases. Taking the sick outside the city proper contributes to its healthiness. But this is also preferable for the sick themselves. Outside the city, comfortable buildings are provided in which, in large wards, each has a bed to himself. No prisons are located either in Selenopolis or its environs—they are all in the interior of the country, as are the insane asylums, institutions for the chronically and incurably ill, and so forth. One last curiosity to note—the astronomical observatory. It is distinguished by the fact that any oval or round line was strictly avoided in its construction. This accentuates still more the predominance of straight lines in Selenopolis. In fact the rectangle, the square, and the cube, as opposed to the circle and the sphere, correspond best to the state of peace, security, and tranquility.[3]

The last city we would like to go through is also on the moon. Lunol has 650,000 inhabitants, and its population never exceeds this limit. In fact, every year there is a census, and as soon as it is noticed that the population has grown too much, all measures permitted by humanity to preserve the balance are taken. For the inhabitants of the moon it is evident that if the extension of a metropolis is not controlled, it can only ruin the country. This limitation of urban growth is insured by legislation. Thus the spatial limits of the city are fixed once and for all by boundary markers in the form of marble columns, which no one would dream of moving and which were installed at the founding of the city. The lands surrounding the latter belong to the state and it is forbidden and, above all, unthinkable that houses be built there chaotically—just as it is forbidden and unthinkable that at the interior of the city rich entrepreneurs would build houses encroaching on the plazas and promenades. So a traveler who approaches Lunol is struck by a double spectacle: the forest and fields that surround it, and, on the other hand, the panorama of an immense city dominated by the towers of the great public monuments. These towers are in the forms of pyramids, domes, cubes, cones, and so forth; some are massive, others very light; some are very tall, others scarcely higher than the houses. There is nothing chaotic and troubling in all that—the effect sought for and attained was the uniting of diversity and order and the elimination of monotony. The royal palace dominates all the other public edifices, each of which is of sober architecture appropriate to its function.

But a stranger has no need to ask for information about the latter—the architecture speaks to him in a universal language, that of well-ordered forms. Private houses each have four stories, which insures a nice regularity as well as free circulation of the fresh air coming from the fields, an essential hygienic requirement. For that matter, everywhere the beautiful is allied with the useful —Lunol is a city built for men. These inhabitants need the air to circulate freely as much as they themselves need to circulate in their city with neither hindrances nor danger. Thus, the streets and avenues are wide and straight, and the principal streets cross the entire city, from one gate to the other. The streets are intersected by others at right angles to them, and it is this regularity that makes the great beauty of the city. But the same can be said for its convenience—no one had the absurd idea of making streets that are narrower than the access routes, in a city where there is a lot of traffic. Circulating freely also means doing so in complete safety, and in Lunol this problem was easily resolved. First, they thought to raise the parts of the streets reserved for pedestrians, but for many reasons this solution proved too awkward. Finally, it was decided to separate these parts of the roadway, which were six feet wide, by installing stone markers and putting chains between them. To allow the pedestrians to move about freely, those who use carriages or horses must restrain themselves. It is thus unthinkable that people gallop at any speed they wish; the rich prefer to wait for a moment rather than put the lives of their fellow citizens in danger. At the crossroads, where there are no chains, panels are set up with the message ''Protect the lives of your fellow citizens''—and a special guard, provided with a bell, does nothing but regulate traffic. In truth, this is not really indispensable—everyone has been educated to respect this order that is as practical as it is necessary. So there are no accidents in Lunol and no street is ever obstructed. There is nothing surprising about the fact that Lunolians so like to walk about their city. They do this with all the more pleasure because they know that they never run the risk of having a chamber pot emptied on their head or having a drainpipe suddenly shower them with cold water. That is all merely a question of good sense and simple order—and yet it is necessary to go to the moon to find it. In Paris, where everyone prides himself on being a philosopher, things are different.[4]

We could continue this voyage but, as we have said, the cities in Utopia resemble one another too closely for it to be worthwhile. Everywhere we will find wide and straight avenues opening on large round or square plazas, which are the scenes of festivals and festivities. There is nothing chaotic in these cities: everywhere a perfect and striking order reigns, in the planning and development of the whole as well as in the architecture of all the houses, public edifices, monuments, and fountains, which embellish the city and are in perfect harmony with one another—they ennoble the city without crushing it, although they are monumental. Everything is built of marble and stone and there is no lack of quarries in the area.[5] They are large and lively cities, often on the order of the Paris of the time, but it is easy to get one's bearings in them, and then one is guided, in a manner of speaking, from the periphery to the center by the streets and plazas as well as by the monuments. They are healthy cities, both physically and morally, and everything in them has been planned to insure the health and convenience of their inhabitants. The water is fresh, the air is pure, and the greenery abundant. There is respect for order everywhere which, when added to the layout of the streets, insures the free flow of traffic as well as the safety of pedestrians. Thanks to many ingenious inventions, a perfect system of pipes insures the circulation of water into all the houses, and a sewer system protects the city from unhealthiness. The metropolises never overrun and crush the country—their expansion is limited by wise legislation; they do not devour the countryside, but rather complement it by their specific activities. This is, briefly described, the urban framework of a happy life—everything in the city is functional, and the beautiful is inseparable from the ideal. Of course, there are differences from one city to another, and they are not all negligible; we shall return to these below. Nevertheless, it is the similarities that predominate. The proof of this is that nearly all the elements of these cities are interchangeable— fragments taken from Lunol could be integrated into Sévariade and vice versa. Nothing indicates that the authors of these works have read those of their predecessors and been inspired by them. It could even be said that throughout the century all they do is continually reinvent the same city. But, on the other hand, it is remarkable that the differences that exist among the socioeconomic and political systems of these imagined societies do not have a great influence on the global vision of the city. The latter fits as well into the quasi-communist society of the Sévarambes as it does into that of the Felicians in which private property and social and economic inequality persist. Let us add yet another example. The ideal city whose principles are fixed by Morelly in his *Code de la nature* is often considered the first charter of city planning. Nevertheless, the same key ideas are to be found there as in several other cities in Utopia. "Around a large plaza of a regular shape, will be erected, with a uniform and agreeable structure, the public shops for all provisions, and the public meeting rooms. Outside this area the sections of the city will be aligned, all equal, of the same form, and regularly divided by streets. . . . All the sections of a city will be arranged so that they can be extended when necessary, without disturbing their regularity, and this growth of the section will not go beyond certain limits. . . . Each tribe will occupy one section and each family will have a spacious and comfortable lodging; all these edifices will be uniform, etc.''[6]

Do these visions of cities in Utopia not anticipate the reality of our contemporary cities or even our dreams of city planning? The anachronism is all the more tempting as these accounts lend themselves to differing readings and offer only too great a choice. In fact, can these cities not be seen as anticipations of our "new cities" with their rationality and their functionalism that are as perfect as they are overwhelming and suffocating? But why not the anticipation of the socio-realistic variation of these same cities—with their enormous plazas prepared in advance for popular demonstrations and parades for which there is never an insufficient crowd, with their monumental public buildings constructed according to a mistaken neoclassicism and surrounded by sculpture that exalts both the civic virtues and the state that both incarnates and inculcates them? But would a more favorable, if not optimistic, reading not be equally possible? Do the cities in Utopia not propose a vision of city planning that still makes us dream? That of city-gardens, which never exceed certain limits, strangers both to wild expansion and land speculation, which harmonize with the environment, cities in which traffic is regulated by the way they are laid out, in which there are neither pollution nor traffic jams, in which one can breathe pure air and walk around?

We must not, however, take what is only the result of projecting our own nostalgia and uneasiness on these two century-old texts for anticipation, presentiments. That would be honoring the ugliness we ourselves have imagined and established too highly by giving it a secular genealogy. That is justifying it while condemning it; one does not do justice to the utopian visions of the city, however imaginary they may be, by attributing a prophetic value to them.

If, on the other hand, we renounce an anachronistic reading of these cities in Utopia, they prove to be even more revealing in another way. In fact, these accounts bring us precious evidence both of the extent and the historical limitations of the field of the imaginary developed by a certain utopian discourse. These limitation have to do, first, with the particular characteristics of the utopian enterprise itself, and, in particular, with the one contained in the paradigm of the imaginary voyage and, second, with the historical realities of city planning with which the social imagination is grappling. In other words, beyond one utopian vision of the city or another, one finds the historical conditions of a certain social imagination whose effect is that at a given time its field is in no way limited. In this sense, the repetition of the same themes, which becomes monotonous, is not devoid of interest. It brings out the key ideas of city planning in Utopia, beyond the imagination of any single author. It could even be said that the more imaginative the author, the more significant the fact that he does not evade this repetition.

This repetition stems, first, from the subordination of the theme of the city to a certain ideal of happy rationality or, if you will, of rational happiness. In fact, what is repeated in these visions is the articulation of a specific representation of the social space on concrete realities of the historical city of the seventeenth and eighteenth centuries. The vision of the city is merely a screen on which to project this ideal, attempting to make it concrete in a series of images, whence the strange mixture of the concrete and the abstract, of the universal vision and the most minute picturesque detail. These details in no way cloud the image. Their function is to bring to the fore the perfect transparency of the city in relation to the principles which are its bases. These are the very principles that govern the universal society, and the city is only a sort of spatialization of a system of social, moral, and esthetic values—their representation in space. Thus, the lines and the regular shapes, the squares, circles, and cubes, are so many signs that allow us to *read* in the space the order, or rather, the idea of order that governs social life. Despite the accumulation of details, the urban space lacks depth—dimension specific to itself.

All these cities have no history—a problem to which we shall return. But just the same, in all these cities, the space is charged with an educational function. Nothing eludes this essential function—neither the organization of the whole of the city nor the slightest details of its architecture. They are, indeed, cities worthy of the societies that live in them, all happy and rational. But they are, as well, cities in which each promenade is a virtual lesson in civic and moral virtues, an apprenticeship in the social order. It could almost be said that everything in them is both reality and symbol at one and the same time. The square or round plazas, the straight and wide avenues, the symmetry and the variety, the paving slabs of marble or stone, do not only give order to the city, but are also and above all the visible signs of the rational order to which it is subordinated. This subordination of the city to the universal vision of the social order does not in any case end in a renewal of the language of architecture and city planning—rather the existing language of forms is taken over and charged with conveying the social message of the New City. Or a completely new and surprising style is merely announced, with the reservation that it will not be described, as "that would take whole volumes." So cities in Utopia are not oriented toward a *city planning of dreams*. What is reiterated insistently, however, is *the dream of city planning*, the image of the city submitted to a rigorous plan. It is a rudimentary and frequently quite timid city planning, yet is inclusive and constrictive, as it lets nothing escape its abstract principles.

These images of an alternative city do not call any of the historical functions of the city back into question—it remains the political, administrative, economic, and cultural center, and it is not by chance that these accounts show a clear preference for capital cities. Similarly, the functions of the city are defined by opposition to those of the countryside and its way of life, and there is no attempt to rebalance the relationship between the two. Of course, the anarchic expansion of the city is checked, yet its size frequently remains that of the large European cities of the time. Thus the urban condition proves to be completely adaptable to the ideal social order, but on the condition that the city *be purified*, as much in the spiritual sense as in a prosaic, down-to-earth, physical or hygienic sense. We have already emphasized water which, thanks to numerous fountains, flows overabundantly in these cities and which is at once the material instrument and the symbol of the pure city. It is, though, characteristic that in many of the utopias, the infirm, chronically ill, and aged (except, of course, for the venerable old man who is acting as guide) are relegated far from the cities or, at least, from the capital. The happy city thus rids itself of everything that might bring its beauty and happiness into doubt. Among the Sévarambes, there is a city, quite as regular, but where were gathered all the hunchbacks of the country. In Selenopolis the houses of the aged are outside the city; this is, of course, good for their health and, on the other hand, one does not meet them when walking through the city. The placing of hospitals outside the city is explained by reasons of health and hygiene; but prisons, too, are placed outside the city limits for reasons having nothing to do with the health of the criminals. The city that wants and intends to be pure thus rejects and casts out anything evil that might soil it.[7]

The rules of city planning are even more abstract and constrictive because the narrative accounts of the cities in Utopia are just that, that is, the cities in question are only *literary* cities—not in the sense that they are unrealizable, fantastic; that is not the aspect that interests us here, nor is it, in our context, the most important. We shall encounter other cities which were not realizable either, because it was historically impossible to link together the social, or even technical conditions necessary to make the proposals concrete. Nevertheless, the representations of these cities could not be reduced to an account, to words; they required plans and drawings. But this was not the case with the cities in Utopia of which it had been a question up to that point. One could, of course, attempt to make a more or less sketchy outline or plan of them, based on one account or another. But it then becomes obvious that one or another of the indispensable elements is missing and, moreover, that this plan adds nothing to the comprehension of the text, or to the image of the city. The cities in Utopia, then, are also literary in the sense that not one of their aspects escapes the *word*. The entire city, in all its dimensions, can be *recounted*; at the very most "that would call for additional volumes." It is also noteworthy that the account is situated on two levels. On the first, there is the statement of the abstract principles that organize the urban space—the square or circular plan, the perfect regularity of the streets, the houses, and so forth. Second, this same urban framework is spoken of on the level of the individual and of actual lived experience—the pedestrian is not run over by carriages, chamber pots are not emptied on his head, etc. These two levels are, of course, complementary. There is a whole play of mirrors between the overall image of the city submitted to a rigorous plan and the fragmentary and limited images situated within the perspective of a single walker. The abstract and rigid principles of basic city planning were thus taking shape in a series of images that had, at the same time, to add picturesque color to the account.

It is useless to stress the fact that yet another reference intervenes on both levels of the account. The realities of the big cities of the time are always implicitly or even explicitly presented, particularly when the text becomes satirical. It is, after all, this opposition to the real city that is the pivot of the account and that gives a certain life to these imaginary cities and to their abstract city planning. The structure of the text supposes a reading that does not confine the reader to the imaginary, but requires that he go on to a permanent confrontation between the imaginary city and the real one. So the imaginary city, however poor in dreams, nevertheless led to dreams of city planning that would be opposed to real cities in their chaotic growth.

Paradoxically, it is by the repetition of a few principles and anecdotal details, which are always the same, that the accounts of imaginary histories approach historical realities more closely. Of course, as we have said, this repetition is part of the paradigm of the imaginary voyage. But, on the other hand, can this not be seen as a negative replica of the constants of the urban reality of the time? The accounts of streams of water which clean the streets paved with marble are not, after all, more monotonous than the long series of petitions and policy regulations "on the bad state of the fountains; despite the precautions taken to deal with the water shortage, we are about to experience a total lack of water"; "forbidding the leaving of pea and bean pods, of artichoke leaves in the streets"; "proposing the installation in the Tuileries gardens of places suitable to the satisfaction of certain needs in order to offer all of Paris an idea of the sought-for cleanliness," and the like.[8] In romantic literature, Paris, a lively city, rich in adventures and numberless surprises, still has as a most monotonous backdrop the image of an anarchic and unhealthy city. In Restif's *Nuits de Paris*, the singular adventures of the owl-man in search of the city very frequently begin by a bone thrown through a window, which barely missed killing the passerby, or by the rightful demand, rightful because it was in conformity with the frequently reiterated policy regulations, of being given, with utmost urgency, the key to the lavatories in a private house. Grappling with realities which only changed very slowly, was it not sufficient, in order to imagine an alternative city, to take up once again the same idea of a city governed by rudimentary city planning, and to support it with a few clichés?

To bend themselves to an abstract and rigorous city planning, the cities in Utopia had, necessarily, to be devoid of all history. In fact, the refusal of history is pushed to extremes. Of course, there was no question of the imaginary cities having a history analogous to that of real cities. Did the historical destiny the latter experienced not materialize in their labyrinths of twisting and unhealthy alleyways as well as in their "Gothic" monuments? Yet it is striking that city planning is imagined and thought of as a refusal of *all* history, even of the wished-for and desired history of the ideal City. It goes without saying that the cities in Utopia were based, from their very beginnings, on a rational plan. They certainly grew—but within limits and based on principles set down in advance. They kept no vestige of their past and the ingenious idea applied to Lunol perfectly sums up this fierce interdiction against any trace of history. The inhabitants of Lunol, it will be recalled, wanted to have the effigy of their king in the center of the city. But kings, even the model kings in Utopia, die and succeed one another and the city can have but one *single* central spot. Besides, there is no question of setting up new plazas in Lunol and of submitting the city to the caprices of history. So the statue in the central plaza becomes a turntable. As soon as the king dies, a new effigy is put on the same pedestal and the old one goes to the museum. In this way the plaza and the city triumph over their own history.

If *cities* in Utopia do not experience history, the imaginary *City* nevertheless undergoes an evolution. In fact, if one attentively compares the accounts quoted, which are spread out over more than one century, one finds some changes which, although minor, are nevertheless revealing. Thus, the walls that surround the city begin to fall and the limits are no longer fixed by markers; the regularity is kept, but there is an attempt to add some diversity to it in order to eliminate too great a monotony; new forms of architecture begin to make their appearance. The imaginary city does not, then, succeed in completely cutting itself off from history—in its own way, it integrates, in its abstract space, some evolutionary elements of urban realities, but also, and above all, ideas and dreams that seek to take over real cities and their historical space.

2
"To Envision the City as a Philosophe..."

"**H**ere is a very wide, big street, in a straight line and bordered by two or four lines of trees. It ends at a triumphal arch, from which it enters onto a large semicircular, semi-oval, or semi-polygonal plaza crossed by several big streets forming the branches of a crossroads, some of which lead to the center, others to the city limits, and all of which have a beautiful object at their end." This image of a sort of triumphal road by which one enters a city is not taken from an account of a voyage into the austral lands or even to the moon. We took it from the work of the Abbé Laugier, published in 1753, and this is not a question of an imaginary city, but of a proposal for the beautification of Paris.[9] Laugier sets his proposal up in opposition to the pitiful state of the gates of Paris. "From whatever side one arrives at this capital, the first objects to present themselves are always some sorry looking palisades more or less raised above wooden streets, moving on two old hinges and flanked by two or three piles of manure. That is what is given the pompous name of the gates of Paris. There is nothing quite so miserable to be seen in the smallest towns in the kingdom. Foreigners who pass through these gates are shocked when told that they are now in the Capital of France. It is necessary to argue with them to convince them, they can hardly believe their eyes, they imagine they are still in some nearby small town. That all proves how indecent it is that the gates of a city such as Paris are so lacking in any sort of ornament. Large triumphal arches should be built where all the *barrières* are." This is only one of the indispensable elements to ensure that Paris has the magnificence and beauty he calls for and which in every city "depend principally on three things: its entrances, its streets, and its buildings."[10] Laugier's book had a great success and gave rise to a good deal of controversy. Twenty years after its publication, J.-F. Blondel still speaks of the influence the book has on architects, while judging it disastrous. "Our

236

young architects are reasoners who do not reason. Because they have read farther Laugier's *Essai*, they think they are educated."[11] The author of the *Essai* was frequently criticized for speaking dogmatically about architecture and city planning—of thinking up, as an amateur, chimerical projects. On the other hand, he was criticized for having borrowed his ideas on the city, and particularly on the beautification of Paris, from diverse authors and for presenting hackneyed ideas as original ones of his own.[12] Does the literary and "reasonable" character of the Abbé Laugier's work not explain the affinity between the imaginary cities in Utopia and his proposals? Blondel was not "literary," and his *Cours d'Architecture* served as a basic text for a whole generation of architects. However, when Blondel formulated the "equally essential considerations that contribute to making a flourishing city," one would think that he only summed up the basic principles of many a city in Utopia or else, if you will, that the authors of the imaginary voyages practiced their city planning based on Blondel's *cours*. In fact, do they not translate into images those conditions the combination of which makes a city happy and prosperous? "1. the advantage of its situation; 2. the ease of access to proper building materials; 3. the fertility of its surroundings, with abundant grain and livestock, for the subsistence of its inhabitants; 4. the peaceful and industrious genius of its citizens; 5. the wisdom and gentleness of its government."[13] Pierre Patte, to whose architectural work we shall return, takes a quasi-utopia as a system of reference when explaining his ideas of city planning. He criticizes Plato for having forgotten "to imagine the plan of a city for its new citizens" when he "composed laws to form a Republic and make men as happy as they could be in the state of society."[14] Social happiness necessarily calls for adequate urban structures; but the inverse is true as well— the city, urban space, must be thought out and imagined in the perspective of a social state that ensures maximum happiness. Would Plato, the city planner, not necessarily have wanted the site of his ideal city to be healthy, with salubrious water, not subject to harmful winds, fogs, or foul-smelling odors, which are liable to cause sickness? He would certainly have thought about the proximity of building materials, the risk of earthquakes, etc. The site of a city is of material importance to the happiness of its inhabitants. What, then, could be said about its layout and its beautification? Alas, they are "causes foreign to the happiness of the men who have guided 'the legislators' in this establishment. . . . One thinks only of political views and almost never about the aim one must have set for themselves in such a case. That is why the cities were never arranged appropriately for the well-being of their inhabitants, who are perpetually victims of the same scourges, dirtiness, bad air, and an infinity of accidents that a judiciously thought-out plan would have done away with." Patte opposes to these urban realities his vision of the ideal city which would combine "all the advantages one might wish for the happiness of its inhabitants. Crossed by a navigable river, surrounded by a canal, separated from the suburbs by promenades, with embankments on all sides as far as the eye could see; its streets arranged in such a way as to present sights that are always varied, always interesting, here a spire, there a fountain or an obelisk, further along a statue, elsewhere plazas, public buildings, colonnades. What residence could ever have been more agreeable?"[15] One would think oneself in Lunol and yet Patte insists on the idea that he is only drawing the "picture of an imaginary happiness one would regret being unable to enjoy." The principles of a city that could be the framework for social happiness are perfectly applicable "to all cities and however defective they are by their physical composition, they could be more or less rectified by following our proposal." This is notably the case of Paris, to which we shall return.[16]

Did the authors of the imaginary voyages read Blondel and Patte? Did Sévariade or Felizia interest them? Is there a return to utopian themes by the architects, or is it rather the utopian authors who transfer into imaginary countries the ideal city that takes shape in the background of architectural treatises? It is difficult to answer these questions if one attempts to clarify one particular work or another, or one particular case or another. On the one hand, we have very little information on the utopians' readings and, on the other, the imaginary voyages were part of the minor literature everyone read, without explicitly mentioning it. And then again, in order to do research in the origins of a particular idea or image, would it not be necessary to extend the field of possible sources and references? Did the utopians and the architects not both draw, each in his own way, from the Vitruves and the Albertis? Be that as it may, these questions of influence seem secondary to us. Beyond the ideas and images, more or less original depending on the particular instance, a common feeling emerges, which is more and more widespread in the second half of the eighteenth century, namely that of the divorce that had been established between men and the constructed space they inhabit.[17] The city becomes the object of a debate which goes far beyond the "specialists," and people become more and more aware of its multiple aspects, functions, and contradictions. The first place naturally goes to Paris, where the contradictions of the urban phenomenon of the time culminate. Both the criticism of and the apologies for the big city are both increasingly influenced by the myth of Paris. The success of the works that study "moral physiology" and the *Tableau de Paris* by Mercier in particular, are so many manifestations of the growing interest in the city as a social space. "The penchant for embellishment has become general," notes Laugier, "and, for the progress of the arts, it is to be hoped that this taste continues and improves. But this taste must not be limited to individual private houses, it must extend to entire cities."[18] A happy phrase of Patte's sums up this need for new attention to be paid to the city and, in particular, to its planning: "Objects were constantly seen from the point of view of a builder, whereas they should have been envisaged from that of a Philosopher."[19] And it is the utopians as well as the architects who apply themselves to "envisioning the city as a Philosopher" and "considering Architecture on a large scale, in its totality," to use another of Patte's formulas. Whence the convergences between the cities in Utopia and the utopia of the city, between the dream of city planning and the city planning that was imagined, between the utopian who plays at being a city planner in imaginary countries and the architect who rethinks the real city, referring to the model of Plato, the founder of an ideal city. But if there are convergences and affinities, there are also oppositions, both between the two approaches to the urban phenomenon and among the languages in which the images of the ideal city are expressed— convergence in the very way of envisaging the city "as a Philosopher." A voluntary construction by men, the city must be the expression of a rational will, which can only be translated by an *order* to which it must submit. "Everything in it is to be reasoned," said Patte. Whence, too, an analogous attitude (but within certain limits and with important reservations, to which we shall return) toward the historic city. We have already discussed the rejection of the historic city peculiar to the cities in Utopia. Nascent city planning, too, looks upon history, as it manifested itself in the city, as an anarchic force, harmful in its effects, and contrary to all rational order. "The majority of our cities," writes Laugier, "have remained in the state of negligence, confusion, and disorder into which the ignorance and rustic simplicity of our elders put them. New buildings are built, but nothing is changed in the bad way in which the streets are laid out or in the awkward disparity of decorations made haphazardly and according to anyone's caprice."[20] "Despite the multitude of cities," writes Patte, "which have been built up to this point in all the parts of the world, there have not been any that can truly be looked on as models. Chance governed their general layout no less than it did their site. To convince oneself of this, one only has to cast a glance at them as a whole, to notice that they are all merely a mass of houses laid out without any order, without following any suitably reasoned plan. . . . What strikes one first, when one attentively examines a large city, is seeing exposed refuse flow from all sides into the gutters before going into the sewers and giving off, along their passage, all sorts of harmful odors; then, it is the blood from the butchers, streaming in the middle of the streets and offering horrible and revolting sights at every step. Here it is a section of the city stinking with wastes from latrines; there, it is a number of filthy tipcarts, which take over the streets daily, in order to take away refuse, and which, independently of their filthy and disgusting appearance, cause all sorts of obstacles; further on, you will observe in the center of the most frequented places the Hospitals and Cemeteries perpetuating epidemics and sending the germs of maladies and death into the houses. . . . In a word, the Cities will present to us on all sides the abode of dirtiness, infection, and lack of comfort and well-being. . . . Who would not believe, seeing the frightening picture of these disasters, that an evil genius, an enemy of humankind, was the motivating force of the gathering of men in the City?"[21] History is not only the disorderly mobility, but even and above all these inert, materially present results which curb any rational change if they do not totally prevent it. "Our cities are still what they were, a group of houses, piled together pell-mell, without a system, without economy, without design. Nowhere is this disorder more obvious and more shocking than it is in Paris. The center of this capital has hardly changed one whit in 300 years; the same number of small, narrow, winding streets are still to be seen there, giving off nothing but filth and wastes and in which meeting vehicles cause constant hindrances."[22] This dream of a city, as rational as it is new, liberated from the "malevolent genius" of history, brings the utopian and the architect dreaming of becoming Plato closer together. But the convergence stops there. The cities in Utopia are empty of all historical substance; on the other hand, the imagination of the city planner is captivated and haunted by the real city, by this "monster Paris," of which he dreams of taking possession, in order to dominate its historical contingencies. Patte forcefully opposes all those who say that it would be necessary to knock Paris down in order to reconstruct it, if one wanted to make it into a beautiful city. "I think, on the contrary, that it would be necessary to preserve everything that is worth saving, as well as all the sections and the edifices that already form particular adornments so as to join it, with art, to a general beautification."[23] Paris, the historic city, with all its "absurdities," is not so much an obstacle to the dream of an ideal city as it is its greatest opportunity. In contact with realities and grappling with them, the dream of an ideal city takes on another orientation and form than those characteristic of the imaginary city in Utopia.

Thus, beyond the convergences of certain key ideas one again finds the fundamental opposition between two forms of utopia, the opposition we have briefly defined as that between city planning in Utopia and the utopia of city planning, between the cities in Utopia and the utopia of the city. The convergences, if not the reciprocal reutilization of themes, conceal the specific characteristics of the respective utopian undertakings and images. The utopia of city planning is not satisfied with opposing an alternative city, in conformity with the principles of the ideal city, to historical Paris; it imagines an *alternative Paris*. This imagined Paris is not a simple variation of the ideal city or even a simple projection of an ideal urban space on the historic city. The undertaking is, rather, the reverse—it is the real city, with its contingencies and historical constraints that is *rethought and revised* in light of the ideal urban space. Whence, too, the different, if not opposing languages, which convey utopian images. As we have noted, the cities in Utopia are only literary cities, the objects of a narrative account. Of course, one could also recount an alternative Paris, the utopia of Paris, and city planners as well as poets have frequently done so. However, the specific language of the urbanistic utopia is that of the spatial structures and architectural forms, and it is the ideal plan that this discourse adopts as its privileged paradigm.

Of course, every city planning program is not necessarily utopian in the sense that it would be the expression of a utopian vision of the city. Not every plan necessarily refers to a system of values opposed to that which is already at work in the real urban space. It is rarer still that it challenges the social structures and types of human relationships of which the city and its arrangement are a tangible manifestation. It has, however, been judiciously noted that between an ideal program of city planning and the urban utopia the relationships are as complex as the dividing lines are blurred, and particularly so when the latter attempts to encompass the entire city. Depending on the circumstances, it is one or the other orientation that is predominant and there are many slight differences between the two formulas as well as mixed variations of the two.[24] This observation is particularly valuable for the eighteenth century, the epoch of the dawn of city planning, when the very idea of a general plan for the layout of a large historic city, and Paris in particular, is inseparable from the theme and image of the ideal city, both of which haunt the imagination of architects. However, "the ideal city implies the projection on a site of a rigid and geometric schema of composition. On the contrary, if the natural conditions of the site and the current needs of a population are given and even if the urban creation aims at imposing a new specialization of the inhabited zones, one find oneself to be in the presence of another type of city planning. In other words, the ideal city creates the urban functions before the arrival of the inhabitants; the modern city of Western Europe rebalances an urban area with the idea of a better adaptation of the setting and surrounding to the human functions evolving according to local conditions, often outweighing the local government."[25] Thus, at its inception, city planning is faced with a dilemma: *utopia or reform*. A decision must be made as to whether "to see the architecture as a whole" and to envisage the reconstruction of the real city in order to make it conform to the vision of the ideal city, or else to adapt the model of this ideal city to the constraints of the historic city, to its spatial and social structures. But is that not *the* dilemma of all city planning? Is its history not one of compromises between the idea-image of an ideal city and the diverse historical constraints and contingencies its materialization comes up against? Compromises in which the utopian component is more or less present and through which the utopia succeeds more or less in inscribing itself in the real city and in modifying it?

The work of Patte is a noteworthy example of such a compromise, and one that is particularly instructive in the context that interests us. In fact, Patte's work marks an important stage in the formation of city planning in the eighteenth century and, at the same time, it is evidence of an intense exchange between the idea-image of the ideal city and the realities of the historic city and, notably, of those of Paris. What is to be done so that the essential reforms are not limited, but take on a dimension such that they can more closely approximate the vision of the ideal city? What is to be done so that the ideal city can be embodied in the real city despite the farrago of absurdities the latter opposes to the rationality of the former? For the man who wanted "to envisage the city as a Philosopher," the utopia and the reform do not present themselves as the terms of an alternative but rather as two convergent if not complementary approaches.

Patte does not speak of city planning—the term, in its present sense, does not yet exist, and this absence translates the level of the language corresponding to an early stage of the formation of city planning itself. In the *Monuments érigés en France à la gloire de Louis XV*, the city is spoken of in the terms of a traditional problem, namely that of the beautification of a city. But the architect—an apprentice philosopher—believes that he is obliged to rethink the very essense of what this "beautification" must be. The essential aspect is to give a new dimension to the "penchant for beautification" and to prevent its limiting itself to an individual house or even to an isolated fragment of the city. The architect cannot content himself with creating a beautiful building or even a beautiful plaza. He must "consider Architecture on a large scale," and that means envisaging the city as *a whole* and conceiving it within the perspective of a *"total beautification."* He must "reason out the means that could be employed to embellish this city (Paris) *in its totality* and to make it as comfortable as it would be agreeable."[26] Up to the present, "the whole penchant for beautification was limited to the houses of individuals. In the last fifty years or so, nearly half of Paris has been rebuilt, without anyone having thought of subjecting it to any *general plan* and without even having attempted to change the bad layout of its streets." This is Patte's major idea—*to reform* Paris in little steps, but from the perspective of a *general plan* which would be that of "the beautification of the city as a whole." Would it not thus be possible to give Paris all the advantages of the model city, such as a "Plato who was an architect" would have conceived it, while keeping what had already been built that did not contradict this model? "In order to succeed in bringing such desirable advantages to a city, it would be opportune to make a general plan of it, one sufficiently detailed to include all local circumstances, both of its site and of its surroundings; in that way, one would be able to judge the respective situation of different objects, their possible relationships, and the help one could expect in the execution of our views. . . . As far as possible, it would be advisable to join the agreeable to the useful, keeping, in the reform of the plan of a city, all that is worthy of being kept, all that already forms particular embellishments, to join them, with art, to the total beautification. . . . Once the plan of a city has been sufficiently meditated, little by little it would be executed not by knocking down, as might be believed, all the houses, but in ordering that as new construction was made, it would be governed by the proposed arrangement."[27]

It is, then, a matter of a prospective plan, the expression of the vision of a Paris of the future, "embellished in its totality," but, at the same time, of a guiding plan, imperative for the evolution of the city so that it would reach its ideal term. And it is noteworthy that Patte envisages such a plan as the synthesis of *two plans* which are different in their orientations and which would have to be complementary: a plan of small reforms and one of the total recasting of the city, the latter plan being the most open to dreams. "The first, in leaving the city as it is, to repair defective spots, embellish it where it may be embellished, and advantageously fill the empty parts, mindful of separating the City and the Suburbs; in a word, it would be necessary to give the best order and the most perfect harmony to all the parts of which it is currently made up, insofar as it is possible to do so, for the useful as well as for the agreeable, and generally for all that must enter into the decoration of a great capital city. In the second plan, there would be full freedom *to transform the City*, and to decorate it as judged suitable, to give it the magnificence that a great and beautiful capital ought to have."[28]

Patte was neither the first nor the only one of his time to demand a general plan for the development of Paris. His merit lies above all in his extension of ideal of "total" beautification; his originality was manifested in the presentation of Paris as the place where the two plans met and could possibly merge. This is the key idea of his magnificent *Monuments à la gloire de Louis XV*. But before speaking of it, some observations must still be made on the moves and countermoves between the dreams of an ideal city and the realities of the historic city, between the utopia and the reform in Patte's work.

Let us note, first, that for Patte the ideal city is by no means a space with rigorous geometric forms, divided by regular lines. The image of the ideal city suggested, so to speak, to Plato-the-architect, is different from that so frequently reproduced in the cities in Utopia. "It is not necessary for the beauty of a city that it be built with the cold symmetry of the cities of Japan and China, and that it be an assemblage of houses regularly laid out in squares or parallelograms. The essential is that all approaches to it be easy, that everything lead from the center to the circumference without confusion."[29] The external form of a city is likewise of little importance and it must be determined according to the constraints of the soil as well as the number of inhabitants. It is to be hoped that it be given octagonal form but this is not in order to translate into images the abstract idea of order. The city is beautiful only when it is functional and that is why it is necessary to give thought to having "its different sections closer together, in closer communication, with less distance from one extremity to the other so that order could be more easily exercised."[30] Subordinate the form, then, to the needs, but also eliminate excessive regularity for purely esthetic reasons. "It is especially advisable to avoid monotony and too great a uniformity in the total arrangement of the plan, but to assign, on the contrary, variety and contrast in the forms, so that different neighborhoods do not resemble one another. The traveler must not perceive it at a glance; he must be constantly attracted by interesting spectacles and by an agreeable mixture of plazas, public buildings, and individual houses."[31] There, too, Patte is not original in his ideas—he only follows the evolution of esthetic principles and tastes.[32] But his vision of the city is particularly enriched by contact with realities—his ideal Paris was to preserve a beauty characteristic of it alone and was not to seek to imitate Versailles. This esthetic ideal is the direct opposite of the agonizing stereotype of the perfect symmetry of the cities in Utopia. Besides, as we have noted, the latter, too, are to undergo an evolution—such as Selenopolis, for example, an imaginary city that seeks to escape monotony and to establish variety.

To embellish the city, in joining "the agreeable to the useful," in "reconciling the beautification with the comfort of its inhabitants," Patte returns many times to this key idea of city planning. Easily recognizable within it is the replica of a certain esthetic of the Enlightenment, one which was so frequently harped on that it became hackneyed. To the agreeable and the useful another key word is added, that of *happiness*. Together they define the finality of the ideal city, which opposes it to the historic city: the latter was subordinated to the search for prestige by those in high places, while the former must satisfy *all* the inhabitants of the city and become the framework in which social well-being can be harmoniously inscribed. "The entire worth of the most highly praised Capitals consists only of a few rather well-built sections, a few tolerably aligned streets, or of a few public monuments, commendable either for their mass, or by the taste of their architecture. It will continuously be noted that all was sacrificed to grandeur, to magnificence, but that no effort was ever made to gain true well-being for men, to preserve their lives, their health, their goods, and to assure the salubrity of the air of their dwelling place."

This notion of happiness nevertheless remains quite vague sociologically. Patte is far from thinking of bringing back into question the social hierarchies translated by the structures of the city. So, for example, there is no question in his work of the restructuring of the relationships between the working-class sections of the city and those of the rich. He does not imagine a city for man as he ought to be, but for men as they are, and men whose most elementary specifically urban needs must be satisfied so that they can enjoy their urban conditions. But are more ambitious utopian orientations, bearing on the totality of social life, nevertheless absent from his work? At the end of his life Patte announces, in a prospectus, a work whose title leaves no doubt that he takes the model of Plato-the-architect seriously. This title, if not concise, is at least explicit: *Fragments d'un ouvrage trés important qui sera mis sous presse incessamment intitulé: L'homme tel qu'il devrait être ou la nécessité démontrée de le rendre constitutionnel pour son bonheur et d'établir, par des lois vraiment conformes à sa nature l'empire absolu que doit avoir son moral sur son physique.*[34]

If the idea of happiness is vague and sociologically abstract, it takes more concrete shape with its application to the problems of reforms that are in urgent demand in the cities and, in particular, in Paris, "one of the cities where there is certainly the most to reform in all respects."[35] Two themes dominate the proposals for reforms put forward by Patte: circulation and hygiene. Thus, it is necessary to widen the streets, to assure good access to the city and at the same time easy and rapid circulation within the city itself. But, above all, to protect the pedestrians from accidents, to insure their safety and to reserve, in every street, two paths for the "people." But what is even more urgent is hygiene—the beautification of Paris is above all a matter of cleaning up and improving living conditions. Therefore, it is necessary to install a sewer system for the entire city; to set up "common places for the needs of the passer-by";[36] to install aqueducts and fountains which would put pure water within reach of all inhabitants; to remove the cemeteries and hospitals from the city; to push butchers, tanneries, and "other unrefined trades and occupations" out into the suburbs, and the like. Have we not seen all these proposals realized? Do they not furnish the accounts of cities in Utopia? Yet Patte does not content himself with advancing them and speaking them—he translates them into a technical language, proposes concrete solutions, plans, and drawings. Does the utopia of city planning not break down under all these large and small pragmatic reforms? The realities are so painful, their weight so crushing that the city planner can only fit "the great dreams and the small complaints" into one another.

As we have said, Patte insists frequently on the idea that the vision of a "totally beautified" Paris is not the picture of an "imaginary happiness." It is not only minds lacking in imagination that see it as a chimera. "If, for example, an able architect in 1620 had proposed to Louis XII making his house in Versailles a place whose magnificence surpassed anything of the kind that had ever been accomplished, it is certain that such a proposal would have been rejected; the genius of the artist would have been admired, while his design would not have been carried out. Yet this idea, however chimeric it may have seemed at the time, is at present realized before our eyes."[38] The dream of a new Paris can become reality only by the action of the government and it is to the king and his top ranking advisors that Patte addresses himself; it is their imagination he seeks to arouse. Louis XIV had Versailles built; it is incumbent on Louis XV to realize a work of even greater scope, to transform Paris. Patte hopes that the foundation of the new Place Royale can get the enterprise under way. It is nevertheless noteworthy that he has confidence not only in the state as a patron, and particularly in the enlightened king who would take on the execution of the proposals of the architect-philosopher. Another factor is touched on, too, namely that of *time*. It is necessary "to bequeath a great idea to posterity" and to show future generations the road which alone can "make them as happy as they can be in their living conditions."[39] This time, which can but improve the plan "of total beautification" as it is accomplished, is no other than the time of progress. The small reforms are inscribed in the same perspective—as they accumulate they will contribute to the realization of the great design. The dream of city planning is not projected only on space but also in time—the different Paris is the one that will be realized by the future.

Patte himself did not develop this "total plan" for the beautification of Paris that he desired his age to leave to future generations. As we have said, his monumental and most original work is the collection of *Monuments érigés en France à la gloire de Louis XV* in which Patte projects an imaginary Paris on the *real* Paris or, rather, clarifies the possibilities of transforming the latter by images of the former.

Let us rapidly recall the circumstances that provided the opportunity for this work. In June 1748, to glorify the peace of Aix-en-Chapelle, a competition was begun on the site of a plaza in honor of Louis XV, where his statue was to be built. This competition aroused deep interest and passionate debate. Not only architects took the floor; the "philosophers" became apprentice architects and their voices "brought" to light the desire of the eighteenth century to raze Paris, nearly totally, to reconstruct it in another way, rational, proud, and theatrical."[40] In July 1748, La Curne de Sainte-Pallaye opened fire in an article published in the *Mercure de France*, in which, despite reservations about his architectural qualifications, he nevertheless expounded on his ideas about this plaza, calling for its foundation to give a new image to Paris.[41] Bachaumont, in his *Mémoires*, joined the battle on the subject, suggesting the most daring proposals, and finally Voltaire himself intervened with his text *Les embellissements de Paris*, followed by another *Des embellissements de la ville de Cachemir*. These texts broaden the scope of the debate still further. A single plaza, even the most beautiful one, cannot, alone, beautify the city; it is necessary to think of the overall layout of Paris and in particular of hygiene, of the reconstruction of aged and "Gothic" sections. The last word, however, was reserved for architects, great numbers of whom participated in the competition, and in particular, Gabriel, Soufflot, Destouches, and Broffrandi. Patte himself presented a proposal as well. In it, he planned on locating the new Place Royale in such a way that it would result in the transformation of the most unhealthy section, namely la Cité. He found "that there is nothing to be saved in this section with the exception of Notre-Dame and the building of the Enfants Trouvés (foundlings)." Otherwise, the Cité is the very example of a section where "badly built, badly decorated" houses, "of Gothic construction" abound. Thus, it would be necessary to raze "seventeen churches that are completely useless because of the small area of this section and which have neither the grandeur nor the dignity suitable to represent the dwelling of the Supreme Being.'' And then it would be necessary to demolish the buildings in the palace courtyard (including the Sainte Chapelle!) and in rue Saint-Louis, as well as ''all the small houses belonging to the different fabrics of the small parishes.'' The Palais de Justice would be transferred ''to a convenient place,'' as would the hospital, since reasons of hygiene impose the latter's being placed outside the city or at its periphery. The proposal calls for clearing the bridges of the houses that obstruct them and joining the Cité to the Ile Saint-Louis. At the site of their junction a market should be set up and ''a circular plaza should finally be constructed at the tip of the Ile Saint-Louis,'' to which the statue of Henri IV would be transferred. Thus there would be a confluence of the conditions necessary for beautification, whose ''principal object would be the construction of a Cathedral on the new place Royale located between the Pont de Change and the Pont Neuf.'' (Notre-Dame ought not to be the parish church of the Cité.) This section-monument demands an appropriate setting, whence the proposal for the reconstructions of houses along the banks of the Seine.[42]

This dream project certainly leaves us dreaming and, judging by it, the plan ''of total beautification'' was not far from that of ''having Paris razed.'' Nevertheless, Patte's great success was neither his own proposal nor the compilation of several other proposals of places honoring Louis XV in a monumental book with magnificent plates, detailed commentaries, and often judicious criticism. His great stroke of inspiration was to bring all the proposals to bear on a single general plan for Paris. The idea was unprecedented and the result struck and stimulated the imagination. Patte did not, of course, seek to suggest by this plan the accomplishment of all the projects, either simultaneously or even spread out over time. His intention, it seems, was to facilitate the comparison of the proposals, ''of their extent, their respective location, and the advantages they would have brought to this City.''[43] The result went a good deal beyond the original objective.

The proposals all transferred together to a plan of the city showed not an ideal city, but an imaginary Paris or, if you will, a Paris suspended between the real and the imaginary. And even more than a single Paris, there were several possible cities of Paris on the map. In fact, starting from one or another proposal or from their diverse combinations, one could easily read several variations of new organization of urban space on the same plan. The map presented the real city as rich in multiple possibilities of transformation, of urban renewal, of beautification and, again, as the privileged place for the implementation of the imagination in city planning. The imaginary was thus inserted into the real even while opposing it. The map of Paris did not transfer Paris into Utopia. It showed it, with all the advantages of the diagrammatic presentation, as the place to which the utopia of the city could be transported, and in which it could be established.

Mercier, in *L'An 2440*, seems to be the first to have taken the step and established, so to speak, the utopian city in Paris itself. The interest of his vision of the Paris of the future is not due so much to the creativity or the strength of the imagination of its author but rather to the endeavor implemented. And, it is a matter of a double endeavor—one which, starting from the historical city, is oriented toward a utopian city and the other, which could be called the reverse, and which models the historic city on the vision of the ideal city situated "nowhere," in an imaginary country. The Paris of the year 2440 is the meeting point of the one which would have undergone "total beautification" and of a Lunol or a Selenopolis that would have been replaced on the banks of the Seine—the meeting point, but not the place of fusion. When all is said and done, these two "cities" remain superimposed on one another. This has to do, of course, with specific weaknesses of Mercier's work, but it is also a revealing example of this play of oppositions and affinities between the two utopian enterprises and between their respective languages, which we have already emphasized.

"Everything was changed—this was the first impression of the walker come from the eighteenth century to visit the Paris of the year 2440. All these sections that had been so well known to me presented themselves to me in a different and recently beautified form. I lost myself in grand and beautiful, properly aligned streets. I entered spacious crossroads where such good order reigned that I didn't notice the slightest hindrance. I heard none of those vaguely odd cries that used to be so ear-splitting. I encountered no vehicles ready to run me over. . . . The city had a vibrant air, without troubles or confusion."[44]

Mercier refers explicitly to the sources that inspired his vision of this Paris in which "everything has changed." The picture of the Paris of the future is intended only to put into images the supposed execution of different proposals conceived in the eighteenth century. "Everything has its time. (The narrator, having come from the eighteenth century, addresses the Parisians of the twenty-fifth century.) Ours is that of innumerable proposals; yours is that of accomplishments."[45] The description of the Paris of the future thus merges with the great preoccupations of the proposals for city planning: circulation and hygiene. "The greatest people forms a free and easy circulation, full of order." That was all the easier to realize as not only are all the streets wide and paved, but all the carriages have disappeared. Was the use of carriages for moving about the city not the sign of a superfluous luxury that was quickly done away with? The city is well lit and the light in which it is bathed also has a symbolic import: Paris no longer has anything of its physical and moral realities to hide. The apartments are huge and clean and all the houses "are furnished with the things most necessary and most useful to life. What cleanliness, what freshness in the air there is as a result!" Thanks to the realization of the "proposal of M. Despacieux of the Academy of Sciences, which has been further improved," there is an abundance of pure, fresh, cool water. So, fountains which "allow pure and transparent water to flow, are to be seen everywhere." Besides washing the pavement, this has a symbolic function: the new Paris is as pure and transparent as is the water. The hospital has been transferred from the Ile de la Cité out of the city, as have the cemeteries."[46]

What about the city plan and the layout of the city? It is notable that from this point of view, the new Paris is, with the exception of a few details, only a repetition of one of the plans to be seen on Patte's map. So, the privileged place from which this new Paris best offers itself "to the enchanted gaze" is the banks of the Seine: and the proposals Patte transferred to the general plan of the city were more or less equally laid out along the Seine, between the Ile Saint-Louis and the place Louis-le-Grand as if "the Seine attracted and polarized all the attention and as though there were the wish to open on it."[47] The plazas are the essential elements of the imaginary organization of the space, which, again, coincides with Patte's map. Thus, between the château of the Tuileries and the Louvre, there is "an immense esplanade where public festivals will be held." The Louvre is complete—a new gallery matches the Perrault gallery and the Hôtel de Ville has been built on the same plaza. The Pont Neuf, which establishes "communication between the two parts of the city," is enlarged and runs into two plazas, symmetrically laid out on each side of the river, adorned with statues of great men. Added to all these public squares is that of Louis XV (that is, the proposal that had won the 1748 competition, the present place de la Concorde). Gabriel's work is the only one judged to be "worthy of our time," that is, of this twenty-fifth century. All the bridges are cleared of houses and thus one's gaze is able to "plunge with pleasure into the far-reaching currents of the Seine"; the wings of the Collège des Quatre Nations which had obstructed the left bank were also demolished. And there was still another new public square, this time located far from the Seine, namely the one laid out on the ruins of the Bastille (after 1789, Mercier will not fail to cite this point as irrefutable proof, if that were necessary, of the clairvoyance, if not the quasi-prophetic character of his work).[48] Had Patte's beautification proposal been put into effect after practically all of the Cité had been razed? We know nothing about it. It is nevertheless striking that in walking about in the new Paris along, so to speak, several hundreds of pages, the narrator never fixed his attention on any ancient monument other than those—very few and far between—of which we have just spoken.

As soon as one moves away from the Seine, one no longer knows in what part or section of Paris one is. With a single exception, that of Montmartre, which is transformed into a sort of sacred hill, both opposed to the city and its complement. Montmartre has become "the faithful image of the Mt. Parnassus of antiquity, the abode of genius, the dwelling place of famous writers." In this "august spot, shaded on all sides by venerable woods," where a formal law forbids all noise, a palace was erected for the Académie Française, "a rather huge edifice, but very simply decorated." Not far from this is "a huge temple that fills the spectator with admiration and respect and on the frontispiece of which is written *Abrégé de l'Univers* (synopsis of the universe)." It is a museum of natural history in which a place of honor has been given to the collection of monsters (the men of the twenty-fifth century quite share the curiosity of their eighteenth-century ancestors for those beings in which nature, the producer of order, seems to contradict herself but at the same time displays a mysterious strength and "energy"). And it is Montmartre as well that is the location of small lodges, a sort of retreat where scholars and artists can devote themselves to meditation, far from the noise of the city. Thus the section of the arts situated at the periphery of the city complements its political and religious center, located on the two banks of the Seine.[49] But what is to be found between the center and the periphery of this city which is said to be more spacious and even larger than eighteenth-century Paris?

Of course, the visitor crosses still more plazas, all "spacious," "broad," "beautiful" public squares, on which avenues, all large and magnificent, debouch; but none of them are in any way localized. They exist only in an abstract space, that of nowhere, in which one searches in vain for a landmark and which is merely the object of a narrative account. This space, though, is overflowing with monuments and temples; it is furnished with a whole fictional architecture. There is a colonnade of statues of great statesmen where next to Sully, Jannin, and Colbert is a whole "line of heroes whose mute but imposing brow cries out to all that it is useful, great, and noble to gain the esteem of the public." Another public square is surrounded with statues of Voltaire, Rousseau, Buffon, and others. On the same plaza rises a marble monument whose dominant figure symbolizes "holy humanity," before which other figures representing women bow in a pose of grief and remorse. "These were representations of the nations which begged humanity's pardon for the harsh scourges they had caused over the course of more than twenty centuries." The public edifices are all monuments and all are constructed in a style that is new to the visitor who has come from another epoch. In fact, sumptuous architecture has been condemned and the antiquities of Rome are no longer imitated either. The architecture is distinguished by the perfect harmony between the building and the commonweal. Its novelty lies specifically in the way in which its forms express moral and civic values.

Together, then, these statues, temples, palaces, and the like form "a book of morality" and, all together, deliver "a public lesson which is both forceful and eloquent." Besides, what is this new Paris, if not a moral lesson, told, if not created, by the stone? Is its entire space not *speaking* and does it not convey the values that govern the New City and the progress that gave rise to it? How remarkable it is that the majority of the monuments and old locations have been rebaptized, for "nothing influences the spirit of the people more than when things have their own specific and real terms."[50] That is still another way in which moral and educational discourse take possession of the city. The urban space is abstract, yet it is not *empty*. Besides being paved with good intentions, it is furnished, so to speak, with values represented in stone. As far as city planning is concerned, the resources of Mercier's imagination do not prove to be too rich. But was this apprentice architect not seeking above all specifically to transfer a moral discourse onto a plan of Paris from which all but an islet along the banks of the Seine had been erased?

All things considered, then, this attempt to fuse the city in Utopia and the utopia of the city ends in failure. But does this very failure not reveal a double movement: that of city planning that approaches the utopia and that of the utopian imagination that seeks to appropriate the language of city planning and architecture?

3
An Architecture for Utopia

In 1792, Boullée drew up one of his last proposals: a *Palais municipal pour la Capitale d'un Grand Empire*. It is a monumental edifice the plan of which consists of a square in which a circle and a cross are inscribed; its "character is proud and virile" and the whole ensemble "offers the most imposing mass," which the artist had attempted to bring out as much as possible. So that the exterior could make its presence felt with "dignity," the architect placed "guardrooms in the four corners of the base to show metaphorically that the foundations of society rest on the authorities charged with the public order." The elevations of this monument posed problems to the architect. They are only "smooth bodies which produced virile effects in the decoration." And this time the use of blind exterior walls, characteristic of Boullée's architecture, proved to be impossible. Their effect would have contradicted the guiding ideal of the project, namely that of "succeeding in making the purpose of this monument recognizable." A *Palais municipal* that "is suitable to the Republican" is not only "a place meant for the magistrates of the commune," but also "a house for all. It is in this house that the citizens make their claims heard and attend the most important deliberations. . . . A house for all must necessarily present a *kind of hive*. . . . The municipal hall is a human hive." Therefore, in order to characterize the specific qualities of this "house for all" and to adapt it to its functions, Boullée makes "galleries communicating on all sides and innumerable openings, so that a swarm of men can freely enter and leave without commotion." That is why its layout is divided; and in order to preserve "the virile effect" at the same time, the architect came up with a clever idea: unable to have smooth surfaces in the width of the building, because the openings, which were necessary, did not permit it, he introduced them into the height.[51]

Where are the "great Empire" and its capital, of which Boullée was thinking in drawing up his proposal? There is a great temptation to locate them, immediately, in one of the countries of Utopia. Would it not tally best with an imaginary city? And was this city not supposed to be ideal too in the sense that the social order governing it would make the *Palais municipal* a "true house for all," a "social hive." Let us recall another of Boullée's proposals to which we have already alluded, that of a gigantic circus. We noted the affinity between the architectural form of this monument and the image of the festival for which it was conceived and which was no other than that of a civic utopian festival. Boullée himself draws the parallel between the style in architecture and the political and social order. Thus he says that Caesar's true coup d'état was to lead up to the change of form of the government by changes made to the architecture of the Roman circus.[52] May we not say, paraphrasing him, that Boullée and Ledouxs' architectural proposals anticipate an imaginary coup d'état, one that they have dreamed for a New City?

Let us, however, be wary of making too rapid and too facile a connection between a style in architecture and a social vision. Of course, in utopian literature it is frequently a question of architecture but, as we have observed, these are only generalities or even mere commonplaces. At the very most, the authors express a vague desire to design edifices that would be the visualization of the ideas and principles governing the utopian City. All attempts to specify this architecture lead nowhere—they never go beyond the level of the word. No real architectural innovation is to be found in the cities of Utopia, much less an innovation that would merit comparison with Boullée's work. Architecture is not merely a matter of the pure and simple translation of an ideology, nor yet of a utopia, even when the architect proposes accomplishing this. Its particular language causes it to say at once more and less than the ideological message it takes on.

Besides, in Boullée's case, it was not a question of making architecture for the utopia. He did not bequeath a social utopia to us, and his written work is an architectural treatise with a pedagogical aim, intended to train future architects. Several proposals in which the innovative style of "Revolutionary" architecture is forcefully asserted were not in the least conceived for an imaginary "great Empire" but really and truly for the Paris of the Ancien Régime, while taking a specific order and its constraints into account. The *proposal for a public library* is a striking example of this. Of course, this gigantic edifice was inspired by the great dream of making a monument worthy of the spirit of the Enlightenment. But, on the other hand, the proposal consisted of utilizing the site of the Royal Library, by covering its large court and transforming it into a reading room. Still, Boullée's work did not meet the cruel fate reserved for Ledoux's gates, one of which was attacked and burned as a warm-up for the 14 July. It could be said that in this case history has voluntarily taken upon itself the task of putting us on our guard against too rapidly bringing together artistic mutation and social transformation.

That having been said, let us remember that utopian themes are often found in Boullée's texts and that Ledoux's written work is full of them. For anyone pondering the relationship between their architecture and the utopia, this is certainly an important indication, even when it is merely a matter of a banal idea or image, having nothing to do with the originality of the architectural work. Questions on the affinity between this work and the utopian social space must necessarily go further than these indications and bear on the schemas of the imaginary at work in the architecture itself, on the fusion of the utopian images with the specific language of the architecture. (Whatever the importance of these written texts, of the *word* that in this specific case forms a complement and an extension to the language of forms, might be, we shall take up this problem in greater detail below.) Revolutionary architecture is an even more notable chapter in the history of the utopia of the Enlightenment because it is in perfecting their art, or rather in *seeking perfection in and by their art* that its masters turn toward utopian horizons. That occurred particularly when the architect thought himself free of all the obstacles caused by a "silent partner" and when he devoted himself to ideal projects. It is then, too, when the architect was able to blossom out even while working within a certain "social vacuum" that the complicity between his architectural vision and a utopia is more clearly shown. It is the utopia of the city that appears to be the context most appropriate to the full exercise of the word by this "speaking architecture." In other words, it is in seeking to affirm its specific functionality that visionary architecture proves to be nostalgic for the utopia and has recourse to a utopian space. Questions on this functionality and its particular characteristics will guide us in our exposition which, however, requires two preliminary remarks.

There is no question of our taking up Revolutionary architecture in its entirety, a task far beyond the scope of this work. Let us parenthetically note, however, that the rediscovery of this architecture is relatively recent and that the breadth and importance of this phenomenon are the object of great debate. As far as we are concerned, we will confine ourselves to speaking only of the the work of Boullée and Ledoux and only from the perspective just defined. We shall attempt, then, to bring out certain aspects of their *architecture considered with respect to art, morals, and legislation*, to use the title of Ledoux's book; that is, those aspects that seem to us to reveal the utopian horizon. Another remark concerns the terminology. We use "Revolutionary," "speaking," and "visionary" alternately; all three are current in the copious literature on the work of Boullée and Ledoux, and only bring to light the diverse and yet complementary aspects of this work.[53]

Speaking of *functionalism* in the case of Revolutionary architecture may seem both anachronistic and paradoxical—anachronistic, because the term is not part of the vocabulary of the era; paradoxical, because this architecture favors the monumental and is overloaded with symbols. Thus it seems to take the opposite course to that of any enterprise that seeks beauty of form as the result of the exact adaptation of an edifice to a utilitarian service. Was the major idea of the speaking architecture not, however, to join the *beautiful* to the *useful*? Or even to fuse the beautiful in the useful by opposing decorations and ornamentation judged to be pointless and which were criticized in rococo architecture as well as in a certain imitation of antiquity? The idea, certainly, was neither new nor original, and the Revolutionary architects were only taking up a commonplace of the esthetics of the Enlightenment. What is in question, however, is, on the one hand, the very definition of the useful in architecture and, on the other hand, the search for forms that would be appropriate to this utility. "Architecture is an art by which the most important needs of social life are fulfilled," said Boullée, completing this definition with another. "Architecture is the art of presenting images by the arrangement of bodies. The effects of the bodies result from their masses."[54] The "functionalism"—let us nonetheless accept the quotation marks—of Revolutionary architecture is dependent first on a certain idea of the social and moral functions of the art and second on a certain idea of the specific language of the forms the architect has at his disposal to achieve these functions. Although these two problems—the language of architecture and the social functions of the latter—are closely linked together, they are so extensive and complex that we shall have to examine them in turn.

The assimilation of architecture to a language is not a tribute paid to fashion. It is a key idea of the architecture intended to be *speaking*. With the bodies and their masses, the architect has a *system of signs*, a language of his own, at his disposition. "The circle and the square," wrote Ledoux, "are *letters of the alphabet* that the authors use in the texture of their best works."[55] This system of signs is governed by the laws and relationships suitable to it, those of harmony, proportion, symmetry, and the like. Neither these signs nor these relationships are arbitrary. Boullée, seeking the unity of his work and the theoretical bases of his style, engages in a long "examination of Perrault's assertion on the constituent principles of architecture." In this, he goes against the affirmation of the creator of the colonnade of the Louvre (a work that he nevertheless admires); Perrault claims that architecture "is an art of fantasy and pure convention." For Boullée, the raw materials, the "rough bodies," their forms and their masses, as well as the relationships they imply, are not invented by the artist; he finds them, rather, in nature itself. Moreover, "men were able to have a clear idea of the bodies only after having had that of their regularity." Therefore, there are "principles which preexist the art" and from which "there is no way that he (the architect) can allow himself to deviate."[56] The architect does not invent his language, he gets it from nature itself. It is in nature that he finds the volumes his art demands and it is nature that establishes "the proportion and harmony of bodies." The spherical body, then, is "in all respects the image of perfection. It joins together exact symmetry, the most perfect regularity, and the greatest variety; it has the greatest development; its form is the simplest; its figure is outlined by the most agreeable contour; finally, this body is favored by the effects of the light, which are such that it is not possible that its gradual moderation be softer, more agreeable, and more varied. These are the unique advantages it gets from nature and *which have unlimited power over our senses.*"[57]

We find these exceptional qualities of the sphere exploited in Newton's cenotaph, designed by Boullée, but also in Ledoux's projects: in the "house of circles" or even in the Chaux cemetery. Or rather "brought into play." "Bringing nature into play" is, in fact, the formula to which Boullée emphatically returned to define the art of the architect. As far as Ledoux is concerned, he proclaims that "the architect is the man faithful to the wish of nature . . . and he has no need of cold and deadening precepts."[58] This architecture, then, refers to a "naturalistic" esthetic, as J. M. Pérouse de Montclos so judiciously noted. But the very term *nature* accentuates that ambivalence that makes it the key word of the diverse or even opposing theories of this era when art as well as politics lays claim to nature as its authority. *Nature*, the immutable model of beauty, order, and truth; *nature*, the archetype of a language; but also and above all *nature*, force and energy. "To bring nature into play," is not to imitate its forms but rather to organize and utilize the "forces" and "energies" available in them. It is just the same with that other "force of Nature," light. While studying the model of the play of light and shadow presented by every forest, the architect "will bring Nature into play" in an "architecture of shadows," exploiting, for instance, the possibilities offered by zenithal light, by the play of shadows on the surface of a sphere, by the utilization of matters that either absorb or reflect light, and so forth. So architecture is, for Boullée, the sole art "by which one can implement Nature and this unique advantage certifies its sublimity."[59]

The organizer of masses, the implementer of energies and forces, the architect is, as well, the operator of sensations and impressions. Indeed, the reference to a force also implies the idea of the action performed by the organization of the masses on the spectator. In producing impressions, the masses inevitably "bear" sentiments "into his [the spectator's] soul." In support of the existence of the affective influence of the action of the "organized masses," Boullée has reference to a rather vague sensualism which is merely a recapitulation of the clichés of the era. But what is more important than the philosophic originality is the way in which he imagines the hold the "masses" have over souls, and hence the field of action thus open to the architect. It is "from the effect of their (the bodies') masses that sensations are born. Yes, of course, and it is by the effect they produce on our senses that we have succeeded in giving them appropriate denominations and that we are able to distinguish massive forms from light forms. It is even by the different sensations they arouse in us that we feel that the bodies that break on the earth sadden us, that those that rise toward the heavens delight us, that soft smooth bodies are agreeable, but those that are angular and hard repel us.'' The art of organizing masses, of creating the play of lights, and so forth, amplifies still more the ''natural'' effects they produce on our emotions and thus gives the architect the means of ''controlling our senses by all the impressions he communicates to them'' (Ledoux says that architecture awakens the apathetic sleep of the feelings). It is not only a question of esthetic impressions and feelings, but also, and above all, of moral sentiments; the two are interdependent. Such as, for example, ''the image of the great which is pleasing to us in all respects, because our soul, eager to extend its delights, would like to embrace the entire universe.'' Thus the architect, in ''bringing nature into play,'' and in bringing his art to perfection, produces works which so affect the spectator that he ''is forced to express himself according to their action on his senses.'' Boullée calls *character* the effect that results from an object and ''causes any impression at all in us.'' It is not, however, ''any impressions at all'' that the architect tries to produce but well-defined moral and esthetic feelings, which are relative to the subject of his work. The sudden impression we feel at the sight of an architectural monument comes from the formation of the whole. The feeling that results from it constitutes its character. What I call putting character into a work is the art of employing in any and every production all the means that are appropriate and relative to the subject one is treating, so that the spectator feels no sentiments other than those the subject ought to involve, which are essential to it and to which it is susceptible. It is thus that the architecture into which ''character was put'' takes possession of our souls, orients and guides our sentiments. ''By the useful monuments this beneficial art offers us the image of happiness; by the agreeable monuments, it presents us with the delights of life; it intoxicates us with glory by the monuments it erects to it; it leads man back to moral ideas by funerary monuments and, by those it dedicates to piety, it raises our soul to the contemplation of the Creator.''[60]

Thus an architectural monument may well convey a moral message. Is the language of the masses and volumes not, however, too poor in relation to the richness of such a message? That would be to forget that the basic forms that compose the vocabulary of this language are all *signs*, and that their signifieds are moral values. Take, for example, the cube. Its form ''is the symbol of immutability; one seats gods, heroes on a cube; it is thus that Neptune is represented; the limits of the sea are supposedly immutable; the ancient towers, the skylines of ancient cities are square . . . morality ought to be accounted an immutable monument in these splendors. The Greeks called a man who could never be turned away from virtue or his duties square.''[61] That is why, when Ledoux designs the "panarétéon, a school of morality where the duties of man are taught," he gives his edifice the form of an assemblage of cubes. Thus every form is considered charged with a symbolic significance or rather with many, stemming from the age-old fund of symbolism that is enriched with new meanings. Thus the sphere lends itself to symbolizing the vault of heaven, the eternity of the universe, and fortune and its wheel, but also—and why not?—equality. The organization of basic forms into a whole, the utilization of their affinities and opposing points, the exploitation of the play of lights (with all the symbolism of light opposed to darkness), the effects of surfaces considered to be "virile," "noble," etc.—all are possibilities for telling a moral message in an architectural language, but also for giving new life to architecture and for seeking novel formal solutions.

It is characteristic of the language of architecture that it "speaks to the eyes," that it dispenses with any translation. Its signs are entirely transparent to moral values, for they do not translate them, but rather give them a material form. Thus architecture, by fully exploiting the resources of its language, can become eloquent, *speaking*, and have its own poetry and rhetoric. It is an *original* language, that of nature itself, and the artist, returning to the sources of his art, frees himself from abstract, ossified precepts and gives free rein to his genius and imagination. This does not in the least mean the reign of disorder, the capricious, and the bizarre. Is not nature itself the supreme order that man seeks to imitate and to recreate in his works? In seeking beauty, the artist cannot infringe the system of rules of his language—symmetry, proportion, etc. Taste, the "method that clarifies all ideas," said Ledoux, is by no means arbitrary or based on convention—there is "a despotism of beauty" which it obeys.[62] There is still another "despotism" the artist necessarily obeys, that of the sentiments his work must express. This "dogmatism of sentiment" imposes the choice of the "masses" and the forms in function of their symbolism.[63] The artist is, then, tuned in to nature, but he is also tuned in to an important moral message. The work attains nobility and greatness only when it makes the noble and the great speak. The ancient monuments we still admire today bear witness to the genius of their creators. But do they not also, in a universal and often forgotten language, tell of the greatness and nobility of their times?

How can this idea of the architectural language not be compared to that of Rousseau's "language of signs," which we have mentioned elsewhere. In fact, similar preoccupations are to be found in both cases: the search for a forceful and transparent language, with a strong affective charge, able to convey a moral message without any distortion, by the play of symbolic representations, and thus to have a direct hold over souls. In making this comparison, we do not by any means think that the sources of the esthetic of "speaking" architecture are to be sought in Rousseau. We have already said that such a search for sources and influences seems without much methodological interest. In this specific case, it would come to a dead end for two additional reasons. First of all, no references to the linguistic ideas of Rousseau are to be found in these texts of Boullée and Ledoux. Of course, the presence of a certain Rousseauism is to be found, but it is merely the diffuse Rousseauism of the time at which these texts were written, that is, the last decade of the century. The references to Rousseau's work are vague and imprecise and are only ideas that had become commonplace. Let us note, next, that while stressing the theoretical developments of our architects, we by no means overestimate their importance; in particular, we do not suggest that their architectural work is the application of an esthetic theory. Historically, the situation seems to be the reverse, and the dates when the texts were written are revealing. Both Ledoux and Boullée wrote their texts at the end of their lives, when they no longer had any practical possibility of constructing.[64] The written texts are only commentaries on achievements or else on ideal proposals. But they are as well their indispensable complements and extensions and that is a revealing phenomenon. Indeed, it is characteristic that this architecture which claims to say everything in a language of forms inevitably has recourse to a *verbal* complement, to a text that is, so to speak, its second word. Ledoux frequently stresses the idea that eloquent architecture must necessarily be accompanied by eloquence about architecture. Boullée joins to his proposals *accounts* in which he tells the effects they should have on spectators. There is, moreover, an isomorphism between the style of architecture and that of writing—the latter is grandiloquent and mixes the lyric with the pathetic. In Ledoux, this "eloquence becomes so dizzying that it prevents the 'reading' of the engraved work as well as of the written work."[65]

In the two architects' work, the writing seeks to give an *a posteriori* unity to the architectural work, to point up and systematize the principles that were the basis of the achievements, but which manifested themselves even better in the ideal proposals. But it also seeks to give a general significance to the work. The accomplishments and ideal proposals are presented only as examples of a whole new style that opens unknown perspectives to architecture and thanks to which this art could fully accomplish the mission incumbent on it. Both Ledoux and Boullée have a clear idea of the innovative and in that sense Revolutionary character of their propositions. They refer, certainly, to the classical heritage, but this is an ambivalent, if not ambiguous, reference. On the one hand, classicism, the reference to the antique, forms a cultural code of the era, and innovation often passes through utilization of that code. On the other hand, this reference can translate the will to take over that heritage, to see and hear it in another way and thence, to put it to the service of innovation.[66]

In the latter context, the search for a "forceful language of signs," which would be at once innovative and primitive, seems all the more revealing to us as it merges with a utopian undertaking and tendency. In the reflections on the architectural language are to be found preoccupations similar to those we have already encountered in discussing the search for a language for the Revolutionary festivals or the new calendar. It is a question of establishing at the very heart of collective life a language of the greatest moral efficacy, which would be due to the singular power it had over souls. It must be iconic in the sense that its signs make the moral values visible, thus assuring their immediate assimilation. The idea of such a visualizing language is part and parcel of that of a lost or forgotten primitive language which, by its energy, its affective and symbolic force, is opposed to "cold," conventional and elitist languages—an idea, if not a vision, of an *alternative language* which proves to be rich in utopian promise. Once it has been discovered, this universal and transparent language should insure perfect communication and thus, unite men in a community of "natural" values and sentiments. The utopia of language underlies several linguistic theories of the era and the ideas of a Court de Gébelin are a striking example of a linguistics nostalgic for utopia. Does Court de Gébelin not hope that the rediscovery of the universal language and of its "allegorical genius" will inevitably set in motion the moral and even physical regeneration of man (along the paths of his research, moreover, Court encounters "animal magnetism" and a certain "social mesmerism" with utopian extensions).[67] The fact that the linguistic utopia of perfect communication is widespread toward the end of the century reveals a whole utopian horizon of the Enlightenment. It underlies, in particular, the interpretation of the architecture of the ancients as a religious, moral, and social message, told in a symbolic language. It could be said that it is a sort of archaeological vision, which is the counterpart of the visionary architecture.

We are thinking of the *Lettres sur l'architecture des anciens et celles des modernes dans lesquelles se trouve développé le génie symbolique qui présida aux mouvements de l'Antiquité*, published in 1774–1778 by Jean-Louis Viel de Saint-Maux. The title of these *Lettres* summarizes their principal idea.[68] Viel's enterprise is similar to that of the Revolutionary architects. In assimilating the architecture to a universal and symbolic language, Viel does not seek, however, to imagine a new architecture, but rather to clarify the old one, to discover its true sense by *reading it as a coded message*. Indeed for Viel the ancient monuments are so many "books whose existence had never been suspected; their language is a fertile source of lessons and enjoyment."[69] The modern seek the perfection of the ancient monuments in their technique ("a base and a capital of so many modules") or else in their respect for a few abstract rules concerning orders, proportions, and the like. However, "the most respectable" antiquity envisaged architecture from a different point of view. "It is a masterpiece which will honor and which truly honors humankind. Its sublime origin, to the greatest astonishment of those who claim to be most skillful in the genre, is Agriculture itself and the cult which followed it; it is its *speaking poem*; it is from it, in its entirety that the Ancients instructed themselves as from a book, not only about primitive theogony, but about the combinations and devices of their cosmogony; in a word, it is in its complement that all knowledge was united and that it was depicted by ingenious allegories and emblems about which there could be no mistake."[70] Therefore, the ancient monuments are so many "sacred archives" and everything in them lends itself to a reading—the columns and their ornaments, the forms of temples and altars ("occasionally circular to express the supreme power and eternity, occasionally quadrangular, to correspond to the cardinal points of the earth"),[71] the plans according to which the monuments are constructed and even entire cities. In them, in a symbolic language that suited their genius, the ancients inscribed a perfectly coherent discourse on their cults and religious rites, on their knowledge and even on their wisdom. The art that corresponds to the needs of social life is also a political masterpiece and Viel makes the legendary legislators if not the first masters of architecture, at least the inspirers and guides of the latter. Let us note, too, the parallel drawn by Viel between architecture and the ancient festivals, their rites, ceremonies, and festivals. It is, once again, a coherent discourse in a symbolic language that he finds in the "celebration of the festivals of the Ancient Peoples . . . which has unfailingly been depicted to us as a mass of ridiculous and contemptible fables."[72] Thus, through a detailed analysis of these symbols and allegories, this "visionary archeology" advances the idealized vision of the ancient peoples— their imagination acquires strength, their soul is raised to the height human weakness allows it to attain.[73] They were agricultural peoples, whose religion was that of nature and whose pure morals harmonized with the institutions, they made of their monuments "indelible evidence of their works and their insight. . . . The earth was never more honored than it was by those masterworks. . . . The monuments of the Nation did not at all resemble one another. That cold monotony was reserved to the moderns. How could they have resembled one another if each depicted by its expressive form one of the causes it was useful to retrace before the eyes."[74] In joining the beautiful to the useful in "expressive forms," the ancients made of their architecture the most effective and sublime means of the scientific, as well as moral and civic, education of the people. It is in the stone that the ancients incorporated their wisdom and it is the stone that they charged with teaching it. What other architecture could better serve a people while expressing its grandeur? Thus it is an example to imitate on the condition that its language be unveiled and its message discovered. But then such a return to the sources could only be an innovation in relation to modern architecture which, "crushed by prejudices," misunderstands this message, disfigures it in abstract and arbitrary precepts. By a detour, visionary archaeology thus intersects the architecture which is also visionary and which seeks to innovate with the forceful language of the symbolic forms.

To summarize our discussions, then, the architecture takes over *from the transparent and universal utopia of language*, whose energy would contribute to communion thanks to the establishment of a communication both perfect and without obstacles. This language of forms which architecture has at its disposal is also synthetic, in the the sense that it encompasses the other arts. Both Boullée and Ledoux insist on the idea that architecture is far more than *the art of building*, as Vitruve defined it. Vitruve "speaks like a laborer rather than like an artist who has knowledge of his art." Of course, the "scientific part," that is, techniques and technology, is of "primary importance," but it is merely a support for architecture, which aims at higher objectives. Arguments with Vitruve's definition were common at the time and the affirmation of architecture as a "noble" art is too frequently combined with an *esprit de corps*. What is striking, however, in Ledoux and Boullée is, on the one hand, the correlation of architecture and the semantic arts and, on the other, the stress put on the moral and social functions it was to take on. Architecture that succeeded in "implementing nature" and in using all the resources of the language it had at its disposal can make tableaux and poems of each of its constructions. Comparisons with the painter and the poet are common in both Boullée and Ledouxs' writing. Ledoux makes Corregio's words: *Ed io anche son pittore* the epigraph of his treatise on the art of architecture.[75] On the other hand, this synthetic language is distinguished by its special *performative functions*—the architect's word is able to arouse in the person to whom it is addressed attitudes that go far beyond the esthetic domain. The architect must look on himself not only as a poet and a painter—he necessarily offers a hand to the educator and to the legislator. This leads us to the other aspect of the functionalism of visionary architecture, namely the problems of its moral and social functions. The redefinition of the latter became compelling with the adaptation of the utopia of language. A field of action was opening to architecture that could and would be *speaking*, which recovered the effectiveness of its word. Indeed, thanks to this language, architecture can enjoy a greater audience and social resonances than those of belles-lettres and painting. The message conveyed by architecture is not shut up in places reserved for the privileged. "All the monuments on earth suitable to the establishment of men are created by means dependent on this beneficial art."[76] Its works accompany and surround men everywhere, in both their private life and their public activities; they "speak to the eyes" of those who cannot read. Is this social art par excellence not also the one that could best join the beautiful to the useful? In taking on this major idea of the esthetics of the Enlightenment and of its social pedagogy as well, the Revolutionary architects give it a new dimension.[77]

There is usefulness in a double sense—first of all in that of building edifices suitable to their functions and which satisfy the needs of those they serve with all that implies insofar as hygiene, conveniences, comfort, and so forth are concerned; second, a useful art means, as well, if not above all, one that touches the "moral man," that contributes to the formation of his soul; in other words, the art that takes charge of moral instruction and pedagogy. As we have said, architecture is particularly suited to these didactic functions. Moreover, it only attains perfection, only rises to the sublime on the condition that it express, that it represent concretely, moral values in all their purity and greatness. In other words, there exists a complicity between the language and the message, due to the symbolic character of the language itself. Pettiness, baseness, and meanness cannot be expressed in forms of monumental scale; rationality, simplicity, and probity do not lend themselves to being "said" by the play of capricious lines and surfaces, or by superfluous ornamentation.

In order to realize its esthetic as well as its moral and social aspirations, this architecture is condemned to being monumental, and in a double sense. It can affirm itself only on a monumental, colossal scale—it is only then that the masses can, by their disposition, deploy all of their energy. And then, it flourishes only in edifices that are *monuments*, works with a strong symbolic charge and which exalt the great values and virtues in all their purity and perfection. The marked preferences shown by Revolutionary architects for funerary monuments has frequently been stressed. This type of symbolic art is a testing ground for Revolutionary architecture, and it is in this genre that it had some of its most notable successes: let us recall the proposal of the cenotaph for Newton designed by Boullée or that of the cemetery of Chaux by Ledoux, of the many examples. This sort of monument opens a nearly unlimited field for the play of symbols. "Temples of death, your appearance must turn hearts to ice! Artist, flee the light of the heavens! Descend into the tombs to trace ideas in them by the pale and dying light of age-old lamps! It is obvious that the aim one proposes to oneself, when one erects this sort of monument, is to perpetuate the memory of those to whom they are consecrated. These monuments then must be conceived so as to stand up to the ravages of time. The Egyptians left us famous examples. Their pyramids are truly characteristic, in that they present the sad image of arid mountains and immutability. This production is more demanding than any other poetry of architecture." It is, as well, the search for a style appropriate to cenotaphs that is at the origin of the most original ideas of Boullée, such as, for example, that of a *buried architecture* with absolutely "naked and bare" walls, as well as that of the architecture "of shadows" which would play the contrasts between light and shadow on large surfaces. Then, too, it is necessary that the man whose memory the monument proposes to perpetuate be worthy of it by his virtues and works. It is only then that his example stimulates the genius and energy of the artist and that a sort of affective and moral affinity is translated in the work. "The homage we are pleased to render to great men is born from the sentiment inspired in us by the height at which our spirit places them. We like to find in one of our fellows that eminent degree of perfection that deifies, so to speak, our nature in our eyes. Oh Newton! Vast and profound genius!

Sublime mind! Deign to accept the homage of my feeble talents! If I dare make it public, it is because of my persuasion that I have surpassed myself in the work of which I am going to speak. Oh Newton! If by the extent of your knowledge, and the sublimity of your genius you determined the figure of the earth, I have conceived the proposal of enveloping you in your discovery."[78] It is noteworthy that effigies are rarely to be found in these funerary monuments or that, if found, they occupy a secondary position. The individual is, as it were, uprooted from history and from his biography. The monuments are temples raised to the universal virtues, values, or even truths.

That establishes a parallel between the funerary monuments and the large public edifices, another favorite subject of visionary architecture. As Boullée says, the former present "subjects that are indicated, and therefore susceptible of being grasped and characterized by the skilled hand." Boullée even considers that "residences" are only "sterile subjects," since "one can only make them distinguished by greater or lesser sumptuousness but it is difficult to introduce the poetry of architecture into them."[79] The architect seeks to represent the functions of the public edifice—to express in the language of forms the social and moral values that must preside over these functions. The mortuary monument commemorates what has already been accomplished, while the public edifice glorifies what must be done in society. The two types of monuments, then, are placed differently in relation to the time of history, but are less opposed than it might at first seem. Indeed, in both cases the artist seeks the degree of idealization that would join that of simplification of forms and would encroach on the time of the origins which creates the models of institutions and human activities.

The search for an equivalency between the form and the purpose of the building is governed by an educational objective—looking at such a monument, the spectator becomes imbued with its moral message. If the idea of such "appropriateness" is not new, the Revolutionary architects give it innovative ramifications which are as much the product of a concern for symbolism carried to the extreme as of the choice of symbolic forms. Thus a court of law must present a clear visual image of justice, in all its purity, majesty, and severity. In seeking a "majestic and imposing ornamentation" appropriate to the functions of the edifice and in order to introduce into it, at the same time, the "poetry of architecture," Boullée proposes "placing the prison entry under the building. It seemed to me that by presenting this august edifice rising above the shady den of crime, I could not only bring out the nobility of the architecture by the resultant oppositions, but even present in a metaphorical manner the imposing picture of vice overwhelmed by the weight of justice."[80] Thus, the symbolism of the function is an integral part of the function itself. As J.-P. Pérouse de Montclos observes, the symbolic system of the Revolutionary architects is certainly one of the most studied and deliberate in the history of architecture."[81]

In seeking to spatialize values, this architecture relinquishes all space that would be emotionally neutral, that would escape the message it disseminates. In linking the signified to the signifier by symbolic relationships, the architecture thus calls for harmony between the *container*, the constructed environment, and the *contained*, the activities performed in it. The will to educate by art inevitably impinges on the moral and the social—the purity and grandeur of the forms demand the elevation of sentiment and actions. Is this architecture not at the same time a criterion of social and moral norms? Boullée's Métropole is not conceived for any religion at all, but rather for the *true* religion, with neither prejudice nor fanaticism and which comes within a hair's breadth of deism: such is the "enlightened" form of sacredness that this church codified in stone. As we have seen, the proposal for the circus likewise supposes that this is the site and setting for an ideal celebration, that of a happy people, representing itself to itself.

At this degree of idealization, simplification, and monumentality, architecture necessarily tends to overlap the sacred, the universal, and the rational. Its works are so many temples, which raise man above himself. To this idea of architecture corresponds the idea thought to be of the mission of the architect. Ledoux does not hesitate to call architecture the imitator, if not the rival, of God. "See all that you owe him," he cries. "He saves suffering humanity from the troubles that afflict it. The rival of God who created the round mass, he will have done more than he, he will have cut it to size, he will have filled in the mountains which frighten the timid; dug ravines to make the limpid waters flow freely; he will have embellished the deserts. Raising man above himself, he will have spread useful knowledge, dipped into the treasures of philosophy, buried under the weight of the barbarous century, drawing forth the true richness that will make ours shine, giving humankind a new brilliance. By associating the hovel to the palace, ignorance to knowledge, how many resources you prepare for us!"[82] Of course, the metaphor is not new, and Ledoux's bombast owes much to his obsession with grandeur as well as to the transports of a romantic before the fact. But is this solemn consecration of architecture not inscribed, so to speak, in the logic of things? Did the old metaphor that said God was the architect of the universe, to which the ideas and rites of the Freemasons had added new meanings, not impose a parallel with the man who defined himself as "the Architect of Humanity"? Did the architect not, thanks to his genius as well as to his synthetic art, implement nature herself in order to join, in a monument, the physical to the moral order? Ought he not to class himself as well alongside that other founder of order whose mission and word are often at the time compared to those of God, namely the ideal legislator? These metaphors and the associations of ideas and images suggested by the very language of the time only express an ideal model of an architect which would correspond to that of ideal architecture. From this perspective, to be an architect is not to practice a trade but to accomplish a mission. The responsibilities of the architect are as extensive as the possibilities of his art and the latter was to be envisaged in its "relationships with morals and legislation," as the title of Ledoux's treatise phrases it.

Between this "consecration of the architect" and the real, historically and socially defined condition of his work, the conflict was fatal. To make speaking architecture is not to speak of it, nor even to design projects, but to accomplish, to realize, to construct. Architecture can imagine the most exalted idea of its mission; to practice it, though, it still needs commissions. And these architectural commissions must be obtained either from the public authorities or from individuals. Therefore, it is necessary to accommodate the tastes and demands of the developer, or else to succeed in persuading him of the values and advantages of the solutions proposed by the architect. And then, how can one get a commission, particularly an important one, without intrigues and contacts? Would Ledoux himself have bequeathed the city of Chaux to us if he had not built the sumptuous pavilion of Louveciennes for Mme. du Barry and Mlle. Guimard's hôtel? Monumental architecture is very expensive, and Ledoux's almost permanent quarrels with his principals are well known. To conflicts of a material nature are added those of a moral and esthetic order.

How keenly and bitterly Ledoux and Boullée feel the dependency of the architect in relation to those who give him commissions, that is, dependency on those with power and money. For Boullée, the young architect finds himself in a nearly inextricable situation. If he meets with some success, he is then "overburdened with a mass of demands and details of all kinds, forced to devote himself completely to the enterprises that have been entrusted to him." The artist then becomes "the businessman of the public and he is lost to the progress of art." But ought not he then "abandon lucrative business" to "do studies of pure speculation"? But the architect's condition is specific. He is not free and independent as painters and men of letters are, who "can choose their subjects and follow the impulses of their genius." The architect must *construct* and have all the means that implies at his disposal. How, then, can he give himself up to the hope of one day being given the responsibility for some great monument? "Opportunities are so rare! How can one flatter oneself, ten or fifteen years in advance, that one will surely be employed by the men who, at that time, will be in authority? The answer will be, perhaps, that the man of merit has the right to expect it. And I will reply: will this justice be done? Does he have obvious grounds for seeing himself preferred? I imagine the organizers, the officials, to have the most honest views, the purest intentions, and I still find myself forced to acknowledge that, for want of knowledge, they often act blindly and that it is a happy chance when their choice falls on an able man. How frequently their preference has been granted to ignorant schemers to the detriment of the man of merit who always works and never engages in intrigue!" Thus, a young architect finds himself forced to sacrifice his talents to "succeed in being known

by people in authority without whose benevolence he cannot develop his talents.''
But suppose he succeeded and found the client, the official who entrusted him
with work worthy of his talent. ''It is known that when the simplest individual
has something built, he subjects the patience of his architect, on whose decision
he only rarely relies, to the greatest ordeals. It is known, too, that the authorities
who order public monuments are not commonly more docile than individuals
are. What happens then? That, to obey higher orders, the architect finds himself
obliged to give up good ideas. . . . Yes, because of not being understood, the
architect will suffer all sorts of discouraging frustrations and, if he wants to be
retained, will be very wary of putting up any resistance; he will no longer listen
to the voice of his genius, but will lower himself to the level of those he must
please. . . . It is obvious that, as a result, it is very difficult for an able architect
to be put in a position where he can produce good work. . . . That is of course
a great source of sharp distress and bitter regrets for one who has a passion for
his art; so I was not surprised when I heard that because of having suffered the
hardships of which I just spoke, a strong man fell into the most frightful despair.''[83] The conflicts between the clients and the architect denounced by Boullée
are not, certainly, specific to his time—they are as old as architecture itself, and
even Boullée did not know the clients who would proliferate with city planning
as widespread as it is wild. Nor is the conflict peculiar to architecture: although
Boullée envies painters and poets their freedom, similar indictments from them
are plentiful at the time. What is, however, noteworthy in Boullée and even
more so in Ledoux is the sharp feeling of a *moral* conflict between architecture,
with its mission inseparable from its specific language, and the moral state of
the society in which the architect is constrained to practice his art. Ledoux is
particularly revealing on this point. In effect, Ledoux poses himself a problem
which can only seem paradoxical to us and which nevertheless arises inevitably
when one seeks a harmony that is both *moral* and *esthetic* between the container
and the contained: how can the architect construct a building for a wicked person
without degrading his art? ''The dignity of the architect is demeaned when he
is obliged to descend the steps of the temple of glory to design the domicile of
the men who fomented common evils.''

''An architect is quite embarrassed when he is obliged to construct the den
of a leech swollen with human substances. What can he do when the authorities
order it? Will he delegate the sublimity of the art to the blind complaisance that
uses durable marbles and perishable wood indiscriminately, will he abandon it
to the enemies of taste? No, of course he cannot be indifferent to the practical
offenses that obliterate the splendor of the arts. What, then, is to be done? In
vain does the architect read and reread the poets to reinforce his spirit; surrounded
by distastes it shares with the majority, genius is mute and inactive, confined
amid the common afflictions which suffocate him. . . . How can one achieve a
house whose particulars are so difficult to fulfill? . . . That is how the thought

of an architect tormented by discordant elements churns. No longer does it take flight; the purity inherent to the cultivation of the arts is incompatible with the greedy passions that demean it."[84]

Thus this architecture, because it wanted to be speaking, could not resign itself to lending its word to anyone at all without repudiating itself, without questioning that unity of the message and the language on which the sublime aspect of its art rests. Its style as well as the idea of its moral and educational mission define an ideal model of the "silent partner," of the developer. For the architecture to be able to be established and to flourish, it needs commissions that go beyond the scale of private residences and clients who think big, and as "philosophers." The ideal developer was necessarily a public person, the state, for several reasons. First of all, construction on a monumental scale called for the commitment of enormous financial means and materials. It involved, as well, the development of the surrounding space so that it would conform to the monument. On the other hand, only a developer aiming at the "general good" could order theaters, gigantic cenotaphs, law courts, temples, and museums. Moreover, this architecture proves to be functional only for the government which will make use of its monuments to communicate the grandeur of its ideas and the values that prevail in it and, hence, to make of them so many means of educating the populace. In other words, it is with a social system which intended to be educational and which sought harmony between the organization of space and the system of social values that Revolutionary architecture could see itself in profound harmony from both the esthetic and the moral point of view.

This aspiration toward the state client which would take on the responsibility for realizing ideal projects fits the idea of the state which was widespread at the time—the privileged instrument of the expansion of the enlightened mind. This is, of course, reminiscent of the traditional ideal of the state-patron, the protector of the arts and sciences, but this "enlightened century" adds specific ramifications. A government which would make the philosophical ideas its own, and would implement them in order to reform society is imagined; occasionally, it is demanded. The political formula of these hopes and dreams most often does not go beyond that of a certain enlightened despotism in which, at most, the government would be only the executor of the "philosophical projects" and ideas. Political moderation, if not timidity, nevertheless allies itself perfectly with the utopian dreams and images of an alternative society to which the reforms and the march of progress which would thus take over social life would lead. In the case of Revolutionary architecture, the texts in which it is a question of the ideal client have no political tenor or specific ideology. However, the very scope of their proposals leads the architects toward the utopian. The specifically architectural dream is combined with that of a perfect harmony between the monuments and a social system which would raise these temples to sacralize the moral and civic virtues. The ancient monuments would serve as a projection screen for this double dream. They were looked on, in fact, as works achieved by great legislators and great peoples who had understood the social and moral role that architecture has to play thanks to its exceptional esthetic and educational possibilities. Of course, in practice, they were resigned to compromise, and Ledoux finally did the project of that "leech swollen with human substances" because he had been given the commission. The comments he made on the occasion of this project are nevertheless very revealing of the ideas and dreams that prevailed in his work as a whole. "The architect plows the future and wants to convince himself; *he sees the good in the purification of the social system everywhere*; adapts it to the edifices he constructs. This is not true of the craftsman; he is the automaton of the creator; the man of genius is a creator himself."[85]

The utopian ideas and images are not superfluously added to Revolutionary architecture in a secondary discourse. The discourse *on* architecture, the commentaries on projects, and the esthetic explanations abound, of course, in utopian images or in allusions to utopia. Nevertheless, the utopian dimension of this architecture is not uniquely or even principally found on this level. The aspiration toward an alternative society, in which this architecture would fully exercise its functionality and where the architect could fully assert his genius is inherent to the "architectural discourse" itself. The aspiration toward the utopia inhabits and inspires the projects themselves, is stated in their specific language, that of *the ordering of masses*. It is in reviving the imaginary in architecture and in its own language that visionary architects turn in a direction where their visions must necessarily meet the images and dreams of an alternative society. It is notable, too, that these architects who for too long were classified as "neoclassic" have a very clear awareness and even an exaggerated feeling of proposing an *innovative* architecture, an alternative architecture. Reference to the future recurs frequently—both to future progress in art and to its insertion into social life. "I admit that I considered it beneath me," Boullée says, "to limit myself to the study of our former masters. I sought to expand, by the study of nature, my thoughts on the art which, after profound meditation, seems to me at its dawn. How little, indeed, have people applied themselves up to the present time to the poetry of architecture, a sure means of increasing men's enjoyment and of giving artists a just celebrity. Yes, I think, our public edifices ought to be, in some way, poems. The images that they offer to our senses should arouse in us feelings analogous to the use to which these edifices are destined." "Before dying," exclaims Ledoux, "I will have the satisfaction of having broken the chains that fettered it (architecture), of having made them fall. There will remain many things to say, but what I have forgotten will be found in an isolated expression of the discussion, which adds to the thought, in the theory formed on different situations, in the liberty to create, in the relinquishment of the Ecole's reservations . . . and in the inexhaustible wellsprings of the imagination without which genius can produce nothing. . . . Then the architect will stop being a copyist, he will develop new forces on earth, annihilate the vault covering the future . . . , he will find the means of forcing new products from nature."[86]

The affinity between the renewal of the architectural imagination and social utopias is even more fully evident if one goes from proposals for isolated monuments to the comprehensive organization of space—urban space, in particular. The Revolutionary architecture which intended to be an all-encompassing and at the same time social art par excellence inevitably tended toward city planning. It did not, however, seek a utopia, an imaginary society in which to set its monuments in an appropriate urban setting. And yet these monuments imply a social arrangement of the space which proves to be isomorphic to that which predominates in the ideal Cities. This isomorphism manifests itself on two levels. On the one hand, the cities implied by Revolutionary architecture are perfectly suitable to the ideal Cities—they give them an architectural setting and an urban social and cultural complex. On the other hand, who could better inhabit the urban space of Revolutionary architecture and enjoy its monuments than those who people the ideal Cities and who live their happiness in the utopia? These observations are valuable for both the ideal cities of Boullée and Ledoux. Each of these nevertheless presents particular characteristics that are worth noting.

Boullée does not work out a proposal for a city. Nevertheless, as J.-M. Pérouse de Montclos judiciously noted, when one considers the mass of projects put together by Boullée, one notices that all those monuments "can be naturally laid out in an overall plan which reconstructs for us the tableau of an ideal city."[87] It is noteworthy, as well, that Boullée joins this tableau to a whole utopian imagery. Thus, on the occasion of Bonaparte's expedition to Egypt, he gives his imagination free rein and dreams of developing "a country that had become a wilderness because of barbarism and in which the unfortunate inhabitants are ignorant even of the means of building cabins for themselves and take shelter under mounds of earth." On this quasi-virgin terrain he dreams of constructing model cities according to "a general plan that would be used to record this great association. . . . I think of this plan as resembling the tree of science; from a common center branch out all the beneficial ramifications whose branches would extend into all of this great establishment adorned by the enchanting poetry of architecture. Do you hear the spectators cry out their admiration? What a sublime image is offered to us in this temple consecrated to piety! What touching simplicity reigns in this house of charity! With what brilliance these monuments erected to the glory of the nation shine! What imposing nobility characterizes the Temple of Thémix! How these agreeable refuges allow us to savor the pleasures of life! Ah, into what profound reflections we are thrown by the appearance of these funerary monuments!"[88]

Let us prolong this reverie, if not as apprentice architects, at least as simple tourists who stop off in Boullée's imaginary city. Let us imagine, indeed, that we are visiting a city where Boullée's great monuments are harmoniously gathered and laid out—the Métropole, the City Hall, the Museum, the Coliseum, the monument for Newton, etc. During this visit, let us adopt the attitude of a model spectator, so to speak—that is, of one on whom these monuments produce all the effects intended by the architect. Let us attempt, finally, in the course of our imaginary visit, to explore the *social space* implied by this architecture. We do not know the plan of this city; Boullée did not leave it to us and it would be presumptuous to want to substitute oneself to him. However, the essential characteristics of the urban space are given us, along with the monuments that form the strong points of the city. The size of the city is already implied by the monumental scale of the public buildings. The Coliseum, for example, is conceived as a setting for celebrations which could house three hundred thousand people and thus serve the population of a city the size of the Paris of the time. The Métropole, the temple of the rational religion, only becomes functional, its "ordered masses" only produce the intended effects, on the condition that an enormous crowd fills it and that by its presence it amplifies the sensation of grandeur and immensity.[89]

Boullée does not indicate the plan of the streets and open squares, but the strong points of the city determine its overall layout. The monumental edifices, to be seen and admired in all their splendor, must be autonomous and surrounded with open spaces whose size harmonizes with the scale of the monument. Broad and long avenues must necessarily open on these plazas, for two reasons. First of all, as means of communication: it is necessary to open access and exit routes for the crowds that fill the amphitheater or the City Hall. But, too, for esthetic reasons which also are linked to moral and social reasons. To make the monument speak, so that the message conveyed by the order of the masses gets through, it is necessary that the edifice present itself to the spectators in its most varied perspectives. First of all, their view must encompass the building in its entirety, in its imposing grandeur; that is, they must see it from a very great distance, which is indispensable for the effect of the volumes organized into a whole to work. "Our emotions arise from the effect of the whole in its entirety and not from the details, whose beauty only adds to the first impressions caused by the masses."[90] Then it is necessary that the effects are constantly renewed as one gets closer to the monument, that it display its greatest developments to the spectators, in playing off its voids against its solids, its decorated parts against its bare ones, shadows against lights, etc. Let us take the case of the Métropole, that temple that was to offer the image of greatness. The latter came not only from its expanse, but also from the application of that "ingenious art by which one extends and expands images, which consists of combining objects so as to present them to us in such a way that the unity of the whole is most obvious to us. . . . The objects are then arranged so that everything contributes to our enjoyment of them. Their multiplicity offers us the image of richness. The greatest magnificence and the most perfect symmetry are what result from the order which establishes them on all sides and spreads them out to our view in such a way that we cannot count them. By extending the paths so that their end is beyond our sight, the laws of optics and the effects of perspective offer us the picture of immensity; with every step, the objects presenting themselves from new angles renew our pleasures by successively varied pictures. Finally, by a happy marvel which is caused by the effect of our movements and which we attribute to the objects, it seems that the latter move with us and that we have communicated life to them."[91]

In moving with us, the monuments "make [us] circulate," they command our movements. They do not for one single moment abandon us to ourselves alone. At no moment will our glance escape the images they offer us, or rather with which they assault us. Of course, it is our movements that communicate life to them but does their omnipresence not impose on us the means of living in the city? No one will stroll aimlessly about in this city because one is always *guided* by the monuments from one place to another, from one perspective to another. How could one lose one's way? We see landmarks everywhere, which orient us, which force us to return to what is essential for this city and its inhabitants. Inevitably our souls will be imbued with the dreams of grandeur, the sense of the ceremonial and the celebration. How can one take a step in this city without the architecture that dominates it exercising its quasi-magical faculties of arousing the most intense emotions in us?

Of course, they are only the most elevated and sublime sentiments. They are not only or essentially esthetic. Is this architecture not endowed with extra-architectural values and do its forms not express moral and civic truths? Each monument confines us within a well-defined interpretation: these poems in stone do not lend themselves to varied readings. In front of the Métropole which offers "the most striking and greatest image of existing things" and which seems to us "enormous and yet simple, like the universe itself," how can we resist the ascendancy the image of the great has over us? "The image of the great has such influence over us that even in supposing it horrible it always excites a feeling of admiration in us. A volcano spewing flames and death is a horribly beautiful image!"[92] Since "man commonly weighs himself up in the space in which he finds himself," how could we not be *shattered* by the entrance of this temple? In order to produce this effect the architect raised the height of the entrance to the apex of its vaults and gave it the width of the large nave. As the beautiful is associated with a sacred terror, the spectator is only an *object* on which the art will exercise its power. Inside the temple, everything is implemented "to inspire all the religious sentiments appropriate to the cult of the Supreme Being." So, by means of the play of lights, the architect "will arouse the feeling of happiness in the spectator's soul" or else will plunge his soul into sadness when the temple presents only somber effects.[93]

If, after the temple, we go on to the library, we shall be struck to the soul by the equally new effect produced by its vaulted court, whose "decoration comes from its immensity." The bookshelves rise above our heads and are extended by a colonnade which seems to span the vault of heaven. The light spreads over the wise who, immersed in their books, are spontaneously arranged, so to speak, in decorative groups. How could such a picture not speak to our hearts? How could it not arouse the desire to follow in the footsteps of the great men who made their epochs illustrious? How could one not, then, feel "those noble transports, those sublime flights of the spirit by which it seems that the soul leaves its envelope behind; one believes oneself to be inspired by the shades of these famous men." These sublime sentiments experienced by the spectator are no other than those that inspired the artist himself and that make the stone live, breathe, and speak.[94] This account could be continued by evoking the impressions made by the funerary monuments whose "appearance would turn our hearts to ice," or the feelings inspired by the national law court which "gives prominence to the laws, the object of everyone's love, because everyone wanted them" through the metaphor of the tablet of the law inscribed on an immense bare facade. In front of this monument, will our feeling be any different than that of Madame Brogniart who, having seen the project, wrote her husband, Boullée's student: "It is so pure and has a certain *je ne sais quoi* that is so great that I get goose pimples looking at it. One has the feeling that it is the painting of the happiness and unhappiness of humans by the laws that emanate from it. . . . I had of course heard you speak of it occasionally, but I could not imagine that moral effects could be produced in architecture as they are in painting. That is quite what I felt on Thursday at your teacher's."[95]

As we have said, one does not wander aimlessly about in this city; one goes from one monument to another as in a sort of pilgrimage. The space one crosses is an initiatory space which at each step introduces us to the moral values that guide the collective life. This city has nothing mysterious about it; from all its diverse perspectives, it offers itself in the same way to our eyes everywhere. By its perfect transparency it takes the opposite course to the myth of the dark and unhealthy big city, the asylum of evil, if not its incarnation. The broad avenues and the large plazas as well as the perspectives on which they open, evoke the crowds that cross them to celebrate their festivals, to go to discuss public affairs at the Palais Municipal, to pay homage to, and initiate themselves into, science in Newton's cenotaph. The architecture serves to cement the social space; it makes it into an educational place where the community is formed by the participation of each of the spectators in the same collective imagination. A speaking architecture, certainly, but also in the sense that it transforms the spectators into simple receivers of this omnipresent word. On the condition, of course, that they do not revolt against this collective imagination constricting every individual imagination, and against these dreams of grandeur which, in order to elevate souls, only crush them. . . .

Boullée's imaginary city does not refer to a defined social system that the ideal City was to incarnate. The art espouses the values and guiding ideas of the Enlightenment and puts itself at their service without, however, having sought to clarify them on the social, political, or institutional level. However, the conjunction of these ideas and the architectural style calls for the utopia or else, if you will, this conjunction reveals the utopian dimension underlying both a dreamed architecture and a moral and social dream that it wanted to represent. Whom would this architecture better suit than the model citizens who identified with the values of the rational and happy City incarnated in the ideal city? And what else could take on the responsibility for this architectural dream, if not the city animated by rational happiness, for which art would be functional only in its didactic effects and would seek to broadcast continuously its moral message by its gigantic mute reproducers which would be the works of *speaking architecture*?

It was necessary to imagine a city based on Boullée's proposals for monuments. Ledoux presents a different case—his proposals for edifices are present from the inception as integrated into the space of an ideal city, the grandiose image of which opens *L'Architecture considérée sous les rapports des arts, des mœurs et de la législation*. "One will see important factories, the daughters and mothers of industry, give birth to populous gatherings. . . . A city will rise to surround them and to crown them. . . . The surroundings will be adorned with dwellings dedicated to rest, to pleasure and planted with gardens to rival the famous Eden."[96] Between city planning and architecture there is perfect agreement. The ideal city brings to the fore the esthetic and social values of the new architectural forms and in such an urban space this architecture proves functional. Ledoux has the very strong feeling that his ideas "are laying the foundations of the future" and that his proposals forestall the "prejudices" of his century. The scoffing and mockery his proposal for the city of Chaux aroused only confirmed his opinion. "I presented the proposals for a city with the enhancements to which it was open; I had foreseen it, I excited a convulsive movement. . . . The dealers, spurred on by indigestible rhapsodies, harp on discordant strings and tire our ears with impotent sounds; interests cut across one another. Everyone says laughingly: *columns for a factory, temples, public baths, markets, bridges, places of business, gambling dens, etc.—what a mass of incoherent ideas*. Then, shrugging their shoulders already bent under the weight of adulation, they call it madness. How much prejudice must be conquered! Everything was opposed to these advanced views, which took away from the century. Impartiality in its tolerance summarized the most diverse opinions and said, stroking the idol of the day: one cannot deny it, *these are great views*, but *why so many columns; they are suitable only to temples and to kings' palaces*."[97]

Fourier, in his observations on the *Modifications à apporter à l'architecture des villes*, only quotes a single example of an architecture that would correspond to his views, namely that of the *hôtel* Telluson, one of Ledoux's creations.[98] This evidence is certainly significant, but to conclude from it that Ledoux was a "Fouriérist" before the fact would be farfetched and erroneous. The interplay between the architectural dream and the social dream is much more complex and subtle. Ledoux's architectural vision is part and parcel of that of an *alternative society*, situated somewhere in the future. He emphasizes that on many occasions, and it is from that perspective that he defines the mission the architect must assume as well as the novelty of his own work. "For the first time, art puts the natural laws together and works out a social system; it imposes well-being in all situations, in all the usual enjoyments; it joins its seductive powers to the innate rights of man, industry to the compulsory luxury which develops the resources of the states; taking all forms to give all impetuses, it forces the rich to accord to the poor the honorable tribute that one owes to work. Art will finally have matched all the nuances of life, with the dignity which does away with unequal fortunes, after having created happiness will force it into retirement (for all values degenerate in idleness which cuts itself off from the public good; I would go even further, they become paralyzed). Such is the effect of imaginations transported beyond the mountains where the apathy that subjugates enthusiasm feebly rules. One works one's way through obstacles."[99] All that is as generous as it is grandiloquent and vague. What is this new "social system," however? Can one find out more about its institutions, its social structures? These vague and hazy images of a "society of the future" take shape only in a certain language. The unity of this utopian discourse is in the language proper to it, that of the *order of the masses* and of the organization of the space. Ledoux's dreamed City is not the representation made of one proposal for an ideal City or another. It could be said to be a monument erected to the *Utopia of the Enlightenment*. More than a utopian city, it is Utopia itself imagined in stone, or even a museum in which the utopian dreams of the epoch are realized in an architectural representation and organized in a spatial whole.

Let us be more specific about this dreamed City, as many versions are to be found in Ledoux's work.

First of all, Ledoux presents us with the proposal for the city of Chaux and its diverse programs. Chronologically, it seems, the first was that of the Saltworks (Saline) of Chaux, to be built based on a square plan. It was only afterward that Ledoux went on to another proposal for the saltworks adopting a semicircular form.

The symbolism of the circle certainly determined the choice of this form. Let us note, however, that the latter is adapted to the nature of the setting, that is, to the loop of the Loue in the spot where the construction was located. The saltworks, and the city which was to form the other semicircle, thus took up the "imperial path of Nature," and the circular form has a double meaning. The perfection and the "transparency" of the circle symbolize the perfect accord between the human work and nature, but the same form represents, too, the domination of nature by man, the utilization of "natural" energy by the creative genius.

Ledoux succeeded in carrying out only the saltworks, and then only in part. The vestiges of this achievement still extant in Arc-et-Senans allow us to get some idea of what the whole was to be. The project of the city of Chaux had high aims.

From the beginning of his work, Ledoux dreamed of grasping the unique opportunity presented by the commission for the saltworks to implement his ideas on architecture and show the possibilities of the art that *encompasses all the social functions*. Whence the successive proposals he collected in his book that go from a small suburb to the plans for a "city and the growth to which it is susceptible," projects which are increasingly ambitious and in which Ledoux takes up the key ideas of the ideal city planning of his time. The city must satisfy the needs of hygiene and of communication. It must assume a moral, "philanthropic" function—the urban form encompasses and is a material representation of the association of work and virtue, it is the place for the initiation by one to the other. Thus, the saltworks, its administrative buildings, its workshops, its dwellings for the workers, etc., become for Ledoux a testing ground for an ideal city. A detailed analysis of the successive proposals shows how Ledoux's dreams grew, how his imagination worked in seeking an urban space which would be at once the foundation and the expression of rational and harmonious social relationships, of the unity of the moral and the social.[100]

In *Architecture*, Ledoux does not, in any case, content himself with gathering and displaying his city planning proposals for the city of Chaux. The space implied by the ensemble of his proposals and his comments is not situated on the banks of the Loue. It is an imaginary and ideal space that defies localization. Indeed, in his book, Ledoux gathers several proposals for monuments which he vaguely relates to an urban project and which nevertheless are not on any of the ideal plans of the city of Chaux.

Moreover, any attempt to integrate them into one of these proposals faces insurmountable difficulties, because these monuments prove to be nonfunctional—such as the Oïkema, for example, a gigantic bordello whose architecture is a mass of phallic symbols. Ledoux explains the moral and, so to speak, moralizing functions both of the edifice and of the institution it accommodates. Sound morality enlightened by reason uses a ruse to put vice at the service of virtue. Seen close up, vice does not have a less powerful influence on the soul; by the horror it imprints on it, it causes a reaction toward virtue. To the fiery youths it attracts, the Oïkema presents naked depravity, and the feeling of the degradation of man reviving dormant virtue leads man to the altar of the virtuous Hymen which embraces and crowns him. . . . The workshop of corruption, under its deep, dark dens, reveals to him the poisoned sources that adulterate the vigor of morality . . . and returns him to daylight with only hatred for what might corrupt morals.''[101] How is this ''workshop,'' which makes sense only where vice is widespread, conceivable in this virtuous city that is to be the city of Chaux? Would it not be only for the recalcitrant young inhabitants? But then why so gigantic an edifice which is by no means a ''workshop'' but rather an enormous factory whose capacity for purification, so to speak, is more than amply sufficient for the entire population of Paris, the young as well as the not-so-young. . . . And why would the virtuous city of Chaux need an enormous prison, the reutilization of a proposal made for Aix? And where along the banks of the Loue was the grandiose cemetery to be located, a veritable city of the dead in flagrant disproportion to the population of Chaux, even with its possible growth?

If all these monuments cannot be found on any of the proposals for the city of Chaux, it is because they are situated elsewhere. The space to which Ledoux attaches them is not that of any definite city but the imaginary space of *the City*. The City is then only the paradigm of an architectural discourse on the global society. No precise political idea, no reasoned principle on the social system governs this discourse. It proves, however, to be bound up with the utopia, both by what it affirms and by what it contradicts. The City is the privileged setting for the practice of architecture as well as the setting for the demonstration of its nearly limitless possibilities for serving the cause of a purified morality, or even for purifying morals. As in Boullée, the City is the exact opposite of the perverted and corrupting city. It is the City of triumphant virtue, as opposed to cities in which vice rules; a transparent and luminous City which contrasts with the opaque and shadowy cities. A City closed on itself, in the sense that it forms a microcosm which harmoniously orders all social activities. But the City of a double opening as well. It is open to nature, which surrounds and extends it, and also to history which, for it, means only a practically indefinite growth. The flourishing of the City can only be harmonious and can only confirm its initial order. The City, with its ''columned factories'' and its ''recreational monuments'' favors the activities typical of Utopia—work, festivals, education. ''The City Hall represents and in its wisdom keeps the balance among individual interests; it is there that rewards are distributed and crimes are punished. The public schools develop the first seeds of virtue and teach sound morality. . . . Further, it is a monument destined for the recreations of the populace, for the exercises that develop its faculties. . . . What movement! Industry, under the vault of the market, brings prosperity; the religious cult placed in the common center calls for piety; The Pacifère amasses the tables of the laws and replaces the temple of Concord; the calendar of the decent, honorable man assembles all the virtues. . . . It is a world isolated from the world; it is a happy people who develop and bring to fruition all the seeds that the earth in its easy contact with humans promised to fertilize.''[102] The city of Chaux is only one of the variations and the possible material representations of the City. Thus, the latter easily accommodates what, either by its dimensions or its function, goes beyond the bounds of the space of the former. In the abstract space of the City, monuments and edifices one would think inspired by the most diverse, if not opposing, utopias of the epoch cohabit. Is that not the case with the *cénobies*, houses made for the wise whose "happiness and well-being can be found in the attractive feeling of common enjoyment" and who, therefore, have no private property? Is the *Oïkema* not the ideal edifice to accommodate that other bordello in the service of virtue that Restif proposed in the *Pornographe*? And for how many utopian Cities would the architectural dream incarnated in the *Panarétéon*, the school of morality, be suitable? "When one erects durable monuments, the principle that directs the artist cannot be immaterial; if he begins with examples which strike the multitude, he surrounds himself with all the means for giving the different establishments he conceives the useful character that honors the present and improves the future. The Platos, the Socrates, Lactance, and Augustine all worked on this vast edifice. . . . They formed the public mind for the need of the day; a lovely job for the Architect destined to succeed them! What good things he can develop in striking the curiosity, in awakening apathy by intentional flights of fancy. How many people who do not know how to read will find by walking around this edifice everything that can save them from the lapses that degrade them. How many people stripped of the spirit of superstition which conceals basic ideals, will find, in this great book of elements, desirable perfection."[103]

A disconcerting work, if there ever was one, is this *Architecture considérée sous le rapport des mœurs et de la législation*. The grandiloquent style and innumerable digressions further muddle the text in which dreams are confused with realizations, the City is mixed up with the city of Chaux, and the principles of architecture are entangled with the architect's confessions. Paradoxically, this confusion stems from the pedagogical intention of the work. The discourse encompasses the written text, the drawings, and the plans; by visualizing the ideas and making the images speak, it seeks to join technical knowledge to moral initiation. It is addressed to the "legislators" who alone can be "ideal promoters" and shows them that architecture in its new developments is able to become the major instrument of the inculcation of civics. But it is addressed above all to the young architects. It is an architecture course which teaches how to practice this art in a creative way; but it is also a treatise of moral education for the architect. It could be said to be a new *Emile* in which the educator seeks to form the personality of the architect by confronting the student with all the aspects of social life through an imaginary architectural experience which is the object of comments and lyrical effusions. But it could be said, too, to be a new *Encyclopédie*, which "gathers . . . all kinds of edifices used in the social order to compose a whole which lends itself to the variety of all the motifs that dictated it."[104] Both this "order" and its "motifs" are raised to the ideal purity. As we have noted, the monuments of visionary architecture are conceived as temples erected to Religion, Justice, Virtue, Work, etc.[105] Dream architecture is thus married to the dreams of a moral and social order that would insure the common happiness. It is the duty of the architectural imagination itself to be social and to go beyond the bounds which stop the politician. "What the government does not dare to do," Ledoux explains on the occasion of his proposal for the *Oikema* "the Architect confronts; he who makes light work of animating stone surfaces, he who called up all the forms in order to contrast them; he who staked his usufruct invested in art can also commit the capital."[106]

Thus this encyclopedia of the architecture of dreams is also that of utopian dreams and visions or even a sort of architectural museum of utopias. One must go to Arc-en-Senans and visit what remains of the city of Chaux to get an idea of what such a museum of utopias based of Ledoux's work can be. The lived experience of this visit teaches more than any discourse on the urban space of utopia. The monumental entrance announces that one is penetrating an *alternative* space. The buildings, constructed in a semicircle, surround the visitor. Enormous decorative elements—distilled drops of salt—assail him from all sides and one cannot for one single moment escape the didactic message the walls spread abroad. There are constant reminders that one lives in this city in order to work and produce. The closer one gets to the Director's house, situated in the center of the axis, a lofty house, composed of cubic masses which "pyramid," the more one has the feeling of becoming smaller and bowing before this mass resting on columns and rising toward the sky. And it is in terms of stones and forms that we get the message: "one of the great motives which link governments to the results involved at all times is the general arrangement of a plan that gathers at an illuminated center all the parts of which it is composed." There is nothing more disquieting than the experience of this visit. One is caught in the trap of feelings that are opposed to one another even while they blend with one another; that of the being dazzled by the explosion of the social and architectural imagination free of all shackles, and that of the agonizing oppression secreted by this space that closes in on itself, in definitively imposing Law and Order on all it contains.

4

"From the Place de la Révolution to the Place du Bonheur": The Imaginary Paris of the Revolution

$\mathbf{A}$n engraving published in 1791 to preserve the accurate recollection of the *pantheonization* of the shades of Voltaire endeavors to give a realistic image of this sublime ceremony, "a unique festival in the splendors of literature and philosophy." In the foreground is the magnificent, antique-style chariot which rises to the height of the second story of the houses. Harnessed with magnificent white horses, it heads toward the French Pantheon (formerly the church of Sainte Geneviève) at the head of the majestic procession in which can be seen young students of the Academies of Painting disguised in Roman costumes. The sky is somber, and torrential rain drenches the participants—nature, alas, is not at the rendezvous of the festival, and the sun does not shine on Voltaire's triumph despite the program for the festival. In the background, the artist engraved the landscape in which the ceremony takes place. Several houses can be distinguished, as well as the masses of the Pont Neuf and the Louvre. To these familiar monuments, however, are added a monumental pyramid and a colossal trajan column. These monuments, however, were never built for the ceremony, not even in plaster. The artist added them to the urban setting the festival demanded and which could only be that of an imaginary city.

Integrating nonexistent monuments into the realistic image of a festive Paris is only an extreme case of a procedure found in nearly all the prints representing Revolutionary celebrations. This festive Paris of the the prints is an *alternative Paris*, different from the historic city and opposed to it. An ideal space and a new architecture are imposed on the city and take possession of it. The urban landscape is dominated by monuments expressly erected for one particular celebration or another: triumphal arches, altars of the country, sacred mountains, temples of immortality, etc. The painters and engravers in no way attempt to bring out the provisional character of these diverse constructions. On

280

the contrary, in the prints the plaster constructions take on the solidity of marble and granite. These prints were proposed to the Parisians, the participants in and spectators of these celebrations, as a material form of their souvenirs; to those from the provinces they offered the image of the city they would have admired had they been at the celebration. Whence the care taken to situate the new monuments in relation to a known setting, to evoke some elements of the historic city as landmarks. But these evocations are even more revealing of the preponderance of representations of the ideal city. Preference is given to the monuments that do not overly evoke the "feudal" past—for example the Pont Neuf or the Ecole Militaire. There are practically no churches, with the exception of those transformed by the *fabriques* they accommodate on the occasion of a ceremony (for example, the interior of Notre Dame where a sort of mountain crowned by a small, round, Greek-style temple is erected). Like the "monuments of despotism," there is yet another Paris absent from these prints, in which are rarely seen "the sad and dirty walls" and the "street corners without symmetry" of which Kersaint said that they weren't worthy of having the sacred laws of liberty posted on them. It is as though all that Paris was has been razed, and if there are still some traces of it to be found, it is only so they can be contrasted with another space that has been established in the heart of the city.

Take the print that represents the Fountain of Regeneration erected for the Festival of the Unity and Indivisibility of the French Republic (10 August 1793) on the place de la Régéneration, at the Bastille. The grandiose figure of Nature rises in the middle of a plaza whose immense *emptiness* is itself a symbol. Some remaining rubble serves as a reminder of what the populace destroyed and eliminated forever of their city. It is only in the distant background that some ugly houses and a sinister wall can be made out; they seem to be the vestiges of an ancient city, which the statue pushed back out of the way of the freed space which surrounds it. In other prints, the crowds gathered around a monument or crossing the city in a procession are spread out on plazas which are always immense or on avenues which are always wide and straight and look out upon an open horizon or on a mass of greenery, on poplars and oaks. Thus, Nature is reinstalled in the very center of Paris, becoming reconciled with the city, if not paying homage to Liberty, which triumphs in it.[107]

Of course, the Revolution had neither the time nor the means to build and it has been frequently said, after Michelet, that it left no monument except the emptiness of the Champ de Mars. It is, however, sometimes forgotten that it left an imaginary architecture and city planning and, in particular, an *imaginary Paris*. The prints of festive Paris are so many postcards, or representations of this Paris which was never constructed. With the Revolution, the imagination takes over the city as though it were an immense building site. It prepares to beautify Paris, to transform it, and to recreate it in order to make it a city worthy of the Revolutionary dream. Like any other city, this imaginary Paris has its system of itineraries and privileged places which unify its space. Like any other city, it is a collective and historical work—it was made and unmade with proposals for monuments, the settings erected for the celebrations, the programs of transformation, the routes taken by the crowds during the Revolutionary days or those drawn up for solemn processions. It was constructed by professional architects who expressed themselves in the language of drawings and plans, but also by sections which, to beautify their neighborhoods, proposed the erection of a statue, the transformation of a church, and so forth.

Can this imaginary Paris be classed with the utopian cities we have frequented? The problem is complex and there can be only a qualified response. There are numerous proposals which compose imaginary Paris and which were possible only by the conjunction and merging of two utopias. On the one hand, it is the utopia of the New City, in search of a city planning and an architecture that would be the material representation of the Revolutionary principles and myths; but, on the other hand, it is the unfulfilled dreams of architecture and city planning in search of a social order that will take them on. Was the Revolution an overall liberating act to unleash talents and found a new art? "Genius," Romme proclaimed, "restored to its own conceptions, will make canvas and marble exude only liberty and equality."[108] It is particularly during the years 1792–1794 that the most remarkable of the utopian cities dreamed of in the eighteenth century is established in an imaginary Paris. Below one partial representation or another, a global discourse is established on an *alternative city* which would demonstrate both the exceptionl epoch which gave birth to it and the future, already deciphered, which was foreseen for it. After this period, the utopia tails off, although it does not completely disappear. Moreover, even when the utopia of the New City is maintained on the surface, it disintegrates in the depths of the imaginary Paris. In fact, the space-time of the latter is irreducible to that of the cities of Utopia. Even in imagination, Paris is never constructed on virgin soil. While seeking rupture with the historical city, the utopia must nevertheless establish itself within it and, hence, subject to the constraints of both its realities and its myths. But what most explodes the utopia of Revolutionary Paris is less the past it inherited than the historical evolution from which the imaginary city emerges and in which it finally founders. Imaginary Paris is subject to a history; on its own modes it reproduces the evolution of the Revolution as well as its contradictions. They dream of a city of marble and granite which will last in time definitely conquered by equality and happiness; but even the plaster constructions prove to be more durable than the moment that gave rise to the dream. And the architecture which takes charge of the message about the city of a free people tells it in terms linked together in a discourse on the institutions incarnating order and power, does it not?

The complete reconstruction of the space-time of imaginary Paris as well as the analysis of the portion that falls to the urban and social utopia would take us far beyond our subject. Let us venture, at most, to present some aspects and fragments of the imaginary city which accommodates the utopia—a rapid visit, similar to our promenades in Boullée and Ledouxs' cities. Besides, we shall recognize some monuments borrowed from the latter.

From the first encounter with imaginary Paris the omnipresence of the *conquering word* comes to the fore. It manifests itself on several levels, beginning with the new names of the streets. The capital itself has not changed its name. As far as we know, there was no proposition of giving Paris a new name, although it was surrounded by Franciades (formerly Saint Denis) and Emilies (formerly Montmorency). Paris did not suffer the fate reserved for cities with "absurd and tyrannical" names—there is even pride in the etymology by which the name derives from that of the goddess Isis. It did not, *a fortiori*, have the destiny of those cities which, because of their federalistic and counter-Revolutionary behavior, no longer deserved that their names stain the map of the one and indivisible Republic—such as, for example, Lyon, which became the Commune-Affranchie or Marseille, the *Ville-sans-Nom*. It is an entirely different story with Paris. "The annihilation of this city was, it must be admitted, a profoundly counter-Revolutionary idea; this city where the arms of reason were tempered, those arms the sight of which alone made the proud despot, the fanatic priest, and all the agitating troublemakers of tyranny, disguised under whatever name, turn pale."[109] *L'Almanach indicatif des rues de Paris* for year II begins by noting that "this city has become the first in the world by the National Convention's choice of it as the site of its sessions, and the source from which spread everywhere the light of virtues and of Reason at the sight of which fanaticism and tyranny will return to the void from which they never should have emerged."[110] It would be all the more incongruous if the names of the streets of this city remained in full contradiction to its moral grandeur and its universal mission. In fact, as the report presented to the Commune in the month of nivôse in year II states, "the names of the majority of the streets of Paris are either barbaric or ridiculous or patronymic. In general, they are insignificant and all together they present no motif."[111] Only the majority, for certain streets have already changed their names, have been rebaptized (or, rather, unbaptized). The rue de l'Observatoire has become that of l'Ami du Peuple; rue de Monsieur, rue de l'Egalité, rue Montmartre, rue Mont-Marat; the square in front of Notre Dame has become the place de la Raison; the place Vendôme has been named the place des Piques; place Louis XV, place de la Révolution, etc. The sixteenth *barrière*, constructed by Ledoux, is called Barrière des Vertus ("much less rare," the *Almanach des rues* commented, "in free men than they are among the slaves and satellites of despots"). These changes arose spontaneously, without any preestablished plan, frequently on the initiative of sections which manifested their civic sentiments in this way. These local initiatives are in keeping with a broader movement. More or less everywhere in the country the detachments of the Revolutionary army which landed in a village imposed a new name on it, after having gotten rid of the church bells and "dechristianized" some statues in the church. The same preoccupations are found in these name changes as in the reform of the calendar or even in the adoption of Republican first names (the most expressive if not the most manageable of which would seem to be *Brutus-sans-culotte-marche-en-avant*). The Revolution has the duty of modifying the everyday, of arranging things so that time as well as space will be invested with a new significance and will diffuse a unique message, that of the egalitarian and fraternal Republic in progress. Faith in the quasi-magic power of the word is found in it as well. Once *Coulanges-sur-la-Vineuse* has been converted to *Egalité-sur-Vertu*, its inhabitants will not delay in feeling the beneficial moral effects the new name exerts on their souls.[112] In symbolically taking possession of the space, in transforming, by words, the streets and towns into Revolutionary monuments, there is an attempt to perpetuate what has been gained by the Revolution and to institute without delay the New City which it announces.

Soon, however, they are no longer content with merely limited and spontaneous changes. The Comité d'Instruction publique takes the responsibility for developing a unique system of appellations of cities and communes for all of France. Likewise, in Paris, there are growing numbers of initiatives for the adoption of a system which would encompass the entire city, that is "approximately nine hundred streets, thirty quais, twelve bridges, twenty-eight passages, cours, or former cloisters, twenty-six places, twenty halles or markets, nine enclosures through which people pass, which are owned by lazy monks, and more than one hundred culs-de-sac."[113] The task is therefore complex and all the more delicate because the sections feel themselves to be directly concerned. Is it not a matter of naming *their* streets and *their* places? There is easy agreement on one point: it is necessary to find a unique principle which "would give a motif to the totality of the streets in Paris." A *rational order* must be substituted for the chaos which had established itself in the city in the course of a history which was itself disorderly if not absurd. This is essential for practical reasons: several streets in Paris have the same name; "this results in letters being misaddressed, the area on top of a letter being insufficient for the prolixity of the address, and business suffers because of this."[114] Other, loftier preoccupations correspond to these pragmatic ones. A unique system of appellation, rationalizing the city and thus making it transparent to its inhabitants, will necessarily be of great moral and educational effectiveness. But this result will be even more enhanced if the new names, in turn, dispense a moral and civic lesson. The city in its entirety must form an educational space no part of which will be without symbolic significance. The space on which a civic discourse will be projected will itself become *speaking*; it will permanently address itself to the Parisians who use the streets every day. The new names must thus "perpetuate the Revolution.'' But in what way, in adopting what nomenclature? Without entering into detail, let us note a few versions of an index of streets for imaginary Paris.

On 14 brumaire year II, a deputation of the section of Arcis presents itself to the Convention and offers a complete proposal for street names ''based on all the virtues necessary to the Republic'' to be applied in all France and, in particular, in Paris. The principles are as clear as the arguments in favor of the proposal are convincing. ''There is an incontestable maxim, known to all legislators, *without morals, there is no Republic*. And by familiarizing the populace with virtue, the taste for pure morality will be easily transmitted to their soul and, consequently, the disposition propitious to its practice. To succeed in this aim *I propose giving the people a mute morality course*, applying to the streets, etc., of all the communes of the Republic the names of all the virtues. . . . *The result of that will be that the people will at all times have the name of a virtue in their mouths and morality soon in their hearts*.'' This all the communes will be divided into districts of which each public square will be the center; each public square will be the name of one of the principal virtues. The streets allocated to the district surrounding this square will be designated ''by the names of virtues having a direct relationship with this principal virtue. When there are insufficient names of virtues, those of great men will be used, but they will be placed in the district of their main virtue.'' And here is an example of the application of this system to the streets of Paris: the Palais National will be called Temple, or Centre de Républicanisme; the adjacent streets will become those of Générosité, Sensibilité, etc. The square in front of the church, the Parvis-Notre-Dame, will take the name of Humanité Républicaine, the place de la Halle that of Frugalité Républicaine; the adjoining streets will be called those of Tempérence [*sic*], Sobriété, etc.[115]

The assembly applauds, gives the petition honorable mention for the patriotic zeal that inspired it, but does not adopt the proposal. The Commune of Paris, which debated it as well, is not without reservations. Do they fear they will lack enough names of virtues—principal and secondary—for the 900 streets, places, and culs-de-sac? Be that as it may, the project proposed by the regional council of the Commune adopts another principle inspired by an already ancient idea and discussed by Teisserenc in his book *Géographie parisienne*, published in 1754. It is a matter of making ''the Commune of Paris a kind of geographic tableau of the French Republic.'' The corners of the quais will have the names of the *départements* of the East and the West, those of the former boulevards, the names of those of the North and the South. ''The street corners will bear the names of the communes of the Republic, depending on the angle the extension of such a street forms on the meridian or the perpendicular. . . . The culs-de-sac will take the names of the communes surrounding Paris, according to the principle adopted for the streets.'' The multiple advantages of this system are obvious. First of all, it is simple, and clear, and has "a unique motif." Then, it has a symbolic significance: it designates Paris as the true center of the one and indivisible Republic. Finally, it is a system that is easy to remember, which will favor public education because "the citizens, barely out of their childhood, will know by routine that a street has a specific inscription because its direction, turning one's back to the center of the City, is the same as that of the City whose name it bears. . . ." The proposal wins the consent of the majority of the sections. Only one obstacle is seen to its immediate application, the fact that in the country several cities and communes still bear the names of saints or even the patronymic names of former princes and aristocrats. An appeal is launched to accelerate the attribution of new names throughout the country so that the new and definitive map of France can be projected on Paris as soon as possible. The proposal anticipates an exception for the "former Cité or île de Paris." At the street corners will be inscribed the names of those who have deserved well of the country. They can appear there "beside the names of those men whose life was of benefit to the universe." And as the stock of these respectable names is, it seems, insufficient, it is decided that "the remaining streets will have numbers while waiting for the name of a virtuous patriot to be given them."[116]

The Comité d'Instruction publique, after having examined the different proposals of the communes, proves to be hesitant. Grégoire, who is responsible for making a synthesis, contests neither the necessity nor the usefulness of a reform. He reports that "the majority of large communes are anxious for the strict uniformity of a system." But why subjugate ourselves to an "exclusive system, the execution of which, repeated in 44,000 communes, would establish a tiresome monotony?" Indeed, there are several systems at our disposal, each of which present incontestable advantages. Each commune could choose one or even combine them since all are in perfect keeping with one another. "The denominations can be geographical, historical, Revolutionary, or taken from the virtues, from agriculture, from commerce, from the sciences, from the arts, and from the men who have made them illustrious." The combination of the two principles, that of the "immortal deeds of our Revolution" with that of the names of virtues, lends itself particularly well to the streets of Paris. Thus, the new names will form a sort of "historical synopsis" of the Revolution, of the actions which cause new values to triumph forever. "Why not put the square of the Pikes next to the street of Patriotism, of Courage, of 10 August, of the Jeu de Paume? *Is it not natural that from the place de la Révolution one approaches the rue de la Constitution which would lead to the the rue du Bonheur?*"[117]

From the place de la Révolution to that of Bonheur (Happiness)—the formula perfectly summarizes the significance with which they mean to invest the network of the major streets of imaginary Paris. To lay out these major axes, they are not content with merely changing the names of the streets. They want to remodel the urban space itself and to thus inscribe if not the New City then at the least an anticipatory vision of it in the framework of the city. We shall attempt to retrace these privileged routes in making use, on the one hand, of the proposals for the development of Paris, in particular of the "artists' proposal," and, on the other hand, in referring to the paths taken by the processions of the Revolutionary celebrations. These two types of plans, in any case, intersect, at least in part.

If Paris becomes, as we have said, an immense building site open to the imagination, that is because, among other reasons, the Revolution seems to offer an exceptional opportunity for proposals planning its development. In fact, with the putting of ecclesiastical property "at the disposal of the Nation," and the later addition of that of the abolished guilds, the émigrés, etc., there are around 400 hectares situated in the heart of Paris (along the left bank in particular) that can be used for its development. Thus, as early as 1790, committees of architects and geometricians are given the responsibility of evaluating these lands, of proposing roads to serve the individual plots of land and facilitate their sale. Thought is given as well, though, to preserving those sites that can be used for widening streets and for the beautification of the city. By the edict of 4 April 1794 (15 germinal year II) a temporary Commission of artists is charged with drawing up an overall plan for the development of the national property. But they want to go still further and they aim even higher. On 10 messidor year II, the Comité du Salut public makes a decision "relative to the preparation of a general plan for the renewal and beautification of Paris and of plans relative to the other communes of the Republic." It could be said that it takes on the idea of envisaging the city as a philosopher and draws conclusions from the half century of debate on the city planning of Paris. Thus it is decided to "establish unity in public works and to begin to deal with renewal of the communes only *according to a general plan*." Several technical measures are taken to insure the creation of this general plan: gathering all the partial proposals drawn up by architects, launching new national competitions wide open to all "artists," creating a jury to examine propositions, etc.

The most important: it is decided than while waiting for the finalization of this general plan "the alienation of the national properties located in Paris" will be suspended, to prevent property speculation and rampant urbanization. The decree finally defines the major objectives of the general plan, thus advancing a global vision of a Paris which is, if not new, at least radically transformed. "A general plan of Paris will be drawn up by the jury, providing for the cleaning up and beautification of this commune, *the whole in order to improve the lot of the citizens*, bringing in abundant water, constructing in it vast esplanades, public squares, fountains, markets, gymnasiums, public baths, theaters, wide streets with sidewalks, sewers, latrines, cemeteries, and in general everything that can contribute to public health and comfort."[118]

Contrary to its habitual practice, the Comité de Salut public does not set rapid time limits for the works to be accomplished. This time, they are aware that it is a long and arduous undertaking. They do not want to work in plaster, but to build an urban setting inseparable from that happiness that the Revolution already establishes for the generations to come. Like the proposals for public education, for a new calendar, for "Republican weights and measurements," etc., this program of city planning translates, on its own individual modes, the global vision of a new society in a discourse announcing the profound transformation of the structures of daily life. What is decreed, all things considered, is the establishment in Paris of an urban utopia. "The decree of 10 messidor is inscribed in a body of edicts which amplifies and explains it. It constitutes one of the aspects of the foundation of a virtuous and democratic, egalitarian and deistic Republic. It is the framework of those great institutions which are to serve as the basis and guarantee of the new regime. It is to lend itself to religious and patriotic uses, it is to assure the attachment of the citizens to their city, to their Country, to the Supreme Being. The Terror would have only a limited time, as would the prisons and the arms works, *after which happiness would reign in this model city. The Paris of the year 2000 would already have been realized as early as year II of the Republic.*"[119]

Besides, the Comité de Salut public anticipates this general plan, by setting up some high points and by thus suggesting, if not imposing, privileged itineraries in the city. A series of decrees of 5 floréal prescribes the rapid erection of several monuments "retracing the glorious epochs of the Revolution." Another edict (of 25 floréal) sets up a vast program of works aiming at the beautification of the Palais national and of its accessories (the cour du Carrousel, the Tuileries, the place de la Révolution, etc.). We shall return to these monuments; let us note, for the moment, that these proposals, the realization of which was to begin immediately, are intended, as well, to contribute to the "common good," as does the city planning program of 10 messidor. However, this time, the "common good" does not materialize in enterprises of "public health" which seek to "improve the lot of the citizens," but in a monumental Paris, a city of prestige and propaganda. Certainly, in the spirit of the authors there was no contradiction between these two orientations. One complemented the other and both merged in the global vision of a cleaned, renewed, and beautified Paris, transformed so as to be worthy of its glorious people. Was Paris, the model city of urban happiness, not to be the most prestigious monument the government would raise for the people and to immortalize the Révolution? And was the virtuous and happy populace not to perpetuate its own grandeur by erecting monuments recalling its victories and accommodating its institutions? However, the formula that wants to link la place de la Révolution to la place du Bonheur via la rue de la Constitution risks falling apart as soon as an attempt is made to give it other than a symbolic meaning or other than a verbal expression. The utopia of the model city at once masks and reveals the contradictions at work in this imaginary Paris, namely the opposition between the city of Happiness, salubrity, security, and that of Power, prestige, and the monumental organization of space.[120]

We shall never know what forms the vision of Paris conceived to "improve the lot of its citizens" would have taken. The image of the city realizing the objectives defined in the decree of 10 messidor is dissipated even before there is an attempt made to translate it into plans and drawings. The Commission of Artists survives Thermidor and continues its works for two more years. The times have nevertheless changed and the artists no longer work in the perspective of the program-vision of the year II. The Commission is told to concentrate on its primary task, the "making of plans, calculations, and reports relative to the division of the large national estates." The artists do not, however, confine themselves to these limits. How ambitious their proposals remain! The commission keeps the idea of a general program of city planning and seeks to arrange that the development of national property will be only the very beginning of such a plan. Thus the commission stresses that it is not sufficient to "follow the method of division into individual plots" which would leave the opening of new streets "to the discretion of the owners of the houses along the roads." While thinking about the sale of these lands and of how it might be "the most profitable to the finances of the Republic," the artists nevertheless refuse to submit their work to the sole demands of profit. They judge it indispensable to proceed according to "a fixed plan in order to lead them (the new streets) toward the aim of general usefulness. Convinced that individual operation in each estate would never attain the proposed aim, the commission thought that its work had to include foundations which could be joined to ulterior changes, which might be necessitated by the formless mass of the old streets, and that it had to present a total group of proposals, which could be partially achieved and which time and circumstances would lead to in succession."[121] Thus the first general program of Parisian city planning is born. Insisting on the opening of new roads, it attempts, by their layout, to check private construction. It will never be realized. The same year, the assembly of the Conseil des Bâtiments (buildings) and that of the Ponts et Chaussées (highways) decides that "operations of the Commission of Artists . . . relating to the beautification and the cleaning up of Paris will only be able to be dealt with at a more opportune time."[122] The "opportune moment" will never come. The lands are sold and some years later a discerning architect finds what has happened to Paris frightful; it is "covered with a prodigious number of edifices," given over to "a building frenzy, which leads to new speculators who acquire the recently released grounds."[123]

It is not up to us to reconstitute the artists' plan or to discuss the developments it proposed.[124] Besides which, it is difficult to specify what the overall vision of "beautified Paris" which governed the Commission's works was. The proposal was marked by the circumstances under which it was worked out and, consequently, the utopia is sacrificed to reform. The artists do not locate any monument and make no decisions about constructions to be built on the vacant lands. They limit changes in the historic center of the city where empty space is rare, to the minimum; on the other hand, they feel much freer when they propose to open roads and lay out esplanades along the left bank, where the bulk of national properties was located. Let us note merely one revealing point. The layout of the new public squares and streets corresponds, at least in part, to the routes followed by the processions of the Revolutionary celebrations. It could be said that in seeking to relieve congestion in Paris, the artists proposed primarily removing the obstacles that hinder the free deployment of the festive processions. Thus the new layouts revalorize the high points of the festivals and facilitate access to them. The site of the Bastille is transformed into a circular plaza from which streets radiate. Around the French Pantheon, they imagine another, widened, circular plaza, at the center of a system of seven roads "arranged according to the principal radii of the cupola." The building of these new roads would facilitate entrance to the plaza for crowds, which up to that point had broken up in the narrow and twisting alleyways. On the left bank, there was a project which was already old, but which took on significance and assumed a new function: a large main street leading from the new place de la Bastille to the place de la Révolution, thus linking the departure and terminal points of many processions. A new bridge is projected in front of the Champ de la Fédération, at the same site where, in 1790, a bridge of boats was built to serve the Festival of Federation.

Of course, the artists' plan did not limit itself to these particular layouts. It is nevertheless notable that by providing the city with "a well-balanced network of spacious routes and ample open areas," the plan orders the historic space of the city so as to adapt it at least partially to the demands made of it by the institution of Revolutionary festivals.

Moreover, was the perfect adaptation of the historic city to the needs of the Revolutionary festivals possible? The ideal space of the Revolutionary festivals, implied by their programs, is imposed by the dream of a space similar to that of the cities of Utopia. "The festival treats Paris as something that can be traversed through and through. . . . All the elements of the utopian city are established by the festival: The straight line, legibility, symmetry, and transparency, with their gracious consequence: the reciprocity of hearts."[126] The organizers of the Revolutionary festivals want to project this utopian space on the historic city. But then the realities of the latter, its narrow, twisting streets, its palaces and churches which evoke tyrants and prejudice, are only so many defects which debase the festive space. But if the historic city is an impediment, it is at the same time the necessary condition for the Parisian Revolutionary festival to be possible. Let us recall Kersaint's words: annihilating Paris could only be a counter-Revolutionary idea. It is indeed in the real space of Paris and in particular in its privileged places, such as the Bastille, the Champ-de-Mars, the Pantheon, and the place de la Révolution, that history took a new departure. Here, in these "sacred spots," were inscribed the fundamental actions that the festivals and the montagnard festivals in particular proposed to celebrate in the rites. Thus came about the complex relationships between the space-time of the festival and the space of the historic city, relationships so well analyzed by Mona Ozouf. The routes of the Revolutionary processions are so many "impossible compromises" between the imaginary space and the constraint of the real city, between the exclusion and the inclusion of the historic city in relation to the utopian space of the festival. Whence the two major typical itineraries of the processions: the ceremonial route that begins at the Bastille, walks around the city by the north, following the line of the "new boulevards," crosses the place de la Révolution and ends at the Champ-de-Mars; the second route, imposed by the pantheonizations: points of departure on the right bank (the Bastille, the Tuileries, the place de la Révolution), crossing of the historic city, arrival at the Pantheon.[127] The ephemeral monuments—the statues and the triumphal arches, the temples and the altars—are essential elements of these itineraries. It is not solely a matter of adding splendor to the festival, but of thereby putting the finishing touches to the real city and of transforming its landscape. The compositions overloaded with meanings are to revalorize the places and to overpower the historic space. The festival does not only oppose an alternative city to the ancient city. It seeks, too, to go beyond the contradiction by creating a space in which the sublimation of the historic city as well as its synthesis with the space-time of the symbolic city would take place.

The end result of this attempt is a sort of theatricalization of Paris in which, as though on an enormous stage, scenery intended to be touching, made of wood, plaster, and words, is set up. But would the effect not have been less artificial if they had succeeded in erecting the monuments in bronze and marble, thus imposing on the real city its readjustment to the dreamed city? Such was, in any case, the intention of the builders of the imaginary Paris. For their constructions, they anticipated using only materials symbolizing the perpetuity of the principles and work of the Republic. "It is with bronze that we found the Republic; it is with bronze that we must transmit to posterity the image of its defenders. Every patriot must truly be astonished that our monuments erected in honor of liberty are still only in clay or in plaster." The Convention is not slow to decree the measure called for. "The Palais National of a people who based its liberty on the eternal rights of man must be constructed of indestructible materials, like reason of which it will be the sanctuary," Kersaint proclaims.[128]

Constructions are called for that are meant to be as durable as they are majestic and grandiose. "The most salutary effect of our Revolution must be to bring everything back to its principle. Let us cease to make the infinitely large smaller and attempt, if possible, to add size to what our pettiness can grasp. . . .

Colossi were frequently used by the ancients; and we have not yet dared to imitate them in that genre. They were convinced that what struck the senses by large images inspired larger ideas as well."[129] Monumentality and gigantic scale organize the imaginary space as much as they overpower it. In the desire for perpetuity and grandiosity, which becomes a true obsession with the colossal, the characteristics of the imaginary Paris are in harmony. It is a city whose finality is educational and the immense volumes are supposed to permanently diffuse a "mute morality course" in which magnitude is an omnipresent metaphor and a most mystifying one. It is a prestige city, as well, in the sense that the new monuments must prevail over the old ones and that their superiority must be visualized. "The Republican regime must replace the effect of church steeples by columns, obelisks, and finally monuments whose elevation, in attesting to the glory of the nation under the empire of reason, is at least equal to those towers and spires that were erected by fanaticism."[130] It is, finally, a city masked by the myth it secretes, that of its people, victorious over tyranny and prejudice. Like the entire monumental city, it is neither the place where the populace lives nor that where it works. None of its colossal monuments contributes to "the improvement of the citizens' lot," to repeat the formula of the decree of 10 messidor. And yet it is a *space for the people, offered to the people* and which becomes functional only by the supposed presence of the people. It is the people who ought to come to it, to admire the colossal monument erected to *their* glory, to use this immense setting arranged for *their* festivals, to frequent the Palais National and to observe how *their* sovereignty is exercised. The colossal scale only veils and amplifies at the same time the ambiguities and contradictions of this space in which the imagination draws the wide, straight avenue leading from the place de la Révolution to that of happiness.

Nearly all the monuments populating Paris fit into three categories: the festive monuments; the places where the political power is exercised; the civic temples which, in a way, combine the functions of the two other types.[131]

More than a hundred "fabriques" were erected to add glamor to the festivals and to serve as appropriate settings. Triumphal arches and altars of the country, "holy mountains," and artificial grottoes: some lasted only a few days, others fell apart over weeks and months, leaving the sad impressions evoked by Romme in his request that the Republic finally be immortalized in bronze. Let us note among these festive monuments only the statues that had so impressed the people, or at least the people's representatives, that the Convention decided to strike medals with their images and to distribute them to its members as well as to "all the envoys of the primary Assemblies." The Comité de Salut public designated the same statues as worthy of being "executed in bronze and in marble." The statues in question are those famous ones which were erected for the festival of the Réunion républicaine on 10 August 1793 and set up on the site of the four "stations" of that "immortal ceremony by which a great people sanctioned its constitution." We have already spoken of this festival, its itinerary and its ritual, on which David, its great architect, particularly left his imprint. The engraving of these statues are only, in a way, pale replicas of a gigantic dream which was to materialize in the city, in marble and in bronze.

At the Bastille, it is the Fountain of the Regeneration, represented by Nature, "in the Egyptian style"; from its "fertile breasts, which it will press with its hands, pure and wholesome water will flow abundantly." On the boulevard de Poissonière, it is "a portico or triumphal arch to the glory of the heroines of 5 and 6 October" on which inscriptions "retrace these two memorable days." Standing on the place de la Révolution is the enormous statue of Liberty, "in the form of a goddess," her head covered with a helmet, a pike in her hand, and surmounting "the remaining debris of the pedestal of tyranny"; "oaks with dense foliage will form a considerable mass of shade and greenery around her and the foliage is covered with the offerings of all the free French." On the place des Invalides, finally, it is at the summit of a mountain "represented in sculpture by a colossal figure, *le peuple français*, gathering in its strong arms the bundle *of the départements*; ambitious federalism, coming out of its miry swamp, moving the reeds aside with one hand, tries with the other to detach some portion of it; the French People notice it, take its club, hit it with it, and make it return to its stagnant waters, never to emerge again." The image of "the People, triumphing over tyranny and superstition" seems to haunt David's imagination. He will present to the Convention still another proposal for a statue destined for the terreplein of the Pont-Neuf, "not far from that church of which the tyrants made their Pantheon." Trampling the debris of the royal effigies underfoot, the monument will represent "the image of the giant people, the French people. On this image, imposing by its character of strength and simplicity, let there be written, in large letters, on its forehead, *light*, on its chest, *nature*, *truth*; on its arms, *strength, courage*. Let the figures of Liberty and Equality huddled together on one of the hands and ready to travel the world, show everyone that they rest only on the genius and the virtue of the people! Let this image of the people *standing upright* hold in its other hand that terrible club with which the ancients armed their Hercules." The Convention, at its session on 27 brumaire year II, adopts the project immediately, decrees that "this monument will be colossal" and rules that the word *work* be added to the hands of the giant People.[132]

As we have noted elsewhere, all these statues were perfectly integrated into the procession and its ritual. In retracing, on the symbolic level, "the glorious epochs of the Revolution, they established the utopia of the New City in a history-myth of the Revolution. In decreeing the erection of these monuments "in bronze and in marble," did the Convention not envisage thus establishing, once and for all, the model itinerary of future processions, tracing an authoritative magnificent festive path along which the populace could admire if not itself, then at least its gigantic effigy?

Both the utopia and the practice of the Revolutionary festival called for the latter to culminate in the assembly of all the participants in an enclosure where the people could see one another and create a spectacle of themselves for themselves—thus the need for a setting in keeping with a necessarily immense crowd. The characteristics of this structure for reception had to satisfy both the ideological and functional demands imposed by the festival program. In order for the key ideas, affective communion, and transparency to materialize, each participant had to take in the assembled crowd with one single glance and, hence, no one should escape the gaze of the others, the "collective glance." On the other hand, the place had to be easily accessible. It was necessary to ensure the rapid entrance and exit of hundreds of thousands of people, at once the actors and spectators of this gigantic production. This need was strongly felt during the festival of Confederation, and the architectural formula of enormous arenas became essential. The transformation of the Champ de Mars into arenas was, however, only a provisional solution. In 1792, Kersaint notes that "this enclosure has been abandoned; the altar of the Country, composed of fragile materials, seems to say to despotism: The oath of the French, which made you tremble, will be fragile and ephemeral like me." The time has come for the Revolutionary government which "is in some way *accountable to posterity which progresses* through public education" to combine "with the lessons of words *the forceful language of the monuments.*" The confidence which it "is so necessary to inspire in the stability of our new laws will be established, by a *sort of instinct*, on the solidity of the edifices destined to conserve them and to perpetuate their duration." It is likewise obvious that the new monuments "considered from their moral and political perspective" must provide "dazzling evidence of the superiority of the new regime over the old."[133] One of these monuments destined to embody this ideological discourse was in fact a gigantic "national circus" designed for the celebration of festivals. Based on the proposal in Kersaint's report and developed by Legrand and Molinos, its dimensions were to be "greater than those set by the Romans for their *circus maximus* . . . This immense monument must be eternal. Only granite is able to impart this great character and give this unique advantage." Of course, it is an enormous undertaking. But is it not made to measure for a people who "in one day overthrew the tyranny of fourteen centuries? . . . *Let us confirm liberty and everything will become easy.*"[134]

Several other circuses appeared in imaginary Paris. As D. Rabreau aptly noted, the circus or Coliseum is "the only architectural archetype that underwent no change of its original function under the monarchy, for two reasons. First of all, because the character of the official festivals of that time did not lend itself to this, and second because such an undertaking would lack sufficient space in the city (or in its proximity) as well as financial support."[135] On the other hand, the antique-style circus became the formula of choice for the accommodation of the populace during festivals.

The feeling of living during an exceptional time, an epoch when victorious liberty makes everything "possible and easy," could only stimulate the imagination. It is again the *colossal* that modulates discourse and sets the scale of projects. De Wailly proclaims that "the instant has come to leave gigantic circuses to our nephews to celebrate the colossus of our glory." Poyet, who declares himself a "Jacobin architect," publishes the proposal for a national circus situated on the Champ de Mars and which was to accommodate 108,000 spectators under cover and 100,000 out-of-doors. Another anonymous proposal also chose the Champ de Mars as the setting for an immense circus; but it also planned for the destruction of the Ecole militaire and its replacement by the Palais National, the seat of the Assembly. Thus, according to this proposal, the two major monuments of a newly transformed Paris would face each other and would be integrated into a single gigantic space, materially and symbolically opposed to the historic city and its monuments, from which "the people today avert their gaze."[136] Finally, the most gigantic Coliseum, the glory of another city we have already visited, of Boullée's imaginary city, is seen transplanted to Paris. Indeed, around 1790, Boullée revives his old proposals for circuses and amphitheaters, giving them a broader scope. He situates his Coliseum in "the place called l'Etoile, beyond the Champs-Elysées, in order to offer the public easy access and convenient outlets." Let us recall the vision of the ideal festival that governs this proposal, "conceived to carry out moral and political views." "It is under the eyes of all that the soul of the citizen is elevated and purified. . . . Imagine three hundred thousand people gathered in amphitheatrical order in which no one can escape the gaze of the multitude. A unique effect will result from this order of things: that is that the beauty of this astonishing spectacle would come from the spectators who, alone, would compose it." The enormous edifice dominating Paris will be surrounded by columns; it will be "open on all sides to facilitate entry into the arena" and an "infinite number of staircases" will allow easy access to the amphitheater; spacious galleries under the amphitheater will allow for shelter for all the spectators in case of bad weather.[137]

The Comité de Salut public, at the time that it established the program of the public monuments to be built in Paris, did not accept the solution of a Coliseum constructed outside the city. The decree of 5 floréal year II "calls on the artists of the Republic to compete in the transformation of the premises that served as the Opera theater, between the rue de Bondy and the boulevard into covered arenas; these arenas are destined for celebrations of the triumphs of the Republic and for national festivals during the winter, with patriotic and martial songs."[138] The instigator of this idea was, it seems, David, who saw in a plaza-amphitheater, located in the middle of the city and on the route of the festive processions, the solution that was, if not ideal, at least the easiest to achieve, because of the lack of means, for setting up a site for popular assemblies. In 1793, David had already suggested to de Wailly to make the semicircular plaza of the Odéon theater into an area for festive ceremonies. De Wailly seemed to be attracted to this idea and he conceived the project of developing the plaza and the theater (of which he himself was the architect, with Peyre). A doric colonnade was to be laid out around the plaza in front of the houses; triumphal arches crowned with symbolic statues world stand at the entrances to the streets radiating from it. The design also called for the construction in stone of amphitheatrical tiers bordering the circular pavements of the plaza and, finally, the covering of the latter with a canopy, a sort of tricolor marquee.[139] This program of de Wailly's was not accepted, resulting in the competition of 5 floréal, in which Lahure, the winner, proposed the erection of an enormous circular auditorium, topped by a gigantic dome. Two immense triumphal arches, projected above the boulevard and supporting the statues of Liberty and Equality, formed the monumental entrance for processions heading majestically for the "covered arenas."[140]

All these proposals, each more colossal than the rest, reproduced, unintentionally and according to their own modalities, the ambiguities and contradictions of Revolutionary discourse on festivals, if not those of the festivals themselves. The moving realities of the latter were contained in advance by the triumphal arches. The spontaneous popular participation was already programmed by the vast emptiness of the gigantic stadiums that had necessarily to be filled by immense crowds; otherwise the festival would not take place. Consequently, someone had to take charge of it or, if you will, had to take charge of the spontaneity. The dream of transparency was submerged in shadow where a manipulative power, the institutor and guarantor of order, was confirmed.

Along with the festive sites where the sovereign people was to provide its own spectacle, another edifice took a privileged place in the imaginary Paris, that in which the *power*, the government, showed *itself* to itself as well as to the people. The idea of a special edifice for the députés of the nation was essential for practical as well as ideological reasons. When, after the days of 5 and 6 October, the National Assembly left Versailles and installed itself in Paris, it found no suitable building. It was finally decided to use the Manège Royal, which was adjacent to the terrasse des Feuillants. An architect of the Menus Plaisirs, given responsibility for fitting it out, installed a sort of gallery for the president and the secretaries in the rectangular auditorium; on the long sides, he set up four rows of banquettes, behind which were two floors of loges, while, on the short sides, several other rows of banquettes rose to the galleries. The public, barely separated from the députés, squeezed into the loges and the galleries.[141] The solution could only be provisional. The acoustics and visibility were bad; neither the character of the building, a former outbuilding of the royal chateau, nor its architecture, destined it to become the major edifice of the new government. As early as 1790, there was a flood of proposals and plans for a special monument. But the députés left the Salle du Manège before having even discussed them. The day after 10 August, the Legislative Assembly discussed the proposal of symbolically taking possession of the palace that the people had taken by force on the preceding day. On 10 September, on Brissot's proposal, it was decreed that the députés will sit at the Tuileries. After discussion, the choice went to the former Salle des Machines and a young architect, Gisors, was given the responsibility of fitting it out. The desires of the Convention were contradictory. On the one hand, they wished to go quickly and to reduce costs; on the other hand, they would not be content with paltry fittings, but wished to create a space which, by its majesty and symbolism, would be in harmony with the spirit of grandeur and virtue which guides the representatives of the people in their work. When, on 10 May 1793, the members of the Convention moved into their new site, they found things never before seen, if not quite unprecedented. The pavillion of Unity (formerly of the Clock) was topped by a huge scarlet serge Phrygian cap, surmounted by a thirty-three-foot long tricolor banner. To reach the chamber where sessions are held, one crossed a sort of vestibule whose name, the Liberty room, is the same as that of the statue erected in its center. Liberty was represented seated; it was leaning on the globe with one hand and holding up, in the other, the Phrygian cap. The chamber formed a space which was to be *speaking* and which was, in fact, at least in the sense of being a replica, in the language of forms, of Revolutionary rhetoric. In this rectangular room, Gisors installed benches for the 750 députés, in the form of a semi-oval. Facing this vast and long amphitheater and in the middle of the lateral wall, was a wooden construction which included the president's office, the orators' rostrum, etc.; two ramps on either side led up to the bar. Opposite this, five large windows, opening on the garden, illuminated the room. On the sides were immense arcades surrounding the galleries, which could accommodate approximately 1500 spectators.[142] Thus the auditorium was conceived after the example of a specific theatrical site in which the most solemn Republican rites took place. Robespierre dreamed, moreover, of an enormous auditorium able to accommodate more than 10,000 people who thus could attend the most noble and most educational performance, that of the exercise of popular sovereignty. The organization of the space translated the ideology of the transparency of public life and the omnipresence of the people—of the people represented by the députés and of the people assembled in the gallery, to whose gaze the députés presented themselves. Let us not, however, forget that during the great days of the Montagnard Convention, this spectacle aspect was often part of the lived experience. Countless deputations, which often arrived with red caps on their heads, and pikes in hand, succeeded one another at the bar, presenting patriotic poems, songs, and the like. (Danton was, as a matter of fact, vigorously opposed to this assimilation of the sessions of the Convention to sites of spectacles and festivals.) Every orator was obliged to strain his voice—the room was immense, the acoustics bad. The public, crammed into the galleries, was not content with watching; by applause, shouts of approbation, or boos, it participated in the proceedings in its own way and, occasionally, exerted real pressure. Even the decorations, which incorporated both the members of the Convention and the public in a symbolic space, contributed to the theatricalization. "The form of this construction is in the best of taste. The decoration presents antique green backgrounds, adorned with antique yellow pilasters. . . . Above the entablature one sees, on plinths of porphyry and among the five porticoes on each side, statues of the illustrious men of antiquity. Beside the president one sees, painted to look like bronze and of large dimensions, Demosthenes, Lycurgus, Solon, Plato; on the opposite side Camillus, Valerius Publicola, Brutus, Cincinnatus; above their heads crowns are suspended. . . . The general decoration of this room is in beautiful antique style, it is pure and of a noble simplicity." The journalist to whom we owe this enthusiastic account nevertheless had his fill and noted somewhat doubtfully: "Basically, this construction has more flashy glamor than solidity; nearly everything in it is in plaster, in canvas, in paint; there is nearly nothing in reality."[143] One might wonder whether the artists, in submission to the force of circumstances, did not, finally, express most faithfully the exceptional realities of the moment in that paradoxical formula that mixed politics and spectacle, the true and the imaginary, and which offered to the immutable and the imperishable the refuge of constructions as fragile as they were temporary.

However, both the government and the architects dreamed of building in indestructible materials. Contrary to the constructions in the Tuileries, the Palais National of their dreams was erected in marble, if not in granite, while the sculptures surrounding it were all in bronze. As we have said, proposals and projects wanting to embody this dream of an ideal monument, worthy of a free nation, started to pour in as early as 1790. They all had common characteristics: they manifested "that taste for the colossal, of which Boullée and Ledoux had furnished examples";[144] they invested the edifice with moral significance; they made use of architectural forms to diffuse, in their own language, the civic message. The proposals diverged on the choice of a site for the Palais National. Sites which were themselves charged with symbolism were, of course, preferred. Thus several projects proposed establishing the Palais on the foundations of the Bastille—the symbol was striking and, furthermore, the site was available. Others suggested the transformation of the Louvre. "Legislators, order it and the Louvre is going to become the French Capitol. The Louvre will efface the Capitol of the Romans and the decree which will draw this monument from the oblivion into which it has fallen will be well received by the Republic and will make the glory of the Arts."[145] Legrand and Molinos proposed utilizing the Madeleine, still unfinished, installing the chamber under the dome and surrounding the edifice with another circular building. Kersaint, who supported this project, demanded that the construction be financed by contributions from all the *départements*. This would, certainly, facilitate the collection of funds but would above all add yet another symbolic qualification to the monument and to the city in which it would be erected. "Each *département*, taking it unto itself to pay this expense, will feel that it possesses a part of the edifice to whose erection it has contributed. I would propose that the plan be brought up in all the assemblies of all the constituent bodies as well as that of Paris, under the title *Paris, or the city common to all the French*. In fact, what is this *Département*? Can it exist by itself? And in circumscribing its territory, did the legislators not implicitly recognize the principle that this great city was the city of no one because it was that of all?"[146]

Most of the time, the room formed a semicircle or even a complete circle, like an amphitheater, as in the theaters of antiquity. This formula of a semicircle, taken up by Gisors, finally became the prototype nearly everywhere (with the exception of England) of chambers of parliaments (with the designations *left* and *right* substituted for those of the *Montagne* and the *Marais*). All the proposals provided for huge galleries, in addition, for a large public; it was almost unimaginable that the Assembly would sit other than in the presence of a populace impassioned by the proceedings. Illuminated from above, the chambers were topped by vast domes. To symbolize the perfect unity of nature and the new history, one particular architect proposed decorating the vault with a fresco representing "the state of the sky over our horizon on 14 July 1789, the memorable epoch of our liberty."[147] By all possible means, the proposals tried, in David's words, "to produce something new, to leave behind known and ordinary forms."[148] Of course, this was easier to postulate than to accomplish. In attempting to make the architectural language the instrument of symbolic communication, in taking up antique models to revive their "energy and noble simplicity," in accumulating geometric volumes on a monumental scale, the authors of the proposals too frequently confused the redundancies of an ideological and esthetic rhetoric with the creation of a new style.

All things considered, it is still Boullée who gave the imaginary Paris of the Revolution its most remarkable Palais National. He considered the Palais an exceptional subject requiring of the artist the practice of an innovative art as well as the search for new forms of expression. "It is useless to show . . . how a Palais National requires more particularly than any other production the presentation not of the tableau of architecture, but indeed the most expressive forms of the art. According to these views, I disdained putting the sterile richness of architecture into this work." Of course, one must not "lose sight of the immortal

Republican works of Greece.'' But one must above all realize that ''ideas become greater in seeking to rise to the level of this subject.'' In his proposal, Boullée implements all the means of *speaking architecture*; he brings into play forms and masses, the oppositions between solids and empty spaces, between the adorned parts and those without decoration. The Assembly room, circular and lit from above, occupies the center of an immense block in the form of a massive rectangular parallelepiped. The whole thing aims to awaken in the spectator feelings of solidity and grandeur, of perpetuity and elevation. But Boullée feels the greatest innovation to be in the introduction of a metaphor at the second degree. He is no longer content with making the masses and the stones speak; he makes the word an integral part of the edifice. ''After having meditated on the means suitable for manifesting the poetry of the architecture in this edifice, I thought that nothing would be more striking and characteristic than to form the walls of this building by the tables of the constitutional laws. What image, I said to myself, can be of such keen interest as that which gives prominence to the laws, the object of everyone's love, because everyone wanted them.'' The pediment of the Palais presents an immense naked wall, with no decoration, on which is written, in immense letters, the text of the Declaration of the Rights of Man and of the Citizen. This monument could be said to be transformed into a gigantic poster, in marble and bronze. Contrasting with the naked walls, two bases, stylobates on which Boullée arranges ''two rows of figures indicating the number of our *départements* and which, each holding the book of decrees, betokens the assent of the people who sent them.'' The attic story is decorated with a bas relief representing the national festivals. Thus it contrasts with the austerity of the walls, and by its theme adds a new metaphor to the whole, the unity of the people celebrating and of the people making laws. The monument is crowned by an immense statue—the triumphal chariot of Liberty symbolizing ''the most beautiful triumph that a nation can desire.'' Thus the edifice attempts to combine verbal preaching with that of the architecture in a single discourse as universal as the message conveyed. History, translated into symbols which are integrated in a synchronic image, is at the same time sublimated, freed from its fears and uncertainties. It is remarkable, as well, that Boullée is not the only one to utilize the metaphor of the printed laws on a wall. In fact, around twenty proposals taking up the same image have been listed.[149] This monotonous repetition seems to provide double evidence—of a style which is born from the encounter between the mythology secreted by the Revolution and the search for new forms of expression, but also of its weakening and wearing out even before it succeeds in being materially represented in real constructions. Be that as it may, nowhere, neither in the streets nor in the plazas of this imaginary Paris, can one escape from the *word* erected in gigantic monuments.

As has been said, the Convention chose none of these monumental projects but fell back on a solution which was admittedly temporary, but could be achieved rapidly and would not occasion too great an expense. Once installed in the Tuileries, it thought about developing the surrounding space in a Republican style. The works were to be included in the general plan for the beautification of the city, and intended to get it off to a good start. So it is that by the edict of 5 floréal year II, citizens Hubert and David are charged with "applying themselves without delay to enclosing the chamber where the sessions of the Convention are held." Hubert rapidly fulfills this mission and twenty days later, according to his proposal, the Comité de Salut public sets up an enormous program of works relating to the terrains of the Palais National as well as the Jardin National and the Place de la Révolution. On the side of the Carrousel, the court of the Palais National will be closed by a circular stylobate on which will be inscribed (yet again!) "in letters of gilt bronze" the Declaration of Rights and the Constitution. Figures representing "the Republican Virtues will be placed on pedestals supported by a single base, the symbol of the Unity of the Republic." To the side of each of the pedestals facing the court will be affixed a blazing star which will illuminate the Palais National during the night. On the dome will be placed "a statue representing Liberty in an upright position, holding the tricolor flag in one hand, and the Declaration of the Rights of Man in the other." In the entrance to the court, two enormous statues of Justice and Happiness which will support "the suspended level of Equality." The garden will be laid out. The terrace "des Feuillants" will be enlarged; the part located over this terrace will be constructed as a portico whose interior "will be adorned with pictures capable of developing and giving direction to the generous passions of adolescence." The terrace will end in a copse, beside the place de la Révolution, in which "a monument analogous to the Revolution" will be installed. In the garden which has been laid out in this way will be arranged "hexahedrons similar to those in which the Greek philosophers gave their lesson." Hubert did not, on the other hand, accept an earlier proposal which consisted of constructing in the garden an amphitheater "destined for public education" and in which would be given only the spectacle which must "be suitable to a people who are free and love equality and provide for accommodating the greatest possible number of citizens, gathered with no sort of discrimination, to see images having reference to the love of liberty retraced before their eyes."

The place de la Révolution will also undergo major modifications. The two colonnades forming the Garde-Meuble (the buildings built by Gabriel) will be linked by "a triumphal arch in honor of victories won by the people over tyranny." It will allow the former church of the Madeleine, which will be completed, becoming a "Temple of the Revolution," to be seen. Another triumphal arch will be constructed opposite, in front of the bridge of the Revolution. The statue of Liberty, which had been erected in plaster in the middle of the plaza, on "the pedestal of the next to the last tyrant of the French people," will be replaced by another, of "larger dimensions." The entire *place* will be converted to a circus, by means of a glacis, "whose gentle slope will facilitate access from all sides" and can thus serve as the site for national festivals. The entrance to the Champs Elysées will be enlarged, and the horses of Marly placed there, flanked by two porticoes adorned with painted and sculpted Revolutionary subjects. There are plans too for the "garden of the national house known as the Beaujon house" (nowadays better known as the Elysée Palace) that will be open to the public beyond the Champs Elysées, where "a statue to Jean-Jacques Rousseau, in bronze," will stand. The ditches and parapets surrounding the garden will be demolished and filled in and in the garden itself will be built a Temple of Equality, of simple architecture and with "Republican ornamentation" appropriate to this monument.[150]

The Temple to the Revolution, the Temple of Equality: the imaginary Paris is filled with new sanctuaries. But the sacred is by no means limited to them. The Republican temples only bring to the fore the sacralization of the same values that the other monuments, in their own modes, allow to "speak." The urban space, marked by values and symbols, closes on a Revolutionary catechism. The Palais National is, of course, the prestigious monument of the Power. But is it not, at the same time, the dwelling inhabited by "sacred Equality" and "sacred Liberty" as well as the center from which "the sacred love of the Country" radiates? And are the other monuments, the *Peuple-Hercule*, Nature Regenerated, etc., not erected to the glory of the same values celebrated in the temples constructed nearby? The discourse which the imaginary monuments recite, is, on a second reading, a discourse on the transference of the sacred, on the sacralization of the innovative time of politics and history. The monuments that dominate the imaginary city, in opposing themselves to the historic city, to its churches and chateaux, take possession of space as well as time. Made of granite, marble, and bronze, they impose on the city the time that "opens a new book to History." Their volumes and their masses, their materials and their symbols, project on the space an ideological discourse on history, on its starting from zero as well as on its finality, which emerge from the fundamental deeds of the Revolution. To perpetuate the Revolutionary experience in bronze and marble is to take definitive possession of the future of the city or simply of the future. With the Revolutionary calendar, the institution of Revolutionary festivals, etc., the universal architecture participates in the struggle in which what is at stake represents one of the essential aims of the Revolution, the "overthrow of relationships of symbolic domination."[151]

New temples are envisioned. But there is also the wish to take over the old temples and to shelter *the new sacred* in them. This movement is particularly accelerated at the time of dechristianization, when many popular societies or assemblies of individual sections hold their sessions in the former churches. This choice is more or less imposed by circumstances. Where else could large enough rooms be found? A decree of the Comité de Salut public of 28 floréal year II sets up a competition for "plans for civic architecture, and first of all for edifices destined for assemblies, for *décadaires*, common houses."[152] Churches were decorated for the occasion by the installation of busts of the martyrs of the Republic and by more or less hiding the altar. The decorations were nevertheless modest, owing to a lack of means. There was nothing to equal the mechanism erected in the former church of Notre Dame during the famous festival of Reason and Liberty, celebrated on the *décadi* of 20 brumaire year II. "A temple had been erected which was of simple, majestic architecture, on the façade of which could be read these words: *To philosophy*; the entrance of this temple had been adorned with busts of the philosophers who had contributed the most to the present Revolution, by their knowledge. The sacred temple was erected on the summit of a mountain. . . . Two rows of girls, dressed in white and crowned with oak, and with a torch in their hand, could be seen descending and crossing the mountain, then going back up the mountain in the same direction. Liberty, represented by a beautiful woman, then emerged from the temple of philosophy, and came, on a seat of greenery, to receive the homage of the men and women of the Republic, holding out her arms to them. Liberty then descended to return to the temple, stopping before going in and turning to cast another beneficent glance at her friends."[153]

But the war on symbols begins well before dechristianization. Even during the period of relative coexistence when masses are celebrated in front of the altars of the country, thought is already given to new sanctuaries. The need is felt more and more keenly and there is no lack of architectural proposals. It is, nevertheless, noteworthy that there is no attempt made to find a style for these temples that would distinguish their architecture from that of the "profane" public monuments. It is not the opposition between the sacred and the profane that the architecture seeks to express but, on the contrary, the unity and coherence of the sacred on which the institutions are based, as well as the spirit of the New City. Thus the repetition of the same symbolic forms—spheres, circles, cubes —are to be found in these projects, as well as the same metaphors: the new sacred table of laws is put on the walls, kept in a repository in the sanctuary, inscribed on the altar of the country, etc. In his report on public monuments, Kersaint proposes the erection on the ruins of the Bastille of "an enormous prytaneum," the major piece of which would be a gigantic altar of the country, made from a block of granite. "On the pedestal, on the granite, the declaration of rights is to be engraved; the constitution is to surround it and, on the square in front of the sanctuary, which can be entered only on 14 July of each year, the plane map of France, showing its astronomical situation, following its con-stitutional division, is to be reproduced. . . . The altar of the country must be infinitely larger than it is now. It must crown the summit of a pyramid of tiers and be close to the vault of the heavens under which it is placed. There is to be nothing else at this height that could destroy the effect of this sacred monument, alone in the world. At the base of the pyramid are to be experienced guards who will share the respect and admiration inspired by this altar. The statues of great men will then be placed there; their genius will watch over the altar of liberty." Similar but more modest pyramids (Kersaint carefully divides them into "three classes") will cover all of France and in these "sanctuaries of liberty" the laws will be exhibited and the names of citizens worthy of the country will be inscribed, or statues in their honor might even be erected.[154] Let us note one other account of the imaginary architecture of these sanctuaries. It is all the more revealing of the mentalities and the affectivity of the epoch, as its author is not one of the professional architects who supported a Kersaint, but an anonymous amateur. He proposes, for the temple of Equality to be built on the Champs Elysées, "a round form . . . because this figure offers the greatest similarity in all its aspects, compared among themselves, which is already a symbol of equality. The temple will be adorned with twenty columns along its circumference, as many outside as in. . . . The sanctuary of this temple, which will occupy the center of the edifice . . . will be formed by a circular balustrade, in which there will be ten entrances, each of which will be across from those of the temple. In the middle of the sanctuary will be a square marble pedestal which will support a globe representing the globe of earth, surmounted by the standing figure of a woman, absolutely naked. The statue is Equality, all its attributes and its action will announce the fact; and it will also be the emblem of nature, there will be a very large garland of flowers and fruits around her horizontally, which she will hold with both hands. . . . Above all these objects, the cupola of time also speaks a language that is interesting to hear; it is occupied in the center by the figure of an immense sun, whose face is in the center of the void by which the interior of the temple is lit. . . . Among the entrance doors, within the temple, will be placed large inscriptions, which will cause Equality to be cherished. . . . This temple is the place where Equality will be presented to society as a salutary dogma, whose importance will be demonstrated to make people love Equality, after it has become well known. By this happy system, men will be freed from the errors of the old ideas; they will learn how liberty is an individual good, without ceasing to be a great general good in all times and for all ages in a Republic."[155] Did the author, in order to express these noble emotions in architectural and symbolic language, carefully study all the proposals for monuments of the time, to the point of drawing up a list of their clichés? The sincerity of his desire to find forms as sober as they are sublime and worthy of *sacred Equality* cannot be doubted. If that were not so, this could be taken for a pastiche of architectural rhetoric.

The Cathedral of civics and its rites is, assuredly, the Pantheon. On 4 April 1791, on the occasion of Mirabeau's funeral, the Assembly decrees that the church of Saint Geneviève be transformed into a Pantheon destined "to receive the ashes of great men." After the mortal remains of the *tribun*, it is the ashes of Voltaire which are brought there in the course of a grandiose ceremony we have already discussed. Soufflot's edifice has to be adapted to new functions. On 19 July, Quatremère de Quincy is named commissioner of the management and supervision of the works, a post he keeps until germinal year II. Contrary to the others, the monument does not remain on paper. Despite the difficulties, the lack of means, the changes in the political situation, etc., Quatremère, with remarkable enthusiasm and tenacity, makes the Pantheon into an immense building site on which, at a certain time, some hundreds of people are working. It is a great artistic workshop as well; sixteen statuaries and a hundred sculptors are recruited to make the bas reliefs and statues, several artists receive commissions (sorely lacking at that time) to work on the ornamentation. Two architects, Soufflot-le Romain and Rondelet, collaborate with Quatremère; Molinos is frequently consulted. But Quatremère is by no means satisfied with merely organizing the works. He draws up an esthetic and ideological program he imposes on the architects and artists by intervening in the slightest details, both in the projects and in their execution. Thus, the entire enterprise is marked by the strong personality of its author, as well as by the contradictions of his political and ideological evolution. Quatremère welcomes the Revolution as an extraordinary opportunity for the revival of the arts, for their liberation from the dominating influence of the routine of the Academies, an institution he fights fiercely at David's side.[156] A lover of the antique, more theoretician than artist, he enters the Revolution provided with a sort of esthetic utopia—he already sees Paris being transformed into a new Rome. The Pantheon offers him a unique opportunity to implement his esthetic ideas which he had already formulated in the *Dictionnaire d'Architecture*. This doctrinarian is nevertheless open to the new esthetic experiences of the Revolution and, in particular, to those of the first Revolutionary festivals. He himself set up the artistic program of the festival of 3 June 1791 in honor of Simoneau, the mayor of Etampes. The choice is revealing, too, about his political options. The festival in question is to affirm order as against *anarchy*; it could be said to be a Revolutionary counter-festival. A man of order and of law (the harmony between his esthetic tastes and his political options is practically perfect), Quatremère wants to codify a style for Revolutionary art, and he imagines the Pantheon as the matrix of an official esthetic doctrine. Of course, he, too, intends to formulate antique verses on new thoughts; he does not want merely to imitate the ancients. But by no means has he the intention of seeking a system of norms leading to perfection in overly audacious experiments which might give way to extravagance. Opposition to change, support of the status quo joined to a methodical approach is thus the end of Quatremère's political evolution. The radicalization of the Revolution repels and frightens him. Therefore, he turns further and further to the right and will be one of the prime movers of the abortive Royalist putsch of 13 vendémiaire year IV.

It was necessary to discuss Quatremère himself before dealing with the work of which he was, if not the sole author, at least the principal instigator. The Pantheon was conceived as the code in stone of a new art. In a sense, it recalls the first Fête de la Fédération; like the festival, it expressed the novelty and dynamism of the Revolutionary experiences while expressing the will to stop them and bring them to a standstill. Grappling with history which is rapidly made and unmade, the Pantheon is at once ahead of and behind the evolution during which it is constructed.

It is not for us to discuss here in detail the successive projects for the Pantheon, nor their always partial achievement. Let us merely bring out some of the key ideas which translate the orientations and the contradictions of a whole search for an architectural and decorative style for the Revolution.[157] Let us note, in particular, these three leading ideas which recur in the successive projects: to make the Pantheon the privileged site for solemn rites and civic ceremonies and, in particular, to establish a close connection between the monument and festive processions; to make the edifice a "representational catechism of the duties of man in society"; and to find a formula which would reconcile the two temporalities in which the Pantheon participates at the same time, that of history in the process of being made and which the monument must serve and that of the Republic of the eras to come, through which it is supposed to last.

The Assembly visualizes the Pantheon as a funerary monument for the ashes of great men, to whom the "thankful country" will render homage. Thus, the monument is to be, so to speak, the counterpart of the royal sepulchres of Saint Denis and, hence, to affirm "that truly universal religion to which all peoples must be won over; that religion is morality." But Quatremère has a larger vision and wants to go further. The Pantheon must not be reduced to "a destination which is, as it were, passive," but it must be given an "active use." In favor of this active use is the economic argument: the enclosed void of its "customary purpose," its "long solitary" precinct, will not justify the crushing expense such construction entails. But there is also an ideological argument supported by the revolutionary experience: no spot better lends itself to being the principal place in which "the diverse institutions of which a civic religion ought to be composed are formed and consolidated." In 1793, Quatremère imagines the Pantheon as an unprecedented formula for a monument that "offers a mixture of uses and characters, combining the ideas of sepulchres and of a temple, of festivals and of historic monuments." A flexible and multi-functional edifice, then, and Quatremère does not tire of inventing the multitude of uses to which it can be put: civic awards will be presented in it; all civil servants will take the oath of the Republic in it; in it, young people will annually receive prizes "for the encouragement of both education and youth." The space of the Pantheon is capable of associating, on every occasion, all its occupants, and particularly the young, with the "great men who surround them." It is to serve not only as cenotaph and temple, but also if not above all, as "a kind of theater often offered to national festivals, the Pantheon will offer in its details, in its accessory features and in the whole enclosure, when it is finished, unsuspected resources." To the multiplicity of functions must correspond a space which today would be called polyvalent.[158] The edifice will be spacious, well lit, and with good acoustics; in it, a large audience will be able to gather around an orator. The upper galleries, which "good taste in architecture might criticize," are justified when one realizes that they will accommodate masses of spectators. A long ceremonial march can be deployed both inside and outside the building. Quatremère is thinking, particularly, of the close connection between the Pantheon and festivals. First of all, of course, those of "pantheonization," of the translations of the ashes, which are to unfold as grandiose spectacles, "French Panathenaea" (for the stylobate of the dome, Quatremère plans and orders a frieze representing this ceremony). But also all the other festivals are to have the Pantheon as an obligatory "station." To respond to these multiple functions, wide means of access must be opened to the monument (remember that the processions broke up along the narrow, twisting streets that surrounded it) and a large, open space be created around it. Thus, the projects propose to clear the Pantheon of the "broken-down hovels infringing on it," to arrange a circular enclosure around it, planted "with an Elysium or a sacred wood, and to surround this itself with a semicircular plaza. Access to the plaza will be by a wide avenue, a sort of triumphal route.[159]

All of these uses of the Pantheon are found in its major function: to instruct, to elevate souls. The entire monument and its décor in particular are conceived to speak directly to souls, using "the forceful writing of signs." Thus, it will furnish a representational civic and laical catechism, a "coherent course on the essential virtues of man and of the citizen." A language "in figures or a writing by signs" will make great use of allegory; what other language would be more universal and better adapted to the telling of this universal message? It is, as well, the language that is "particularly useful for the education of the people," as the Société Républicaine des Arts noted.[160] However, Quatremère proves to be hesitant about the use of allegory in architectural forms. Contrary to the *visionary architects*, he considers that architecture has at its disposal "the most limited means, particularly for the expression of nuances of ideas." Architectural language has no ascendancy over our affections and over the sensitive part of our soul" and the allegories transcribed in this language are understood only by a few.

In belittling the role of architecture as a means of symbolic communication, Quatremère is faithful to his principles, while adapting himself to the circumstances. There is not, in fact, much to be done with Soufflot's edifice, which is "done, if not finished." Its "pagan" form, paradoxical for a church, proves to be perfectly adapted to the new use of the monument. Nevertheless, Quatremère does not hesitate "to suppress everything that could recall the old ideas, either on the exterior or the interior, and to add everything that could make the present intention readable." Therefore, he suppresses the two towers of the apse and the sacristy; the windows are blocked up (light, as in ancient temples, is to enter only from the top); the cross crowning the cupola is taken down. But the most important transformations and innovations have to do with the decoration and, in particular, the sculptures. In the new monument the latter must blend with the architecture "in their relationship of monumental majesty." The old sculptures are consequently immediately condemned and replaced by new ones: Houdon's bas relief, *Saint Peter Receiving the Keys*, will be replaced by Lesueur's *The Benefits of Public Education*, Couston's pediment, *The Triumph of Faith*, is supplanted by Moitte's bas relief, *The Country Crowning Virtues*, etc. In the middle of the temple will rise a colossal, polychrome statue of the Country, "that veritable idol of a free people," supported by Liberty and Equality. Around the dome, the colonnade of which will be removed, will stand thirty-two enormous statues, and the cross will be replaced by a gigantic statue of Renown, cast with the bronze of the cannons that had been won, and dominating, along with the edifice, the whole city.[161] The description of Moitte's bas relief, installed on the pediment, gives a striking idea of this explosion of the "sober and republican" allegorical language. "The Republic or the Motherland, in the form of a large and imposing woman, accompanied by emblems which show it to be France, rises from its throne; its two outstretched arms bear crowns; to the left, a winged young man holding the club, the symbol of force, in one hand, seizes the crown; from his features one knows him to be Genius. The other hand of the Country holds a crown which rests on the head of a girl, whose reserved bearing distinguishes her as Virtue. She is followed by the genius of Liberty leading a team of lions attached to the chariot, in which the emblems of all the virtues are enclosed. A figure brought down by this chariot occupies the lowest part of the pedestal; its attributes, its regrets, show it to be Aristocracy subjugated.[162]

The unity of this monumental and educational organization of the space depends on the *active use* of the Pantheon. The speaking stone, or, if you will, the patriotic and revolutionary eloquence fixed in stone, assumes the almost permanent presence of a public listening to this message. The works of art are not artificially assembled and in no way function as objects of esthetic curiosity. They are conceived for this particular space and to be harmoniously integrated into its functions—on condition, of course, that the space itself not be empty, that the forms address their words to a crowd eager to receive the message, that the allegories of the tympanum be attentively and emotionally deciphered by the people in a procession, assembled on the plaza of its "station."

In the entire decor, there is no figure, no motif borrowed from history or ancient myths. "In this first national monument, it was necessary to finally abandon the idea of seeing ourselves as dependent on the ancients; it was necessary finally to belong to ourselves. The effigies of the Greeks and Romans had to cease appearing where those of the French who have become free would begin to shine.'' This declaration of principle in no way contradicts the *return to antiquity* which governs the overall program. Antiquity furnishes only the universal language of forms; it does not determine the discourse, which must be completely new and original, like the history of the French, *"which begins only with the Revolution."* Quatremère refuses to have any event or motif drawn from this recent history represented in the decoration. The *system of allegories* does, of course, evoke the new time, but only on a second reading. ''The events of history so closely reproduced resemble objects seen through a magnifying glass'' and that is why ''local and fortuitous truths'' must be sacrificed ''to general truth.'' What is behind these equivocal formulas? Does Quatremère already sense the ''depantheonizations'' to come, beginning with that of Mirabeau? Does he refuse entry into the Pantheon to events which are happening at a faster and faster pace and pushing the Revolution beyond the limits he would set? Is he seeking ideological justification for his esthetic preferences? Be that as it may, he formulates the opposition as clearly as he concludes it. ''Here (in the Pantheon) the *effects* of Liberty and not its *actions*'' must ''be sung, and its *reign* celebrated rather than its *conquest.*'' Thus, the history being made is opposed to accomplished and sublimated history. Liberty in action is ejected by the symbolism of its accomplished and immobile reign.

Fleeing turbulent, evolving history, seeking refuge in a vague utopia postponed to the end of history, does the program for the Pantheon not, in some way, sum up the contradictions exercising the whole of this imaginary Paris and, hence, a whole architecture, and its esthetics and ideology? On the one hand, they are present at the extraordinary explosion of an architectural imagination which espouses the social imagination and is inspired by a renewed collective imagination. But, on the other hand, this rapid development is set in a symbolic language believed to be as universal as it is finished, and which leads to the monotonous repetition of the same forms, metaphors, and allegories. An architecture that ''sings of'' the city of happiness and equality, but which, by its monumental organization of space, overwhelms the ''city of happiness'' and makes of it, at the most, only a setting for the ''city of prestige.'' An architecture which postulates a community of values and of imagination with those who use it, a permanent communication between the ''speaking'' monuments, constructed to the glory of a free people, and this people itself. And yet, an architecture which expresses the possession, by the new power, that historic materialization of the ideal promoter of utopias, of the monopoly of the educational word dispensed to the people, thus reduced to admiring muteness. Does it not, in its monumental immobility, paradoxically express a movement, the transformation of a dream stirring people into action into an object of oppressive discourse? There is nothing more opaque than its intended transparency which disguises history as the utopia and masks the historic realities on which the utopia breaks down.

If construction could have been accomplished as rapidly as it was decreed, part, at least, of this imaginary Paris would have been realized. Would it have been later suppressed, as was the case with Moitte's bas relief? Or else, because stone is durable, would it have resisted destruction and been assimilated to the living city? Symbols which no longer speak to anyone and whose message has ceased to be picked up do not necessarily disappear. The Pantheon stands in the middle of Paris. One can visit it, as I myself have done several times. A few lost tourists, their Michelin in hand, stray through its overwhelming void, visiting this museum of curious tombs under the somnolent gaze of the guardians. By a conjuring trick that history alone can manage, the Pantheon has joined that other type of monument so beloved and admired at the time of its construction. It seems, in fact, to be a ruin, a very decorative moral ruin, solidly built of stone. It rises like the vestige of an imaginary city, of *the city called Liberty*, in which the shortest road linked the place de la Révolution to the place du Bonheur.

VII
The Flying Man

Every epoch has its modes of imagining, reproducing, and renewing the collective imagination, as it has its own ways of believing, feeling, and knowing. The imagination, with its orientations and activities that are as diverse as they are multiple, constitutes a dimension of mentalities and sensitivities whose importance would be difficult to overestimate. We have qualified it as *social* in order to designate the specific orientation of its activity *in the direction of the social*. Oriented in this direction, it produces imaged representations of *ourselves* and of *others*, images of society taken as a whole as well as of the institutions and groups which compose it, of the hierarchy and social divisions, etc. The field of expectations which surrounds individual and collective experiences, is stocked by the social imagination with hopes and fears, dreams and obsessions, and so many "fantasies" associated with the cohesion or the disintegration of a society, with its stability or its conflicts. The social imagination plays a stabilizing role—it contributes to the legitimization of a power as well as to the working out of a social consensus, which calls for symbols and myths, dominant models of behavior, and systems of values and prohibitions; it is at work in the comprehension of social life, as it is in the occultation of its mechanisms. A regulating and stabilizing factor, the social imagination is nevertheless also the faculty which allows for not considering the existing modes of sociability as being definitive and the only ones possible, but for imagining other formulas and models. It exercises an autonomous activity in the sense that its uses and products are not reducible to an intellectual or even cognitive activity. Of course, the social imagination does not work in isolation; it is nourished with knowledge and experiences that it transforms and expresses according to its own modalities. The imaginary formations, the "fantasies" it produces are only "unreal" specifically in quotation marks. If the social actors do not act acccording to the scenarios they themselves imagined, their actions are no less separable from the images they give themselves of themselves and their adversaries, of their dreams and myths, of their haunting fears and hopes. The social imagination gives evidence of inertia and it operates in the long term; it reproduces a sometimes age-old collection of symbols and stereotypes, enmities and hopes. But it also goes through "hot" periods which are characterized by a particularly intense exchange between the "real" and the "fantasies," by a greater pressure of the imaginary on the way of living everyday life, by explosions of passions and desires. This is notably the case of Revolutionary crises. To mobilize large masses, to snatch them away from "normal" life, to project them from *immobile history* toward an accelerated history cannot be accomplished without the production of great social dreams that stir them to action and the symbols that incarnate them, without the expansion of tasks to be accomplished and objectives to be reached. Neither the ideas nor the dreams make revolutions, but how could they be made without the dreams they exude? A revolutionary crisis necessarily goes through the renewal of the social imagination; it is, as well, a combat in which domination and power in the symbolic sphere are at stake.

An essential factor of all historic change, the social imagination nevertheless is hidden when sought, as it does not refer to any group of specific sources. It seems to be just about everywhere and nowhere. According to Hegel, the history of men can only be written based on their dreams. But how very fleeting these dreams are, how rare to find a trace of them in the archives! The hopes and fears accompanying the birth of a baby are not inscribed on his baptismal certificate. The sale of a steer has much more chance of being chronicled than do the dreams produced, lived, and exchanged by men.

As far as we're concerned, we let ourselves be guided in our investigation by an interrogation of the social imagination and utopias. In fact, one of the functions—and not the least of these—of utopias, is to be a setting and a specific mode of the exercise of the social imagination. In and by utopian representations, the imagination leads the exploration of *social otherness*. In and by utopias, the individual and collective social dreams take on consistency; they are organized in coherent groups of idea-images of an alternative society, in opposition to and in rupture with the dominant order. Let us recall, in recapitulation, the essential of our definition of the utopia: imagined representation of a society which is opposed to that which exists: 1. by the alternative organization of the society envisioned as a whole; 2. by the otherness of the institutions and relationships that compose the global society; 3. by the alternative modes according to which everyday life is lived. This representation, whose details are more or less developed, can be envisaged as one of the possibilities of the real society and it is then valorized in relation to the latter, positively or negatively.

The sphere of the social imagination is, of course, much broader than that of utopias, and the utopian enterprise is merely one of the paths of the formation of the social imagination. A specific and partial manifestation of the latter, the utopian phenomenon is nevertheless a very precious symptom of it.

In questioning the relationships between utopias and the social imagination, we have been led to reject several of the traditional frameworks to which the study of the utopian phenomenon are sometimes relegated. We were not exclusively attached to certain forms of utopian discourse; we sought utopian representations just about everywhere they were developed and at work, where they effectively oriented an intellectual, political, or artistic activity; where they served as receptacles and poles of crystallization for social dreams. For the same reason, we did not respect the fetishism of the ''chronological threshold'' which supposedly separates the Enlightenment from the Revolutionary period. It is, once again, the force of things that led us to approach this period which is particularly revealing of the intervention of the utopian imagination in the organization of collective time and space, as well as of the fusion of utopian representations and political myths in the crucible of Revolutionary ideas.

As we have proceeded only by thematic probes or sections, our conclusions can only be of provisional value. But, in truth, the very idea of ''concluding'' is completely foreign to us. The formulation of queries for research to be accomplished as well as questions on the validity of the hypotheses we have drawn throughout our investigation is sufficient for us. It is only for ease of expression that we will avoid the repetitious use of the interrogative form.

Let us point out, first, the most obvious deficiencies. The predominance of one particular theme or another is due to the fortuities of research that sometimes led us further than we had foreseen. As an indirect consequence, it was necessary to resign ourselves to leaving aside, at least for the moment, other themes and problems of equal importance. We shall cite only a few of them.

We did not even approach the theme of education, a domain favored by the utopian exercise. It would be necessary to consider education in the utopia, all these imaginary Cities that set up educational systems for themselves which are as perfect as they are effective and which transform the entire society into a continuously running pedagogical machine. But it would also and above all be necessary to examine the utopias of education and, in particular, the projects of public education which convey the dreams of a new man for the New City or even the dream of the regeneration of the City by the reeducation of its citizens. This history of the controversy on public education during the Revolution would have to be gone into in its entirety. Utopian representations would be found at work in these projects which proliferate at the time and which go as far as suggesting the almost total suppression of any specialized and institutionalized school system. Did the Revolutionary experience not prove itself by teaching the people more in just a few years than the schools had during centuries? It is in living history as rupture, and not as continuity, that the new man can be formed. A system of specialized schools can only develop new privileged people, those of knowledge; it is only the experience of the transformation of life that is the true and only school of free and equal men. One would think it was May 1968; but, as we have already pointed out, utopias more frequently anticipate other utopias than they do realities—proposals, but also some practical achievements. Education is conceived for the utopia; but it ought also to be accomplished *by the utopia*, as at the Ecole de Mars, which was intended to be the breeding ground of the new man and which, in the middle of Paris, had kids living in a sort of Spartan-style sansculotte republic.

Nor have we noted the utopias on which the hopes conveyed by Knowledge, the flourishing of the sciences, were fixed. Science in the utopia is, besides, much less interesting than the utopian expansions given to the sciences. Unfulfilled utopian dreams focus on their unlimited and regenerative social effect. Thus the discovery of "universal magnetism" would promise the cure not only of physical ills but of moral evil as well. Humanity is already seen as renewed; morals and institutions transformed; a social order, in conformity with the eternal laws of nature, established; and all of that thanks to the most powerful spiritual energy having been put to the service of man. Another promise behind the universal grammar. It would not only seek the common foundations of all languages; it was motivated by the dream of finding once again the lost universal language, the restoration of which would ensure perfect communication, the true basis of transparency and social communion. These are peculiar sciences, parasciences, if you will. Let us note, however, how very similar these "peculiarities" are to an idea whose history we touched on and which was to have the greatest success. We are thinking, in particular, of the great rational promise of making human evolution the object of a science that would be as universal as it was rigorous and which, thanks to the discovery of the immutable laws of history-progress, would encompass both the past and the future in which the City of Happiness and Justice is inevitably situated. Does an epoch not, in its "extravangances," give evidence which, however frequently deformed and grotesque, is nevertheless revealing of its problems, anxieties, and hopes?

We have only lightly touched on the case of utopias directly associated with programs of Revolutionary political action. Two examples, at least, would be worth special attention. Think, in particular, of Saint-Just, who married his Revolutionary experience to the utopian dream he codified in the *Institutions républicaines* and of Babeuf, who installed his utopian dreams in the program of Equals.

The list could be extended. What about sexuality in Utopia and the utopias of sexuality? Or prisons in Utopia and the utopia of the penitentiary system?

We limited ourselves, then, to certain themes and authors. Our point of departure was literary texts espousing a "classic" paradigm, that of the imaginary voyage. As one reads them and discovers in them the most diverse and divergent proposals, one is struck by the presence of a foundation of common feelings.

An anxiety, a malaise, if not a feeling of denial prevails: the discontent, the discomfort, the embarrassments of someone who is more or less frustrated by the religious, intellectual, moral, and other contexts of social life, or fails to find his place in it. In certain texts, these feelings remain vague and imprecise; they are expressed only in a movement of escape from reality. In others, they are more specific and are expressed in a more or less radical critique of the mores, morals, political institutions, religion, and so forth. In still others, they are accompanied by the desire, if not the will for change. If these utopias derive from a similar state of mind, they contribute as well, by the play of their interaction, to an awareness of it. Proposing a sociological or ideological qualification of these diffuse feelings, in which malaise merges with hopes and fears, would be unwarranted. The most unexpected encounters are possible on the roads of utopias: moderate reformers meet radical protesters, disillusioned aristocrats rub elbows with minor writers, representatives of a growing, if not overly numerous, *intelligentsia*, seeking to make a name for themselves, to make a career.

The historian is struck both by the proliferation of these texts and by their incontestable monotony. How marked is the repetition of the same themes and ideas in this literature! To visit one city in Utopia is to have seen nearly all of them. The imagination suffers from the rules of this discourse. One notes, first of all, the attrition of the literary genre under the effect of an excessive paradigmatic rigidity. But there is more: the desire to deny reality, to give proof of an unfettered social imagination can lead to the paradoxical effect of repetition and uniformity. The utopians, when they want to emphasize the free rein given the imagination to better challenge the existing society, its institutions, and its morality, always find themselves attracted to the same themes. Whence the inflexibility of spirit which hinders and even paralyzes the enterprise of the social imagination. Whence the repetition of certain themes: the rational religion, reduced to a vague deism or to a sort of social ethic; the liberalization of the relationship between the sexes, if not total sexual freedom; the invention of rational languages; the transparency and simplicity of political institutions; and so forth. The utopias are part and parcel of and inspired by the philosophical and moral problem that fascinates this "enlightened century," that of evil, of its origin, and its existence; they reproduce a more or less secularized theodicy, oriented toward history and the social. The utopia does not, nevertheless, content itself with diminishing *evils*; it envisages suppressing *evil*, striking it in its very principle. As an indirect consequence, by wanting to reduce all the evils denounced to a single principle, they fabricate the aggregate image of an ideal society which would be as simple as its founding principle. It is therefore sufficient to deduce and imagine, based on this principle or on a limited number of convergent principles, daily life in all its details. Insofar as one finds evil rooted in history, one is tempted to make it disappear, with these absurd and irrational conflicts. As we have noted, these imaginary cities live in an insular time, cut off from our own. The monotony and repetition of their evocation comes from the fact that they are societies with neither conflicts nor contradictions to be resolved, so many responses to one single problem perfectly defined by Morelly: to find a situation in which it would be nearly impossible that man be depraved, or evil, or, at least, *minima de malis*. One might well wonder whether this specific, limited, and restricted utopian enterprise should not be related to a certain structure of the thought of the Enlightenment. This "enlightened century" is, on the one hand, in search of a totality, of a rational and universal order; on the other hand, it is fascinated by the exploration of the concrete and of the individual, in their richness and diversity. The quasi-novelistic accounts of the imaginary cities harmonized, in their way, the two preoccupations: the concrete and the partial keep a semblance of richness and autonomy, while being merely manifestations and symbols of the social whole.

Frequently flat and mediocre novels, less rich in ideas and new images than might have been expected, the imaginary voyages are nevertheless enormously successful. What perhaps counted most was mobilizing the social imagination, standing aloof from the established society, its order of values and hierarchies, exercising the sense of liberty and independence. This literature, which often has no precise social object and seems to lose itself in escape and monotonous dreams, is nevertheless a *practiced activity*. Is it not, in fact, the manifestation of a specific intellectual activity which marks the culture of this century, particularly at first? Pierre Francastel spoke of this with pertinence in his analysis of the work of Watteau. In the "Embarkation for Cythera," the imaginary dreamland, the painter does not, as one might have thought, flee from reality. It is precisely by representing imaginary places that are located nowhere, where one enjoys oneself, that he is the faithful and concrete painter of the social elites who were to produce and diffuse the great ideas of the Enlightenment. Before formulating the principles of a political, social, and economic transformation, they sought only to develop the mental context of an imaginary culture. It is in these conversations, which were both philosophical and gallant, that "more liberty and less mental conformity" were sought, that the imagination and spirit that wished to be free were exercised and took pleasure in that exercise.

The imaginary voyages, in overwhelming majority, can be put in this category. It could be said that in these utopias the pleasure of traveling is often more important than the interest in the countries to be discovered.

The wear and tear suffered by the imaginary voyages, clearly notable in the second half of the century, reveals the profound and complex changes the field of social expectations undergoes, as well as a reorientation of the imagination at work on it. The *elsewhere* of the utopia moves and changes its face. It leaves the *nowhere*, inhabited by exiles from our society, who live their own time, their own history which is not connected with ours. This *elsewhere* had as a condition of its existence the imaging activity which was announced from the inception in its aptitude for "fictionalizing" and which was recognized as such. It was only *the possible of the imaginary*, the manifestation and affirmation of the possibility of freely imagining the social. More and more, social hopes and dreams postulate other forms of expression with a different epistemological and cultural status. The *elsewhere* of the social otherness is established at the very center of the field of expectations; it is conceived more and more as the latent possibility of experiences to have. The utopia espouses a certain pragmatism, giving it a specific tonality and taking it beyond the limits of its "realism." We have observed several examples of this slow and tortuous movement of transformation: going from the festival in the utopia to the utopia of the festival, from cities in Utopia to the utopia of the city, from power and government in the utopia to the power and government envisaged as the agent of the utopia and the executor of social dreams. The distances between the dreamed and imagined society and the real society, between the wanted and desired history and the lived history, seem to lessen. But then, the utopia is no longer recognized as the dreamed image; it is announced and presented as something other than itself: a proposal of reforms as lucid as they are practical, an extension or application of science; the ultimate truth that deciphers history; an anticipation of the future. This sociological and epistemological change is easily noticeable on the semantic level. Utopian discourse with scientific, political, or ideological garb no longer accepts being called *utopia*.

The term is negatively valorized and reserved to the *others*, all those who merely fabricate "chimeras." The utopian dreams thus refuse to recognize the work specific to the imagination as the condition and support of their existence. The gap between the imaginary and the real is reduced—social otherness is no longer offered within the scope of the *dream*, but within that of *knowledge* and *action*. The utopia is thus established in the extensions of the time of history; on the one hand, it verges on science; on the other, on politics.

The most striking case, and that most revealing of this transformation, is offered by the intervention of utopian representations in the development of the ideal of history-progress. As we pointed out, this process is only at its beginnings in the eighteenth century, when Progress as such, with a capital P, is still spoken of only rarely. Nevertheless, a double movement is already under way. History, on which are projected the cult of change and of accelerated innovation, of progress that has already been made and that remains to be achieved, is inevitably opening on a great promise of the future. The idea and the certitude that the New City incarnating happiness is found at the term of historical evolution thus underlay the interrogation of the past, which is presented under a new light. But, at the same time, the utopias are opening to history and its time. The vision of an alternative and better society is not only projected on the future; with the future, it is joined to the present and past by an overall ideological discourse summarizing the orientation of History. The latter is conceived as not only decipherable but as already deciphered. Reinforcing its coherence, the discourse on Progress establishes itself as rational and scientific. Thus, it accepts the utopia only as its second, indirect, and concealed object. It is History, the object of a science, which is charged with producing and establishing the utopias. The images of an *alternative* City and History, situated in the time of Progress and integrated into a discourse with scientific sheathing, are inevitably remodeled. They are no longer either offered or accepted as dreams and aspirations, but as *anti-chimeras*, not as *visions*, but as *predictions* of the future, if not as truths endowed with all the prestige of science. The utopian representations thus become receptacles and places for the crystallization of new attitudes toward historic time, of the dreams and hopes focused on History and Knowledge to which indefinite possibilities are accorded. Becoming enriched with new themes and gaining in social resonance, they also become relay stations and resonance chambers of the conquering ideological discourse. This play of interaction and exchange between the utopias and the ideologies tends, if pushed, to blur the outlines of both. It is under the transparency, the rationality, and the happiness of the New City that the ideologies dissimulate their shadows; it is in the opacity of the ideologies that the creativity of the social imagination which produced utopian representations is lost and frozen.

The opposition between history and utopia, in which only a pure and simple denial of history is seen, is occasionally exaggerated. Recently, this seems to have become nearly an intellectual mode. Things seem more complex to us, however, and we feel we have given several examples of that complexity. The opposition utopia/history is by no means absolute: the terms as well as their relationship are variable and historically defined. If there is an opposition, it by no means excludes a complementarity. The assimilation of utopian ideas and images form the very condition making possible the existence of certain historical discourse and myths. But it is also in opening itself to history, rejoining its time, and charging the latter with great promise that the utopian representations are renewed and remodeled. In other words, it seems indispensable to us in the study of utopias always to specify which ideas or which images of history are confronted, or even refused or assimilated by and in the dreams of a model City and of a wanted and desired history. The utopias and the utopians are not grappling simply with history, or even with that History priding itself on a capital H and which has but a single sense and a single logic. Besides, is this History not a quite recent invention and would it have been possible without the contribution of the utopias? Beyond the utopian images are found men whose social imagination is grappling with the realities of their times. The dreams of the ideal City harmonize readily with those other dreams of a history of which men have already taken possession, once and for all. But the reiterated images of the societies established in the immobility of their outcome only reveal, by dissimulating them, the conditions of their own historical existence, as well as their insertion into realities which were themselves moving.

The changes and reorientations of the utopian enterprise take shape throughout the eighteenth century, becoming more pronounced in the second half, and are inscribed in the broader context of the modifications of its social and mental framework. These changes coincide at a given moment with the great Revolutionary upheaval whose impact on the creativity of the social imagination and, in particular, on the production of utopian representations, would be difficult to overestimate. We are alluding to a coincidence and not a cause-and-effect relationship, without entering into the eternal debate on the Revolution—rupture or continuity, rupture and continuity. That seems to us as useless as it is presumptuous. However, it is patent that one does not involve oneself in the Revolution with a virgin social imagination or, more precisely, with neither dreams nor hopes, one is not *carried away* by the Revolutionary exploit. Let us recall once again de Tocqueville's remarkable observations on the social imagination at work during the decades to which the Revolution gave the light of a "pre-Revolutionary" epoch. "Above the real society, whose constitution was still traditional, confused, and irregular, where laws remained diverse and contradictory, classes and ranks clearly defined, conditions fixed and responsibilities unequal, little by little an imaginary society was built, in which everything seemed simple and coordinated—uniform, fair, and in conformity with reason." Gradually the imagination of the crowd deserted the first to withdraw into the second . . . and one finally lived through the mind in this ideal City the writers had constructed. Did the idea-images of this ideal City actually mark the imagination of the "crowd" or rather primarily, if not solely, that of certain elites and, in particular, of the intelligentsia of the epoch? We have insisted on the "scholarly" character of utopian discourse throughout the century. Nevertheless, it is certain that the utopian activity supported this edifice Tocqueville speaks of and that it furnished its architectural plans. But the utopias contributed to the formation of the social imagination during the pre-Revolutionary era only by following the very tortuous road by which the century succeeded in inventing its own formulas of liberty. The utopias neither anticipated nor predicted the Revolution and the utopians are by no means either "pre-Revolutionaries" or "precursors" of the Revolution. Every utopia does not imply a political project and is not a call to action. (On the other hand, it is obvious that not every political proposal of the epoch assimilated utopian representations.) Even when there was a rapprochement between the utopia and politics, as was the case, as we have seen, during the second half of the century, it did not lead up to a Revolutionary project. During the eighteenth century, before the Revolution, utopias with other than reformist extensions were rare. No utopia imagined a scenario which even distantly resembled the political and social upheaval for which the utopian activity had, indirectly and in its own particular way, prepared minds and spirits. With and through the utopias, the social imagination, of course, manifested its dynamism, but its inertia and its limitations as well. The men of this "enlightened century" did not approach their history with all the social imagination it required, any more than did any others.

The relationships between the utopia and political projects change at the epoch of generalized political and social crisis that is the Revolution. Of course, the Revolutionary exploit is neither produced nor provoked by the imagination, but once begun, it gives a new élan and a particular dynamism to the imaginary. The Revolutionary realities and experiences generate a great burst of political hopes and myths. More than ever, the social actors are inseparable from their "fantasies," from those dreams that elevate, glorify, and magnify the actions accomplished, and the work that remains to be done.

We have brought out the examples of a Babeuf or a Saint-Just, who did not separate their political actions from the development of a model of the Ideal City set out and organized in a text. But during the Revolutionary period especially, utopias cannot be confined to a particular text that follows a rigid paradigm. It is by their diffuse presence that the utopian representations profoundly mark the Revolutionary mentalities. The images of an *alternative* community, a fraternal and egalitarian union of free men, are responses given, particularly by militant minorities, to the collective hopes awakened or engendered by the Revolution, but also to the anxieties provoked by its vicissitudes. Images, certainly, as global as they are vague, but for that very reason all the more dynamic and mobilizing, as they leave a relatively wide field for the exercise of individual and collective dreams. The exceptional function of symbols in Revolutionary mentalities is due, among other reasons, to the strong utopian charge. Their polysemy signifies, among other things, the announcement of a New City and of the new man. Abstract figures of abstract values which serve as the basis for the promised City, the symbols of the regenerated Country, the victorious and sovereign People, Equality and Fraternity, etc., function as both receptacles and generators of energies, hopes, and social dreams.

The utopia of the Revolutionary City in this symbolic language is coupled with the Revolutionary myth. Those who fabricate it while participating in it live and recount their acts and the evolution of the Revolution in the specific mode of a founding and creative time. They glorify the absolute beginnings and the primordial events of the time when, in Michelet's words, "everything becomes possible." But this time which "opens a new book to history" can be conceived as such only because it is lived as the vector of its own finality. Its sole and unique significance is deciphered in the images of the New City which it already establishes for eternity. The Revolutionaries recount the utopia to themselves as an integral part of the myth secreted by their own experiences. They need the "forceful language of signs," a means of communication and communion, in order to tell what they believe but also in order to believe what they tell. The fusion of the utopia and the Revolutionary myth will leave a durable mark on the collective imagination far beyond the survival of the Revolution itself. It will be revived and reproduced, in particular, in the account of the *unfinished* Revolution, which did not succeed in accomplishing its ultimate objective or which was diverted from it. This account, in its diverse versions, will nourish the imagination of the "professional" Revolutionary, that new historical figure making its first appearance only with the French Revolution and particularly in the era that succeeded it.

The utopia of the Revolutionary City, coupled with symbols and the political myth, contributes to the formation of a certain community of social imagination. Thus, the utopia is found at work in the new Revolutionary rites, and it is lived as a spectacle in the Revolutionary festivals. It intervenes directly in the modeling of time and space as well as in proposals for the education of a new man worthy of the New City. The unfulfilled dreams of architects and painters, scholars and educators, and schemers of all kinds seek to take possession of realities wide open to the imagination. This community is, of course, more extensive or more limited at different stages of the Revolution. The idea that it encompasses the entire population, everyone with the exception of traitors and aristocrats, is only an additional expression of the way of living and perceiving realities which substitutes, for the complex and contradictory people, the reassuring images of the victorious and sovereign people, or of the nation, free and regenerated.

Thus, in the course of the Revolutionary experiences, the utopias gain in specific sociological reality. Of course, the society is not *utopianized*; it has not actually become transparent, conforming to reason and nature. The gap, if not the gulf, between the utopias and the Revolutionary dreams, is inevitable. No revolution ever marks a total rupture with the society which preceded it, none ever turns the time of history back to zero, none satisfies the hopes it awakens or the utopias it stimulates. Sociologically and historically, the *reality of the imaginary* is in its existence itself, in the diversity of social functions it exercises as well as in the intensity of that exercise. Utopias gain in "reality" and in "realism" insofar as they are durably inscribed in the field of expectations of an epoch or social group, and, above all, insofar as they emerge as guiding ideas and key points which orient and mobilize hopes and appeal to collective energies. Thus during the Revolution, and in particular during its rising phase, an intense exchange between utopian representations and collective hopes is established. The experience of Revolutionary realities itself stimulates the discovery of new uses for the utopia, considered by some as reassuring and encouraging and by others as harmful and fearsome.

The Revolution necessarily goes through the conflict and combat in which power and domination, if not monopoly, in the sphere of the imaginary, are at stake. How frequently those who think themselves the spokesmen of the Revolution, the ideologues, the politician, and the militants, demand, in urgent appeals, that the Revolution take over imaginations in order to guide the passions and elevate the souls! However, it is not the imagination which comes to power, but is rather the Power which thus surrounds itself with a new imagination. It seeks to take it over, to make it into its stabilizing instrument, a necessary element of its prestige, a tool of propaganda, mobilization, and manipulation of the masses. The Power "utopianizes itself" only in the sense that it aims at institutionalizing the utopia in images and discourses which it monopolizes.

During the Revolutionary epoch, the utopias maintain complex relationships with the ideologies and politics. If a certain orientation of political action were possible without the perspectives and objectives formed in and by the utopias, it would be naïve, if not incorrect, to see in the programs and political actions simple extensions or conclusions drawn from utopian visions. If the utopia marks certain Revolutionary ideas and mentalities, it is the very course of the Revolution which forces the utopian imagination to draw closer to history and political action. From the Revolutionary event the utopia draws new hopes and encouragement: does it not seem to reveal that all social reality, including that which had been thought stable and definitive, could be abruptly changed and shattered? But the confrontation of the utopia with history and politics is also full of disappointments and bitter experiences. For some, the Revolutionary experience compromises any utopia; for others, the Revolutionary image of the City of happiness, equality, and fraternity will remain the great promise of history and will nourish their hopes and plans of action.

These hopes and disappointments have perhaps never been more dramatically expressed than they were by the great painter whose work seems to embrace all the hopes and disillusionments of the Age of Enlightenment. Toward the end of his life, Goya presents, in an enigmatic painting, a fantastic vision. In the center are flying figures who escape from earth and head toward a City whose vague outline, seemingly a mirage, takes shape on a lofty and distant rock. These flying men will not succeed in reaching the City of their dreams. They are hit, in full flight, by bullets shot from below, from the earth they wish to flee and on which men kill one another. Let us not superfluously add to the vivid metaphor a univocal sense that would kill it. Let us not crush it with comments as moralizing as they are futile, and which would be either optimistic: would the man have taken flight without the mirage toward which he is headed? or pessimistic: was taking flight only to be massacred worth it? Let us take the painting as it is: it locates the flying man in the foreground and on him it fixes our gaze.

Notes

I: The Social Imagination and Utopian Representations

1. Cf. A. Découflé, *L'an 2000*, Paris. The author distinguished six ways of "speaking of the future": divination, prophecy, futurology, prospective, science fiction, and utopia. We will study below how utopian discourse becomes a way of "speaking to the future."

2. Fourier, *Œuvres*, Paris, 1969, vol. X, p. 9. (Manuscripts published by la *Phalange*.)

3. L. Febvre, *Pour une histoire à part entière*, Paris, 1962, pp. 736–742.

4. C.-G. Dubois, *Problèmes de l'utopie*, Paris, 1968. p. 7.

5. This ambiguity of More's neologism was recognized as early as the sixteenth century.

6. *Dictionnaire de Trévoux*, 1771. In English the meaning is extended throughout the seventeenth century. *The Oxford English Dictionary* gives the following sequence: "An imaginary Island depicted by Sir Thomas More as enjoying a perfect social, legal, and political system (1551); Any imaginary, indefinitely remote region, country, locality (1610); An impossible ideal scheme esp. for social improvement." A detailed analysis in H. Schulte-Herbrügen, *Utopie und Anti-utopie; von der Strukturanalyse zur Strukturtypologie*, Bochum, 1960.

7. *Dictionnaire de l'Académie*, 1795. We will return to the polysemy of *utopia* in the eighteenth century.

8. L. Reybaud, *Etudes sur les réformateurs sociaux*, Paris, 1856, pp. 1–2. In the *Grand Dictionnaire Universel du XIX$_e$ siècle*, P. Larousse adopts a more qualified attitude toward the utopia and utopians. *Utopia* is, certainly, "a synonym of reverie, of ideal which *seems* unrealizable"; one is "rather considerably inclined to see

utopians as finding themselves in a state of mind akin to madness." However, *ideal* is not to be made synonymous with *fictive* or *imaginary*. Only "routinists," creatures of habit whose mind is "rebellious to any conception of the ideal" think that way. The ideal is necessary to progress; often, what was described as "utopia at one era becomes a tangible reality at another time." Of course, there are excesses, and one sees "men whose mind is constantly occupied with unfeasible proposals. . . . But that only shows that one must keep the *juste milieu*; and it is not a reason to mock or to paralyze inventors." Utopians "are sometimes singular beings, but do not resemble poets or soothsayers."

9. The first bibliography, to my knowledge, of "all utopias," a sort of bibliographic *guide raisonné* for militants, was published in 1923 (W. Swiatlowski, *Katalog utopij*, Moscow, 1923). In the early 1920's Volguine began to edit his remarkable collection of utopian texts whose title alone deserves a historical semantic analysis: *Les précurseurs du socialisme scientifique*. . . .

   A. Kopp compiled a number of extremely rare documents from this period in his book *Changer la vie, changer la ville*, Paris, 1975.

   The "anarchist" republic of Makhno, in the Ukraine, represents a singular and particularly complex chapter of the "utopias put into practice" of this period. Cf. N. Makhno, *La révolution Russe en Ukraine, mars 1917–avril 1918*, Paris, 1927; P. Arscinov, *Storia del Movimento Makhnovista, 1918–1921*, Naples, 1954.

10. Cf. G. Sorel, *Réflexions sur la violence*, Paris, 1908, pp. xxviff.

11. K. Mannheim, *Ideology and utopia*, London, 1952. Let us recall, without going into detail, that Mannheim distinguishes four historic structures of the utopian mentality: the chiliasm, the humanitarian-liberal idea, the conservative idea, the socialist-communist utopia.

12. There is an excellent bibliographic introduction in H. Desroches, "Petite bibliothèque de l'Utopie," *Esprit*, 1974, no. 4. This is the second special issue of *Esprit* devoted to utopias, the first having been published in February 1966. Note also the special issues of several other journals, evidence of the consistency of a similar interest: *Dædalus, Journal of the American Academy of Arts and Sciences*, Spring 1965; *Revue des sciences humaines*, no. 155 (1974); *Littérature*, no. 21 (1976), including a pertinent updating of the most recent studies: F.-P. Bowman, "Utopie, imagination, espérance."

13. Cf. H. Desroches, *Sociologie de l'espérance*, Paris, 1973, pp. 195ff. R. Kosoelleck has shown the importance of the study of the changing relationships between the "field of experiences" and the "horizon of expectations" of an era, of a social group, etc., to the history of ideas and mentalities. Cf. "Geschichte," "Historie," and "Fortschritt" in *Historisches Lexicon zur poliitischensozialen Sprache in Deutschland*, Stuttgart, 1974. On the "horizon of expectations," see H. R. Jauss, *Litteraturgeschichte als Provokation*, Frankfurt/Main, 1975, p. 175.

14. In these developments on the concept of the utopia I take up again ideas I have expounded in my earlier works, clarifying or rectifying them. Cf. in particular, B. Baczko, *Rousseau. Solitude et communauté*, Paris-The Hague, 1974; idem, *Czlowiek i swiatopoglady* (The Man and his Visions of the World), Warsaw, 1966. I have been greatly inspired by the works on utopias and by the utopias of my friends, Polish historians of ideas (including Kolakowski, Pomian, Walicki, Garewicz, and

Skarga). On the ideological and intellectual activity of this group of historians and philosophers, see R. C. Fernandes, *The Antinomies of Freedom. On the Warsaw Circle of Intellectual History*, unpublished thesis, Columbia University, 1976. It goes without saying that I am solely responsible for these developments.

15. "A good utopian . . . is reduced to being first of all a consistent realist. It is only after having looked reality in the face, as it is, without any illusions, that he turns against it and attempts to transform it along the lines of the impossible," Ortega y Gasset, *Vom Menschen als Utopischen Wesen*, Stuttgart, 1951, p. 136.

16. It would be presumptuous to enter here into the extremely complex and exciting debate on the imagination taking place at the present time. Thus we deliberately observe a certain reserve when referring to current institutions. The adjective *social* is only meant to qualify the specific orientations of imaging activity that particularly concern us here. We will return to the concept of *social imagination* at the end of this study (cf. the chapter "The Flying Man"). On the concept of imagination and its history, cf. J. Starobinski's noteworthy study, "Jalons pour une histoire du concept d'imagination," in *La relation critique*, Paris, 1970. On the sociological aspects and tendencies of the imagination, cf. W. C. Mills, *Sociological Imagination*, London, 1970; H. Desroches, *La sociologie de l'espérance*, loc. cit., pp. 191ff.

17. Cf. B. de Jouvenal, "L'utopie dans des buts pratiques," in his *Du Principat*, Paris, 1972, p. 235. "The designation 'utopian' ought to be refused to any presentation of a *new model* lacking in images of daily life."

18. The role of ritualization in utopias has been brought out by N. Frye, "Varieties of Literary Utopias," in *Dædalus*, Spring 1965. Cf. F. P. Bowman, *Utopia, imagination espérance*, loc. cit. The supremacy accorded rites is not only a matter of the structural characteristics of the utopia. In certain utopias, this supremacy converges with the intention of dissolving the political into the social or even into the moral, a problem to which we will return. Cf. the judicious observations of G. Benrekassa, "Le savoir sur la fable et l'utopie du savoir," *Littérature*, no. 21, February 1976.

19. H. Desroches, *Sociologie de l'espérance*, loc. cit., p. 217. R. Trousson, *Voyage aux pays de nulle part. Histoire littéraire de la pensée utopique*, Brussels, 1975, gives a notable analysis of the evolution of the utopia as a literary genre.

20. Cf. N. Eurich, *Science in Utopia*, Cambridge, Mass., 1967, pp. 134–135. The author calls attention to the strange personality of Samuel Hartlib, and his "group" (including in particular R. Boyle and W. Petty). Hartlib, a Polish emigrant himself, creates a strange mixture of the utopia of science with millenarian and initiatory ideas he got from J. W. Andreae, one of the founders of the Rosicrucians, and author of a utopia: *Reipublicae Christianopolitanae Descriptio* (1619). Hartlib also wrote other utopian texts and, in particular, *A Description of the Famous Kingdom of Macaria* (1641); he planned to establish a model colony in Virginia.

21. On the utopias put into practice in England, see W. H. G. Armytage, *Heavens Below: Utopian Experiments in England* 1560–1960, London, 1961. Ch. Hill studied the utopian practice of the diggers in *Le Monde à l'envers*, Paris Payot, 1977. J. Séguy did a noteworthy study on Peter Cornelisz Plockjoy van Zurik, a Mennonite, who set out to establish a utopian community in America. Cf. J. Séguy, *Utopie*

coopérative et œcuménique, Paris–The Hague, 1968. Many of these demi-prophets and demi-utopians are found in the authoritative work of H. Desroches, *Dieux d'hommes: Dictionnaire des messies, messianismes, et millénarismes de l'ére chrétienne*, Paris, 1969. H. Desroches demonstrated how blurred, in certain movements of the modern era, are the frontiers between utopias on the one hand, and on the other, prophetisms, Messianisms, and millenarianisms. Thus, he speaks of differentiated populations of "utopianistic millenarianisms" and of "millenarian utopias." Cf. H. Desroches, *Sociologie de l'espérance*, loc. cit., pp. 214ff. J. Szacki proposes a typology of utopias that defines the two main types of utopias by the specific nature of its rejection of reality as well as by its sociological implications. In "escapist utopias," the dream of the New City does not imply the moral obligation of personal (or collective) commitment to an attempted achievement of the utopia. On the other hand, "heroic utopias" lead to that obligation and a program of action. This action can take different forms: it is political action, but also a retreat from the world for closed communities that, by their example, ought to win society over to the cause of utopia ("cloistered utopias"). During the eighteenth century and before the Revolution, when these "heroic utopias" flourish in England and America, there are none in France. We will discuss this problem further below.

22. A. Tocqueville, *L'Ancien Régime et la Révolution*, Œuvres complètes, Paris, 1952, t. II., p. 199.

23. Cf. *Dictionnaire de Trévoux*, 1751; *Dictionnaire de l'Académie*, VIᵉ edition (1795). The term *utopia* is not in Diderot's *Encyclopédie*. It is only the *Complément du Dictionnaire de l'Académie française* that introduces the word *utopian*: one who believes in a utopia; the creator of a utopia.

24. Leibniz, *Essais de théodicée*, Paris, 1969, p. 109.

25. Rousseau to Mirabeau, 26 July 1767, in J.-J. Rousseau, *Lettres philosophiques*, presented by H. Gouhier, Paris, 1974, p. 167. Rousseau, *Lettres de la montagne*, in *Œuvres*, Paris, éd. de la Pléiade, t. III, p. 810.

26. J-P. Brissor, *Mémoires*, Paris, 1912, t. II, p. 275.

27. *Encyclopédie méthodique. Economie politique et diplomatique*, by M. Demeunier, attorney and royal censor. Paris, 1784–1788, vol. IV, p. 814. The term *Staatsroman* was widely used in German as a synonym for utopia.

28. More, *Utopia*, Guedevill translation, Paris, 1730, p. XIV. Cabet created another neologism; he said, in effect, that it is necessary to *utopianize* the universe. Quoted from H. Desroches, *Les dieux rêvés*, Paris, 1972, p. 147.

29. L. S. Mercier, *Néologie*, Paris, An IX, p. 266.

30. The complete title is much longer and more detailed: *Histoire des Sévarambes, peuples qui habitent une partie du troisième continent communément appelé la terre Australe, contenant une relation du gouvernement, de la religion et du langage de cette nation inconnue jusqu' à présent*, Amsterdam, 1677–1679. In *Candide* the description of Eldorado is in large part a pastiche of the *Histoire des Sévarambes*. Cf. Chr. Thacker's commentary in his critical edition of the philosophical tale in Voltaire, *Candide*, Geneva, 1968.

31. *Memoires du marquis d'Argenson*, published by René d'Argenson, Paris, 1825, pp. 342–343.

32. *Réflexions sur quelques ouvrages faussement appelés ouvrages d'imagination*, dis-

sertation read to the Académie française in 1741, in Moncrif, *Œuvres*, Paris, 1751, t. II, pp. 163–172. In his criticism, Moncrif makes a single exception for the *Voyages de Télémaque*.

33. *Bibliothèque impartiale*, t. VIII, November 1753. In response to these objections, Morelly wrote the *Code de la Nature*. Cf. R. N. Coe, *Morelly. Ein Rationalist auf dem Wege Zum Sozialismus*, Berlin, 1961, pp. 351–352.

34. Ch.-P. Duclos, *Considérations sur les mœurs*, in *Œuvres complètes*, Paris, 1820, t. I., p. 21. J. Terrason, *Séthos, histoire ou vie tirée des monuments et anecdotes de l'ancienne Egypte*, Paris, 1732, t. I., pp. IXff.

35. *Encyclopédie méthodique: Economie politique et diplomatique*, loc. cit., t. I., p. V; t. III, p. 702; t. IV, pp. 814, 840. At the end of the fourth volume is a table raisonnée of the entire "Administration théorique" section. Articles on utopians are also found in the volumes of the *Encyclopédie méthodique* devoted to history. Two other dictionaries with important articles on utopias should be mentioned here: G. Réal de Curban, *La Science du gouvernement*, Paris, 1764, vol. VIII; Robinet et Castilhon, *Dictionnaire universel des sciences, morale économique, politique et diplomatique ou Bibliothèque de l'Homme d'Etat et du Citoyen*, London, 1777–1783, 30 vol. Castilhon himself had composed a few small utopian texts. G. Benrekassa furnished a remarkable analysis of these dictionaries' discourse on utopias in his article: "Le savoir de la fable et l'utopie du savoir: textes utopiques et recueils utopiques, 1764–1788," *Littérature*, no. 21, February 1976. He does not hide his disappointment at the repellent character of this discourse that lacks all utopian ardor. But one might ask oneself whether, for the same reason, but from another perspective, these texts don't hold a certain interest. In fact, the mixture of utopianism and reformism we have drawn from them furnished the historian with important evidence of the diverse manifestations of the utopia's presence in the ideas and mentality of the era.

36. G.-B. de Mably, *Droits et devoirs du citoyen*, critical edition by J. Lecercle, Paris, 1972, p. 214.

37. "Observations concernant l'*Utopie* de Thomas More," *Journal encyclopédique*, 1784, t. VII. Brissot reproduced large excerpts from utopian texts in his *Bibliothèque philosophique du législateur . . .* , Berlin (Neuchâtel), 1782–1785. More, *Du meilleur gouvernement ou la nouvelle isle d'Utopie*, new translation, second edition with notes, by M.-T. Rousseau, Paris, 1789, pp. VII-IX.

38. Our overall estimate of approximately 80 texts of *imaginary voyages* is based on the following bibliographies, to which we have added through personal research: W. Krauss, *Reise nach Utopia*, Berlin, 1964; idem., *Französische Drücke in den Bibliotheken der DDR*, Berlin, 1970; R. Falke, *Versuch einer bibliographie der Utopien, Romanistisches Jahrbuch*, VI., 1954–1955; R. Messac, *Esquisse d'une chrono-bibliographie des utopies*, Lausanne, 1962 (1962); L. Versins, *Encyclopédie de l'Utopie, des voyages extraordinaires et de la science-fiction*, Lausanne, 1972. None of these bibliographies gives indications of editions, unauthorized or pirated editions, etc. We have not done extensive research on this subject; our few investigations came up with numbers than Werner Krauss's estimates. They were, however, only limited surveys, and Krauss is the authority on this subject. If one goes beyond the domain of *imaginary voyages*, the rough estimate changes radically.

Thus, for example, one comes up with 200 texts (imaginary voyages, proposals for reform, etc.) considered "utopias" by A. Lichtenberger, in his authoritative thesis that, eighty years later, remains an indispensable tool. Cf. A. Lichtenberger, *La socialisme au XVIIIe siècle. Etudes sur les idées socialistes dans les écrivains français du XVIIIe siècle, avant la Révolution*, Paris, 1895. According to a recent bibliographic essay, and the criteria therein applied, there are approximately 150 titles for the period 1700–1789. Cf. I. Hartig et A. Soboul, *Pour une histoire de l'utopie en France, au XVIIIe*, Paris, 1977.

39. A. Cioranescu points out that the first "uchronia" dates from 1659. Cf. A. Cioranescu, " 'Epigone,' le premier roman de l'avenir," *Revue des sciences humaines*, 1974, no. 3.

40. The anti-utopia and its evolution would call for a deeper analysis. Let us limit ourselves to some rapid observations: In taking the opposite course to that of the utopia, the anti-utopia is not inventing new formulas; it is not creating, so to speak, an "anti-voyage." It furnishes the description of a "utopian space" where the disastrous consequences of the realization of utopian ideals compromises the utopia itself. Nevertheless, this said, the anti-utopia is not necessarily an apologia for the established order, but it is often the opposite. It occasionally presents a more radical and more bitter critique of the present than any utopia. It therefore compromises the present *with* and by means of the utopias that it produces. It is one thing to oppose the utopia as an apologist for the established order, and another to compromise the utopia by means of the anti-utopia. The latter aims at utopias in general and not a specific utopia. That is why it must be shifted into the "realm of the impossible": it is the negation of the utopia in the domain the utopia opens up for itself. The anti-utopia in the eighteenth century is a complex phenomenon. Several works merit close attention. First is *Gulliver's Travels*. For the historian of utopias, this book is a veritable laboratory: Swift mixes and uses all existing utopian genres and turns them against themselves. Thus, he bursts open the genre from within; imaginary societies are "counter-societies" because they are grotesque visions of real social life. But the model counter-utopia is the land of the wise and virtuous horses, the Houyhnhnms, where the men, the Yahoos, drag out their miserable, beastly lives. The truth about man that the imaginary society brings proves crueler than reality. The "true" human society, the one that corresponds to human nature, is precisely that of the troop of Yahoos. Justice, like virtue, is above the human condition; it is within reach only of the Houyhnhnms, because they are horses, anti-men. Mandeville's *Fable sur les abeilles* is another case at the frontier of the counter-utopia. This is an ambiguous work, that escapes a univocal interpretation and yet, the anti-utopian tenor of the allegory of the society of bees is clear. Every society exists and prospers *thanks to* its vices and evils, and not *despite* them. Every utopia that wants to eliminate vice and evil undermines social life itself, and precisely because it aims at the reign of the good. Finally, a third case, particularly complex, that of Sade. In Sade, one finds the classic paradigm: the happy island of Tamoé described in *Aline et Valcour*. But, in the same text, Sade presents two other imaginary societies: a tyrannical society that finds its philosophical and moral justification in naturalism and atheism, and a community of "established disorder,"

of anarchism in revolt, that finds its justification in a Manichean vision of the world. It would be necessary to add, at least, the vision of society in *Philosophie dans le boudoir* (the famous text *Français faites encore un effort et vous serez républicains*) and no doubt the "society of the friends of crime" as well. J.-M. Goulemot has done a noteworthy analysis of the complexity and ambiguity of Sade's political and social options and, in particular, of his attitude toward the Revolution (Cf. J.-M. Goulemot, "Lecture politique d'*Aline et Valcour*," in *Le Marquis de Sade*, conference in Aix en Provence, Paris, 1968). It seems nevertheless that a certain drift emerges through these ambiguities and hesitations, such that, in Sade, the refusal of existing society is the opposite of the utopian refusal. Sade's discourse does not even lead up to an anti-utopia but, rather, to a social *anti-system*, an anti-society. He doesn't dispute one vision of society or another, but challenges any possibility of justifying the social link as a human value. Let us point out, finally, that the anti-utopia of the eighteenth century is, like the contemporary utopia, centered on the idea of human nature. It is a pessimistic confrontation between human nature and the ideal, that concludes that the ideal is *above* man. In the contemporary anti-utopia, that of the twentieth century, the perspective changes. The utopia is denounced as being *beneath* man; at the center is found, in effect, the conflict between the oppressive utopian society and the irreducible values of individuality. This latter theme appears in the eighteenth century in an anti-utopia by Prevost. In fact, an episode telling the story of the *Ile heureuse* is found in Cleveland. (*Cleveland . . .*, Amsterdam, 1744, t. II, pp. 68ff.). The people inhabiting this island know equality, justice, collective happiness, etc. However, this society does not allow individual love—the choice of companion is ruled by drawing of lots, taking no account of individual preferences. This is the obstacle that thwarts the integration of the narrator into the perfect society. "There is," according to Prevost, "a contradiction between individual happiness and social happiness"; we are dealing with "the commonplaces of the era being challenged by an anti-utopia." Cf. the pertinent observations of J. Ehrard, *L'idée de nature en France à l'aube des Lumières*, Paris, 1970, pp. 406–407.

41. Turgot, *Œuvres*, Paris, éd. Dupont de Nemours, 1808, t. II, p. 345.

42. Cf. F. Venturi, *Utopia and Reform in the Enlightenment*, Cambridge, 1971, pp. 95ff.: *Utopia et institutions au XVIIIe siècle. Le pragmatisme des Lumières*, text compiled by P. Francaster, The Hague-Paris, 1968, pp. 8–9.

43. P.-J. Garat, *Mémoires historiques sur la vie de M. Suard, sur ses écrits et sur le XVIIIe siècle*, Paris, 1820, t. I, pp. *163–164*.

44. *Le Thésmographe*, Restif de la Bretonne, *Œuvres*, Paris, 1931, t. III, p. 174.

45. *Correspondance de Babeuf avec l'Académie d'Arras*, published under the direction of M. Reinhard, Paris, 1961, pp. 23, 29, 80ff. The author of the *Avant-coureur* is, probably, Claude-Boniface Collignon, an attorney in Orléans, who wrote several works showing reformist leanings, such as the *Essais de bien public* (1776). Moreover, he posited as a condition of the publication of his salutary proposal, that "the King and the Republic of Poland give him, in their State, along with the rights of citizenship one or more starosties that will bring in an income of a million Polish florins or so, and enough to maintain a guard of six or seven hundred men at his

expense." It is not clear whether this is intended to be a modest reward for the remedies he proposed in the *Avant-coureur* or, rather, as a testing ground for their application (ibid., pp 22–23).

46. Cf. J. Séguy, loc. cit., p. 21.

47. Cf. H. G. Armytage, *Heavens Below; Utopian Experiments in England 1560–1960*. London, 1961; M. Holloway, *Heavens on Earth; Utopian Communities in America 1680–1880*, New York, 1966.

    The experiment of the "Fareinists," a sect of Jansenist inspiration, whose activities extend from 1775 to the year XIII, is very revealing on this point. Its Messianism is never at one with the utopian representations of the era and is not translated into attempts at communal life. Cf. C. Han, *Le messie de l'an XIII et les fareinistes*, Paris, 1955. Among the "imaginary voyages," we have found only one narrative of Jansenist inspiration: *Relation du voyage de l'île d'Eutropie* (1771). The narrator, whose work is intended for "pious and wise people," describes how he discovered on an unknown island a church and believers practicing an austere and pure Catholicism, totally at variance with the one that, under the harmful influence of the Jesuits, had been established in France.

48. We have analyzed the utopia of Clarens in our work *Rousseau. Solitude et communauté*, Paris-The Hague, 1974, pp. 349ff.

    Let us take this opportunity to point out a problem. Jean Ehrard attracted my attention to the problems posed in the eighteenth century by the relationship between the idyll and the pastoral, on the one hand, and the utopia on the other. Indeed, occasionally, the boundary line is unclear and the play of reciprocal influences would call for a special study. Schematically, the following distinction could be established: there is in the idyll and the pastoral a movement of escape from reality toward a certain ideal, which occasionally establishes a parallel between these literary genres and the utopian enterprise; however, the utopia is not possible without an orientation of the imagination toward the *social*, without an imagined social otherness. The pastoral dream can be an escape and a refusal of any social problematic: it can be situated on a purely esthetic, moral, lyric, or other plane. In other words, the idyll reduces the social to a distant and vague setting or else dispenses completely with any reference to the social. Nevertheless, these two enterprises were, in the eighteenth century, often complementary, and the play of divergences and convergences, that "utopian frontier," is of particular interest.

49. Cf. Restif de la Bretonne, "Les vingt épouses des vingt associés," in *Œuvres*, loc. cit., vol. II, pp. 10–25. "Les statuts du Bourg d'Oudan," that form the last pages of the *Payson perverti* are reproduced by G. Rouger in his critical edition of the *Vie de mon père*, Paris, 1970, collection Classiques Garnier, pp. 242ff.

50. Cf. *Journal d'agriculture*, September-December 1755; *Encyclopédie*, the "Moraves" article, reprinted in the *Encyclopédie méthodique*, in the "History" section. Faiguet, the royal treasurer, was also the author of a brochure, *Economie politique. Projet pour enrichir et perfectionner l'espèce humaine*, London, 1773. In it, he expounded his ideas on the creation of a sort of insurance fund against sickness and old age, that would produce all the effects mentioned in the title of the work. A. Lichtenberger mentions still more writings in praise of the *Quitards-Pinons* and even proposes the institutionalization of their example (A. Lichtenberger, loc. cit.,

p. 340ff.). On the economic and distinctive social characteristics of the peasant communities in Auvergne in the eighteenth century, see A. Poitrineau, *La vie rurale en Basse-Auvergne au XVIIIe siècle*, Paris, 1965.

51. J.-A.-V. d'Hupay de Fuvéa, *Maison de réunion pour la communauté philosophe dans la terre de l'auteur de ce projet*, Euphrate, les associés Frères Dumplers, and Utrecht, at the expense of the communal house of the Moravians, 1779. Some of the arrangements proposed in the project are directly inspired by More's *Utopia*, but the author refers to other utopian texts as well. We have found nothing further about the author beyond Quérard's indication that Hupay de Fuvéa was thereafter regarded "as an ardent disciple of Swedenborg."

52. J. Servier, *Histoire de l'utopie*, Paris, 1967, p. 313.

53. Y. Bercé, *Croquants et nu-pieds*, Paris, 1974, pp. 131ff.

54. Cf. R. Mandrou, *De la culture populaire au XVIIIe siècle*, Paris, 1975; G. Bollème, *Les almanachs populaires aux XVIIIe et XVIIIe siècles*, Paris, 1969.

55. Cf. J. Meslier, *Œuvres*, Paris, 1971, vol. II, pp. 60ff. On Meslier's prophetism, see the observations of J. Proust and J. Ehrard in *Etudes sur le curé Meslier. Actes du colloque international d'Aix en Provence*, Paris, 1966.

II: Utopia and Politics: An "Imaginary Voyage" by Rousseau

1. It is only Jean Fabre who, by his notable works as well as by his critical edition of *Considérations*, paved the way for a new reading of this text and demonstrated its capital importance. See J. Fabre, "Jean-Jacques Rousseau et le destin polonais," *Europe*, no. 391–392, 1962; idem, "Réalité et utopie dans la pensée politique de Rousseau," *Annales J.-J. Rousseau*, t. XXXV, pp. 181–216; idem, Introduction and Notes to *Considérations sur le gouvernement de Pologne*, in J.-J. Rousseau *Œuvres complètes*, Pléiade, t. III. (Further references to this edition will be abbreviated *O.C.*)

   May the references to these inspirational works, throughout these pages devoted to *Considérations* serve as homage to this "maître" and friend who died prematurely.

2. Rousseau, *Emile*, in *O.C.*, t. IV, pp. 548–549; *Contrat social*, in *O.C.*, t. III, p. 425.

3. On the composition date of *Considérations*, see W. Konopczynski, *J.-J. Rousseau doradca Polakow, Themis Polska*, 1913, pp. 1–28. J. Fabre, *O.C.*, t. III, p. ccxxv.

4. J.-J. Rousseau, *Lettre à d'Alembert*, Paris, Garnier-Flammarion, 1967. pp. 142–143.

5. *Lettres écrites de la Montagne*, *O.C.*, t. III, p. 810; *Jugement sur le Projet de paix perpétuelle*, ibid., p. 599.

6. *Fragments politiques*, *O.C.*, III, p. 494.

7. Here and below the numbers in parentheses refer to pages in Jean Fabre's critical edition, in *O.C.*, t. III.

8. *Jugement sur le Projet de paix perpétuelle*, *O.C.*, t. III, p. 159. On the Abbé de Saint-Pierre's "proposals," see the chapter below "History as a Pretext for Utopia."

9. *Contrat social*, O.C., t. III, p. 351; Rousseau à Mirabeau, letter of 26 juillet 1767, J.-J. Rousseau *Lettres philosophiques*, edited by H. Gouhier, Paris, 1974, p. 167.
10. *Contrat social*, first version, O.C., t. III, p. 317.
11. Ibid.
12. Machiavelli's influence is found in the developments on the legislator; however, contrary to the author of *Discorsi*, Rousseau limits the great legislator's possibilities of action to the dawn of history. In his reflections on the hero of antiquity, as well as on the epic of antiquity, Hegel was greatly inspired by Rousseau's ideas. On the concept of the legislator in Rousseau, see the studies of B. Gagnebin in the proceedings of the Dijon conference of 1962 and of R. Polin in the proceedings of the conference at the Collège of France in 1963. On the idea of the legislator in Rousseau and Hegel, see our study "Hegel and Rousseau," in B. Baczko, *Czlowiek i swiatopaglady*, Warsaw, 1965.
13. *Emile*, O.C., t. IV, p. 858.
14. In the *Dialogues*, Rousseau establishes another parallel between his personal destiny and that of Poland, which he calls a "miserable nation" (see O.C., t. I, p. 836).
15. On Rousseau's documentation, see J. Fabre's analyses in O.C., t. III, p. CCXXXV, as well as p. 953.
16. Recent studies have shown to what point Polish romantic literature was marked by the myth of the Confederation of Bar. See *Przemiany tradycji barskiej*, Warsaw, 1972. There is still research to be done on the destiny of *Considérations* in Polish Romanticism.
17. O.C., t. III, p. CCXLIII.
18. *Dialogues*, O.C., t. I, p. 836.
19. *Contrat social*, II, 10, O.C., t. III, pp. 390–391.
20. See E. Dedeck-Héry, *J.-J. Rousseau et le "Projet de constitution pour la Corse,"* Philadelphia, 1932; S. Stelling-Michaud, introduction to the *Projet de constitution pour la Corse*, O.C., t. III, pp. CCII–CCIII.
21. *Contrat social*, II, 8, O.C., t. III, pp. 384–385.
22. Ibid., II, p. 394.
23. See ibid., IIII, 10–11, pp. 23ff.
24. Ibid., III, 12, p. 425.
25. The problem is more fully discussed in the collective paper on "Modèles antiques et préromantisme" delivered at the conference on pre-romanticism at Clermont-Ferrand, in June 1972, by a group of which we were a member, along with J.-P. Bouillon, A. and J. Ehrard, J. Joly, L. Perol, and J. Rancy. See *Le préromantisme: hypothèque ou hypothèse?*, Paris, 1975.
26. See J. Fabre's remarks in O.C., t. III, p. 957. In *Considérations*, Rousseau takes up his own ideas previously sketched in a handwritten fragment on Moses and the Jewish people, O.C., t. III, pp. 498–500. Was this text to be part of the *Institutions politiques* Rousseau proposed to write? In any case, it is attached to a page of the *Contrat social*, but nowhere in Rousseau's work is the "Jewish model" so extensively discussed as it is in *Considérations*.
27. O.C., t. III, p. 499.
28. *Emile*, O.C., t. IV, p. 250.
29. *Essai sur l'origine des langues*, ed. Ch. Porset, Bordeaux, 1970, p. 31.

30. *Emile*, *O.C.*, t. IV, p. 647. Rousseau here takes up, with some changes, a passage of the *Essai sur l'origine des langues*, loc. cit., pp. 31–33.
31. Ibid., pp. 29, 35, 645.
32. Ibid., p. 647.
33. Ibid., p. 646.
34. Ibid., p. 645.
35. Thus, Ch.-V. Bonstetten notes at the beginning of the nineteenth century that "the theory of imagination is so little known, that the majority of the moderns see in this faculty only the power to envision absent objects. . . . The imagination everyone speaks about . . . only shows itself veiled." Ch.-V. Bonstetten, *Recherches sur la nature et les lois de l'imagination*, Geneva, 1807, pp. 2–4.
36. Cf. Ch. Porset's pertinent remarks in his introduction to the *Essai sur l'origine de langues*, loc. cit., p. 23, and J. Starobinski's note to his edition of the *Discours sur l'origine de l'inégalité*, *O.C.*, t. III, pp. 1330–1331.
37. *Essai sur l'origine des langues*, loc. cit., p. 93.
38. *Emile*, *O.C.*, pp. 304–307.

III: Utopia and Metaphysics: Dom Deschamps

1. E. Beaussire, *Antécédents de l'hégélianisme dans la philosophie française. Dom Deschamps, son système et son école d'après un manuscrit et des correspondances inédites du 18ᵉ siècle*, Paris, 1865, p. 232.
2. One almost gets the impression that it is an accursed text, one that brought misfortune to those dealing with it in the Soviet Union. Zaïtseva did not succeed in publishing either his copy of the manuscript or his translation. During the 1920's, another Russian scholar, Naguijev, came to Poitiers; he made another copy of the *Vrai Système* and began to prepare his complete edition in a Russian translation. He did not accomplish his project—he seems to have committed suicide before 1930. It was his friend, S. Vasiliev, who continued his work and published the first volume of Dom Deschamps's *Œuvres* in Baku, in 1930.

   The edition was to comprise four volumes, but ended with the first, which was, moreover, withdrawn from circulation at the time of the "great terror" of the 1930's and which became as rare as the two pamphlets published by Dom Deschamps during the eighteenth century. Zaïtseva's translation has recently (1975) been published posthumously. The latter text was revised and extremely well annotated by L. S. Gordon, an eminent historian of the social ideas of eighteenth-century France. Gordon accomplished this work after his liberation from the camps of the "Gulag archipelago," where he spent several years, gravely ill, never having been able to return to Leningrad or to realize the dream of his life—to see France and to work at the Archives Nationales and the Bibliothèque Nationale. He did not even have the joy of seeing his edition of Deschamps published—yet another posthumous work. F. Venturi dedicated to Gordon's memory a moving necrology that is also a notable contribution to the study of the dramatic destiny of the Russian intelligentsia (*Rivista Storica Italiana*, 1973, n. 2).
3. J. Wahl, "Cours sur l'athéisme de Dom Deschamps," *Studies on Voltaire and the Eighteenth century*, vol. III, Geneva, 1967. The proceedings of the Poitiers con-

ference were published in *Dom Deschamps et sa métaphysique*, Paris, 1974 (published under the direction of J. D'Hondt). A. Robinet's *Dom Deschamps. Le maître des maîtres du soupçon*, Paris, 1974, includes an excellent bibliography, prepared by F. Bastien, of manuscript sources and editions of texts, as well as of works on Dom Deschamps. The latter have begun to snowball during the last ten years.

4. Y. Belaval, "Apologie de la philosophie française au 18ᵉ siècle," *Dix-huitième siècle*, n. 4, 1972.

5. In putting the names of these utopians one after the other, we are speaking of a *presence* and not of a *continuity* since in fact there is no proof of the latter. There is no more trace in Morelly's work of his having read Meslier than there is in Dom Deschamps of having read either of them. And there are as many conflicts as there are affinities among the ideas of these authors.

6. Let us briefly recall the most essential biographical data. Léger-Marie Deschamps was born 10 January 1716 in Rennes. In 1733, he made his profession and having completed his *scolasticat* he remained until his death with the Benedictines of the Congregation of Saint-Maur. In 1762, he was named *procureur* of a small priory in Montreuil-Bellay, near Saumur, where he died 19 April 1774. It is impossible to specify, barring new discoveries of unknown sources, either when and how Dom Deschamps began to develop his "true system" or the stages of his success. For several years, he participated, in keeping with the Mauristes traditions, in historical scholarship, analyzing and recopying charters and deeds. The "key to the enigma" was found as early as 1761, when Dom Deschamps entered into epistolary contact with Rousseau, trying to win him over to his ideas. Seventeen sixty-three marked the the first contacts with the Marquis Marc-René de Voyer d'Argenson, who lived in the château d'Ormes, not far from Montreuil-Bellay. This event marked a turning point in the life of Dom Deschamps. The Marquis, after a brilliant military career, inherited, in a manner of speaking, the disgrace of his father, the Count d'Argenson, former Secretary of War, and retired frequently to Ormes. He was a confused and disturbed individual who allied great intellectual curiosity and broad culture to a libertinage that had become legendary, although his contemporaries were not easily impressed on that point. The circumstances in which the Marquis began to take an interest in Dom Deschamps's ideas are unknown; he adopted them not without hesitations and reservations, and became the faithful disciple and even the patron of the author of the "True System." Through the intermediary of the Marquis, Dom Deschamps entered into correspondance with Helvetius, D'Alembert, Voltaire, and J.-B. Robinet, trying to win them over to his ideas. All his attempts led to failure; on the other hand, Dom Deschamps made a strong impression on Diderot, whom he met, with the Marquis's active encouragement, on the occasion of a trip to Paris, in 1769. It was again the Marquis who took it on himself to furnish pupils to Dom Deschamps from among those who frequented the château. (Among the very numerous visitors, let us note the presence of Talleyrand and Dumouriez.) Thus, a sort of philosophical salon (it was called "the Academy of Metaphysics"), or lodge (the Marquis was a Freemason), or even sect with several grades of initiation was formed at Ormes. Dom Deschamps grouped some proselytes at Montreuil-Bellay as well (it is one of his proselytes, Dom Mazet, who transcribed the papers of Dom Deschamps that are preserved at the Municipal Library at Poitiers). Pierre

Méthais, basing his work on unpublished documents preserved at the château of Ormes, furnished a remarkable analysis of Dom Deschamps's activity, as well as of his milieu at Ormes and in Montreuil-Bellay. See P. Méthais, "Montreuil-Bellay. Paris. Les Ormes," in *Dom Deschamps et sa métaphysique*, loc. cit., pp. 29–85.

7. Diderot, *Correspondance*, ed. Roth-Varloot, Paris, 1963. t. IX, pp. 123, 245.

8. *Réflexions métaphysiques préliminaires*. (The unpublished texts of Dom Deschamps, cited from manuscript (145) 200 of the Bibliothèque Municipale of Poitiers, are indicated below only by their titles.)

9. *Réponse à l'abbé Yvon qui me demandait ce que je pense de la demande faite par l'académie de Mantoue pour le prix de 1773 d'assigner les causes des crimes, d'indiquer les moyens de les détruire, si possible.*

10. Dom Deschamps, *Le vrai système ou le mot de l'énigme métaphysique et morale*, published by J. Thomas and F. Venturi, Geneva, 1939, p. 101. (Hereinafter referred to as "Thomas-Venturi," citing the title of the text.)

11. *Les observations morales*, Thomas-Venturi, p. 126.

12. *Chaîne des vérités développée*, Thomas-Venturi, p. 101.

13. Ibid., pp. 101–102.

14. *Observations morales*, Thomas-Venturi, pp. 126–127.

15. The dialectic of these three stages has often been emphasized, comparing it to that in Hegel. This comparison seems doubtful to us; we will return below to the relationships among these stages of history as well as those between history and the utopia.

16. W. Krauss, "Der Jahrhunderthegriff im XVIII Jahrhundert," in *Studien zur deutschen und französischen Aufklärung*, Berlin, 1963.

17. On the evolution of these concepts and their ideological functions in the seventeenth century, see the noteworthy work of K. Koselleck, *Kritik und Krise*, Freiburg, 1959. See, too, B. Baczko, *Rousseau, solitude et communauté*, loc. cit., pp. 39ff.

18. "Le mot de l'énigme métaphysique et moral appliqué à la théologie et à la philosophie du temps par demandes et par réponses," publié par B. Baczko and F. Venturi, *Dix-huitième siècle*, nos. 4 and 5, Paris, 1973, 1974. Cited below as "Demandes et réponses," with respective paragraphs indicated.

19. *Observations morales*, Thomas-Venturi, p. 121.

20. *Réponse à l'abbé Yvon . . . sur la demande de l'académie de Manoue.*

21. *Observations morales*, p. 176.

22. Ibid., p. 111.

23. Ibid., p. 114.

24. Ibid., p. 185.

25. Ibid., pp. 115–116.

26. *Demandes et réponses*, III.

27. Ibid., XVI. Our italics.

28. Ibid., XXX.

29. *Réflexions métaphysiques préliminaires.*

30. *Demandes et réponses*, XXX.

31. This is the harangue Dom Deschamps has a man deliver when he meets a woman he finds attractive: "This object is a good to which I have as much right as any other. Attempting to deprive me of it would be usurping it from me: I find in it all

that I can desire in a woman, I want to enjoy it.'' Woman is an object with the remarkable quality of being able to satisfy the needs of several individuals. On the other hand, it doesn't seem as though Dom Deschamps excludes homosexual relationships from the "state of morals." *Observations morales*, pp. 127–128.

32. Ibid., p. 147.
33. Ibid., pp. 122–123, 141, 169.
34. *Observations morales*, p. 130; *Demandes et réponses*, XIV.
35. *Additions à ce qui précède*. . . .
36. Demandes et réponses, XVIII.
37. Ibid., XXIV.
38. *Observations morales*, p. 157.
39. Ibid., p. 166. "They would not use either meat or fish, or salt, or spices, or any strong liquor, but they would feed themselves simply on bread and water, vegetables, fruits, milk, cheese, butter, honey, and eggs. This way of eating, the healthiest and most reasonable, would require little preparation, care, or work, while ours, which impairs our faculties and shortens our days, requires an incredible amount. . . . There, on the contrary, one would eat the most substantial bread, and drink the best water." Ibid., pp. 186–187.
40. Ibid., pp. 177–178. Dom Deschamps adds that the consumption of iron would be so low that the ore already mined by men would suffice for centuries. Moreover, utensils would be of earth or wood.
41. Ibid., p. 183.
42. Ibid., p. 163.
43. "Women who have milk without being pregnant, will nurse babies indiscriminately, without caring whether or not they are theirs. . . . There will be none who is not a nurse, either of children, or of the elderly, who will be strengthened, rejuvenated by their milk." Ibid., p.171.
44. Ibid., pp. 182–183.
45. Ibid., pp. 122–123, 162.
46. Ibid., p. 166.
47. *Colloque entre Mme la marquise de Voyer, M. L'abbé et dom Deschamps*; see, also, *Observations morales*, pp. 184–185, 149, 158–159.
48. *Observations morales*, pp. 181–182.
49. Ibid., pp. 163–164; *Demandes et réponses*, IX.
50. *Observations morales*, p. 119; *Observations métaphysiques*, II, XVII.
51. *Observations morales*, p. 195.
52. Ibid.
53. *Observations métaphysiques*, II, 16. One is struck by the affinity between these developments and the ideas of Diderot, in the *Rêve de d'Alembert*, on the relationship between the "great whole" and its elements. Cf. Diderot, *Œuvres philosophiques*, Paris, 1961, pp. 311–313.
54. *Observations morales*, p. 187.
55. *Demandes et réponses*, XXXII; *Réponse à la demande: comment une partie peut être le tout?*, edited by J. Wahl, *Revue de Métaphysique et de Morale*, 1964 (69); *Observations métaphysiques*, II, V. Dom Deschamps thinks about gravitation when he affirms that "the forces that physicists have discovered in nature" and in which

"they want to see an enigma" are only one of the manifestations of the universal tendency of beings to a perfect unity.

56. See *Colloque*. . . . In another text, Dom Deschamps wrote: "One can only be a Nothingist insofar as one believes in nothing; that is, in the negative existence that is inseparable from the positive." Cf. *Revue de Métaphysique et de Morale*, loc. cit., p. 247.

57. *Réfutation courte et simple du système de Spinoza*, *Revue de Métaphysique et de Morale*, loc. cit., p. 247.

58. We have discussed this interplay of the esoteric and the exoteric more completely in B. Baczko, "Les discours et les messages de Dom Deschamps," Dix-huitième siècle, no. 5, 1973.

59. C. B. Macpherson, *The Political Theory of Possessive Individualism*, Oxford, 1964.

60. Cf., e.g., *Colloque* . . . , *Réfutation simple et courte* . . . , loc. cit., p. 241.

61. *Réfutation simple et courte* . . . , p. 241.

62. *Précis en quatre thèses du mot de l'énigme métaphysique et morale*, Thomas-Venturi, p. 77. Dom Deschamps affirms that man has a metaphysical cognitive faculty. The universal whole is given to us in the specific senses "of harmony and agreement." "The senses of harmony and agreement, the senses metaphysically taken, are the harmony and the agreement of everything that exists. They do not convey to us that which appears, as each of our senses renders it to us; and they only convey to us what they are, what we are in what we have strictly in common with all beings, in what excludes any and every difference between them and us." *Précis en quatre thèses* . . . , p. 79. See also *Demandes et réponses*, XIII.

63. *Demandes et réponses*, XIII.

64. There would again be good grounds for a comparison of Dom Deschamps's developments with the ideas expressed in Diderot's *Rêve de d'Alembert*, op. cit., p. 312.

65. "The more comparable the beings are to us in milieu: are simple, beautiful, harmonic, great, etc.; and the closer they approach, in relation to us, the absolute milieu of perfect simplicity, of beauty, of harmony *par excellence*, of sovereign greatness and of all the qualities that one can give to the being who is always present to us in a hundred different aspects, that is the first phenomenon, the first image, in which we see the sensible things." *Observations métaphysiques*, I, XV. *Demandes et réponses*, XXXII.

66. *Précis en quatre thèses* . . . , Thomas-Venturi, p. 80.

67. Ibid.

68. *Précis* . . . , Thomas-Venturi, p. 74.

69. *Réponse à la demande: comment une partie peut être le tout?*, loc. cit. p. 240.

70. *Observations métaphysiques*, II, VI.

71. *Demandes et réponses*, XXXII.

72. *Réfutation simple et courte* . . . , loc. cit., p. 241.

73. *Précis en quatre thèses* . . . , Thomas-Venturi, pp. 89–90.

74. *Controverse avec Robinet*, *Revue de Metaphysique et de morale*, loc. cit., p. 246.

75. For Dom Deschamps, the relationship is, obviously, inverse—it is the idea and the image of the Holy Trinity that foreshadow the "metaphysical truth." Because of

this presentiment, manifest in the dogma of the Trinity, Catholicism is superior to Islam or to the orthodox religion.

76. R. Barthel in his unpublished thesis *Métaphysique et politique chez Dom Deschamps* (1975) judiciously showed the presence in Dom Deschamps of several themes and ideas certainly taken from the texts he studied during his *scolasticat*. Cf. A. Robinet, loc. cit, pp. 320–323 on negative theology.

77. Y. Belavel, in *Encyclopédie de la Pléiade, Histoire de la philosophie*, Paris, 1974, t. II, p. 6; A. Robinet, loc. cit, pp. 9–10.

78. Letter about Dom Deschamps, by J.-B. Dubuc, undersecretary to the Colonies, to the Marquis de Voyer, quoted by M. Méthais, loc. cit., p. 29.

79. Cf. F. Lebrun, *Les hommes et la mort en Anjou*, Paris, 1971. Ch. Tilly, *La Vendée*, Paris, 1970.

IV: Utopia and the Idea of History-Progress

1. C. A. Helvétius, *De l'Esprit*, IV, speech, ch XXVI, Paris, 1973, p. 199.

2. Sylvain Maréchal, *L'almanach des honnêtes gens*, Paris, Year one of reason (1788?). In the *Almanach*, a proposal for a secular calendar that substituted for the names of saints those of "great men produced by the human race," the names of some important utopians, particularly More, Campanella, and the Abbé de Saint-Denis, are found among the new patrons. On S. Maréchal's proposal, see M. Dommanget, *Sylvain Maréchal, précurseur du calendrier révolutionnaire*, in idem, *Sur Babeuf et le babouvisme*, Paris, 1970, pp. 238–239.

3. These are the definitions given in the "histoire" entry in the *Dictionnaire de Trévoux*. On the semantic field of *histoire* in the eighteenth century, see F. Furet, *L'ensemble "histoire,"* in *Livre et société dans la France du XVIIIᵉ siècle*, t. II, Paris, 1970.

4. D. Veirasse, *Histoire des Sévarambes, peuples qui habitent une partie du troisième continent appelé la Terre Australe . . .* , in *Voyages imaginaires*, Amsterdam, 1787, vol. V, pp. 170–171.

5. Ibid., pp. 172–173.

6. Ibid., pp. 236ff.

7. Ibid., pp. 171, 232.

8. Restif de la Bretonne, *La découverte australe par un homme volant ou le Dédale Français*, Leipzig, Paris (1781), pp. 470ff.

9. On the links between the utopia and historical fiction, see L. Versins, *Encyclopédie de l'utopie et de la science-fiction*, Lausanne, 1972, pp. 8ff.

10. Thus, two variations of their history circulate among the Sévarambes: an exoteric one that sees in Sévarias the envoy and interpreter of the Sun, the divine star, and an esoteric one that considers him a purely secular figure making "the gods speak" in order to give more authority to the laws. This is only a transposition, in the imagination, of the opinion advanced by certain libertine scholars that the ancients, the Egyptians, for example, practiced this kind of double history. Cf. F. L. Manuel, *The Eighteenth Century Confronts the Gods*, Harvard, 1959.

11. Rousseau, *Jugement sur la paix universelle*, in *Œuvres complètes*, Pléiade, t. III, pp. 592–593.

12. It is even more difficult to situate Morelly's other texts, in particular the *Basiliade*, in relation to the *Code*. Is there a rupture between these two texts because of the evolution of the author's ideas? Or was Morelly's aim perhaps not to oppose to the real society a sole valid model, but rather to demonstrate, precisely by appealing to different, "alternative" models, *that more than one society free of social evils is possible?* In order to see more clearly into this "Morellian" world, we will have to await the publication of Nicolas Wagner's thesis. I take this opportunity to say how indebted I am to him for having been able to read his work in manuscript. It is obvious, of course, that he is in no way responsible for my commentary on Morelly.

13. Morelly, *Code de la Nature*, Paris, 1953. p. 40.

14. Ibid., pp. 69–70.

15. Ibid., p. 120.

16. Ibid., p. 40.

17. Ibid., pp. 125–126.

18. Ibid., pp. 127.

19. Ibid., pp. 127–131.

20. Ibid., pp. 150–152.

21. See H. Schulte-Herzügen, *Utopie und Anti-utopie; von der Struktursanalyse zur Strukturtypologie*, Bochum, 1962.

22. The author does not, moreover, completely hide behind the narrator of the dream. In numerous notes, Mercier discusses contemporary problems, situating himself outside the imaginary time. Thus the text has two narrators placed in two different times. Beginning with the title—*L'An 2440, rêve s'il en fût jamais*—the fictional character of this narrative is emphasized, and the reader invited to seek in it not psychological verisimilitude but the pleasure of a game that rests on the permanent exchange between dream and reality. R. Trousson, in his introduction to the critical edition of *L'An 2440* (Bordeaux, 1971), gives a remarkable analysis of the structure of the text.

23. *L'An 2440*, op. cit., p. 332.

24. Ibid., p. 330.

25. Ibid.

26. Ibid., pp. 138–139.

27. Ibid., p. 270.

28. Ibid., p. 140.

29. Ibid., p. 249–250.

30. Ibid., p. 259.

31. Cf. R. Trousson's comments, ibid., p. 246.

32. Cf. the "Nouveau discours préliminaire," the preface to Mercier's work that was published in the year VII. "A *Dream* that announced and paved the way for the French Revolution. . . . Never, I dare say, had a prediction been closer to the event and yet, at the same time, explained in more detail the astonishing series of all the specific metamorphoses." Vol. I, pp. I–III.

33. J. Ehrard, *L'idée de nature en France à l'aube des Lumières*, Paris, 1970, p. 389.

34. A. Burguière, "Histoire et structure," in *Annales E.S.C.*, 1971, nos. 3–4, p. IV.

35. Voltaire, *Défense de Louis XIV contre les "Annales Politiques de l'abbé de Saint-*

Pierre," *Œuvres*, Moland edition t. XXIX, p. 267. Besides, Voltaire had personal reasons for mocking the Abbé and his work. He was furious that Sabatier de Castres, in his book *Les trois siècles de la littérature française*, had accused him of having taken the idea for his *Siècle de Louis XIV* from the *Annales* of the Abbé de Saint-Pierre, a totally unfounded accusation.

36. Panckouke's *Encyclopédie méthodique*, vol. II, History, Paris, 1790, p. 681.

37. Rousseau, Emile, in *Œuvres complètes*, Pléiade edition, t. IV, Paris, 1969, p. 851. Rousseau knew the Abbé de Saint-Pierre personally, having met him in Madame Dupin's salon shortly before the latter's death, certainly in 1742. In his *Confession*, he calls the Abbé "that rare man, the honor of his century and of his species" (*Œuvres complètes*, t. I, p. 422). In 1754, solicited by Madame Dupin, Rousseau took on the task of making an extract from the Abbé de Saint-Pierre's works, to make them more readable and accessible to a wider audience. Disappointed by the Abbé's ideas and discouraged by the mass of his writings, Rousseau never completed the job. Nevertheless, his encounter with the Abbé de Saint-Pierre's ideas played a certain role in the crystallization of Rousseau's political and social thought. Cf. S. Stelling-Michaud's pertinent analyses in his introduction to the edition of the *Ecrits sur l'Abbé de Saint-Pierre*, in Rousseau, *Œuvres complètes*, t. III, pp. cxxff.

38. Rousseau, *Œuvres complètes*, t. III, pp. 592, 595, 635.

39. Montesquieu, *Pensées et fragments inédits*, Bordeaux, 1899, p. 102.

40. D'Alembert, *Histoire des membres de l'Académie française*, Paris, 1787, t. I, pp. 113–115.

41. *Mémoires du marquis d'Argenson*, published by René d'Argenson, Paris, 1825, pp. 342–343. Cf. above, chapter I, p. 107.

42. *Lettres de Bolingbroke*, published by Grimoard, Paris, 1808, vol. III, p. 469. On the collaboration between Bolingbroke and the Abbé de Saint-Pierre, see *L'Abbé de Saint-Pierre, l'homme et l'œuvre*, Paris, 1912, pp. 75ff.

43. Cf. S. Siegler-Pascal, *Un contemporain égaré au XVIIIᵉ s. Les projets de l'Abbé de Saint-Pierre*, Paris, 1899.

44. D'Alembert, *Eloge . . .* , loc. cit., p. 117.

45. Cf. J. B. Burry, *The Idea of Progress*, New York, 1955, pp. 126ff.

46. Ch. I. de Saint-Pierre, *Ouvrajes (sic) de morale et de politique*, Rotterdam, vol. XV., p. 259.

47. Manuscript quoted in J. Drouet, loc. cit., p. 33. On the evolution of the Abbé from morality to politics, cf M. L. Perkins, *The Moral and Political Ideas of the Abbé St. Pierre*, Geneva, 1959, pp. 32–33.

48. Such as, e.g., Mably: "Do not imagine . . . that following the traces of Plato or of the Abbé de Saint-Pierre I go astray among the maxims that were not made for beings who have our passions. My morality is so little austere that I don't ask for people of breeding as readers, but simply for the ambitious who somewhat use their reason." Mably, *Œuvres*, Paris, an III (ed. Arnoux), vol. V, p. 38. Let us note that in dissociating himself from the utopianism of the Abbé de Saint-Pierre, Mably is merely taking up the latter's ideas on this point. Has the Abbé, like all good utopians, not repeated many times that he is addressing men as they are and not as they ought to be? Thus he repeats, in reference to several proposals, that he is appealing "to the passions, to the ambitions, to the interests, to the forces of nature

as they are today and not to their (his readers') goodness or generosity." Cf. *Projet pour rendre la paix perpétuelle en Europe*, Utrecht, 1713, vol. I, pp. 56–57, 96–97.

49. *Observations sur le progrès continuel de la Raizon Universelle (sic)*, in *Ouvrajes politiques*, Rotterdam, 1737, vol. XI, p. 269.

50. Ibid., pp. 275–276.

51. Ibid. The image of humanity compared to one man who will never degenerate plays an important role in the formation of the idea of history-progress. It is found in several texts (including the preface to Pascal's *Traité du vide*); the Abbé de Saint-Pierre took it, certainly, from Fontenelle. "The comparison of the men of all the ages with a single man can be extended to our whole question of the ancients and the moderns. . . . A good cultivated mind is, so to speak, composed of all the minds of the preceding ages, it is only one same mind that has become cultivated during that time. . . . That man will have no old age. . . . That is, to leave the allegory, that men will never degenerate and that the healthy views of all the good minds will succeed one another, always adding themselves to each other." Fontenelle, "Digression sur les Anciens et les Modernes," *Textes choisis*, Paris, 1966, p. 256.

52. Ibid., pp. 277–278. "Projet pour perfectionner le gouvernement des Etats," in *Ouvrajes de politique*, Amsterdam, 1733, vol. III, pp. 226–227.

53. "Projet pour perfectionner le gouvernement des Etats," loc. cit., pp. 231–232.

54. Cf. *Observations sur le progrès continuel . . .* , loc. cit., pp. 300–315; *Supplément à l'abréje du projet de paix perpétuelle*, in *Ouvrajes de politique*, Amsterdam, 1733, vol. II, pp. 242–250. *Projet pour rendre la paix perpétuelle*, Utrecht, 1713, vol. II, pp. 216–217. The Abbé also attaches great importance to the café, a new institution, and predicts the greatest future for the café as a place for communication and for the diffusion of new ideas. "The conversation in our cafés is beginning in truth to improve our oral tradition. . . . Our cafés will continue to improve, and soon some will be established in Paris for the people of quality, and that is a great advantage for the city over the country." *Observations sur le progrès continuel . . .* , loc. cit., p. 290.

55. Ibid.

56. On these editions and contemporary reaction, see the introduction by J. Drouet to the critical edition of the *Annales Politiques*, Paris, 1912.

57. Grimm, *Correspondance litteraire . . .* , ed. Tourneux, Paris, 1882, vol. III, p. 474.

58. *Annales . . .* , loc. cit., p. 283. Demarets's memoir, taken up in its entirety in the *Annales Politiques*, criticizes the unfortunate financial consequences of Louis XIV's war policy.

59. Cf. the *Préface* and the *Discours préliminaire*, in *Annales . . .* , loc. cit.

60. *Annales*, loc. cit., p. 7.

61. *Observations politiques sur le gouvernement des Rois de France*, in *Ouvrages politiques*, vol. IX, 1734, p. 2.

62. Condorcet, "Avertissement qui doit être placé à la tête du prospectus," *Œuvres*, Arago, Paris, 1847, t. VI, p. 281 (referred to below as "Avertissement"). There is not yet a critical edition of the *Esquisse*. Monique and François Hincker's recent

edition is based on manuscript 835 of the Bibliothèque de l'Institut, which is, according to the editors, "the only complete authentic text." See Condorcet, *Esquisse d'un tableau historique des progrès de l'esprit humain*, collection Classiques du peuple, Paris, 1968, p. 68. (This edition will be referred to below as *Esquisse*.) Condorcet's other texts, including the fragments and variants of the *Esquisse* not included in the Hincker edition, are cited from the Arago edition.

63. *Esquisse*, pp. 76–77.
64. Ibid., p. 253.
65. Ibid., p. 259.
66. This is the title of an important fragment not included in the final version of the *Esquisse*; cf. *Œuvres*, loc. cit., t. VI, p. 245.
67. *Esquisse*, pp. 252–253.
68. Ibid., p. 276.
69. *Fragment de l'histoire de la dixième époque*, *Œuvres*, loc. cit., vol. VI, p. 596.
70. *Esquisse*, pp. 251–252.
71. Ibid., p. 153.
72. Ibid., pp. 250–251.
73. *La vie de M. Turgot*, *Œuvres*, loc. cit., vol. 5, pp. 222–224.
74. "Avertissement," p. 281.
75. *Fragment de l'histoire de la dixième époque*, loc. cit., p. 516.
76. "Avertissement," loc. cit., p. 287. *Fragment de l'histoire de la quatrième époque*, *Œuvres*, loc. cit., pp. 383, 391. On the symbolic significance of the new system of dating as well as on its utopian function, see the following chapter.
77. *Esquisse*, p. 265.
78. *Fragment sur l'Atlantide, ou efforts combinés de l'espèce humaine pour les progrès des sciences*, *Œuvres*, vol. VI, p. 604.
79. Cf. G.-G. Granger, *La mathématique sociale du Marquis de Condorcet*, Paris, 1955; S. Moravia, *Il pensiero degli idéologues. Scienzia e filosofia in Francia 1780–1815*, Florence, 1974, pp. 675–715.
80. Fragments sur l'Atlantide . . . , loc. cit., pp. 645–646.
81. *Esquisse*, pp. 274–275.
82. Ibid., p. 265.
83. Ibid., pp. 265, 274.
84. Ibid.
85. Cf. L. Cahen, *Condorcet et la Révolution*, Paris, 1904.
86. We are, here, taking up the formula proposed by L. Kolakowski at the conference on *Utopia, critique et Lumières*, Brussels, 1972. Cf. *Tijdschrift voor de Studie van de Verlichtung*, 1974, no. 1, pp. 8–21.
87. The best and most meticulous reconstitution of this vision is in G. Temkin's *Karola Marksa obraz gospodarki komunistycznej* (Marx and his image of the communist economy), Warsaw, 1962.
88. Cf. F. Engels, *Socialisme utopique et socialisme scientifique*, Paris, 1969, pp. 114–118. We have discussed the utopian concepts in Marx and Marxism elsewhere (cf. *supra*, p. 5). Let us add a remark which seems obvious but which might prove useful in avoiding some possible misunderstandings. It is by no means our intention to reduce Marx to his utopian dimensions. But, on the other hand, we believe that

the utopian image of the New City is an integral part of his entire work (with, of course, the exception of the mathematical manuscripts). To conceive of Marx's texts as a "scientific discourse" par excellence, is a hackneyed idea, but one which is readopted by certain readers of *Das Kapital*. To see in his utopia a "foreign body" or even a "youthful sin" is, of course, to propose a certain reading of Marx, but one which is short-circuited. If no account is taken of the presence of the utopia in Marx's work, it is actually impossible to explain certain of its most important functions, and, in particular, its impact on the social imagination. It likewise becomes impossible to understand why the opposition utopia/science and everything it covers in the Marxist discourse breaks out with new force at each political and ideological turning point of the evolution of Marxism. It seems futile for us to insist on the fact that the *social* model proposed in Marx's utopia is opposed, in many fundamental points, to that of Condorcet. We have frequently noted that the same mode of utopian discourse is used to convey socially, even politically opposed utopian visions.

89. *Fragments sur l'Atlantide*, loc. cit., p. 596.
90. Ibid., p. 598.
91. Cf. E. Faure, *La disgrâce de Turgot*, Paris, 1961, pp. 78–80. The idea of history-progress in Turgot and, particularly its utopian and reformist extensions, deserves further study.
92. *Mémoires sur l'instruction publique, Œuvres*, loc. cit., pp. 184–185.
93. Ibid., p. 183. Of course, the aspiration toward the utopia is not specific to Condorcet's proposal for public education. The debate on public education and the innumerable proposals it gave rise to are particularly revealing of the utopian dimension of Revolutionary mentalities (we are thinking, in particular, of the proposals of the year II–III). Together, they form a collective utopian discourse on the new man worthy of the New City.
94. In his report to the Convention, wherein he presented the *Esquisse*, Danou did not fail to point out this polemical intention and to exploit it against the "terrorists." "It is at the moment when Condorcet vanished from this assembly that he began this work; he ceased to live after having finished it. At first, he had undertaken an apology for his political conduct; soon he abandoned it, perhaps disdaining this work which would then have been futile, and that today would be superfluous. While its enemies were devastating France, he wreaked vengeance on them by enlightening it, and by erecting to the most useful truths a monument more stable than the powers of its oppressors, more durable even than the memory of their infamy." P.-C.-F. Danou, *Rapport fait à la Convention Nationale dans sa séance du 13 germinal an III, imprimé par l'ordre de la Convention Nationale*, Paris, no date, pp. 2–3.
95. *Esquisse*, pp. 283–284.
96. Part of this chapter was published, in homage to Sven Stelling-Michaud, in *Pour une histoire qualitative. Etudes offertes à Sven Stelling-Michaud*, Geneva, Presses Universitaires Romandes, 1975.
97. R. Cobb, *Les armées révolutionnaires instrument de la terreur dans les départements*, Paris, 1963, pp. 634–635.
98. G. Romme, *Rapport sur l'ère de la République fait à la Convention Nationale dans*

la séance du 20 septembre de l'an II de la République, of the same date. On Romme and his eminent role in the activities of the Comité d'Instruction publique, see the excellent monograph by A. Galante-Garrone, *G. Romme. Histoire d'un révolutionnaire*, Paris, 1971.

99. G. Romme, loc. cit.

100. Ibid.

101. Fabre d'Eglantine, *Rapport sur le nouveau calendrier fait à la Convention Nationale dans la séance du 3 de second mois de l'an II de la Republique*, Paris 3/2/II.

102. Cf. *supra* the chapter "Utopia and Politics: an "Imaginary Voyage" by Rousseau." Rousseau's ideas on the imagination were circulating like so many platitudes; cf., *infra* the chapter "Utopia and Festivals."

103. Fabre d'Eglantine, loc. cit.

104. On the proposals for "systems of festivals," see Part V: "Utopia and Festivals."

105. This was a commonplace of the "philosophical" criticism of religious festivals. Certain projects of Revolutionary festivals proposed to so increase the number of new festivals that they provoked strong criticism.

106. Romme, loc. cit.

107. On the ideological justifications of the reform of weights and measures as well as on its "militant" character, see the excellent analyses of W. Kula, *Miary i ludzi* (Measures and Men), Warsaw, 1970, pp. 511–571.

108. Cf. W. Kula, loc. cit., pp. 526, 535. Moreover, the abolition of the Republican calendar had negative consequences on the assimilation of the metric system which, at the time, was still considered a Revolutionary novelty and whose existence hence remained very weak sociologically.

109. "Instruction sur l'annuaire républicain," in *Annuaire du cultivateur pour la troisième année de la République, présenté à la Convention Nationale le 30 pluviôse de l'an II*, by G. Romme. Paris, year III.

110. "Instruction," loc. cit.; Romme, *Rapport sur le calendrier*, loc. cit.

111. "Instruction," loc. cit.

112. Ibid.

113. Ibid.

114. Cf. the illustration and comment in J. Guillaume, *Procès-verbaux du Comité d'Instruction publique*, Paris, 1894, vol. II, p. 427.

115. Romme, *Rapport*, loc. cit.

116. Cf. M. de Vissac, *Romme le Montagnard*, Clermont-Ferrand, 1888. J. Guillaume, loc cit., pp. 580–581.

117. Romme, loc. cit.

118. The nomenclature of the days paralleled that of the months. "Every citizen, every friend of the country and of the arts that make it flourish, must surround himself daily with the attributes of industry and liberty. It is from this reflection that the names we proposed to you for the days of the *"décade"* come:

    1. The day of the *Level*, symbol of Equality.

    2. The day of the *Cap*, symbol of Liberty.

    3. The day of the *Cockade*, symbol of the national colors.

    4. The day of the *Pike*, the arm of the free man.

    5. The day of the *Plow*, the instrument of our earthly riches.

6. The day of the *Compass*, the instrument of our industrial riches.

7. The day of the *Bundle*, the symbol of the strength born of unity.

8. The day of the *Cannon*, the instrument of our victories.

9. The day of the *Oak*, the emblem of generation and the symbol of the social virtues.

10. The day of *Rest*.

119. Manifestations of the same spirit are found in certain proposals of public education and particularly in their ideas on the teaching of history. The latter comes only after moral education and civics, being considered only its complement. The chronological order is turned upside down: the initiation to history begins with the study of the history of the Revolution. For the young citizen, it is the only history that is *his* and in which he again finds civic virtues brought into play. It is only afterward that they go on to other epochs studied in chronological order; the history of the latter is clarified only in light of the new era opened by the Revolution.

120. *Journal des décrets et des débats*, no. 384, Romme's intercession.

121. Cf. H. Guillaume, loc. cit., p. 586.

122. Ibid.

123. Fabre d'Eglantine, loc. cit.

124. Thus, the *Annuaire du cultivateur* is composed of short essays on animals, plants, etc. The abstract and bookish nature of these texts is striking. Under the date of quintidi, the 3 nivôse, which is "dedicated" to the dog, for instance, the citizen-farmer learns: "Dog, a quadruped of different sizes, colors, and characteristics. Its varieties include upright or drooping ears, a round or elongated head, pendulous lips, a raised back, bent legs, short, long or curly hair, or hairless. The dog has a keen sense of smell, laps his drink, eats avidly, sometimes jealously," etc. This *Annuaire* style is in keeping with the evolution of almanacs at the end of the eighteenth century. To use the fashionable language of today one could say that almanacs were then undergoing an epistemological mutation. So, in a 1720 Polish almanac, the article on the horse opens with the phrase "Everyone knows what a horse is" and goes on to summarize the "signs" by which one recognizes a "good horse." In 1784, the article on the horse consists only of a one-page summary of Buffon and begins by a taxonomy: "Horse, quadruped, of different shapes and sizes," etc.

125. Fabre d'Eglantine, loc. cit., *Instruction sur le Calendrier Républicain*, loc. cit., p. x. The five *sansculottides* were to be celebrated each year as, respectively, the festivals of Virtue, Genius, Labor, Opinion, and Rewards. Robespierre amended Fabre's report, asking that the Festival of Virtue be placed before that of Genius. "Caesar," he noted, "was a man of genius; Cato was a virtuous man, and certainly the hero of Utica is worth more than the butcher of Pharsale" (*L'Antifédéraliste*, n. 311). The idea of the Festival of Opinion is worth noting. It contrasts strongly, in fact, with the institutional and bureaucratic spirit with which the proposals for "systems of festivals" were imbued. Fabre proposed that it be a sort of Republican "feast of fools." During this *sansculottide* the citizens were to judge the civil servants by "a tribunal, which would be gay and terrible at the same time. . . . During the unique and solemn day of the Festival of Opinion, the law would open all citizen's mouths on the morality, the personnel, and the actions of civil servants;

the law would give scope to the comic and gay imagination of the French. On this day, opinion would be allowed to manifest itself on that score in all ways imaginable: songs, allusions, caricatures, *pasquinades*; the salt of irony, the sarcasm of folly, would on that day be the salary of the one among those elected by the people who had betrayed them or who had given them reason to have little regard for him, or to hate him. It is, consequently, by its very nature, by its natural gaiety that the French people will preserve its rights and its sovereignty. Tribunals can be corrupted, opinion cannot be . . . . The most terrible and most profound French arm against the French is ridicule.'' Fabre d'Eglantine, ibid.

126. We have been unable to identify the recent research to which Fabre was alluding. Nevertheless, an author, who was not very recent and who never suspected he had discovered the ancestors of the *sans-culottes*, uses the expression *Gallia bracata*. This phrase is found, in fact, in Pliny's *Natural History*.

127. *Almanach d'Aristote ou du vertueux républicain*, Paris, years III. In his *Néologie*, Mercier point out the existence of a counter-calendar of the Vendée; Saint Louis de Bourbon was the patron of 21 January; Saint Elizabeth of France of 11 March; September was called the *month of crimes*; 2 September was to be the *Festival of the martyrs of Paris*. Cf., too, J. and E. Goncourt, *La société française pendant la Révolution*, Paris, 1864, pp. 277–279.

128. *Rapport fait au Comité d'Instruction publique*, by Urbain Domergue, head of the Bibliography Department, in J. Guillaume, *Proces-verbaux . . .* , loc. cit., vol. II, pp. 798ff.

129. *Rapport par G. Romme au nom du Comité d'Instruction publique sur les abus qui se commettent dans l'exécution du décret du 18 du premier mois, relatif aux emblèmes de la féodalité et de la royauté, fait à la séance du 3 du deuxième mois*, Paris, l'Imprimerie Nationale, n.d.

130. On the recasting of the festivals, cf. M. Ozouf, *De thermidor à brumaire: les discours de la Révolution sur elle-même*, in *Au siècle des lumières*, Paris, 1970, pp. 157–189.

131. See W. Kula, loc. cit., pp. 663–664.

132. The analogies with the October Revolution are quite instructive. Revolutionary Russia initiated two reforms at the same time—it adapted the metric system as well as the Gregorian calendar. The only ideological correction to the latter was limited to changing the denomination of the ''first year.'' In effect, there was no longer a reference to the birth of Jesus Christ but, rather, to the ''beginning of our era,'' yet without having specified why, beginning on that day, time is more ''ours'' than was the time preceding it. . . . Sunday was suppressed by introducing the six-day cycle—five working days, the sixth a holiday, while keeping the old names for days. This system lasted only twenty years. It was abandoned above all in order to increase the number of working days, but also to readapt to Sunday which, despite the decrees, remained a holiday, particularly in the country.

It must not be forgotten that the introduction of the Gregorian calendar fulfilled, in the given context, a double objective. On the one hand, it had an anti-religious aspect insofar as it made time advance in relation to the orthodox liturgical year. On the other hand, it was ''unifying'' in relation to the Western calendar. Thus, the ''new style'' began November 7, 1917, and consequently the revolution is called, alternately, the October or the November Revolution. . . . And the New Year is celebrated twice in Moscow: one falls on 1 January and the other, celebrated in private, but by the nonpracticing as well, thirteen days later, is commonly known as "the old New Year."

V: Utopia and Festivals

1. Saint-Simon, in *L'Organisateur*, 1820; quoted from H. de Saint-Simon, *Le nouveau christianisme*, Paris, 1969, pp. 136–138. Cf. F. Gentile, "La festa nell'invenzione saint-simoniana," *Nuova Antologia*, August 1975.

2. F. Bakhtine, *Rabelais*, Paris, 1969.

3. E. LeRoy Ladurie, *Paysans du Languedoc*, Paris, 1969, pp. 225–230; 246ff. On the relationship between festivals and revolts in the mentalities of the common people in the eighteenth century, see Y. Bercé, *Fêtes et révoltes*, Paris, 1976.

4. Restif de la Bretonne, *L'andrographe* . . . , Paris, 1782, p. 13.

5. Restif de la Bretonne, *L'andrographe*, loc. cit., pp. 86–87; idem, *Le paysan perverti*, ch. CCLXXXVII, in Restif de la Bretonne, *La vie de mon père*, Paris, 1970, pp. 248–249.

6. Morelly, *Code de la Nature*, Paris, 1955, pp. 129, 137, 144.

7. D. Veiras, *Histoire des Sévarambes*, loc. cit., pp. 450ff.

8. *La République des Philosophes ou histoire des Ajaoiens*; a posthumous work of M. de Fontenelle, Geneva, 1768, pp. 51, 110–115.

9. L.-S. Mercier, *L'année 2440*, text edited and annotated by R. Trousson, Bordeaux, 1971, pp. 248–249.

10. On the attitudes of the *"philosophes"* to traditional festivals, see Jean Ehrard's analysis, "Les Lumières et la fête," in *A. H. R. F.*, July-September 1975.

11. This is a distinction made by Cl.-G. Dubois, in his article "Eléments pour une géométrie des non-lieux," *Romantisme*, n. 1–2, 1971.

12. G. Bachelard, *Le poétique de l'espace*, Paris, 1975, p. 17.

13. Rousseau, *Lettre à d'Alembert*, Paris, 1967, pp. 232–234.

14. We have only treated the theme of festivals in Rousseau schematically, limiting ourselves to certain aspects. This theme is treated more extensively in J. Starobinski, *J.-J. Rousseau; la transparence et l'obstacle*, Paris, 1957, pp. 114ff; B. Baczko, *Rousseau. Solitude et communauté*, loc. cit., pp. 358ff.

15. E.-L. Boullée, *Architecture. Essai sur l'art*. Texts collected and presented by J.-M. Pérouse de Monclos, Paris, 1968, pp. 120–121. On the relationship between the utopia and visionary architecture, see *infra* the chapter entitled "An Architecture for the Utopia."

16. Diderot, entry under "Beau," *Œuvres*, ed. Assézat-Tourneux, t. III, p. 497. On the relationship between art and politics in the esthetic of the Enlightenment, cf. J. A. Leith, *The Idea of Art as Propaganda in France 1750–1799*, Toronto, 1965.

17. P. Ricôeur, *La métaphore vive*, Paris, 1975. p. 265.

18. J.-F. Rabaut de Saint-Etienne, "Projet d'éducation nationale," in J. Guillaume, *Procès verbaux du Comité d'Instruction publique de la Convention nationale*, Paris, 1891–1894, vol. I, pp. 231–235.

19. Ibid.

20. Ibid.
21. A. Decouflé, *Sociologie des révolutions*, Paris, 1970, p. 87.
22. To cite merely one example, H. Fox, *The Feast of Fools*. This noteworthy book is based in large part on the entanglement of the realities and myths of the festival.
23. Cf. A.-Ch. Gruber, *Les grandes fêtes et leurs décors à l'époque de Louis XVI*, Geneva, 1972, pp. 147–148. F. Herecques, *Souvenirs d'un page de la cour de Louis XVI*, Paris, 1873, p. 287; Mme Campan, *La cour de Marie-Antoinette*, Paris, 1971, p. 209.
24. Letter from Robespierre to Buissart, 23 July, 1789, in Maximilien et August Robespierre, *Correspondance*, Paris, 1926, pp. 43–45.
25. M. Vovelle, *La chute de la monarchie*, Paris, 1972, p. 221. After the present book was written two essential works on the history and anthropology of the Revolutionary festival were published: M. Ozouf, *La fête révolutionnaire. 1789–1799*. Paris, 1976; M. Vovelle, *Les métamorphoses de la fête en Provence de 1750 à 1820*, Paris, 1976.
26. M. Vovelle, *La chute de la monarchie*, loc. cit., p. 221.
27. A. Mathiez, *Contributions à l'histoire religieuse de la Révolution Française*, Paris, 1907, pp. 31–34; idem, *Les origines des cultes révolutionnaires*, Paris, 1904, pp. 40–41.
28. *Travail sur l'éducation publique trouvé dans les papiers de Mirabeau*, published by Cabanis, M.D., Paris, 1791, pp. 82–83.
29. *Instruction publique: spectacles*. Opinion of Anarcharchis Cloots, farmer and *député* of the Département de l'Oise, Paris, nivôse, second year of the Republic.
30. M. Robespierre, *Rapport sur les idées religieuses et morales du 18 floréal an II*, idem, *Discours*, Paris, n.d., pp. 205–208. Scarcely a few months earlier, Robespierre had opposed the institutionalization of festivals, and warned against their bureaucratization. "Public honors as well as national festivals are the luxury of liberty; nothing obliges the populace to delegate the responsibility of awarding them; nothing prevents leaving to the citizens the responsibility of expressing their thanks and their joy as they like. And there is more: in the hands of the magistrates, this institution can only degenerate." It is true that Robespierre gave this warning in specific circumstances when, for several reasons, both personal and political, he opposed Marat's "pantheonization." Speech of 17 July 1793, quoted in Robinet, *Le mouvement religieux à Paris pendant la Révolution*, Paris, 1898, vol. II, p. 553. Cf. F.-A. Aulard, *La société des Jacobins*, Paris, 1895, t. V, p. 303.
31. The examples cited above are from the following texts: *Projet de décret pour établissement de l'Instruction Publique présenté par le Comité d'Instruction publique le 25 juin 1793*. Paris, the same date (a proposal by Lakanal to which Sieyès contributed a great deal; he was the author, in particular, of the chapters on festivals); Robespierre, Speech of 18 floréal . . . , loc. cit. Saint-Just, "Institutions républicaines," in *Œuvres choisies*, Paris, 1968, pp. 350–353.

Other examples of proposed festivals are to be found herein, in the chapter on the Republican calendar. Mona Ozouf studied discourse in the festivals in an important article: "De thermidor à Brumaire: le discours de la Révolution sur elle-même," in *Au siècle des lumières*, Paris-Moscow, 1970, pp. 157–189. Let us take the opportunity to note that before the adoption of the Republican calendar, the idea of a "system of festivals" encountered opposition, which manifested itself in particular during the rather stormy debate occasioned by the Sieyès-Lakanal proposal. Coupé, for example, was afraid that the inflation of festivals would increase "the sterile nonworking days of the calendar." Léquinio criticized the abstract and artificial character of the festivals proposed by Sieyès. Hassenfratz went further in his criticism: "The essential part of public education is the development of national industry and this useful education is replaced by festivals. . . . The institution of festivals is a beautiful metaphysical idea. . . . They were useful among the peoples of antiquity who did not have relationships among themselves which were as intimate as those of the peoples of Europe; who did not have printing and the postal service to propagate their ideas in an instant." But this is not the case in France, "a manufacturing and agricultural people, surrounded by industrious peoples. Let us take care lest while we are occupied with organizing our festivals, our neighbors organize their industry and destroy our manufacturing and commerce." Cf. J. Guillaume, *Procès verbaux* . . . , loc. cit., vol. I, pp. 535, 546, 580–581.

32. Mona Ozouf analyzed the relationship between the "utopian" space of the festival and the constraints of the real city in a noteworthy study of "Les cortèges révolutionnaires," *Annales E.S.C.*," no. 5, 1971. We will show below how festivals mark the imaginary city planning of Revolutionary Paris; cf. the chapter "From the place de la Révolution to the place du Bonheur: the Imaginary Paris of the Revolution."

33. For the reconstruction of the festival of August 10th, we have used, essentially, the following documents: *Rapport et décret sur la fête de la Réunion Républicaine du 10 août présentés au nom du Comité d'Instruction publique* by David, député of the *département* of Paris. Printed by order of the National Convention and sent to the *départements* and the armies, Paris;

"Instruction pour l'ordre de la fête nationale à observer le jour du 10 août, l'an II de la République Française," *Journal de la Montagne*, no. 70, 10 August 1793 (this text was published in a brochure as well as printed on posters put up on the walls of Paris);

Détail de la fête de l'Unité et de l'Indivisibilité de la République, qui a eu lieu le 10 août, décrétée par la Convention nationale. With the inscriptions drawn on the stones of the Bastille and the monuments destined for this ceremony, Paris, year II of the French Republic;

Procès verbal des monuments, de la marche et des discours de la fête consacrée à l'inauguration de la constitution de la République française, le 10 août 1793. Printed by order of the National Convention, Paris, year II of the French Republic.

Let us point out a fact as noteworthy as it is revealing. In fact, these are only more or less reworked versions of the first document, that is of David's *initial proposal*. The third text literally reproduces this proposal with one sole modification: it substitutes the past for the future. The other texts specify details, add commentaries, indicate administrative orders, etc. In our work, all the quotations are from one of these four texts; we, too, have therefore used the past as well as the present indicative.

Note, finally, that the festival was to be surrounded by other symbolic acts.

They anticipated finishing the demolition of the royal tombs at Saint-Denis by 10 August. It was on the same day that the National Museum, at the Louvre, was to be inaugurated. For many reasons, however, these time limits were not met.

34. L.-S. Mercier, *Le Nouveau Paris*, Paris, year VII, t. I, p. 73.

35. Quoted from J. Tiersot, *Les fêtes et les chants de la Révolution Française*, Paris, 1902, p. 22. The counter-Revolutionaries responded to these songs:

> Toujours de l'eau! Quel temps maudit!
> Disait, au Champ de Mars, Damis le démocrate.
> C'est fait exprès, je l'avais bien prédit
> Que le Père Eternel était aristocrate.
>
> Always water! What damned weather!
> Said, on the Champ de Mars, Damis the Democrat.
> It's on purpose, as I'd predicted
> That the Eternal Father's an aristocrat.

Text quoted by M. Reinhard, *Nouvelle Histoire de Paris. La Révolution*, Paris, 1971, p. 185.

36. All quotations taken from documents published by N. Becquart in the *Bulletin de la Société Historique et Archéologique du Périgord*, t. XIX, 1972, pp. 278–285.
   A. Duruy quotes numerous documents of the festivals of the same time, and the varied evidence from all departments is corroborative. "The national festivals are celebrated in the majority of communes only by public employees and only in order to obey the law" (Ariège). "Financial penury does not allow of adding pomp to these national festivals. The forms that have been employed for ten years are worn out" (Hautes-Pyrénées). Moreover, there is more and more the call for a link "to the solemnity of the religious cult." A. Duruy. *L'Instruction publique pendant la Révolution*, Paris, 1882, pp. 499–500. Moreover, in the reports, a new personage begins to emerge, one to whom homage is paid—the hero to whom the populace is indebted for his victories in Italy.

37. "Festivals! Give us festivals! That is the cry that arose one hundred times from my oppressed heart while walking in the humid and monotonous streets of the industrial sections of Paris, Rouen, or Nantes, in those obscure abysses of the deep streets of Lyon." J. Michelet, *Le Banquet*, Paris, 1879, p. 227. Michelet explains the "somber" character of his own childhood, which was "nervous and defiant, precocious in imagination" by the fact that it had no festivals. "It never expanded in the great day, in the warm expansion of a sympathetic crowd, where the emotion of each individual increases five-fold with the emotion of all, where the young soul flourishes under a burning sun." Ibid., p. 218. These pages where Michelet evokes as well his childhood memories of the imperial festivals—"it was noisy, grand, and lugubrious"—deserve a choice place in an anthology of texts on the history and sociology of the festival, as do the pages of the *Histoire de la Révolution* to which we refer hereinafter, dealing with the models of festivals. It is a question, in particular, of the account of the Fête de la Fédération in 1790, and as well, of the images of the festival of Reason and of that of the Supreme Being (cf., *Histoire*

de la Révolution, Pléiade edition, t. I, pp. 218ff.; pp. 418ff.; t. II, p. 546ff.). It would be as useless as it would be imprudent to invalidate the historical value of these accounts-tableaux because of their lack ''of objectivity.'' Michelet himself does not attempt to hide the fact that he brings the event back to life with all the strength of his imagination, but also with all his partialities.

I am anxious to express my thanks to Paul Viallaneix, whose remarkable knowledge never transforms Michelet's texts into the ''object'' of a dead science, for having led me, in a friendly dialogue, in the reading of these pages of Michelet.

38. A. Monglond, *Le préromantisme français*, Paris, 1930, p. 406.

VI: "A City Named Liberty": Utopia and the City

1. Cf. D. Veiras, ''Histoire des Sévarambes,'' in *Voyages imaginaires . . .* , Amsterdam, 1787, vol. 5, pp. 153–170.

2. Marquis de Lassay, *Recueil de différentes choses*, Lausanne, 1756, vol. IV, pp. 357–381.

3. De Listonai (Villeneuve), *Le voyageur philosophe dans un pays inconnu aux habitants de la Terre*, Amsterdam, 1761, pp. 73–93.

4. L. A. Beffroi de Reigny, *Les lunes du Cousin Jacques*, Paris, 1787, pp. 167–177.

5. ''While they wait, they are shown the city, the public buildings raised to the clouds, the markets embellished with hundreds of columns, the fountains of pure water, the fountains of rose water, that of sugar syrup, all of which flowed continually in the large plazas paved with a kind of stone from which emanated an odor similar to that of cloves or of cinnamon''—this is the pastiche of the utopian city Voltaire has Candide and Cacambo visit in Eldorado. Voltaire, *Candide*, C. Tacker edition, Geneva, 1968, p. 168.

6. Cf. the ''Edile Laws'' in the *Code de la Nature*, op. cit., pp. 132–133. Cf., too, A. Doré, *La cité idéale au cours des âges*, Paris, 1944.

7. It seems that toward the end of the century, the image of the purified city takes on the sense of a counter-myth opposed to the mythology of the big city which, as we know, is at that time becoming more and more established, and in the constitution of which the work of Rousseau played an important role. Cf. B. Baczko, *Rousseau. Solitude et communauté*, loc. cit., pp. 25ff.

8. A recent exhibit of documents organized by the Archives Nationales gave an excellent idea of this ''monotony'' of urban realities. Cf. *La vie quotidienne à Paris dans la deuxième moitié du XVIIIe siècle*, the catalogue of the exhibit, Paris, 1973.

9. I. M. A. Laugier, *Essai sur l'architecture*, revised, corrected, and augmented edition, Paris, 1755, pp. 218–219. On Laugier, see W. Hermann, *Laugier and the 18th Century French Theory*, London, 1962.

10. Laugier, loc. cit., pp. 210, 214–215.

11. J.-F. Blondel, *L'homme du monde éclairé par les arts*, Amsterdam, 1774, vol. II, p. 13.

12. Cf. L. Hautecœur, *Histoire de l'architecture classique en France*, vol. IV, Paris, 1952, pp. 50–53; K. P. Pawlowski, *Francuska mysl urbanistyczna epoki Oswiecenia*, Warsaw, 1970, pp. 84–85.

13. *Cours d'Architecture ou Traité de la décoration, distribution et construction des*

bâtiments, containing the lessons given in 1750 and the following years by J.-F. Blondel, Paris, 1771–1774, vol. I, p. 170.

14. P. Patte, *Mémoires sur les objets les plus importants de l'architecture*, Paris, 1769, p. 3.
15. Ibid., pp. 3, 59–60.
16. Ibid., p. 61.
17. P. Chombart de Lauwe, *Des hommes et des villes*, Paris, 1965, p. 209.
18. Laugier, loc. cit., p. 209.
20. Laugier, ibid.
21. Patte, loc. cit., pp. 5–6.
22. Laugier, loc. cit., pp. 209–210, P. Patte, *Monuments érigés en France à la gloire de Louis XV*, Paris, 1765, p. 213.
23. Patte, ibid., p. 221.
24. Cf. H. Rosenau's observations in *Social Purpose in Architecture. Paris and London Compared, 1760–1800*, London, 1970, pp. 120–130.
25. P. Francastel, "Paris et la création urbaine en Europe au XVIIIe siècle," in *L'urbanisme de Paris et l'Europe 1600–1680*, works and documents presented by P. Francastel, Paris, 1969, pp. 14–16.
26. Patte, *Monuments*, loc. cit., p. 212.
27. Patte, *Mémoire*, loc. cit., p. 65.
28. Ibid., p. 64. Patte repeats the conditions defined in the competition launched by Catherine II for the beautification of Saint Petersburg.
29. Patte, *Monuments*, p. 222.
30. Patte, *Mémoires*, pp. 8–9.
31. Ibid., p. 11.
32. Thus Laugier, taking his inspiration from the art of gardens, asks that one "look at a city as a forest. The streets of the former are the paths of the latter. Let us apply this idea and let the design of our parks serve as a plan for our cities. . . . We have cities whose streets are in perfect alignment; but as the design was made by people of little intellect, an insipid exactness and a cold uniformity prevail, which makes us miss the disorder of our cities that have no sort of alignment. It is a long parallelogram traversed in both length and width by lines at right angles. Everywhere one sees only a boring repetition of the same objects, and all sections resemble one another to the point that one mistakes his surroundings and gets lost. A park that would be only a large collection of isolated and uniform sections and whose paths would differ only numerically would be something quite tedious and quite dull. Above all things, let us avoid the excesses of regularity and symmetry." Laugier, loc. cit., p. 224. L. Hautecœur discusses at length the influence of the evolution of the art of gardens on the ideas of city planning (L. Hautecœur, loc. cit., vol. V, pp. 5–50). The study of gardens and of *fabriques* would provide subject matter for a whole chapter of the history of utopias in the eighteenth century. Gardens were often conceived as the setting or even the figurative representation of a certain idea of happiness situated somewhere between the utopia and the idyll. Such a study would be even more promising if it took into account, as well, imaginary gardens and *fabriques* and, in particular, those in the paintings and novels

of the time. Cf. the stimulating observations of R. Demoris in his work on "Les fêtes galantes chez Watteau et dans le roman contemporain," *XVIIIe siècle*, vol. III, 1971.

33. Patte, *Mémoires*, loc. cit., p. 5.

34. Paris, year XII. According to this prospectus, it is difficult to define the social orientations of this utopia. In vague terms, it is a question of establishing in it "social well-being . . . that is founding the reign of justice, of reason, and of humanity." That cannot be done without a government that "would make man what he ought to be or what his own nature requires that he be" (pp. 21–26). It is striking that in this prospectus Patte makes no reference to the city or to architecture—in it he speaks as "politician" and as a "philosopher," not as an architect.

35. Patte, *Mémoires*, p. 161.

36. "With the aid of these establishments it would follow that the surroundings of the great wall, and especially of the temples, which ought to be approached with respect, would not continually be contaminated with excrement. The courtyards of palaces and hôtels, the porches of private houses and their landings are now merely so many receptacles for the needs of passersby." Ibid., p. 15.

37. G. Bardet, *Naissance et méconnaissance de l'urbanisme*, Paris, 1951, p. 333.

38. Patte, *Mémoires*, pp. 225–226.

39. Laugier, loc. cit., p. 225; Patte, *Mémoires*, p. 66.

40. Bardet, loc. cit., p. 273.

41. "Give me the colonnade of the Louvre, the Luxembourg, the Tuileries, and the Saint-Gervais portal (and I regretfully leave out the fountain on the rue de Grenelle and the portal of Saint-Sulpice) to place in the two streets that traverse the center of Paris and that do not intersect, so that I may place them at the extremities of these two streets; when these four edifices, being continually and easily seen by all who come and go by these very frequented streets, fix the attention of strangers, they pay little attention to the rest and are struck only by the viewpoints that have taken possession of their complete admiration." (*Mercure de France*, July 1748, pp. 147ff.) This idea of beautification limited to a decorative architecture which would conceal the deplorable state of the city was strongly fought by Voltaire as well as by numerous architects. The history of the "philosophical" debate as well as the proposals presented at the competition are studied in G. Bardet, loc. cit., pp. 273ff.; K. P. Pawlowski, loc. cit., pp. 76ff.; P. Lavedan, *Histoire de l'urbanisme*, Paris, 1959, pp. 194ff.; S. Granet, *Place de Louis XV*, Paris, 1962; R. S. Tate, Jr., "Voltaire, Bachaumont and Urban Renewal for Paris." *Romance Notes*, vol. XI, no. 1, 1969.

42. Patte, *Monuments*, loc. cit., pp. 222ff.

43. Ibid., p. 187.

44. L.-S. Mercier, *L'An 2440*, Paris, year VII, vol. I, p. 14.

45. Ibid., p. 38. Mercier was well documented on these beautification proposals, to which his *tableau de Paris* bears witness. A vision of Paris beautified underlies the "moral physiognomy" of the capital that Mercier proposes to establish in the *Tableau*. It would be interesting to reconstruct this image and then to compare it

with the one present in *L'An 2440*; although there are similarities and repetitions, the two images are not identical. Cf., e.g., *Le tableau de Paris*, Hamburg-Neuchâtel, 1792, vol. I, pp. 176ff., vol II, pp. 114–115.

46. *L'An 2440*, vol I, pp. 26–27, 44–47, 278–279, 286, 287; vol II, pp. 218–219; vol. III, p. 214.

47. Cf. Bardet's analyses, loc. cit., pp. 284–285.

48. *L'An 2440*, vol. I, pp. 36, 44.

49. Ibid., vol. II, pp. 12–37. Cf. R. Quellet and H. Vachons' pertinent analyses in *La ville au XVIIe siècle*, Symposium in Aix-en-Provence, Aix-en-Provence, 1975, pp. 83–90.

50. Cf. ibid., vol. I, pp. 37, 68, 90, 139, 162, 178, 182, 266; vol. II, pp. 130ff.

51. E. Boullée, *Architecture. Essai sur l'art*, texts collected and gathered by J. M. Pérouse de Montclos, Paris, 1968, pp. 116–117. Drawings and plans reproduced and analyzed in J. M. Pérouse de Montclos, *E. L. Boullée 1728–1799. De l'architecture classique à l'architecture révolutionnaire*, Paris, 1969.

52. Boullée quotes the text of Abbé Brotier, "Premier mémoire sur les jeux du cirque considérés dans les vues politiques des Romans, lu le 23 janvier 1781," printed in *Mémoires de l'Académie des inscriptions et belles-lettres*, vol. XLV. Cf. Boullée, *Architecture*, loc. cit., p. 124.

53. A third reservation should be added here about the particular aspects of our approach as well as the limits of our scope. It is from the perspective of the history of utopias and not that of art and architectural history that we approach the work of the visionary architects. Let us, nevertheless, at least point out some works to which we are particularly indebted and in which the reader will find detailed and excellent information on the questions of architecture and city planning. E. Kaufmann, "Three Revolutionary Architects," in *Transactions of the American Philosophical Society*, v. 42, 1952; idem, *Architecture in the Age of Reason*, Cambridge, 1955; J.-M. Pérouse de Montclos, *E. L. Boullée . . .*, loc. cit. (includes an important bibliography); idem, "Ch. F. Viel, architecte de l'Hôpital et Jean-Louis Viel de Saint Maux, architecte, peintre et avocat au Parlement de Paris," in *Bulletin de la Société de l'Histoire de l'Art Français*, 1967; M. Raval and J.-M. Moreux, *Cl. N. Ledoux*, Paris, 1945; J. Langner, "Ledoux und die Fabriques," in *Zeitschrift für Kunstgeschichte*, 1963; H. Rosenau, "The Functional and the Ideal in Late 18th Century Architecture," in *Architectural Review*, 1966; R. Rosenblum, *Transformations in Late Eighteenth Century Art*, Princeton, 1967; Y. Christ and J. Ohayon, *L'oeuvre et les rêves de C. N. Ledoux*, Paris, 1971; M. Ozouf, "Architecture et urbanisme; l'image de la ville chez C. N. Ledoux," in *Annales E.S.C.*, 1966; J. Starobinksi, *1789. Les emblèmes de la Raison*, Paris, 1973.

54. Boullée, *Architecture*, loc. cit., pp. 32–33, 160–161.

55. C. N. Ledoux, *L'architecture considérée sous le rapport de l'art, des mœurs et de la législation*, Paris, 1804, pp. 223–224.

56. Boullée, loc. cit., pp. 64–65. J.-M. Pérouse de Montclos points out, as does H. Rosenau, the Platonic character of these propositions: similar principles are current among several academic architects of the era and are to be found, in particular, in Soufflot. Cf. ibid., p. 62, note.

57. Ibid. Ledoux similarly praises the sphere and the circle. "Everything is a circle in

nature! The stone that falls into the water propagates infinite circles; centripetal force is constantly combated by a movement of rotation; the air, the sea, move in permanent circles; the magnet has its vortexes; the earth has its poles; the zodiac presents, in succession to the sun, its heavenly signs, the satellites of Saturn and of Jupiter revolve around them, finally the planets trace their immense orbit.'' *L'Architecture*, loc. cit., p. 223.

58. Ledoux, ibid., p. 6.
59. Boullée, loc. cit., pp. 33–34, 135–136.
60. Boullée, loc. cit., pp. 32–35, 65–66, 73–74, 159. Ledoux, loc. cit., p. 179.
61. Ledoux, loc. cit., p. 184.
62. Ibid., p. 11.
63. Cf. Y. Belavel, "Le scepticisme de la raison et le dogmatisme des sentiments," in *Annales J-.J. Rousseau*, vol. XXXVII, Geneva, 1974.
64. Both Ledoux and Boullée put the final touches on their respective "treatises" during the revolutionary years. The dating of one specific fragment or proposal is often a problem, particularly with regard to Ledoux. Cf. E.W. Herman, "The Problem of Chronology in C. N. Ledoux's engraved work," in *The Art Bulletin*, vol. XLII, 1960.
65. *Lecture d'un texte illisible* is the subtitle of M. Ozouf's pertinent essay on the image of the city in Ledoux. See the bibliography in note 53 above.
66. On "neoclassicism," the antique models and their functions, see B. Baczko, J. P. Bouillon, A. and J. Ehrard, J. Joly, L. Pérol, J. Rancy, "Modèles antiques et 'préromantisme,' " in *Le préromantisme, hypothèque ou hypothèse*, Paris, 1974.
67. An entire chapter on the utopia and language remains to be written, in which the imaginary languages in Utopia but also and especially the utopias of language which profoundly mark the linguistic debate of the era, ought to be studied. A whole *visionary linguistics* is, thus, to be exhumed. On Court de Gébelin, his visionary linguistics and its utopian implications, see R. Darnton, *Mesmerism and the End of the Enlightenment in France*, Harvard University Press, 1968; B. Baczko, *Lumières et utopie*, loc. cit.; J. Roudaut, *Poètes et grammairiens au XVIIIe siècle*, Paris, 1971.
68. J. P. Pérouse de Montclos showed the importance of these texts for the analysis of the theories of revolutionary architecture. (See the bibliography in note 53.)
69. We are limiting ourselves to pointing out several broad lines, and only in the context that interests us.
70. Viel de St. Maux, *Seconde lettre sur l'architecture*, Bruxelles, 1780, p. 10.
71. Idem, *Première lettre sur l'architecture*, Bruxelles, 1779, p. 16. Italics in the text.
72. Idem, *Cinquième lettre . . .* , Paris, 1784, p. 5.
73. Idem, *Troisième lettre . . .* , Paris, 1784, p. 7.
74. Idem, *Sixième lettre . . .* , Paris, 1784, p. 5.
75. Boullée, loc. cit., pp. 45, 49, 73. Cf. Ledoux's words: "Architecture is to building what poetry is to belles-lettres." (loc. cit., p. 15.) "You who want to become an architect begin to be a painter: how many variations you will find spread over the inactive surface of a wall whose picturesque eloquence does not move the apathetic crowd" (ibid., p 113).
76. Boullée, loc. cit., p. 38. Cf. Ledoux, pp. 16–17.

77. On the relationships between the *beautiful* and the *useful* in the "moralizing functionalism" of the Enlightenment, see J. A. Leith, *The Idea of Art as Propaganda in France. 1750–1790*, Toronto, 1969; H. Rosenau, loc. cit., in note 53.

78. Boullée, loc. cit., pp. 132–137. Cf. Ledoux, in his discussion of the cemetery of the city of Chaux, in *Architecture considérée* . . . , loc. cit., pp. 196–197.

79. Boullée, loc. cit., p. 118. On the other hand, Ledoux moves in another direction both in his ideal proposals (for example the *Cénobie*, the house of an employee, the dwelling and the workshop of the coalmen) and in certain projects that were carried out (the buildings for Hosten and Saiseval). "It is not sufficient to erect the monuments that announce the splendor of the arts. . . . He who has not disdained the house of the poor person, he who has protected him from the difficulties that spread destruction . . . will be the Architect of humanity" (*Architecture considérée* . . . , p. 5). "Every subject takes on the color of the person who treats it. . . . Believe me, nothing is indifferent; it is nearly always the fault of the artist when the century does not move in the direction he would like. . . . Is there anything the artist can disdain? Thermal baths, the merchant's warehouse, the farmer's barn, must all bear his fingerprint" (Ibid., p. 210).

80. Boullée, loc. cit., pp. 112–113. A similar metaphor is found in Ledoux's proposal for a law court for Aix. Ledoux seeks in addition to reconcile the austere and threatening appearance of the exterior with the interior layout that is in conformity with the humanitarian and reformist spirit inspired by the work of Beccaria.

81. J.-P. Pérouse de Montclos, *Boullée* . . . , loc cit., p. 203. Cf. J. Starobinski's pertinent remarks in *Les emblèmes*, loc. cit., pp. 70–72.

82. Ledoux, loc. cit., pp. 103–104. Cf. Boullée's comment on his proposal for *Métropole*, in which he speaks of the play of light and its effect on the spectators. "I tell myself, then, and I admit it with a certain pride: Your art is going to make you master of these means and you, too, will have some grounds for saying *fiat luxe*; at your wish the temple will be lit with light or will be merely the abode of darkness." Boullée, loc., p. 91.

83. Ibid., pp. 54–56.

84. Ledoux, *De l'architecture considérée* . . . , pp. 174–175.

85. Our italics. It is noteworthy that many of Boullée's comments on his projects begin with a sort of definition of the moral qualities of the user of the building. Thus the monumental proposal for the Public Library begins with an appeal to the "enlightened sovereign who will always favor the means that can contribute to the progress of the arts and sciences." Loc. cit., p. 127. The *palais de souverain* is inspired by the ideal model of the prince who was to inhabit it and, hence, ensure the project's being carried out. Therefore, it projects the academies' being clustered together within the ensemble formed by the palace so that the young princes might be brought up in the sanctuary of the sciences" and so that the monarch "might enjoy the conversation of the most enlightened men of his kingdom." Ibid., p. 112. It is even more remarkable that Boullée quite frequently stressed the education in architecture that ought to be given "people in authority" who decide on commissions.

86. Boullée, loc. cit., pp. 18–47. Ledoux, loc. cit., pp. 34–35.

87. J.-M. Pérouse de Montclos, *E.-L. Boullée*, loc. cit., p. 183.

88. Boullée, loc. cit., pp. 35–37.

89. We have proposed another imaginary walk above (chapter II), in a city that would serve as a setting for Rousseau's "reformed Poland." We said then that monuments in the style of visionary architecture would harmonize perfectly with the social space of such an imaginary city. We can, at this point, qualify our thesis somewhat. There is, in fact, a discrepancy between the size of the city implied by visionary architecture and Rousseau's intention of reducing the importance of the capital and making it into a village. In other words, revolutionary architecture implies an urban space of a certain scope.

90. Boullée, loc. cit., p. 31.

91. Ibid., p. 83. Boullée adopts the commonplaces of the era on the layout of the city and, in particular, on the hygienic conditions and on easy and rapid communications. So, in an ideal city, the water will be distributed to the entire city by special aqueducts and reservoirs. On the other hand, "everything that could facilitate commerce will be provided for by numerous communications and by the establishment of canals, ports, etc." Ibid., pp. 36–37.

92. Ibid., p. 84. J.-P. Pérouse de Montclos notes "the audacity of the romantic vocabulary" this passage evokes, and likens it to Diderot's famous phrase about poetry, which "wants something enormous, barbaric, and savage." Ibid., note.

93. Ibid., pp. 90–91.

94. Ibid., pp. 126–131.

95. Ibid., pp. 114–115, p. 183 (Madame Brogniart's letter to her husband, 19 prairial Year II). Boullée takes up the idea formulated by Kersaint in his report on the great monuments to be constructed in Paris, a text to which we shall return below. The same metaphor is is taken up in numerous proposals for monuments of the revolutionary period.

96. Ledoux, *De l'Architecture* . . . , loc. cit., p. 1.

97. Ibid., p. 40.

98. Cf. M. Ozouf, loc. cit., p. 1291. Madame Thélusson's *hôtel*, and its façade in particular, strongly impressed contemporaries. Fourier's admiration was by no means unanimous. The author of a *Note sur C. N. Ledoux*, Paris, no date (after 1806), probably the Count Choiseul-Gouggier, the illustrious archaeologist, quotes Caraccioli's witty remark about this edifice "whose huge door seems to be a huge mouth, which opens widely to utter a foolish remark." Cf. *La vie quotidienne à Paris* . . . , loc. cit., pp. 18–19.

99. C. N. Ledoux, *L'Architecture considérée sous le rapport de l'art, des mœurs et de la législation. Prospectus*, Paris, 1803, p. 24.

100. As we have pointed out, the dating of the successive proposals for the city of Chaux poses delicate problems, as does the evolution of these proposals. We based our discussion on K. P. Pawlowski, *Francuska mysl urbanistycznz* . . . , loc. cit., pp. 140–152.

101. Ledoux, *L'Architecture considérée* . . . , loc. cit., p. 2.

102. Ibid., p. 72.

103. Ibid., p. 184.

104. Ledoux, *De l'Architecture* . . . *Prospectus*. The "encyclopedic" objective was to be achieved with the fourth volume of the work the complete outline of which was explained in the *Prospectus*, but which was never finished. "I shall execute in a

second city what I have conceived in the first; the wealth of ideas will be seen there reproduced on the antique volume of nature and if one day my shackles are broken, new conceptions, well ripened by the summer sun, will be seen there.'' This ''last leaf'' was to include ''four hundred aspects.'' Ibid.

105. Cf. supra, pp. 000–000.

106. *De l'Architecture*, loc. cit., p. 200; *Prospectus*, loc. cit., p. 13.

107. *Les fêtes de la Révolution.* Catalogue of the exhibit at the Bargoin museum, 15 June-15 September 1974, Clermont-Ferrand, 1974. Our references are to numbers 21, 33, 35, and 43 of the catalogue.

108. *Rapport de Gilbert Romme à la séance de la Convention du 25 XI 1792 sur la suppression de la place du Directeur de l'Académie de France à Rome.* Cf. J. Guillaume, *Procès verbaux du Comité d'Instruction publique de la Convention Nationale*, t. I, loc. cit., p. 88.

109. A.-G. Kersaint, *Discours sur les monuments publics*, Paris. 1792, pp. 16–17.

110. *Almanach indicatif des rues de Paris*, Paris, year III.

111. *Rapport au Conseil Général de la Commune sur quelques mesures à prendre en changeant les noms des rues.* Printed in accordance with the order of the Comité d'Instruction publique of 17 nivôse year II. Imprimerie Nationale, no date.

112. Cf. R. C. Cobb, *The Police and the People. 1789–1820.* Oxford, 1970, p. 303.

113. *Rapport au Conseil Général de la Commune*, loc. cit.

114. Ibid.

115. *Moniteur*, 16 brumaire year II.

116. *Rapport au Conseil Général de la Commune*, loc. cit.

117. *Système de dénominations topographiques pour les places, rues, quais, etc. de toutes les communes de la République*, by Citizen Grégoire, printed by order of the Comité d'Instruction publique, de l'Imprimerie National, no date (pluviôse, year II). For details on the debate at the Comité d'Instruction publique, see J. Guillaume, *Procès-verbaux*, vol. III, pp. 339ff.

118. *Moniteur . . .* , 26 messidor, year II.

119. M. Reinhard, *Nouvelle histoire de Paris. La Révolution*, Paris, 1971, p. 371.

120. Ibid., p. 380.

121. Letter written by the Artists' Commission Members responsible for the division, beautification, and cleaning up of the commune of Paris to the Ministry of Finances, 27 frimaire year IV. Document quoted by G. Bardet, *Naissance et méconnaissance de l'urbanisme*, Paris, 1951, p. 367.

122. Ibid., p. 371.

123. Cointeraux, *Paris tel qu'il était à son origine. Paris tel qu'il est aujourd'hui*, Paris, year IV, pp. 3–4.

124. The reconstruction of this plan poses several problems. In his book, G. Bardet provides a detailed analysis as well as extensive documentation (loc. cit., pp. 366–386). While showing the novelty and originality of the *Artists' plan*, due, among other things, to the new possibilities opened to city planning by the nationalization of lands, Bardet emphasizes the fact that the plan is not an *ex nihilo* creation and that it integrates several earlier proposals (e.g., de Wailly's proposal for the development of the place Vendôme, Corbet's for around the Bastille, etc.).

On the controversy aroused by this plan at the end of the nineteenth century, see M. Reinhard, loc. cit., pp. 369ff. and the reconstruction of the plan, pp. 374–375 (Bardet offers a slightly different variation of the plan, loc. cit., p. 373). Let us recall, finally, the names of the principal architects of the plan: Inspector General Verniquet of the highways department, and the architects de Wailly, Brogniard, Peyre, and Vaudoyer.

125. D. Rabreau, "Architecture et fêtes révolutionnaires," *Architecture d'aujourd'hui*, no. 177, 1975.

126. M. Ozouf, "Le Cortège et la Ville. Les itinéraires parisiens des fêtes révolutionnaires," *Annales ESC*, no. 5, 1971, pp. 893, 901.

127. Ibid. Appended to this is a map which shows all the itineraries followed in 1789–1799 by the processions of the Parisian festivals, as well as diagrams of 20 specific routes. Certain of the convergences with the *artists' plan* are revealing.

128. G. Romme to the National Convention, session of 16 nivôse year II; A.-G. Kersaint, loc. cit., pp. 6–7. Likewise for the monument in the Champ de la Fédération. It is imagined that it will be constructed "of indestructible materials; granite from the coasts of Normandy, so easily transported on the Seine to the base of the altar of Liberty, is to be accumulated for this construction." Ibid., p. 29.

129. A.-G. Kersaint, loc. cit., pp. 35, 69.

130. "Commentaire au projet (anonyme) d'élévation sur le terre-plein du Pont-Neuf d'une colonne de 78 mètres d'hauteur, 13, 60 mètres de diamètre et surmonté d'un trépied atteignant 90 mètres." Cf. G. Bardet, loc. cit., p. 345.

131. This corresponds to the subjects of the competitions proposed by the Comité Salut public in a series of decrees issued in the spring of year II. We quote from numerous examples taken from these competitions, which certainly bring out one of the possible versions of an imaginary Paris. Let us stress the fact that these are only examples and that we claim neither to give a complete inventory of the imaginary architecture nor to follow its entire evolution.

132. The descriptions of the statues are quoted from *Rapport et décret sur la fête de la Réunion Républicaine du 10 août présentés au nom du Comité d'Instruction publique par David, député du Département de Paris, imprimés par ordre de la Convention et envoyés aux Départements et aux Armées*. Paris, no date (1793). The decree of the Comité de Salut public of 5 floréal year II on the competition in the *Moniteur* of 21 prairial year II (reprinting of the *Moniteur*, vol. 20, p. 676). The description of the statue of the *Peuple Hercule* based on the report of the session of the Convention on 17 brumaire year II. Paragraph II of the decree of the Convention on the erection of the statue is as laconic as it is significant: *This monument will be colossal* (cf. J. Guillaume, op. cit., vol II, pp. 778ff.). The statue was never erected. In 1798, B. Poyet proposed erecting another monument on the same spot, a column 400 meters tall, surrounded by a spiral symbolizing the ascending and victorious movement of the Republic. The column was to serve at one and the same time as an observatory, a water tank, and a beacon (see L. Hautecœur, *Histoire de l'architecture classique en France*, t. V, Paris, 1953, p. 138). This same metaphor of the ascending spiral is found in Russian revolutionary architecture, in particular in Tatline's famous proposal for a tower destined to be the seat and monument of the Third Internationale. This time, the spiral was to symbolize the irresistible ascent of the international proletariat (cf. A. Kopp, *Ville et révolution*, Paris, 1967).

Let it be noted, in passing, that in the imaginary space of revolutionary Paris, several monuments appeared on the same privileged sites. Thus, to celebrate the festival in honor of Marat, the section of the faubourg de Montmartre has erected on the boulevard Poissonière "a large stylobate surmounted by the statue of Liberty; on an altar in front will be placed, one against the other, the busts of the first two martyrs of Liberty; on the bases raised four feet from the ground will be placed four candelabra; at the four extremities of the corners will be raised four sepulchral columns, crowned by four flaming torches. The circular background of the exhibit will end in a panorama of poplars." "Section du Faubourg Montmartre: fête en l'honneur de Marat. Rapport à faire en Assemblée Générale de la Section du Faubourg Montmartre le 5ᵉ jour de la 1ʳᵉ décade du 2ᵉ mois de la deuxième année républicaine, une et indivisible (!)," in G. Markow, A. Soboul, *Die Sanskulotten von Paris*, Berlin, 1957, pp. 190–192.

133. Kersaint, loc. cit., pp. 3–6, 28–29, 40.

134. Ibid. According to the calculations of the authors, the *circus maximus*, according to Pliny, measures . . . 1,983 × 871 feet; the new monument will thus be 2,694 x 1,032 feet."

135. D. Rabreau, *Architecture et fêtes révolutionnaires*, loc. cit. The author of this noteworthy study observes that the word *Coliseum* is habitually used as a synonym of circus, amphitheater, or arena, without any clear-cut distinction being made among the archaeological forms of these constructions. M. Rabreau remarks that the theme of the circus appears in the second half of the century and that "one cannot avoid thinking that the programs of the revolutionary festivals answer some unfulfilled architectural desire." In 1783, the Academy proposed the circus as the theme of a competition and it is certainly on that occasion that Boullée presented his first Coliseum project.

136. Cf. J. Lavallée, *Notice historique sur Charles Dewailly*, Paris, year VII, p. 25. B. Poyet, *Projet de cirque national*, Paris, 1792; *Les fêtes de la Révolution*, loc. cit., p. 41. D. Rabreau identified a certain Thomas as the author of the latter program (cf. D. Rabreau, loc. cit.).

137. E.-L. Boullée, *Essai sur l'art*, loc. cit., pp. 121–122.

138. *Moniteur*, 21 prairial, year II (reprinting of the *Moniteur*, vol. 20, p. 676).

139. On de Wailly's project, see D. Rabreau, loc. cit., as well as M. Steinhauser, D. Rabreau, "Le théâtre de l'Odéon de Charles de Wailly, et Marie-Joseph Peyre," *Revue de l'Art*, 1973, no. 19, pp. 31–32. D. Rabreau stresses the fact that de Wailly's program which "very closely imitates the theaters of antiquity, represents an exceptional example of *speaking architecture* conceived, a priori, on the scale of the city."

140. See the drawings and their analysis in L. Hautecœur loc. cit., pp. 132–133.

141. Cf. A. Brette, *Histoire des édifices où ont siégé les Assemblées parlementaires de la Révolution Française et de la première République*, Paris, 1902.

142. *Le Thermomètre du Jour*, 13 May 1793; G. Lenôtre, *Paris révolutionnaire*, Paris, 1896, pp. 103–105. Gisors's construction was demolished in 1800.

143. Ibid.

144. L. Hautecœur, loc. cit., p. 116.

145. The petition of the artists Lemoine, Mully, Gottelet, and Poissent to the Comité d'Instruction publique of the National Convention, J. Guillaume, loc. cit., p. 91. Two architects, Corbet and Magnin-père, proposed going still further, demolishing Châtelet, designing an enormous plaza on the vacated space, installing the Assembly in the Louvre, joined by galleries to the Tuileries. This project, which dates from 1790, thus attempted to symbolize the links between the nation and the royalty.

146. Kersaint, loc. cit., pp. 17–18; L. Hautecœur, loc. cit., pp. 117–118; and D. Rabreau, loc. cit., find other proposed sites: The Invalides, the Augustinian convent (opposite the Louvre, now the Ecole des Beaux-Arts), the Champ de Mars.

147. Combes Proposal, cf. J-P. Pérouse de Montclos, *E.-L. Boullée*, loc. cit., p. 202.

148. L. Hautecœur, loc. cit., p. 128.

149. E.-L. Boullée, loc. cit., pp. 114–115. Drawings and plans in J.-P. Pérouse de Montclos, loc. cit., p. 182, fig. 107. Kersaint, loc. cit, p. 34; Boullée conceived his project around 1792; he first thought of putting it on the terrain of the "convent of the former Capucine nuns" (now the rue de la Paix) in order to use "the most economical means." He noticed, however, that the lack of available space would "imprison the genius of an artist in a straitjacket" and so he composed an ideal project, with no specific site.

150. Cf. the decree of the Comité de Salut public on the beautification of the Jardin National (25 floréal year II) as well as those of 12, 13, and 29 floréal (Reprinting of the *Moniteur*, vol. 20, pp. 674–675); F. Boyer, *Les Tuileries sous la Révolution, 1792–1799*, Paris, 1935. M. Reinhardt notes that part of the planned transformation is explained by the desire to isolate the Palais National to the north, thus taking account of the conditions in which the Assembly chamber was blocked during the "day" of 30 June. Cf. M. Reinhardt, loc. cit., p. 370. Only the hexahedrons in the Tuileries were built, after Bernard's designs; the horses of Marly were also replaced.

151. Cf. P. Bourdieu, L. Boltanski, "Le fétichisme de la langue," *Actes de la recherche en sciences sociales*, no. 4, July, 1974, pp. 7–8. Cf. M. de Certeau, D. Julia, J. Revel, *Une politique de la langue. La Révolution Française et les patois*, Paris, 1975.

152. *Arrêtés du Comité de Salut public relatifs aux monuments publics, aux arts et aux lettres*, Paris (year II). The same edict calls on architects to "compose plans" for other civic constructions—theaters, public baths, fountains, and . . . prisons. The need for that latter was, certainly, as keenly felt as was the need for public baths. We have been unable to find, for the period that interests us, any proposals for model prisons. The New City made do, provisionally, with the old prisons.

153. Sylvain Marechal's article in the *Révolutions de Paris*, no. 215 (23–30 brumaire year II). Cf. *Les fêtes de la Révolution*, loc. cit., p. 27 (pos. 37). In this latter work is to be found the description of the decoration, as remarkable as it was unusual, installed by Brogniart in the cathedral of Saint-André in Bordeaux, for the festival of 20 frimaire. The negation of the former cult is spatially translated by an inversion of the configuration of the church. Brogniart thus wants to "substitute to the axial chapel a vast portal in the form of a triumphal arch dedicated to Reason, the choir would be used for the public, the orchestra and the tribune of the civic authorities

would occupy the arms of the transept, while the scenic apparatus was spread out along a rather steep slope along the narrow nave.'' Ibid., pp. 27–28 (no. 30 and plate).

154. Cf. Kersaint, loc. cit., pp. 28, 31, 69, as well as Legrand and Molinos's appended drawings.

155. *Programme d'un temple de l'Egalité*, anonymous, no date or place of publication, BN Lb⁴¹3863. A note seems to suggest that the author published this program as a commentary on the drawings sent to the competition for the temple of Equality to be constructed on the widened Champs Elysées. The project abounds in symbols, several of which seem to originate in the Masonic repertoire (the pendulum, for instance, installed in the middle of the temple; the flame symbolizing ''the soul of nature'').

156. In congratulating Quatremère on his election to the Legislative Assembly, Pastoret, president of the Electoral Assembly of Paris, praises his fight against the Academies: ''You have rendered the arts services they will never forget. They were slaves; you sought to free them. They were the patrimonies of a few talents, you demanded they become the patrimony of all. . . . For too long they had been subserviently complaisant to power and wealth; all the people must enjoy them and find in them, along with a more just glory, a living lesson in patriotism and virtue.'' Quoted in R. Schneider, *Quatremère de Quincy et son intervention dans les arts (1788–1830)*, Paris, 1910, p. 348.

157. Quatremère's successive reports are doctrinaire documents showing the overall program as well as the ideological and esthetic discourse which supports it. The reports also allow us to follow the enrichment of the initial project. From here on, we will quote primarily from the following texts: *Rapports sur l'édifice dit de Sainte-Geneviève, fait au directoire du département de Paris par M. Quatremère-Quincy*, Paris, Imprimerie Royale, 1791; *Extrait du premier rapport présenté au Directoire en mai 1791 sur les mesures propres à transformer l'église dite de Sainte-Geneviève en Panthéon Français*, Paris, 1792; *Rapport fait au Directoire du Département de Paris le 13 novembre 1792, l'an II de la République Française, sur l'état actuel du Panthéon Français, sur les changements qui y sont opérés, sur les travaux qui restent à entreprendre, ainsi qu sur l'ordre administratif établi pour leur direction et comptabilité* by Ant. Quatremère, commissioner of the Department of Administration and Supervision of the French Pantheon, Paris, 1792; *Rapport fait au Directoire du Département de Paris sur les travaux entrepris, continués et achevés au Panthéon Français depuis le dernier compte rendu le 17 novembre et sur l'état actuel du monument, le 2ᵉ jour du second mois de l'an II de la République Française une et indivisible*, by Ant. Quatremère . . . , Paris, 1792.

    For a complete bibliography as well as numerous archival documents, see R. Schneider's thesis, loc. cit. On the works executed, see Ouin-Lacroix, *Histoire de l'Eglise Sainte-Geneviève*, Paris, 1852; J. Mouval, *Le Panthéon*, Paris, 1940; L. Hautecœur, loc. cit., pp. 121–123.

158. The same tendency is found in proposals for a plaza-amphitheater. Cf. D. Rabreau, loc. cit.

159. Soufflot was already thinking of surrounding his edifice with a plaza. Quatremère seized the occasion represented by the confiscation of the terrain and demanded

that the national properties be reserved for the realization of his project. The *plan des artistes* retains the idea of laying out a plaza around the Pantheon.

160. H. Lapauze, *Procès verbaux de la Commune des Arts*, Paris, 1903, pp. 331, 337; R. Schneider, loc. cit., p. 40.

161. This latter idea encountered opposition and provoked controversy. It was feared that the dome would not support the weight, and the remark was made, as well, that this gigantic decoration bordered on the ridiculous. And they had not yet captured the cannons to be melted down and used for the bronze casting. Cf. J. Guillaume, loc. cit., vol. III.

162. Moitte's tympanum will be executed; Napoleon veils it with a thick cloth in 1806; it will be destroyed in 1823.

Index